P9-CJK-431

THE
SCRIBNER
WORKBOOK
FOR
WRITERS

Marie-Louise Nickerson

Bronx Community College

Allyn and Bacon

Boston   London   Sydney   Toronto   Tokyo   Singapore

Copyright 1995 by Allyn & Bacon
A Simon & Schuster Company
Needham Heights, Massachusetts 02194

All Rights reserved. No part of the material protected by this copyright notice may be
reproduced or utilized in any form or by any means, electronic or mechanical,
including photocopying, recording, or by any information storage and retrieval
system, without written permission from the copyright owner.

ISBN 0-02-387482-1

Printed in the United States of America
10 9 8 7 6 5 4 3 2 1 99 98 97 96 95

CONTENTS

PREFACE

The *Scribner Workbook for Writers* follows the overall format of the *Scribner Handbook for Writers* by Robert DiYanni and Pat C. Hoy. The first ten parts of the *Workbook*, consisting of forty-five chapters, closely parallel Parts I through V of the *Handbook*: "Writing," "The Essay," "Reading," "Thinking," "Paragraphs," "Grammar," "Clear and Effective Sentences," "Sentence Style," "Words," and "Punctuation and Mechanics." The *Workbook*'s final section, Chapter 46, "Avoiding Plagiarism: Using Sources Correctly," presents guidelines for correct use of sources and exercises in using quotation, paraphrase, and summary.

How to use the *Workbook*

Parts I through X of the *Workbook* may be used independently or in conjunction with the *Handbook*. In the latter case, students studying various sections of the *Handbook* can complete the corresponding exercises in the *Workbook*. It includes numerous exercises of various types not found in the *Handbook*. Independent use of the *Workbook* is made possible by the detailed coverage and illustrations of grammar, clear and effective sentences, sentence style, words, and punctuation and mechanics. Thus, instructors may use the *Handbook* and *Workbook* simultaneously or separately.

Special Features

A major feature of the *Workbook* is its inclusion of numerous writing exercises and hundreds of writing topics. These exercises, which generate student writing, appear not only in the chapters on writing, reading, and thinking, but also in most other chapters of the book. The writing exercises are designed to give students practice in writing sentences, brief paragraphs, and longer responses. They also cover a wide range of writing situations, from reverse relationships, basic sentence grammar, idiomatic expressions, and grammar for ESL writers, to freshening stale cliches, using appropriate words, and choosing correct punctuation.

Another important feature of the *Workbook* is Chapter 19, "Grammar for ESL Writers." The areas covered in this comprehensive chapter include the following: count nouns and mass nouns, determiners, articles, quantifiers, demonstratives, possessive forms of pronouns, word order for modifiers, present and past participles as adjectives, modal auxiliaries, gerunds and infinitives, phrasal verbs, prepositions, direct and indirect discourse, and idiomatic expressions.

Various types of exercises are throughout the *Workbook*. In addition to writing exercises, the book includes exercises that ask students to identify sentence elements, to edit sentences and paragraphs for faulty usage, and to select from multiple choices the correct answers to grammatical situations. The exercises geared toward generating student writing are particularly useful in determining whether students have mastered an area of grammar or writing skill. In addition, most exercises are preceded by an example that shows students what is expected from them.

The *Instructor's Answer Key* includes answers to all exercises except those that ask students to write paragraphs or longer responses.

Acknowledgments

I am very grateful to Joe Opiela and Carol Alper of Allyn and Bacon for their help and patience.

MARIE-LOUISE NICKERSON

PART ONE
Writing

CHAPTER 1

Writing—A Way of Expressing Ideas

We write to convey ideas to an audience. Writing an essay involves a series of tasks: accumulating evidence, forming ideas, considering the audience, organizing, drafting, revising, editing, and proofreading. This list of activities may make the writing process seem linear; it is not. The writing process is often recursive.

1a | Assessing audience and purpose

(Section 1d in the *Handbook*)

Your readers make up your audience. What you say, how you organize it, and how you say it will depend greatly on your audience and its makeup, interests, experiences, and needs. When you plan a piece of writing, keep the following Audience Checklist in mind.

AUDIENCE CHECKLIST

- Who are my readers? Are they experts in my subject? Are they generalists with an interest in my subject but no special knowledge?
- What does my audience know? Should I give detailed background information or brief summaries? Will my audience understand technical language, or should I give definitions of specialized terms?
- What response do I want? Do I want my audience to gain understanding, or do I want my audience to respond to my ideas with actions?
- Will audience members be friendly or hostile? If they are friendly, how do I sustain their interest? If they are hostile, how can I make them more receptive to my ideas?

1

- What does an objective look at my writing tell me? If I look at my own writing as if I were a member of the audience, what do I discover? Have I left out anything? What might my audience object to? How can I anticipate those objections?
- What attitudes and opinions does my audience have? What tone would be most appropriate and produce the desired effect with this audience?

1b   Preparing to write

(Section 1e in the *Handbook*)

Ideas for writing are everywhere; the trick is knowing how to find them. A reading journal or a personal journal can provide you with many ideas.

1   Keeping a reading journal

A reading journal can be an excellent source of ideas for writing. In a reading journal, you can record not only facts and ideas found in your reading, but also your reactions to and your reflections on those facts and ideas. The format for a reading journal can vary. You can keep a journal in a notebook, on pads of paper, or on a computer. In your journal, you may wish to use freewriting, letting your mind play over what you have read, recording your ideas as they occur to you. You may wish to keep a double-column notebook, with summaries of the text on one side and your reactions and reflections on the other.

2   Keeping a personal journal

Another valuable source of ideas for writing is the personal journal. (Note that this sort of journal is not supposed to be a diary that records everything you did.) The personal journal is a place to record interesting experiences, things you observed that set you thinking. While you may wish to include detailed descriptions in your personal journal, it is more important to write about your reactions, feelings, responses, and ideas.

1c   Organizing

(Section 1f in the *Handbook*)

Deciding how to organize an essay will depend on how you wish to present your ideas. There are a number of organizational methods: organizing from general to specific, specific to general, climactic order, time order, and spatial order. Outlining before writing can help you organize and present your ideas so that readers can follow your argument easily. Depending on which format works best for you, you may choose mapping as a way of organizing ideas, a formal sentence outline, a topic outline, or an informal outline consisting of a few phrases and key words or of ideas arranged in groups.

The following chart lists the steps that you may go through in producing a piece of writing. While the process is not strictly linear—you may may find yourself returning to an earlier step that you thought you had completed—the list is helpful.

STEPS IN THE WRITING PROCESS

- Gathering ideas (in journals, through research, and so on)
- Organizing
- Drafting
- Revising
- Editing
- Proofreading

EXERCISE 1   Writing for Specific Audiences

For each topic that follows, write a brief paragraph aimed at the specified audience. Example:

Topic: Failing a quiz

Audience: Your family

When I got my last math quiz back, I was upset by the low grade, a 56, the lowest grade I've had so far this semester. When I looked over the questions that I had the most difficulty with, I noticed that the ones I got wrong all had something to do with exponents. Obviously, I need to know more about exponents and how to handle them in equations, so yesterday I went to the math lab and got a tutor.

1. Topic: Failing a quiz
   Audience: Your best friend

2. Topic: Failing a quiz
   Audience: Your advisor

3. Topic: Quitting your job
   Audience: Your boss

4. Topic: Quitting your job
   Audience: Your family

5. Topic: Being in a car accident
   Audience: Your classmates

6. Topic: Being in a car accident
   Audience: Your grandparents

7. Topic: How to watch baseball (or any other sport)
   Audience: Eight-year-old children

8. Topic: How to watch baseball (or any other sport)
   Audience: Adults with limited knowledge of sports

9. Topic: Your favorite music
   Audience: The average newspaper reader

10. Topic: Your favorite music
    Audience: Your close friends

EXERCISE 2   Reading Journals

1. Keep a reading journal, and make entries in it at least once a day for a month or more. You can write in a special notebook, on loose paper, or on a computer. Whichever format you choose, for each entry record the date and some information about what you read. Write down your reactions to each reading, the thoughts and feelings it evokes in you. Allow your mind to wander—if you think of something that at first seems unrelated, write it down and explore it. Later, that idea may be just the topic you want for an essay.

2. If you prefer, keep your reading journal in a double-column notebook. Date each entry. On one side of your notebook, summarize the text you have read, listing the most important points. On the other side, record your ideas about and reactions to the reading.

3. After at least a month of keeping your reading journal, read over all the entries. Do you notice any patterns? What topics tend to evoke especially strong reactions from you? What themes do you tend to write about most often? Can you find new connections between readings that you did not notice before?

EXERCISE 3   Personal Journals

1. Create a personal journal, and make entries in it at least five times a week for a month or more. Each time you write, record the date. Remember that a personal journal is not a diary for listing your daily activities. Instead, write about events, sights, sounds, ideas, and feelings that seem important to you. You can explain the events, but put more emphasis on your reactions, thoughts, and feelings.

2. After you have kept your personal journal for a month or more, look back through it to find connections and patterns. What topics do you tend to write about most often? Can you find new connections between two events that you did not notice before? Did they evoke similar reactions from you?

3. Add to your journal the ideas you discover through rereading it. In approximately five hundred words, discuss the connections between journal entries and what you learned about yourself and your interests through journal writing.

CHAPTER 2

Developing Ideas by Questioning and Writing

2a Considering the evidence—Inferring

One way to develop ideas is to make inferences. To infer is to draw a tentative conclusion based on the available evidence. The conclusion you come to may not necessarily be correct, but it should be a plausible explanation.

Consider this example: You see a car proceeding down the street, weaving from side to side, nearly crashing into fences and trees. Based on what you observe, you might come to one of the following tentative conclusions or inferences:

The driver of the car is drunk.

The driver of the car is having a heart attack.

The driver of the car has just been stung by a bee.

The driver of the car is very inexperienced.

Something is wrong with the car's steering.

Something is wrong with the brakes.

Something is wrong with the tires.

These inferences are not necessarily true, but they are plausible. In order to reach a higher degree of certainty about any one of them, you would need further evidence. However, making these inferences means using your imagination to create ideas, which, in turn, can lead to other ideas.

2b Questioning evidence to find an idea

(Section 2c in the *Handbook*)

Sometimes people think they need answers to find ideas, but what they really need are good questions. A good question is one that leads to a detailed answer and then to more questions. One set of questions that many writers find useful is the journalist's *who, what, when, where, how,* and *why* list. News reporters' stories are considered incomplete unless they answer all six questions. In addition, consider the following questions when you are looking at evidence:

QUESTIONS TO ASK YOURSELF ABOUT EVIDENCE

1. What do I notice first about the evidence? What is most obvious?
2. How do I feel about what I am seeing or reading?
3. Are there any obvious patterns in the evidence?
4. When I look at or read the evidence again, can I find things that were not so obvious on first consideration?
5. What is this evidence about? What can I conclude about it?

As you ask yourself questions about the evidence, write down your answers. You may find that the answers suggest new questions.

2c	Writing about evidence to find an idea—Drafting and revising

(Section 2e in the *Handbook*)

As mentioned in Chapter 1 of the the *Workbook*, the work involved in producing a piece of writing is not usually linear but recursive. For example, it is not always possible to create a thorough, organized list of ideas that can be easily turned into sentences and paragraphs. Indeed, many writers are not sure of their subject until they have done a good amount of writing about it. All writers find it useful to freewrite or to keep a journal, allowing their minds to find connections and ideas that they may not have discovered otherwise. Often, writers discover that their first ideas about a topic are conventional and boring and that what seemed like a small point at first could become the major focus of a piece of writing. Here are some guidelines for writing to discover ideas:

WRITING TO DISCOVER AND CLARIFY AN IDEA

1. Look carefully at the evidence, and begin writing about whatever notion strikes you as interesting.
2. Open your mind to intrusions—to new ideas that push themselves into your writing.
3. Stop. Consider what you have written. Look at what your writing reveals to you about the evidence.
4. Write a second draft, this time beginning with the new idea.
5. Make connections. If the new idea reminds you of other things you know or have read, write about those connections. See what they reveal as you write and think about them.
6. Question your draft. Put yourself in the position of your audience. Ask about the relationship between the evolving idea and the evidence:

    —Is that relationship clear to my audience, which has to read about it without the benefit of everything that I know?

    —Are my intentions clear?

    —Are there aspects of the idea that need to be clarified?

    —What else could I learn about my idea if I question my evidence using the guidelines in section 2b of the *Workbook?*

EXERCISE 1   Inferring from Evidence

For each of the following, make two or more inferences based on the evidence provided. Example:

You see a car with several serious dents in it.

Inferences:

The owner of the car is a poor driver.

The owner bought the car used, in its present condition.

The car is used in drag races.

1. Newspapers are piling up on your neighbor's front lawn.

2. All the houses in a small town are painted yellow or beige.

3. A neighbor has put three locks on the front door.

4. In restaurants, a friend of yours never orders meat.

5. Someone you know reads the *Wall Street Journal* and *Investor's Business Daily* every day.

EXERCISE 2   Questioning Evidence to Find Ideas

Use the questions in section 2b of the *Workbook* to develop ideas about each of the following topics.

1. A painting you saw in a museum or book

2. A short story you read

3. A poem you read

4. A movie that disturbed you

5. A public figure you admire

EXERCISE 3   Writing about Evidence to Find Ideas

Use the guidelines in section 2c of the *Workbook* to write about and discover new ideas about each of the following topics.

1. The televising of real wars

2. Fashions in shoes

3. Simple foods (e.g., rice and pasta)

4. Learning to drive

5. Listening to music

CHAPTER 3

Developing Ideas through Connections and Controversies

3a | Connecting—Another way to find an idea

In general, you can better understand one idea or concept if you think of it in relation to another. To make connections between ideas, you compare and contrast, looking for similarities and differences. The attempt to find connections between things not only gives you a better understanding of each but also leads you to new ideas. Often, the most interesting ideas come when you are trying to find connections between seemingly unrelated subjects. For example, researchers who had studied the behavior of chimpanzees decided to study dolphins because there seemed to be certain similar patterns in both groups; such research could lead to interesting conclusions about mammals. In another example, a student found connections between her childhood trips to baseball games with her father and her interest as an adult in the mechanisms people use to function in work groups. The following guidelines are useful in making connections.

GUIDELINES FOR MAKING CONNECTIONS

1. Recall a significant event, memory, or object of interest to you.
2. Put your ideas about that event, memory, or object of interest into writing.
3. Put the writing aside for a while (for a few hours or several days). Distance yourself from it. Then go back and read it again, objectively, as if it had been written by someone else. Ask questions about it. What new ideas does it suggest to you?
4. Write down those new ideas. Then explore the connections between your first writing and the new ideas. In what ways are they alike? In what ways are they different? What do the similarities mean? What do the differences mean?
5. Revise what you have written so that your audience can understand your ideas and the connections between them.

3b | Researching controversies to find ideas

(Section 3d in the *Handbook*)

A useful way of finding ideas is to look for subjects that are controversial, that stir up conflicting feelings and opinions. You may already have a strong opinion about a given topic, or you may develop an opinion in the course of researching and writing about that topic. In your research, you can turn to many sources—books, articles, interviews, newspapers, government studies, documentaries, pamphlets, and so on—of facts and information about the views of special interest groups. The following guidelines may be useful.

RESEARCHING TO FIND IDEAS

1. Select a controversy that interests you.

2. In the library, locate sources for conflicting points of view on the topic. Do not limit yourself to only two opposing opinions. Remember that most issues cannot be divided neatly into right and wrong, good and bad. Look for a variety of opinions. Outline or summarize each point of view.

3. Question your sources. Look for weaknesses in the various arguments. Look for connections.

4. Start to formulate what you consider is a reasonable conclusion about the controversy. Write down your thesis and the reasons behind your viewpoint. List questions that still need to be answered.

5. Broaden your reading in order to answer the questions that remain and to test your conclusion.

6. Finally, considering all of the evidence you have gathered, formulate your thesis.

EXERCISE 1   Connecting to Find Ideas

Using the Guidelines for Making Connections in section 3a of the *Workbook,* write about the connections you discover and the ideas they lead to for each of the following topics.

1. Two significant memories—one from childhood, the other from later in your life— that seem to be related in some way

2. Two memories that seem to be unrelated

3. Two courses you are taking (or have taken) that seem to have a strong relationship to one another

4. Two courses you are taking (or have taken) that seem to have little or no relationship to one another

5. Two friends who seem similar

EXERCISE 2   Researching Controversies to Find Ideas

Using the guidelines in section 3b of the *Workbook,* research and then write about one of the following controversial topics.

1. Environmental waste
2. Civil disobedience
3. Abortion
4. Pornography
5. Single-sex schools

6. Gun control
7. Illegal immigration
8. Legalization of drugs
9. Religious cults
10. Sex education

CHAPTER 4

The Exploratory Essay

Like analytical and argumentative essays, the exploratory essay has a beginning, a middle, and an ending, but it is not as highly structured or as restricted as the other two essay types. The exploratory essay may have an ambling, storytelling quality; the writer may bring into it anything that makes readers pay attention. Rather than proving a point, the exploratory essayist is interested in examining ideas to see where they lead.

One way to begin an exploratory essay is with a story, a memory, or an experience from your life. The story, memory, or experience need not be a particularly significant one, but one that is interesting, unusual, or meaningful. After you identify it and write it down, ask yourself whether there is the germ of an idea in it. If possible, ask a classmate or friend for feedback. Then write again, perhaps telling another story, one suggested by your classmate's responses or your own rereading.

You can continue this process, adding to your stories; however, the purpose of an exploratory essay is to examine an idea, not to string together a series of stories. Therefore, examine what your stories reveal to you, the similarities they share, and the main point or idea they lead you to. Then you will be ready to form your stories into an essay that explores an idea.

EXERCISE 1   Developing an Exploratory Essay

Choose one of the following topics or another that interests you for your exploratory essay. Ask for feedback from classmates, friends, or family members. Using that feedback, write again, perhaps telling another story. Then shape your ideas and stories into an exploratory essay.

1. A fight with a childhood friend
2. Something in a commercial that seems silly to you
3. A walk in the park
4. An embarrassing moment in class
5. A childhood memory of delicious food
6. The unlikely behavior of someone you know well
7. An irrational fear
8. A time you helped someone you had never met before
9. A time you were treated unfairly
10. A time you made a mistake

CHAPTER 5

The Analytical Essay

An analytical essay can be about a written text, an art object, a family or other social group, an event, a concept—any topic complex enough to lend itself to interpretation. Think of all these different subjects as texts. Your first task in writing an analysis is to find out what the text means and how it conveys its meaning.

FEATURES OF THE ANALYTICAL ESSAY

- Focuses on the writer's interpretation of a text
- Develops an idea about that interpretation in a formal way
- Defends an idea rather than inquiring about it
- Depends primarily on the text itself for evidence
- Has a beginning, a middle, and an ending

GUIDELINES FOR DEVELOPING AN ANALYTICAL ESSAY

1. Read the selected text. Notice details in the text—an image, a phrase, anything that strikes you. Record insights, connections, and reactions in a reading journal or a double-column notebook. If you come across something you do not understand, turn it into a focusing question to answer later when you read and reread. That question should lead to other questions.

2. Reflect on your questions and observations. Think about how the text works and what it means.

3. Reread the text, this time considering your observations in relation to one another. Note the connections you find.

4. Select one detail from the text that interests you, and write one or two paragraphs explaining its relevance to the text. These paragraphs may later become part of the middle section of your essay.

5. Use the one detail you chose to lead you to others. Groups or clusters of details often lead to deeper insight. Keep writing to reveal the relationship between textual details and meaning. This writing may also become part of the middle of your essay.

6. Think about your readers. Can they understand what you have written? Can they follow your train of thought?

7. If possible, collaborate with other students and incorporate their suggestions.

8. Write a beginning for your essay that focuses readers' attention on what your analysis will reveal. Make sure readers can understand your thesis.

9. Revise the preliminary middle paragraphs that analyze details and meaning.

10. Write an ending that gives a final perspective on your interpretation.

EXERCISE 1   Developing an Analytical Essay

Using the preceding guidelines, develop an analytical essay on one of the following topics or another that interests you.

1. A painting or photograph
2. A movie or play
3. A short story or poem
4. A sporting event
5. A speech
6. A concert or opera
7. A family tradition
8. A social group
9. A sculpture
10. An election

CHAPTER 6

The Argumentative Essay

In an argumentative essay, the writer's task is to persuade readers to accept a certain point of view about a given issue. Although the topic may range from local problems to national or international issues, the most persuasive arguments focus on significant or controversial topics.

When you write an argumentative essay, part of your task is to research and consider conflicting points of view on the topic, and part of it is to develop and present your own point of view. Your investigation may require you to conduct library research, to interview local experts, to do field or laboratory experiments, or to rely on your own experience. Only after researching your topic will you be able to form your conclusion.

FEATURES OF THE ARGUMENTATIVE ESSAY

- Makes reasonable conclusions
- Presents adequate supporting evidence
- Provides a clear explanation of conflicting points of view
- Is thorough and complete

The following guidelines, while not a step-by-step system, will help you develop an argumentative essay.

GUIDELINES FOR DEVELOPING AN ARGUMENTATIVE ESSAY

1. Select a controversial topic that interests you.
2. Consider different points of view.
   —As evidence leads you to a particular conclusion, look for contradictory evidence.
   —Question evidence from your own experience just as you do for evidence from other sources.
   —Do not jump to conclusions; be suspicious if your evidence leads to only one way of looking at your topic.
   —Consider how your audience will interpret your evidence.
3. Write a short account of what you have discovered about your controversy. Include various points of view.
4. Based on the evidence you have gathered, formulate a tentative thesis.

5. Think about your audience. What background knowledge will the audience need in order to understand both your point of view and the views of others? How can you best organize and present your evidence?
6. Write the first draft.
7. Collaborate with classmates. Ask them to identify your thesis and to point out the weak spots in your argument.
8. Revise the draft based on the feedback you receive.

EXERCISE 1   Developing an Argumentative Essay

Using the preceding guidelines, develop an argumentative essay on one of the following controversial topics or another that interests you.

1. Gun control
2. Smoking in public places
3. Distributing condoms in high schools
4. The death penalty
5. Life imprisonment after three violent felony convictions
6. Violence on television
7. The passivity of American students
8. The commercialization of collegiate sports
9. Making English the official language of the United States
10. Inappropriate role models chosen by youth

PART THREE
Reading

CHAPTER 7

Critical Reading

Most of the reading you do in college is critical reading, which requires careful analysis and thoughtful response. Here the word *critical* does not mean being disapproving; rather, it means being perceptive and analytical. Critical reading involves reacting to what you read, analyzing it, interpreting it, and evaluating its ideas and values.

7a | Adjusting to different kinds of texts

Not all reading is alike. You read different kinds of texts in different ways. For example, you may skim a newspaper in order to pick up information quickly, but that approach is inappropriate for textbooks. Reading fiction and poetry requires you to do more interpretative work than you do when reading expository prose. To understand some texts, you need to preview, annotate, and reread.

7b | Writing from reading

Writing while you read and after you have read has many benefits. First, it is an excellent way to remember what you have read and therefore a useful way to study for exams. In addition, it prepares you for college writing assignments, such as essays, research papers, and reports. As you read, try the following techniques.

1 | Reacting to a text with annotations

Annotations are brief notes you make while reading. You can underline, circle, or highlight passages that seem significant to you. You can write comments in the margins indicating your reactions to the text. You can use symbols as a kind of shorthand—a question mark to indicate disagreement or confusion, for example, or a star to indicate that you feel a point is important.

2 | Reflecting on a text in freewriting

Freewriting is a way to develop your thoughts about a text. In freewriting, you record your ideas without arranging them in any special order. You aim to get your ideas down on paper, in the order in which they occur to you. You do not worry about spelling, grammar, organization, or the relative importance of your ideas. Freewriting lets you spill out your ideas so that you have a record of them; the time to rethink, evaluate, organize, and edit comes later.

3 | Using a double-column notebook

On the divided pages of a double-column notebook, you use the left-hand pages to summarize what you have read and the right-hand pages to respond to what you have read. The following chart outlines what to do.

HIGHLIGHTS OF THE DOUBLE-COLUMN NOTEBOOK

SUMMARY (LEFT-HAND COLUMN)	COMMENTS (RIGHT-HAND COLUMN)
—Summarize the text.	—Respond to your summary.
—Interpret the author's idea.	—Reflect on the author's idea.
—Explain the idea succinctly.	—Consider whether you agree or disagree, and why.
—Identify important details.	—Raise questions about the details.
—Relate the details to the main idea.	—Relate the main idea to other readings or to your own experience.

4 | Writing a summary

A summary is a condensed version of a text in which you explain the author's ideas in your own words. A summary should present the writer's ideas accurately; it should not include your own interpretation of those ideas.

7c | Analyzing what you read

Analyzing a text involves looking closely at its parts and determining the meanings of those parts. First, of course, you must notice what is in the text, and that means taking note of its details. Simply observing details, however, is not enough. You must also connect the details with each other. In doing so, you will notice patterns and connections that are important in interpreting the reading.

7d   Formulating an interpretation

An interpretation is your tentative or provisional conclusion about a text based on your analysis of it (your observations and the connections you find). To arrive at an interpretation, first you must make inferences. Inferences are guesses, explanations of evidence; inferences are not always correct, but they are reasonable explanations based on the available evidence. You make an inference by discovering what is implied rather than explicitly stated in the text. Your inferences then lead you to an interpretation.

7e   Evaluating a text

Interpretation and evaluation of a text are not the same. In interpreting, you attempt to arrive at an understanding of the text, recognizing that the writer's meaning is paramount. In evaluating, however, you bring into the process your own judgments of the text's quality and values. In doing so, you must be aware of your own personal and cultural values. Evaluation is affected by your likes and dislikes, by what appeals to or repels you, and by your feelings about the subject.

7f   Discussing your reading with others

It can be interesting as well as useful to discuss your reading with others. Doing so can give you a chance to explain what you think and why, often thereby clarifying your understanding of a text. In addition, others' interpretations and evaluations as well as their reasons for thinking as they do can enrich your own understanding.

EXERCISE 1 Writing While Reading

Choose one of the following reading suggestions. As you read, do these critical reading tasks: annotate the text; freewrite in response to the text; take notes about the text in a double-column notebook; and write a summary of the text.

1. A newspaper editorial

2. An op-ed article in a newspaper

3. A Shakespearean sonnet

4. A chapter from a sociology, history, psychology, or economics textbook

5. A short story by Edgar Allan Poe

6. A poem or a story by Gertrude Stein

7. The Declaration of Independence

8. A recent law passed by your state legislature

9. Excerpts from the journals of Henry David Thoreau

10. A chapter from *Down These Mean Streets* by Piri Thomas

EXERCISE 2 Observing and Connecting Details

Choose another reading assignment from the list in the preceding exercise. Make lists of the details in the text and of your observations about them. Then group the details and your observations to see what connections emerge. Explain the connections you find in writing.

EXERCISE 3 Responding to, Interpreting, and Evaluating Texts

1. Record your subjective responses to a text assigned by your instructor or to one of your own choosing. Respond by annotating or freewriting.

2. Make a list of observations about the text.

3. Identify one or more connections or sets of relationships among the details on your list. Categorize the items and create headings for them.

4. List the inferences you can make on the basis of the textual details you observed and the connections you saw among them.

5. Prepare a double-column notebook entry on the text.

6. Write a summary of the text in which you offer an interpretation based on your evidence and inferences.

7. Write an evaluation of the text in which you discuss (a) how well the text achieves its purposes, (b) the cultural values the text displays, and (c) your assessment of those values.

CHAPTER 8

The Experience of Reading

Reading reflectively means to think about, or reflect on, what the writer of a text is saying. One focus for your reflections should be other things you have read or learned that relate to the details of the text. In addition to making connections between details within the text itself, you make connections between the text and other readings and your own observations and experiences. By engaging in reflective reading, you make your experience relevant to the text.

Reflective reading often requires rereading. Reading, like writing, is a recursive process. Not only do your thoughts loop back mentally over what you have read, but you may also go back and reread specific sections of the text. You reread for different reasons. Sometimes you do it to make sure you have thoroughly understood a complex idea. Other times you reread to experience again an enjoyable section. Occasionally, you reread to confirm connections you perceive between sections of a text. The following guidelines can help you read reflectively.

HOW TO ENHANCE YOUR EXPERIENCE OF READING

1. Read actively, annotating the text.
2. Read attentively, focusing on each paragraph or section.
3. Reflect on the text and question it.
4. Interpret the text by observing and connecting details, drawing inferences, and formulating a conclusion.
5. Evaluate the text, considering its effectiveness, persuasiveness, and cultural values.
6. Read intertextually, bringing in other texts and experiences. Write down the connections you find between the primary text and the other texts and experiences. Write about the significance of the connections you discover.

EXERCISE 1   Reading Reflectively

For one of the following topics, find and read at least two related essays, articles, newspaper columns, or book chapters. Read critically, annotating the texts, observing details, making connections between details. Then react reflectively, making connections between the texts and other texts as well as your own experiences.

1. An ethnic stereotype in the movies

2. Encouraging more high school girls to take science courses

3. The First Amendment

4. Fluoridation of water supplies

5. Sports scholarships

6. Life-support systems in hospitals

7. The resurgence of tuberculosis

8. Gender differences in the use of language

9. Religious cults

10. Mail-order catalogs

PART FOUR
Thinking

CHAPTER 9

Creative Thinking

9a Comparing creative and logical thinking

Although creative thinking and logical thinking differ, each is as important as the other. Creative thinking puts things together, generates new ideas, explores all alternatives and possibilities, moves backward as well as forward, and withholds judgment. Logical thinking, in contrast, analyzes, selects, moves linearly, and makes judgments. Despite their differences, creative and logical thinking complement each other.

9b Using techniques of creative thinking

1 Establishing a quota of alternatives

When making a decision or solving a problem, you look for the single best alternative or answer. When thinking creatively, however, you do not stop after identifying one reasonable alternative. Although that one alternative may be satisfactory, by generating instead a quota of reasonable alternatives (such as five possible solutions to a problem), you are more likely to find a better alternative than the one you formulated initially. Consider, for example, that you are asked to select your own topic for a research paper. Rather than limiting your choice to the first topic that occurs to you, you list three or four very different possibilities and then choose the one that interests you most. Then, once you settle on a topic, you list several different ways you might develop and organize the paper.

2 | Reversing relationships

When you reverse relationships, you turn something around and approach it in an unconventional way or from an unusual direction. The purpose of reversing relationships is to see things in a way that your usual perspective does not allow you to perceive. Some examples of unconventional reversals of relationships include thinking about how a dog trains its owner, how children influence their parents, and how television viewers influence programming.

3 | Using analogy

An analogy is a comparison of two different things that have some similar features. Writers use analogy to clarify and explain their ideas. In creative thinking, analogy can help you generate ideas by pushing you to look at things in ways that might not have occurred to you. For example, to illustrate how knee joints work, you might make an analogy with a hinge. In another example, arranging ideas in logical groups in an outline might be compared to sorting clean laundry into similar piles of clothing.

4 | Shifting attention

Sometimes in writing you run out of ideas because you focus too narrowly on only one aspect of your subject. Deliberately shifting attention away from the dominant element to other elements can help you generate additional ideas. For example, while writing a paper about a proposed lengthening of the school year, you might initially concentrate on the effects of the proposal on students. But by shifting attention to the effects of a longer school year on parents and teachers, you can stimulate further thought and additional ideas. So can other kinds of shifts, such as to the broader effects on college preparation, the economy, competitiveness in the job market, and so on. Shifting attention may also cause you to adjust the focus of your paper, in which case you may need to rethink your initial purpose and emphasis.

5 | Denying the negative

Unlike logical thinking, creative thinking does not reject ideas. It encourages ideas. It says "Yes, maybe," not "No." Creative thinking does not make judgments; it is open to all possibilities, and it avoids such labels as unrealistic, inadequate, silly, or wrong. Useful discoveries have been made in experiments whose premises were wrong. Considering an idea that is seemingly unpromising can sometimes lead you to better ideas that would have otherwise remained unexplored.

6 | Asking questions

A student once inquired why the instructor was asking questions rather than conveying to students the material they needed to know. The student had assumed that education was simply a process of transferring a finite body of knowledge from one mind, the teacher's, into the minds of students.

The boundaries of knowledge are always expanding, and an important part of education is learning how to explore and find knowledge on your own. Knowing how to ask good questions is an important skill, one that can lead you to many new ideas.

A question that leads to a single, conclusive answer is a dead end. Such a question does not encourage the exploration of new ideas. The most productive kinds of questions lead to further thought. Questions beginning with the word *why* or *how* generate new ideas. Questions that ask "What if?" also stimulate thinking. So do questions about questions—that is, answering one question by asking another.

Let us consider the topic *bilingual education* and where various kinds of questions about that topic will lead. Questions beginning with *what* or *who* may not generate many ideas: "What is bilingual education?" "Who needs bilingual education?" But questions beginning with *why, how,* or *what if* can generate interesting answers and more questions: "Why is bilingual education an issue?" "Why do we need bilingual education?" "How can we discover the need?" "How can such education be structured?" "What if bilingual classes are provided?" "What if they are not?"

9c   Overcoming obstacles to creative thinking

To become a more skilled creative thinker, you need to overcome various obstacles such as ingrained habits, fears, and anxieties. Perceptual blocks, for example, keep you from understanding that which you know little about. Acquiring more knowledge about a subject helps you see it better. Other kinds of blocks may include cultural blocks; ingrained thinking habits about ethnicity, race, gender, and class; intellectual blocks (lack of knowledge); and emotional blocks (especially the fear of being wrong). Recognizing such blocks to creative thinking is the first step to overcoming them.

EXERCISE 1   Using a Quota of Alternatives

For each topic that follows, list at least four alternative ways of interpreting or approaching the topic.

1. A poem by Langston Hughes

2. A movie you saw recently

3. A short story by Jamaica Kincaid

4. An introduction to a paper you wrote for a course

5. A conclusion to a paper you wrote for a course

EXERCISE 2   Reversing Relationships

Practice reversing relationships by completing at least two of the following assignments.

1. In reading an article, essay, or book chapter, begin with the final paragraph and work your way back to the beginning, one paragraph at at time. Write about what you discovered by reversing your reading of the text.
2. In writing an essay, report, or paper, write the conclusion first, the body next, and the introduction last. What did you learn in doing so?
3. In preparing an assignment, write the paper first and the outline last. What happened because of this reversal?
4. Write a list of the advantages of breaking traffic laws.
5. Write a list of the disadvantages of studying hard in school.
6. Explain the advantages of being a chronic liar.
7. Explain the disadvantages of being a kind person.

8. List the positive consequences of being rude.

9. List the benefits of being sick.

10. List the drawbacks of having perfect health.

EXERCISE 3   Shifting Attention

For each of the following topics, list at least three different elements that could be emphasized in an essay.

1. Alcoholism

2. Child abuse

3. Sales tax increases

4. A longer school day

5. The death penalty

EXERCISE 4   Denying the Negative

For one week, record how often you hear people using the negative to deny a prospect or a possibility. Note also how often you do this yourself. At the end of the week, consider which of those things may be possible after all. Write about the possibilities.

EXERCISE 5   Asking Questions

For each of the following topics, list five initial questions. Then list five more questions that emerge from those in the initial list.

1. Improving your grades

2. Shoplifting in department stores

3. Cheating on exams

4. Saving time

5. Choosing a major

CHAPTER 10

Logical Thinking

Logical thinking applies principles of reasoning to develop arguments and judge their validity. Important aspects of logical thinking include inductive and deductive reasoning, causal explanation, analogy, authority and testimony, and avoiding logical fallacies.

10a   Using inductive and deductive reasoning

Inductive reasoning, or induction, is reasoning from the particular instance to the general principle. Deductive reasoning, or deduction, is reasoning from a general principle to a particular instance by applying a general rule, law, or principle to specific circumstances.

1   Understanding inductive reasoning

Induction is used to attribute causes to events or circumstances, rather than to determine the truth about them with absolute certainty. For instance, if you get a headache each time you drink coffee, you will most likely generalize that something in the coffee causes the onset of a headache. Your generalization about the cause may be right or wrong, but you cannot be certain because inductive reasoning depends on probability—the likelihood that something is the cause rather than complete conviction of its truth. Therefore, the conclusions you reach through inductive reasoning are reliable or unreliable rather than simply right or wrong.

You base your judgment about reliability or unreliability on the quantity and the quality of the available evidence. One instance of a headache that may have been caused by drinking coffee is not a sufficient sample of evidence. Several instances could lead to a more reliable decision, but not necessarily a conclusive one. There could be other factors that you have not yet considered, such as ingestion of caffeine in other foods, stress in your life, high blood pressure, and so on. Errors in inductive reasoning usually involve oversimplification—that is, by reading too much into too little evidence.

ELEMENTS OF INDUCTIVE REASONING

- Begins with a specific observation
- Continues with additional specific observations

- Arrives at a general claim or reasonable conclusion based on the available evidence
- Attributes causes to events or circumstances, resulting in a hypothesis that can be tested further
- Offers probability rather than certainty

2 | Understanding deductive reasoning

In deductive reasoning you reason from a general principle to its application in a more specific instance. For the coffee example cited earlier, you would begin with the generalization that coffee causes you to have headaches. Reasoning deductively, you would conclude that if you drink coffee, you will indeed experience such a reaction.

Deductive thinking is essentially syllogistic reasoning. A syllogism is an argument arranged in three parts: a major premise, a minor premise, and a conclusion. The premises can be facts or assumptions. A major premise states a general principle or rule. A minor premise states a specific instance. A conclusion follows from the major and minor premises. Look at the following examples:

MAJOR PREMISE   A flea is a wingless insect. [fact]

MINOR PREMISE   The creature on your desk has wings. [fact]

CONCLUSION   The creature on your desk is not a flea. [valid]

MAJOR PREMISE   When Bob eats eggs, he gets a rash. [fact]

MINOR PREMISE   Bob is eating eggs. [fact]

CONCLUSION   He will break out in a rash. [valid]

The major premise in this case is a fact, one based on the individual's repeated experience. The minor premise is also a fact. As a result, the syllogism is valid, or true. The premises and the conclusion correspond with reality, with what actually happens.

When the conclusion does not follow logically from the premises, a syllogism is invalid, even if its premises are facts. Consider the following example:

MAJOR PREMISE   When Bob eats eggs, he gets a rash. [fact]

MINOR PREMISE   Bob has a rash. [fact]

CONCLUSION   Bob must have been eating eggs. [invalid]

The reasoning here is faulty because the rash might have been caused by something other than eating eggs. The syllogism is thus invalid.

In some syllogisms, the major premise is an assumption rather than a fact. For example:

MAJOR PREMISE   Varsity athletes are popular. [assumption]

MINOR PREMISE   Claude is on the varsity basketball team. [fact]

CONCLUSION   Claude is popular.

When a premise is an assumption rather than a fact, you must be able to support the premise with evidence. The major premise of this example rests on a shaky assumption, so the argument is not true. Popularity comes from a variety of qualities, not just team membership.

ELEMENTS OF DEDUCTIVE REASONING

- Begins with a general idea or major premise
- Continues with a minor premise applied to a particular case
- Concludes with a specific statement derived from the premises
- Can be true or false, depending on the truth or falsity of the premises
- Can be valid or invalid, depending on whether the structure of the syllogism is sound
- When true, provides certainty rather than probability

10b   Understanding causality

Causality refers to a situation in which one event is responsible for another event that occurs after it. In the case of a headache always occurring after drinking coffee, it is easy to see the relationship between the cause and the effect. However, in many cases causality is not as easily identified. For example, consider your decision to major in a particular area of study. You may be able to point to the specific advice you were given, the experiences you had, and the situations you heard about that influenced your choice. You cannot, however, state with complete certainty that any one single thing "caused" you to make your career choice. To do so would be a great oversimplification.

In the same way that you explain your career choice with multiple causes, you should consider multiple causes when writing and reasoning. Single-cause explanations oversimplify and thus are false. They cannot explain complex historical events and social circumstances. For example, there is no single cause for the decline in reading levels among American school children. The decline has been blamed on, among other things, the two-income family, changing school curriculums, bilingual education, and the number of hours children watch television. Causality is rarely easy to establish. Therefore, in your writing, exercise care in using causal explanation, and do not oversimplify.

10c   Using analogy in arguments

As discussed in section 9b-3 of the *Workbook*, an analogy makes a comparison. Writers often use analogies to explain something unfamiliar to readers by comparing it with something more familiar. For example, to explain how cholesterol narrows the arteries in arteriosclerosis, a writer might compare the deposits of cholesterol on the walls of major blood vessels to the buildup of soap and mineral deposits on a shower wall. Analogies of this type help readers understand what writers mean.

Be careful, however, when using analogies to develop an argument. From a strictly logical viewpoint, arguments from analogy lack persuasive rigor because analogies do not prove a point. They provide alternative ways of seeing or saying things, to enhance understanding, but analogies cannot prove a point because the two things they compare are not actually identical. Cholesterol deposits are in some ways similar to soap and mineral buildup on a shower wall, but in other very important ways the two things are very different. Comparing them may help readers visualize the one they know less about, but the comparison does not prove anything about either one.

10d   Using authority and testimony

Authority refers to the expertise of an individual whose knowledge, rank, position, or accomplishments can lend credibility to an assertion. Testimony refers to someone's support of a claim by standing up for or witnessing to it. Authority and testimony can give powerful support to an argument—as long as the testimony is credible and the authority is convincing. Be careful when using authority and testimony in your writing; always use them credibly and honestly. Authorities do not always agree with each other, sometimes because they consider complex problems with various explanations and validity, as in the case, for example, of the causes of the American Civil War. Also take into account authority bias: to what extent should you believe a medical expert testifying about the safety of a new drug if that expert was paid to do research by the company that produces the drug? In the same way, be skeptical about testimonials that rely on illogical attempts to influence decisions.

10e   Avoiding fallacies

A fallacy is an error. A logical fallacy is an error or a mistake in logic. Be aware of the most common logical fallacies so that you can recognize them in others' arguments and avoid them in your own writing.

1   Non sequitur

Non sequitur is Latin for "It does not follow." A *non sequitur* is a conclusion that does not follow logically from an argument's premises.

I came to class every day this semester. I deserve to pass.

The statement may sound reasonable if we believe the missing premise—that anyone who shows up for every class automatically deserves to pass. Instructors, however, determine grades on more than attendance, and therefore the conclusion is illogical.

2   Hasty generalization

In a hasty generalization, one jumps to conclusions on the basis of too little evidence.

In the last month, in separate incidents, three police officers were arrested for trafficking in drugs. It seems that most police officers are corrupt.

The conclusion is illogical because there is insufficient evidence to support it.

3 | Stereotyping

Stereotyping is a form of hasty generalization because it involves making assumptions about things, places, events, or people based on insufficient evidence.

College professors are unrealistic, absent-minded people.

People who live in New York City are rude.

Most Haitians have AIDS.

Stereotyping is not only illogical; it can often be prejudicial and malicious as well.

4 | *Either-Or* thinking

Either-or thinking limits the possibilities or solutions to just two—either A or B—and ignores other alternatives. Such a view is polarized; it sees things as either good or bad, right or wrong. No other possibilities are considered.

Either Congress must pass the president's health care proposal, or the nation's economy will sink under the weight of health care costs.

The president's proposal is just one of many; the American economy has other stresses besides the cost of health care. *Either-or* thinking is limiting. It oversimplifies complex issues, reducing them to extreme explanations.

5 | *Post hoc, ergo propter hoc*

Post hoc, ergo propter hoc is Latin for "After this, therefore because of this." This fallacy results from the assumption that because event A happened first and event B happened second, event A must have caused event B to occur. Such assumptions are clearly the result of faulty cause-and-effect reasoning.

Shortly before the 1994 Winter Olympics, the skater Nancy Kerrigan was attacked and clubbed on the knee. At the Olympics she narrowly missed winning the gold medal and had to settle for second place. The injury must have affected her skating ability.

Such reasoning ignores most of the factors that led to Kerrigan's silver medal, including her own excellent skating performances, the abilities of the other skaters, and the preferences of the skating judges.

6 | Begging the question

To beg the question involves assuming the truth of an issue without providing evidence or arguments in its support.

Students should not have representatives on the committee on instruction because the committee should be composed only of faculty members.

The statement does not provide reasons. It simply repeats its viewpoint and assumes that it is valid.

7 │ Circular reasoning

Similar to begging the question, circular reasoning asserts the same thing in different words, without introducing evidence or reasons in support.

Students should have representatives on the senate because they deserve to be represented.

The sentence provides no support for its claim.

8 │ Special pleading

In special pleading, a writer presents a one-sided argument while ignoring contradictory evidence and opposing viewpoints.

People should make cheese a part of their daily diet. Cheese contains protein, which is essential for good health. It also contains calcium, and most Americans get far too little calcium in their diets.

The claims made for cheese are true; it does contain protein and calcium. The problem is what is left unsaid: many cheeses are quite high in fat and sodium, which in excess can lead to serious health problems.

9 │ Red herring

Bringing a red herring into an argument deliberately sidetracks the discussion by introducing an irrelevant matter. The fallacy derives its name from criminals' practice of dragging a herring across their path to confuse the scent of the bloodhounds once used to track them down.

This police officer should not be giving me a ticket for failing to stop at a red light when there are drug dealers everywhere selling drugs to young children. The police should be spending their time on important things and not harassing law-abiding citizens like me.

The issue is not drug dealing, but whether the speaker ran a red light.

10 │ Appeal to ignorance

In an appeal to ignorance, the speaker or writer argues that a situation is true simply because there is little strong contrary evidence. It assumes that the assertion must be true because it cannot be proved untrue.

Nobody can prove that God does not exist, and therefore that must mean that God does exist.

Matters like the existence of God can be neither proved nor disproved; they are matters of faith. In an appeal to ignorance, the speaker or writer substitutes belief for logic.

11 *Ad populum*

Ad populum, Latin for "to the people," is a fallacy that appeals to people's emotions and prejudice rather than to reason.

> My opponent cannot possibly understand the feelings of working-class and middle-class people the way I can because he is rich and sends his children to private school.

The speaker appeals to the audience's assumed mistrust of the wealthy. The speaker is assuming that the audience will be swayed more by emotion than by an interest in the opponent's performance record.

12 *Ad hominem*

Ad hominem, Latin for "to the man," is an attack on an individual's character. It attempts to discredit an idea by attacking the person rather than by addressing the actual issue.

> The senator wants us to support the Equal Rights Amendment, but he himself is divorced and has been involved in various scandals involving women. So why should we listen to his views on equal rights for women?

The issue is not the senator's personal life, but his views on a particular bill.

13 False analogy

A false analogy misleads by comparing situations that have more differences than they do similarities. False analogies are also sometimes based on irrelevant similarities.

> Legalizing drugs will decrease the involvement of organized crime in the drug trade, just as happened when Prohibition was repealed.

This analogy ignores not only the vast differences between illegal liquor in the 1920s and illegal drugs in the 1990s, but also the medical, social, and economic consequences of widespread drug addiction. The situations are not parallel.

EXERCISE 1   Analyzing Deductive Arguments

Analyze the following deductive arguments by identifying their major and minor premises and conclusions. When necessary, supply the missing premises.

1. Caring for a pet can teach responsibility. All children should have pets.

2. Marian exercises twice as often as I do. She must be in much better shape than I am.

3. People today watch television much more than they read. How can we have an enlightened citizenry if people do not read?

4. I think; therefore, I am.

5. He must be very intelligent since he has a straight A average.

EXERCISE 2   Constructing Arguments

The following statements are minor premises. Use each statement to construct a valid syllogism. Example:

Housing starts were up for the fifth month in a row.

MAJOR PREMISE   Housing starts are an important indicator of a strong economy.

MINOR PREMISE   Housing starts were up for the fifth month in a row.

CONCLUSION   The economy must be improving.

1. Secondhand smoke can cause health problems.

2. Swimming for an hour three times a week provides excellent cardiovascular exercise.

3. The software company reported substantial losses for the four quarters of 1994.

4. Speaking a foreign language can enhance the possibility of getting a job.

5. The average price for houses in this area has risen steadily in the last two years.

EXERCISE 3   Examining Causes and Effects

Choose two of the following items, and for each make one list of causes and another list of effects.

1. The American Civil War
2. World War I
3. The Depression
4. Declining SAT scores
5. The rise in professional athletes' salaries
6. The popularity of television talk shows
7. American involvement in Somalia
8. The tendency to regard criminals as celebrities
9. The rise of health maintenance organizations (HMOs)
10. The increase in GEDs

EXERCISE 4   Using Causality in Writing

Choose of one of the topics from Exercise 3. In two paragraphs identify its causes, and in two other paragraphs explain its effects.

1. Your choice of a college
2. Your choice of a major
3. The severe winter of 1994
4. Global warming
5. The prevalence of drugs
6. Gun-related deaths
7. The discovery of X-rays
8. The discovery of mitochondria
9. The invention of television
10. The invention of dynamite

EXERCISE 5   Identifying Fallacies

Identify the fallacies of reasoning in the following statements. Explain what, if anything, might be wrong with each one.

1. Something terrible must have happened to him. He would have called if he were going to be this late.

2. The school got a new math teacher. Passing rates declined the next year. He must be a poor math teacher.

3. Evolution cannot be true because no one has actually seen it happening.

4. I was ticketed for speeding in two small towns. All small rural towns must have speed traps.

5. Why should we listen to the mayor's views on the drug problem when his own son was arrested for possessing marijuana?

CHAPTER 11

Fundamentals of Paragraph Development

11a Creating unified and coherent paragraphs

A paragraph has unity when it develops a single idea. All sentences within a paragraph pertain to that main idea; there are no unrelated topics that introduce a different theme.

A paragraph has coherence when its sentences are arranged in a logical order and its ideas are conveyed clearly to readers.

11b Achieving paragraph unity

Paragraph unity can be achieved by staying focused on the idea, placing the topic sentence in an effective position, and giving sufficient explanation.

1 Staying focused on the idea

You can achieve paragraph unity by staying focused on the main idea expressed in your topic sentence. When you lose track of the main idea and bring in unrelated subjects, you create disunity that can confuse readers. In the following example, the *italicized* sentence digresses from the subject specified in the topic sentence and thus destroys paragraph unity:

Many of the English names for months of the year have Latin derivations. September, October, November, and December, for example, derive from the Latin words for seven, eight, nine, and ten. July is named for Julius Caesar, August for Augustus Caesar. *Wednesday means "Woden's day," after Woden, the supreme god in the pre-Christian Germanic religion.* January is named after the god Janus and March after the god of war, Mars.

The subject named in the topic sentence is the names of months derived from Latin words. Unity is destroyed by the sentence referring to Wednesday; that sentence belongs in another paragraph.

2 | Placing the topic sentence

The topic sentence that states the paragraph's main idea can be placed anywhere in the paragraph, depending on how you want to lead readers to an understanding of your main idea. Placing the topic sentence at the beginning of a paragraph is effective in argumentative essays and essay exams. In such cases, you defend your position on a given subject; it is therefore helpful to state at the outset what you will try to prove.

Placing the topic sentence at the end of a paragraph can be effective in an exploratory essay, which leads readers through evidence to a conclusion. A topic sentence can be placed in the middle of a paragraph when you need to prepare readers or provide background information.

3 | Explaining the idea

In addition to remaining focused on an idea and including a well-placed topic sentence, a unified and coherent paragraph must offer enough evidence to convince readers. Do not rely solely on your topic sentence to carry the weight of your idea. Always offer enough explanation to make your idea clear to your readers. Note the difference between these two paragraphs:

UNDEVELOPED   Many people think the phrase "survival of the fittest" means that those who are in the best physical health are those who will survive. Such an idea is a misinterpretation of the theory of natural selection.

DEVELOPED   Many people think the phrase "survival of the fittest" means that those who are in the best physical health are those who will survive. Such an idea is a misinterpretation of the theory of natural selection. These people assign the wrong meaning to the word *fit*, believing that it means being in excellent physical condition, being bigger and faster and stronger than others. In fact, according to Darwin, organisms survive to reproduce when they are adapted to their environment. Adaptation for survival and thus reproduction may for some species mean protective coloration, ability to hibernate, or ability to regulate internal temperature.

11c | Achieving paragraph coherence

You can achieve paragraph coherence in the following ways.

WAYS TO ACHIEVE PARAGRAPH COHERENCE

- Use pronouns to replace nouns.
- Repeat and develop key terms.
- Link sentences with transitional words.
- Include visual details.
- Use parallel structures.

1   Using pronouns

Overuse of nouns can cause a paragraph to seem choppy and to lack coherence. By substituting pronouns for nouns, you can make paragraphs easier to read. Note the difference between these two paragraphs:

CHOPPY   Born in Corning, New York, in 1883, Margaret Sanger was a pioneer in the birth control movement. From personal experience and work as a nurse, Sanger came to believe that family limitation was necessary for social progress. Sanger's promotion of birth control led to indictments and arrests, but Sanger persevered.

COHERENT   Born in Corning, New York, in 1883, Margaret Sanger was a pioneer in the birth control movement. From personal experience and work as a nurse, *she* came to believe that family limitation was necessary for social progress. *Her* promotion of birth control led to indictments and arrests, but *she* persevered.

2   Repeating key terms

The repetition of key terms can have a positive effect on paragraph coherence. You need not repeat a single term; rather, you can use related words to develop your idea and to keep your reader's attention. As a general rule, repeat words sparingly. Note the repetition of key terms in the following paragraph:

Some critics argue that watching too much *television* makes children *passive*. Not only do children *sit* physically inactive in front of the *television* set, but unfortunately they *sit* there mentally *passive* as well. Watching *television* does not require decoding skills, as reading does. It does not ask viewers to reflect on what they are seeing and to compare it to other experiences. *Television* is not interactive; children cannot offer contributions and suggestions, nor can they receive a response to their own ideas. The *passivity* engendered by too much *television* watching will not serve children well either in school or in the world.

3   Linking sentences with transitional expressions

Transitional words can enhance paragraph coherence by indicating the relationships among sentences and among the ideas in sentences. Use transitional words sparingly; too many in one paragraph can create a pretentious, mannered tone. The following chart provides a list of commonly used transitional words and expressions.

TRANSITIONAL WORDS AND EXPRESSIONS

- To suggest continuity and sequence

and then, next, again, finally, furthermore, besides, in the first place, also, moreover

- To illustrate with examples

  for example, for instance, the following example, such as, after all, specifically, that is

- To suggest comparison

  in the same way, likewise, similarly, once more, also

- To indicate contrast

  on the contrary, but, yet, although, despite, nevertheless, notwithstanding, on the other hand, even though, instead, in spite of, for all that

- To show a result

  consequently, therefore, thus, as a result, hence, so, then, to this end, because

- To signal time

  after a while, afterward, after a few days, at that time, before, earlier, immediately, in the meantime, in the past, now, presently, lately, later, shortly, simultaneously, when, since

- To indicate place

  out there, beyond, below, above, under, closer to, elsewhere, there, to the left, to the right, to the north, opposite, nearby

- To offer concessions

  although, granted, of course, let me concede that, but I admit, it may seem that

- To clarify and conclude with emphasis

  thus, in conclusion, in other words, on the whole, in summary, therefore, in any event, as we have seen, to sum up, finally

4 | Including visual details

Often, to help readers understand an idea, you can provide visual details or images. You may give an analogy, for example, providing a comparison between your idea and a physical image. Readers familiar with the physical image are thus led to a better understanding of your idea. In describing how to solve a math problem, you might refer to a jigsaw puzzle. To explain the feeling of discovery, you might compare it to opening a door to a room you had never seen before.

5 | Using parallelism

Using parallel structures is another way to make your paragraphs coherent. Parallelism results when you repeat the same grammatical form. Parallel structures within a paragraph call attention to an idea and create a rhythm that underscores the idea. Note how the following paragraph uses parallelism:

Constant progress is not a feature of real life. On the contrary, life is full of *growth, setbacks, progress,* and *regressions.* A child learns *to tie her shoelaces one day* and has forgotten *how to do it the next.* A dieter *loses some weight one week* and *gains some back the next.* A sprinter *sets a world record in one race* and *loses to an unknown runner in the following race.* There is always movement, but not always in the direction we would choose.

11d   Organizing paragraphs

There are five organizational patterns that can be used within paragraphs: general to specific, specific to general, climactic order, time order, and spatial order.

1   From general to specific

Paragraphs using the general-to-specific organizational pattern open with a general, abstract statement or a broad, inclusive claim and then move to a specific, detailed discussion. Look at the following example:

> Because of language, human beings can have abstract ideas. Like humans, some animals can communicate, but their communication is at a very basic level. Using noises, animals can convey warnings. Using body gestures, animals can tell others about the location of food sources. But only humans can talk to each other of "love, honor, truth, and justice."

2   From specific to general

Paragraphs using the specific-to-general organizational pattern start with particulars and details and then move to a general, broad conclusion. Here is an example:

> *Cane,* Jean Toomer's collection of stories, poems, and sketches, was published in 1923. Langston Hughes's *The Weary Blues,* a collection of poetry, came out in 1926. The novel *God Sends Sunday,* by Arna Bontemps, was published in 1931. The year 1934 saw the appearance of Zora Neale Hurston's novel *Jonah's Gourd Vine.* These works are just a few of the many that were created in the 1920s and 1930s by black American writers, many of whom lived in New York City's Harlem. The flowering of black American literature that took place in the 1920s is termed the Harlem Renaissance.

3   Climactic order

Climactic order arranges information within a paragraph from least important to most important. Climactic order (both within a paragraph and an essay as a whole) is especially effective in argumentative essays. Note how the following paragraph uses climactic order:

> Succeeding as an actor is the dream of many people, but only a few ever achieve that dream. Talent is, of course, the first necessary quality, but there are thousands of talented people who never make it. Persistence is mandatory; one must continue going to audition after audition, even after dozens or maybe hundreds of disappointments. Perhaps the most important component in the mix that leads to acting success is the one not within the person's control: luck.

4   Time order

In narration, time order, or chronological order, can help readers follow the sequence of events and the writer's thinking. Consider the following example:

When Liz first moved to San Francisco, she did not have a job and she knew nobody. For a while she stayed in a youth hostel and looked for a job so that she could find her own place to live. Her first job was in a pizza place, where she made pizza dough and eventually ran the cash register. Next, during the holidays she worked in a department store, where she had to dress up as a ballerina and direct people to the toy department. Some time later, after she had become familiar with the city, she worked for a messenger service. She eventually found a job that she considered perfect; she worked backstage at a dinner theater. The job paid well, and since she worked in the evenings, during the day she could take ballet classes.

5 | Spatial order

Spatial order, moving from one point in space to another within a given scene, can help readers see what happened there. Note how the following paragraph uses spatial order:

He walked slowly into the living room and edged around the brown corduroy sectional sofa, one section of which jutted out about a foot beyond the others. He didn't push it back into place, but instead walked past the coffee table, with its usual collection of magazines and junk mail covering the surface. Behind a large easy chair, he spotted his son's football helmet, which he picked up and absent-mindedly swung back and forth as he surveyed the rest of the room. The room looked comfortable, slightly messy, perfectly normal, except for the view of the front lawn and the street, where the earthquake had neatly sliced away the front wall of the house.

11e | Developing ideas within paragraphs

In developing paragraphs, you have many options. The following list describes some of the techniques that can be used.

TECHNIQUES FOR DEVELOPING IDEAS WITHIN PARAGRAPHS

1. Enumeration: listing or enumerating a series of points or reasons.
2. Illustration by example: using one or more specific examples to prove a point.
3. Definition: explaining the meaning of a word or concept.
4. Cause-and-effect analysis: explaining how or why something happened the way it did (the causes) and showing the results or consequences (the effects).
5. Process analysis: explaining how to do something step by step, or explaining how something works or how something happened.
6. Comparison and contrast: looking at the similarities and differences between two (or more) things in order to understand both of them better.
7. Classification: grouping or categorizing things according to their similarities or class.
8. Division and analysis: breaking something down into its component parts so that you can put it back together and better understand its significance.
9. Description and analogy: description involves appealing to the senses to convey an experience or describe a place. Analogy is the comparison of one thing to another, dissimilar thing in order to make readers' understanding of the first thing clearer.

EXERCISE 1   Paragraph Unity and Topic Sentences

For each topic sentence that follows, write a paragraph that is unified. Every sentence in the paragraph should work toward developing the central idea stated in the topic sentence.

1. When a person is sitting still, it does not necessarily mean that he or she is doing nothing.

2. ____ (*fill in the blank*) is a place that always makes me edgy and worried.

3. Every detail of that childhood experience is still fresh in my mind.

4. _____ (*fill in the blank*) was the worst job I ever had.

5. _____(*fill in the blank*) was the best job I ever had.

EXERCISE 2   Achieving Paragraph Coherence

For each topic that follows, write a coherent paragraph by using pronouns, repeating key terms, using transitional words, supplying visual details, and using parallelism.

1. A relative who has done something unusual

2. An inner quality you would like to develop in yourself

3. An event that frightened you

4. A place that calms and soothes you

5. An activity you do well

EXERCISE 3   Organizing Paragraphs

For each topic that follows, write a paragraph using the specified pattern of organization.

1. The most important quality in a friend (*general to specific*)

2. The most important quality of a good teacher (*specific to general*)

3. What you learned at your first job (*climactic order*)

4. Your first day of college (*time order*)

5. A depressing place (*spatial order*)

EXERCISE 4   Developing Ideas within Paragraphs

For each topic that follows, write a paragraph using the specified technique of development.

1. Reasons for choosing your major (*enumeration*)

2. A person who showed unexpected generosity (*illustration by example*)

3. Intelligence (*definition*)

4. Why you are doing better (or worse) than last semester (*cause-and-effect analysis*)

5. How to study for a test (*process analysis*)

6. Two friends (*comparison and contrast*)

7. Different kinds of professors (*classification*)

8. The people in your neighborhood (*division and analysis*)

9. A time you were surprised (*description*)

10. An emotion (*analogy*)

CHAPTER 12

Types and Functions of Paragraphs

12a Developing beginning paragraphs

A beginning—sometimes called an introduction—can consist of one or more paragraphs, depending on the length of the essay and the complexity of the idea. An opening paragraph may be brief, containing a few sentences, or it may have one hundred to two hundred words. The first paragraph performs two functions: it introduces readers to the idea that will be developed in the essay, and it implies how the essay will be organized.

1 Beginning paragraphs in exploratory essays

Beginning paragraphs in exploratory essays often read more like a story than a formal argument, more like an inquiry into an idea than a defense of a conclusion. These opening paragraphs (introductions) usually reveal the essay's idea and its overall plan of development subtly. Some beginning paragraphs in exploratory essays may include a story that at first seems to be only an anecdote; the writer uses the anecdote to work toward revealing the central idea.

2 Beginning paragraphs in analytical and argumentative essays

The opening paragraphs of analytical and argumentative essays need a clear statement of the central idea and a pattern of organization. Compared to those of exploratory essays, their language is more direct and formal. A beginning paragraph in an analytical or argumentative essay informs readers of the essay's purpose and direction.

12b Developing ending paragraphs

An ending—sometimes called a conclusion—has a close relationship to the beginning (introduction). Beginnings and endings frame an essay, one leading into the essay, the other leading out. The ending pulls all of the parts of the essay together, reminding readers how the idea or thesis was developed in the middle paragraphs of the essay.

Many of the details in a conclusion point back into the essay, reminding readers of important aspects of the main idea.

1 Ending paragraphs in exploratory essays

The ending of an exploratory essay often uses the same image, idea, or anecdote that began the essay. Thus, readers are reminded of the importance of the image or idea. In addition, the ending can remind readers of details described more fully in the middle paragraphs.

2 Ending paragraphs in analytical and argumentative essays

The ending paragraphs of an analytical or argumentative essay can contain references to the examples and evidence used in the middle paragraphs, pulling those details together into a more coherent whole. The conclusion should also remind readers of the central, unifying idea (thesis) developed in the essay. In addition, the ending is an appropriate place to offer suggestions, recommendations, or general statements about your topic.

12c Developing middle paragraphs

The middle paragraphs develop the main idea of an essay. There are two types of middle paragraphs. Informational paragraphs, the most commonly used type, provide evidence and analysis necessary for understanding the essay's thesis. Transitional paragraphs, in contrast, serve as a bridge between informational paragraphs.

1 Using informational paragraphs

Informational paragraphs do the major work of developing an essay's main idea. Each informational paragraph takes an important aspect of the main idea and develops it. In each of these paragraphs, you make sure the subtopic is related to your overall theme. You also let readers know what each paragraph is about, either by conveying the idea implicitly or by stating it in a topic sentence. Most important, in informational paragraphs, you substantiate your main idea by using evidence. Your evidence can come from a variety of sources: experience, observations, books, experiments, newspapers, interviews, and other types of research. The information can be presented as examples, illustrations, quotations, charts, and so on. You should present enough evidence to convince readers that you know what you are writing about.

2 Using transitional paragraphs

Transitional paragraphs are especially useful in lengthy essays. They are used to link or pull together sections of an essay to make it more coherent. These paragraphs often repeat or summarize information that has already appeared or they alert readers to what is coming up in the essay. Transitional paragraphs help readers follow your thinking. Because their function is to link or clarify, transitional paragraphs rarely contain new evidence.

EXERCISE 1   Writing Beginning Paragraphs for Essays

Using a topic from the following list, write a beginning paragraph.

TOPICS

1. A happy memory
2. An unhappy memory
3. A book that affected you positively
4. A book that affected you negatively
5. An important childhood experience
6. Tutoring as a learning experience
7. Unrealistic goals
8. Pain as a part of growth
9. Seeing significance in something ordinary
10. Defining maturity

EXERCISE 2   Writing Ending Paragraphs for Essays

Using your topic from the preceding list, write an ending paragraph.

EXERCISE 3   Writing Middle Paragraphs for Essays

Using your topic from the preceding list, write several middle paragraphs.

PART SIX

Grammar

CHAPTER 13

Basic Sentence Grammar

A sentence is a group of words that expresses a complete thought. Every sentence has (1) a subject, the central topic of the sentence, and (2) a predicate, which indicates something about the subject. Subjects and predicates may be very simple, containing perhaps just one word, or they may be quite complicated, containing many words. This chapter explains the various elements that may be found in a sentence, and it defines and illustrates the following terms:

Subjects	simple, complete, compound
Predicates	simple, complete, compound
Objects	direct, indirect, of prepositions
Complements	subject complements: predicate noun, predicate adjective
	object complements: nouns, adjectives
Phrases	noun, verb, prepositional
Verbal phrases	gerund, participial, infinitive, absolute, appositives
Clauses	adjective, adverb, noun
Functional sentence types	declarative, interrogative, imperative, exclamatory
Grammatical sentence types	simple, compound, complex, compound-complex

13a Recognizing subjects and predicates

1 Subjects

The subject of a sentence is a noun, a pronoun, or another kind of word that functions like a noun. The subject indicates what the sentence is about, and it may have just one word or many words. The simple subject is the single word that indicates the main subject. The complete subject is made up of the simple subject and all the words that modify the simple subject. In the following examples, the complete subjects are italicized and the simple subjects are underlined.

Rats have spread many diseases from one continent to another.

Everybody in the crowded room was overheated and irritable.

The writers I admire most are Gloria Naylor, Ann Tyler, and Alice Hoffman.

Several children dressed in snowsuits waited outside the school.

Sewing all that torn clothing took quite a long time.

A compound subject has two or more subjects joined by a conjunction. In the following examples, the complete subject is italicized and the simple subjects that form the compound subject are underlined.

Both Ms. Tran and Mr. Tirado are studying electrical engineering.

The banks and the schools are closed because of the holidays.

Teachers, parents, and voters have different opinions about the new tax proposals.

Neither vitamin A nor vitamin D should be taken in large doses.

Two abandoned cars and a ruined truck were found next to the highway.

2 | Predicates

The simple predicate of a sentence is the verb. The complete predicate contains the verb and its modifiers, complements, and objects. The predicate tells something about the subject. The simple predicate (verb) may contain only one word or it may contain several words (the main verb and an auxiliary verb). In the following examples, the complete predicate is italicized and the simple predicate is underlined.

Both dancers and athletes *need strength and stamina to perform at their best.*

Several sheep *had broken through the fence.*

Nobody *could understand the instructions on the application form.*

That letter *should have arrived yesterday.*

Taking care of small children *is often exhausting.*

A compound predicate has two or more verbs with the same subject. The verbs in the compound predicate may be joined by a coordinate conjunction or a correlative conjunction. Sometimes, the parts of a compound predicate may be separated by other words. In the following examples, the complete predicate is italicized and the simple compound predicate is underlined.

Most of the spectators in the gym *shouted* and *applauded* each basket scored by the home team.

The dissatisfied customer *not only* *complained* but also *wrote* a letter to the company president.

Max *woke* at six o'clock, *dressed* quickly, *ate* breakfast, and *left* for work.

Mr. Dominguez *lives* in Massachusetts but *works* in Rhode Island.

The heavy rain *decreased* visibility and *made* the roadways slippery.

13b │ Recognizing objects and complements

In addition to a subject and a predicate, a sentence may contain objects and complements.

1 │ Direct and indirect objects

Objects, direct and indirect, are part of the complete predicate in a sentence. A direct object is a noun or pronoun that receives the action of the verb. To find the direct object in a sentence, ask the question *what?* or *whom?* after the verb. The answer to that question is the direct object. Consider the following examples:

The quarterback threw the football out of bounds.

In this example, the verb is *threw.* To find the direct object, ask "Threw what?" The answer, *the football,* is the direct object in the sentence.

The reporter's personal question annoyed the governor.

To find the direct object in this sentence, ask "Annoyed whom?" The direct object is *the governor.*

In the following examples, the direct objects are italicized:

A messenger brought *the package* to the office this morning.

We planted *crocuses* and *daffodils* in the backyard.

The horror movie scared *my children.*

She enjoys *playing tennis* on the weekends.

Rude salespeople infuriate *me.*

The indirect object in a sentence is the recipient to whom or for whom (or for what) the action of the verb is done. If a sentence has both a direct object and an indirect object, the indirect object always comes first. In the following sentences, the direct objects are italicized, and the indirect objects are underlined.

Mr. Chang sent <u>me</u> *his resume.*

Did you give <u>the personnel director</u> *your address and phone number*?

The supervisor gave <u>Ms. Khan</u> *a new assignment.*

Television brings <u>us</u> *world news* every night.

Tell <u>me</u> *the answer* quickly.

2 | Objects of prepositions

A sentence may have an object of a preposition, which is a noun or pronoun that follows a preposition and completes its meaning. Some common prepositions are *of, to, for, in,* and *from.* (See 17a in the *Workbook* for a full discussion of prepositions.) In each of the following examples, note the preposition and its object:

He sent a letter of resignation *to the company president.*

I lent my umbrella *to Harold.*

Last night, he prepared dinnner *for me.*

Did you give your keys *to the superintendent*?

Ms. Wyatt bought a computer *for her daughter.*

Using an object of a preposition instead of an indirect object changes the meaning of a sentence. Look at the following examples:

indirect object   direct object
The director gave *her* an important *assignment.*

object of
direct object   preposition
The director gave an important *assignment* to *her.*

These two sentences contain almost exactly the same words, but their meanings are slightly different. In the first example, the words *an important assignment* are emphasized by being put last in the sentence, after the indirect object. In the second example, the recipient of the action (*her*) is given more emphasis by being made the object of a preposition and by being put last in the sentence.

3 | Complements

A complement is a word that completes the meaning of a verb. It may be either a subject complement or an object complement.

A subject complement can be either a noun or an adjective. It follows a linking verb and identifies or describes the subject of the sentence. If the subject complement is a noun, it is also called a predicate noun. If the subject complement is an adjective, it is also called a predicate adjective. Note the subject complements in the following examples:

Mark's mother is a *judge.* [predicate noun]

Mrs. Anderson looked *furious.* [predicate adjective]

This melon feels *ripe.* [predicate adjective]

After drinking too much coffee, he becomes *nervous and jittery.* [predicate adjectives]

Mr. Ebreo became a *respiratory therapist.* [predicate noun]

At today's meeting, you seemed *worried.* [predicate adjective]

An object complement follows the direct object and renames or describes it. The object complement can be a noun or an adjective. In the following sentences, the direct objects are italicized and the object complements are underlined.

The president declared *the flooded state* <u>a disaster area.</u> [noun]

The dehumidifier keeps *the room* <u>dry.</u> [adjective]

I consider *that remark* <u>an insult.</u> [noun]

We found *the streets* <u>silent and empty.</u> [adjectives]

The rules committee elected *Mr. Corniel* <u>chairman.</u> [noun]

13c Recognizing and using phrases

A phrase is a group of words that is part of a sentence but that does not form a complete sentence. There are various kinds of phrases: noun, verb, prepositional, verbal, absolute, and appositive.

1 Noun, verb, and prepositional phrases

Noun phrases

A noun phrase contains a noun and all its modifiers. A noun phrase may function as a subject, an object, or a complement in a sentence.

    subject   object of preposition
Heavy, gray clouds rolled across *the sky.*

               direct object
The accident injured *many people.*

     indirect object   direct object
He sent *all the employees a lengthy memo.*

      subject   complement
The newspaper columnist called the mayor's speech *a rousing success.*

      subject   complement
High textbook prices were *the students' major complaint.*

Verb phrases

A verb phrase contains the main verb and its auxiliary verbs. Note the verb phrases in the following sentences:

You *should have answered* the letter as soon as it *had arrived.*

We *could* not *use* that room because it *was being painted.*

By next June, she *will have graduated* from law school.

The job *would have been finished* if we *had been given* enough time.

Newspapers and magazines *were strewn* all over the table.

Prepositional phrases

A prepositional phrase contains a preposition, its object, and any modifiers of the object. The prepositional phrase can function as an adjective or as an adverb in a sentence.

You can use the computer *on the front desk.* [adjective modifying the noun *computer*]

The ball rolled *into the street.* [adverb modifying the verb *rolled*]

The plants *on the front porch* need to be watered. [adjective modifying the noun *plants*]

The sound *of children laughing* [adjective modifying the noun *sound*] could be heard *in the distance.* [adverb modifying the verb *could be heard*]

She threw the ball *across the infield.* [adverb modifying the verb *threw*]

2 | Verbal phrases

Verbals are verb forms that do not function as verbs in sentences. They function as nouns or as modifiers, usually as adjectives. Verbals cannot stand alone as sentences. There are three kinds of verbals: participial phrases, gerund phrases, and infinitive phrases.

Participial phrases

A participial phrase contains a participle and all its accompanying words. Participial phrases always function as adjectives, modifying nouns or pronouns. In the following examples, the participial phrases are italicized and the participles are underlined. Note that each participial phrase is next to the noun or pronoun it modifies.

<u>Angered</u> by his boss's criticism, he quit his job.

The person *<u>driving</u> that green van* is my cousin.

Mr. and Mrs. Tran, *<u>married</u> in 1986,* have two children.

She wanted to examine the painting *hanging* on the back wall of the store.

Exhausted after a long day's work, they took the bus home.

Gerund phrases

A gerund is a word ending in *-ing*. It looks like a participle, but instead of functioning as an adjective, a gerund functions as a noun because it names an activity. Note the gerunds in the following sentences:

Swimming is excellent aerobic exercise. [subject]

The management of this restaurant does not allow *smoking.* [direct object]

A gerund phrase contains a gerund and all its related words. Gerund phrases, like gerunds, are always nouns. Note the gerund phrases (italicized) and the gerunds (underlined) in these sentences:

Walking four miles a day is good for the heart. [subject]

My hobby is *making quilts in traditional patterns.* [subject complement]

She likes *knitting sweaters for her children.* [direct object]

He is tired of your *complaining about the boiler.* [object of preposition]

Commuting forty miles each way is certainly exhausting. [subject]

Infinitive phrases

An infinitive is made up of the word *to* followed by the the main form of a verb. Examples of infinitives include *to think, to be, to have, to do, to discover,* and *to wonder.* Infinitives can function as nouns or as modifiers.

To win was his only goal. [noun, used as subject]

She wanted *to succeed.* [noun, used as direct object]

I have no time *to waste.* [adjective, modifying the noun *time*]

He is eager *to participate.* [adverb, modifying the adjective *eager*]

An infinitive phrase contains an infinitive and all its related words. Like infinitives, infinitive phrases can function as nouns or as modifiers. In the following examples, the infinitive phrases are italicized and the infinitives are underlined.

To revise your plans now would be unwise. [noun, used as subject]

Your job is *to discover the perpetrator of these crimes.* [noun, used as subject complement, a predicate noun]

This would be a good time *to review the basic steps.* [adjective, modifying the noun *time*]

He is not willing *to answer any of our questions.* [adverb, modifying the adjective *willing*]

To enter college at age forty was courageous. [noun, used as subject]

Absolute phrases

An absolute phrase contains a noun and a participle or complement, along with any related words. An absolute phrase does not modify a particular word in a sentence; rather, it modifies the whole sentence. The absolute phrase can appear in various places in a sentence, and it is always set off by commas.

The floor having been varnished, we shut the door so no one would walk into the room.

The players walked slowly off the field, *their hopes for victory dashed.*

The passengers, *passports clutched in their hands,* waited on line for the customs inspection.

Anxiety over his test results building almost to the breaking point, he paced the floor for hours.

No one could reach Sue, *her phone being off the hook.*

Appositive phrases

An appositive is a noun that renames the word it follows. An appositive phrase is a noun phrase that renames the noun or pronoun it follows. It is set off by commas.

The book, *a lengthy description of her travels,* was fascinating.

Mr. Delgado, *the supervisor of this unit,* has worked here eight years.

This newspaper, *an afternoon daily,* has wide circulation.

Appositive phrases can be used to combine two short, choppy sentences into one longer, smoother sentence, as in the following examples.

On the reading list is *One Hundred Years of Solitude.* The book is a novel by Gabriel Garcia Marquez.

On the reading list is *One Hundred Years of Solitude,* a novel by Gabriel Garcia Marquez.

I am looking for coconut, mustard seeds, and lemon juice. They are ingredients in a special rice recipe planned for tonight's dinner.

I am looking for coconut, mustard seeds, and lemon juice, ingredients in a special rice recipe planned for tonight's dinner.

13d | Recognizing and using clauses

A clause is a group of words containing a subject and a predicate. A clause may be independent or dependent (subordinate). An independent clause can stand alone as a sentence. A dependent clause (subordinate clause) cannot stand alone. In a sentence, a dependent clause must be accompanied by at least one independent clause. Look at the following examples:

August was a very dry month. [independent clause]

Because August was a very dry month [dependent clause]

Because August was a very dry month, water levels in the reservoirs are down. [dependent clause followed by independent clause]

Clauses can be identified according to their function; there are adjective clauses, adverb clauses, and noun clauses.

Adjective clauses

An adjective clause modifies a noun or pronoun in another clause. The adjective clause is always a dependent clause. Usually, it appears immediately after the word it modifies and is introduced by a relative pronoun—*who, which, that, whose,* or *whom.* (See 15b in the *Workbook* on types of pronouns.) When a dependent clause begins with a relative pronoun, it is also called a relative clause. Note the adjective clauses (relative clauses) in the following examples:

The reporter wanted to interview the people *who witnessed the incident.*

Lavender, *which is a perennial plant,* attracts bees to the garden.

The directions *that you gave me* were very helpful.

Zora Neale Hurston, *whose books were ignored for years,* is now well known.

Incumbents are the candidates *whom most voters seem to prefer.*

Adverb clauses

An adverb clause modifies a verb, an adjective, or another adverb. It tells how, where, when, why, in what circumstances, with what results, or to what extent an action happens. An adjective clause begins with a subordinating conjunction and, therefore, is always a dependent clause. It can appear in different places in a sentence. In the following sentences, notice how changing the position of adverb clauses varies the rhythm and emphasis:

Ms. Tirado's blood pressure has gone down *since she has lost weight.*

Since Ms. Tirado has lost weight, her blood pressure has gone done.

If the team has two more victories, it will win the division championship.

The team will win the division championship *if it has two more victories.*

Interrupted *while he was explaining the new schedule,* Alex lost his train of thought.

Alex, interrupted *while he was explaining the new schedule,* lost his train of thought.

Punctuating adverb clauses

If an adverb clause begins a sentence, put a comma after it.

        dependent clause   comma
If he eats anything containing wheat, he has a severe allergic reaction.

If an adverb clause is in the middle of a sentence, place commas around it only if the clause is nonrestrictive (see 36c in the *Workbook*).

comma   nonrestrictive adverb clause   comma

The hurricane, *because it occurred during high tide,* caused extensive damage.

If an adverb clause appears at the end of a sentence, do not use a comma unless the comma gives the clause emphasis.

no comma   adverb clause

They rushed out the door *as soon as the bell rang.*

Noun clauses

A noun clause usually begins with a relative pronoun—*who, whom, whoever,* or *whomever*—or with *when, where, whether, why, how, what,* or *however.* A noun clause can be a subject, an object, or a complement.

That the meeting actually began on time astonished everyone. [subject]

The article explains *how viruses invade human cells.* [direct object]

The reason for the delay was *that heavy rains had flooded the roads.* [subject complement]

He paid no attention to *what the other people were doing.* [object of preposition]

13e | Using the basic sentence patterns

Sentences in English can be constructed many different ways. The following chart identifies the five most common and simplest sentence patterns.

FIVE BASIC SENTENCE PATTERNS

1. Subject/verb

   subject   verb
   Babies sleep.

2. Subject/verb/direct object

   subject   verb   direct object
   Most people enjoy their vacations.

3. Subject/verb/subject complement

   subject   verb   subject complement
   Chimpanzees are primates.

4. Subject/verb/indirect object/direct object

   subject   verb   indirect object   direct object
   The company gave Ms. Jackson a bonus.

5. Subject/verb/direct object/object complement

   subject   verb   direct object   object complement
   The scientist called her experiment a success.

All sentences contain at least one subject and at least one verb; most sentences also have an object or a complement.

13f   Using different types of sentences

Sentences can be classified in various ways. They may be classified according to their function; for example, as questions or commands. Or they may be classified according to their grammatical construction, as compound or complex.

1   Functional sentence types

Sentences can be classified into four types according to their function. A declarative sentence makes a statement. An interrogative sentence asks a question. An imperative sentence gives a command. An exclamatory sentence expresses strong feeling.

DECLARATIVE   They signed a two-year lease.

INTERROGATIVE   Have you read this morning's newspaper?

IMPERATIVE   [You] See Mr. Eng to get an application. [The subject *You* is unstated but understood.]

EXCLAMATORY   What a shock you gave me!

Using the four sentence types in writing

Declarative sentences state facts, give opinions, make assertions, present evaluations, and offer solutions. Most of the sentences in your writing (especially in your college writing) are declarative because in that writing you describe, analyze, explain, or argue a position. Interrogative sentences, which ask questions, are not used frequently in academic or professional writing; an occasional interrogative sentence, however, can introduce a topic or inject a personal note. Imperative and exclamatory sentences are seldom found in academic writing. The use of too many imperative sentences creates an insistent, even bullying tone. Exclamatory sentences make writing seem overly emotional.

2   Grammatical sentence types

Sentences can be classified grammatically into four types: simple, compound, complex, and compound-complex. Grammatical classification of a sentence is based on the kinds of clauses, independent or dependent, a sentence contains. (See 13d of the *Workbook* on clauses.)

Simple sentences

A simple sentence has one independent clause and no dependent clauses. Length alone does not determine whether a sentence is simple; a simple sentence may be quite short, as in the first example that follows, or it may have a compound subject, a compound verb (or both), and many modifiers, as in the last example.

We must finish the project.

My brother and I went fishing last weekend.

Mr. Vogel quit his job and moved to Hawaii.

New students and those transferring from other schools must file financial aid applications and submit health forms.

Compound sentences

A compound sentence has two or more independent clauses and no dependent clauses.

They had hoped to play baseball yesterday, but rainy weather spoiled their plans.

He walked the dog, and I fed the cat.

She wants to go to medical school, so she is taking science courses.

Music and math may seem very different; Jean, however, enjoys both.

Complex sentences

A complex sentence has one independent clause and one or more dependent clauses. In the following examples, the independent clauses are italicized and the dependent clauses are in regular type.

As soon as the alarm rang, *the fire fighters raced to their truck.*

He gave his first piano concert when he was only six years old.

It is difficult for some children to believe that their grandparents grew up without television.

Although the reservoir levels were low, *the town did not have any problems* because residents carefully followed water conservation guidelines.

Compound-complex sentences

A compound-complex sentence has two more more independent clauses and at least one dependent clause. In the following examples, the independent clauses are italicized and the dependent clauses are in regular type.

She began law school when she was twenty-two, *and three years later she was hired by the district attorney.*

The heavy rains had ceased, and people wanted to return to their homes, but they could not because their houses were flooded.

Whenever the pollen count is high, *his eyes become red, and his breathing is labored.*

Because the home team was losing badly, *many people left the stadium in the seventh inning, but they were sorry* that they had done so because in the bottom of the ninth the team scored six runs and won the game.

EXERCISE 1   Recognizing Simple and Complete Subjects

In the following sentences, underline the complete subject once and the simple subject twice. Example:

Beautiful <u>trees</u> <u>with graceful, drooping branches</u> lined the riverbank.

1. Students with questions about financial aid should see Ms. Banks.

2. Large flakes of snow drifted slowly from the sky.

3. Mr. Aranda opens his pharmacy every morning at eight o'clock.

4. I read an interesting article on health care in the morning paper.

5. Several batteries for the remote control are included with your new television.

EXERCISE 2   Recognizing Compound Subjects

Underline the compound subjects in the following sentences. Example:

<u>A squirrel and some chipmunks</u> were on the ground underneath the bird feeder.

1. Records and tapes filled most of the shelves in the living room.

2. Two women and several children were sitting in the pediatrician's waiting room.

3. Both chemistry and physics require some mathematical ability.

4. Both Gloria Naylor and Barbara Kingsolver have written sequels to earlier novels.

5. Either you or I must clean up this office.

EXERCISE 3   Recognizing Simple and Complete Predicates

In the following sentences, underline the complete predicate once and the simple predicate twice. Example:

The books on that cart <u>should be returned</u> to the shelves.

1. The prolonged drought will lower the reservoirs to dangerous levels.

2. The morning newspaper is lying on the front doorstep.

3. Toni Morrison won the Nobel Prize for literature in 1993.

4. Jazz and the blues are original American art forms.

5. This musuem has an excellent collection of Impressionist paintings.

EXERCISE 4   Recognizing Compound Predicates

In the following sentences, underline the simple compound predicates. Example:

During the night, the guards <u>walk</u> around and <u>check</u> the doors.

1. The dog across the hall barks at night and disturbs the neighbors.

2. The line started at the entrance to the theater and continued down the street and around the corner.

3. He reads his letters but never answers them.

4. Mr. Reed and Mr. Hill fought over a property line and later became good friends.

5. The Alaska pipeline not only brought wealth to the region but also caused environmental concerns.

EXERCISE 5   Recognizing Direct and Indirect Objects

In the following sentences, underline the direct objects once and the indirect objects twice. Example:

> Lisa gave <u>Carlo</u> a <u>tape</u> of his favorite opera arias.

1. Loud noises give Fred a headache.

2. Richard Wright wrote novels and an autobiography.

3. She took one chemistry course and two biology courses.

4. The day care center accepts children as young as two years, eight months old.

5. Ms. Ruiz gave Alice the leading role in the school play.

EXERCISE 6   Recognizing Objects of Prepositions

In the following sentences, put parentheses around the prepositional phrases and underline the objects. Example:

> One (of your <u>books</u>) is (on the <u>table</u>) (in the <u>hallway</u>).

1. The last game of the World Series was played in late October.

2. Children in first grade show great differences in their reading levels.

3. Piles of dusty old newspapers lay on tables and shelves in every room of the house.

4. A group of concerned citizens is protesting the lack of security at college athletic events.

5. By day, Mr. Ebreo is a student at the community college, and at night he is a guard in a downtown office building.

EXERCISE 7   Recognizing Subject and Object Complements

In the following sentences, underline and label the subject complements and object complements. Example:

> This salad is <u>delicious.</u>   subject complement

1. Your voice sounds hoarse.   _____

2. The critic called the new play a fiasco.   _____

3. Several layers of clothing will keep you warm.   _____

4. After sixteen miles, the marathon runner became tired.   _____

5. Mr. Tirado is a newspaper reporter.   _____

EXERCISE 8   Using Sentence Elements in Writing

Choose one topic and write a brief paragraph. Then identify the elements you used in each sentence as simple subject, simple predicate (verb), direct object, indirect object, object of a preposition, subject complement, or object complement. Example:

Topic: A vegetarian meal

     subject   verb   direct object   object complements   subject verb
Many people consider vegetarian meals boring and tasteless. They are

subject complement   subject   verb   subject complements
wrong. Vegetarian dishes can be both nutritious and delicious. Cold

subject   object of preposition   verb   direct object
noodles with sesame and peanut sauce not only provide complete protein

         verb   subject complement
but also taste wonderful.

1. Your favorite room
2. Your favorite food
3. The food you dislike most
4. Your best talent
5. A movie you have seen recently

6. A book that interested you
7. Your most interesting relative
8. A family tradition
9. Your strongest opinion
10. An irritating experience

EXERCISE 9   Recognizing Noun Phrases

Underline the noun phrases in the following sentences. Example:

> Mr. and Mrs. Da Parma have traveled all over the world.

1. Many people actually enjoy rainy weather.

2. A large, friendly dog wagged his long, feathery tail.

3. The old oil furnace finally stopped working.

4. The mail carrier delivered heavy stacks of holiday catalogs.

5. Impatient customers waited outside the bronze doors of the huge store.

EXERCISE 10   Recognizing Verb Phrases

In the following sentences, underline the verb phrases. Example:

> The letter should have arrived by now.

1. If you had asked me earlier, I would have driven you to the airport.

2. The package might have been delivered to the wrong address.

3. The Andersons are moving to Juneau, Alaska.

4. A large bus was blocking the street.

5. Nobody can predict the date of the first frost.

EXERCISE 11   Recognizing Prepositional Phrases

In each of the following sentences, underline the prepositional phrase and state whether it functions as an adjective or an adverb. Example:

He works <u>in that office building.</u>

adverb modifying *works,* indicating "where"

1. Ragweed grew beside the highway.

   _____

2. The red light on the answering machine is blinking.

   _____

3. The student in the front row dropped his pen.

   _____

4. Thunder echoed across the valley.

   _____

5. Fifteen chattering sparrows landed on the front lawn.

   _____

EXERCISE 12 Using Noun, Verb, and Prepositional Phrases in Writing

Choose one topic and write a brief paragraph of three to five sentences. Then, in each paragraph, identify at least one noun, one verb, and one prepositional phrase. Example:

Topic: Waiting on line

   Waiting on line is usually tiresome, and it is especially irritating at the Motor Vehicle Bureau. The last time I was there, I stood on one line for nearly an hour, but by the time I had reached the front of the line, the person on duty was on his lunch break. When he returned from lunch and called me to his window, he informed me that I was lacking one document and would have to stand on another long line in order to get it.

Noun phrase: lunch break
Verb phrase: had reached
Prepositional phrase: on another long line

   1. An inspiring experience

   2. An irritating experience

   3. Keeping one's temper

4. Losing one's temper

5. An interesting object (a leaf, a piece of jewelry, an oddly shaped stone)

EXERCISE 13 Recognizing Participial Phrases

In the following sentences, underline the participial phrases once and the nouns or pronouns that the participial phrases modify twice. Example:

> Touched by a newspaper story about the homeless, he began to work at a local shelter.

1. Distracted by a sudden noise, the horse pranced nervously.

2. Sacked by the defense, the quarterback had no time to throw the football.

3. The child doing an arithmetic problem at the board is learning long division.

4. He sent me the books wrapped securely in heavy brown paper and thick twine.

5. Circling slowly and silently in the sky, the hawk looked for mice in the field below.

EXERCISE 14 Recognizing Gerund Phrases

Underline the gerund phrase in each sentence that follows. Then identify the gerund phrase as a subject, a subject complement, a direct object, or an object of a preposition. Example:

> Many people are afraid of going to the dentist.   object of preposition

1. Baking an apple pie should take less than an hour. _____

2. Eliot really enjoys teaching third grade. _____

3. More people should be concerned about lowering their blood pressure.

   _____

4. Her rather unusual hobby is collecting old weather vanes.

   _____

5. Swimming two miles a day has kept her in excellent health.

   _____

EXERCISE 15   Recognizing Infinitive Phrases

Underline the infinitive phrases in the following sentences. Then state whether each infinitive phrase is used as a noun, an adjective, or an adverb. Example:

<u>To retain the material in lectures,</u> review your class notes daily.   <u>adverb</u>

1. The team tried to repeat its success of last season.   _____

2. To lose weight permanently is difficult for most people.

   _____

3. Doing volunteer work is a good way to gain skills and experience.

   _____

4. To avoid a penalty, mail your tax returns by April 15.   _____

5. A bad time to start studying for a test is the night before.

   _____

EXERCISE 16   Using Participial, Gerund, and Infinitive Phrases in Sentences

Use the following participial, gerund, and infinitive phrases in sentences. Examples:

   Driving a car with a stick shift (*gerund phrase; use as a noun*)

   Driving a car with a stick shift is a little more complicated than driving a car with an automatic transmission.

   Driving the tour bus (*participial phrase; use as an adjective*)

   The man driving the tour bus is a retired police officer.

1. To keep the children happy (*infinitive phrase*)

2. Cooking lentils with garlic and tomatoes (*gerund phrase*)

3. Sleeping in the hammock (*participial phrase*)

4. To attend every home game of the basketball team (*infinitive phrase*)

5. Driving an hour to his office every day (*gerund phrase*)

6. Planning to major in chemistry (*participial phrase*)

7. To avoid personal questions from the reporters (*infinitive phrase*)

8. Excited about his trip to Brazil (*participial phrase*)

9. Repairing antique watches (*gerund phrase*)

10. Elated by the election results (*participial phrase*)

EXERCISE 17   Recognizing Absolute Phrases

Underline the absolute phrases in the following sentences. Example:

> <u>Our reservations having been confirmed,</u> we were ready to start our vacation.

1. Compost and peat moss having been dug in, it was time to plant the garden.

2. The jack o' lantern, its candle burning brightly, was placed in the front window.

3. Her term paper typed and printed, she finally went to sleep.

4. The dog having been bathed, we had to dry ourselves off.

5. Their parachutes having been carefully inspected, the paratroopers climbed into the airplane.

EXERCISE 18   Recognizing Appositives

Underline the appositives in the following sentences. Example:

> Ms. Richards, <u>the president of the student government,</u> is majoring in chemistry.

1. Alice Hoffman, the author of *Turtle Moon,* has written several other novels.

2. A resident of the neighborhood for twenty years, Mr. Perez owns a local jewelry store.

3. An article about traffic safety appeared in the *News-Record,* the town's weekly newspaper.

4. Ms. Eng, the chairperson of the PTA, called a special meeting to discuss extracurricular projects.

5. Mr. Riley owns an old-fashioned piece of athletic equipment, a wooden tennis racquet.

EXERCISE 19   Using Absolute Phrases and Appositives in Writing

Combine the following pairs of sentences by converting the second sentence into an absolute phrase or an appositive. Remember to set off the absolute phrase or the appositive with a comma (or commas). Examples:

> People had to use the building's back entrance.
>
> The front entrance had been damaged in the 1989 earthquake.
>
> People had to use the building's back entrance, the front entrance having been damaged in the 1989 earthquake.
>
> Mr. Kaltvedt worked for several years in Saudi Arabia.
>
> Mr. Kaltvedt is an engineer.
>
> Mr. Kaltvedt, an engineer, worked for several years in Saudi Arabia.

1. The football players were sliding and falling on the field.
   Rain had made the astro turf very slick.

2. Many national parks were closed that summer.
   The prolonged drought had increased the danger of forest fires.

3. He specializes in the treatment of sickle cell anemia.
   Sickle cell anemia is a disease afftecting people of African and Mediterranean ancestry.

4. We had to take the subway to Roosevelt Island.

The aerial tramway had been closed because of electrical problems.

5. Zora Neale Hurston studied anthropology at Barnard College.

Hurston was the author of several novels and an autobiography.

EXERCISE 20   Using Absolute Phrases and Appositives in Writing

For each topic that follows, write a sentence using the suggested absolute phrase or appositive. Example:

Topic: College registration

Suggested phrase: the computer having crashed

It took me longer than usual to register for my courses this semester, the computer having crashed.

1. *Topic:* Learning a new language

   Phrase: idioms in the two languages being so different

2. *Topic:* Yoga

   Phrase: one of the choices for gym class

3. *Topic:* Toni Morrison

   Phrase: the author of *Sula*

4. *Topic:* Lateness

   Phrase: the bus having left without me

5. *Topic:* Jury duty

   Phrase: The defendent never taking the stand

EXERCISE 21 Recognizing Adjective Clauses

Underline the adjective clauses in the following sentences. Example:

> The mayor, <u>whose reelection is in doubt,</u> is campaigning energetically.

1. Dick Francis, who had been a jockey earlier in his life, became a writer of mystery novels.

2. The tree that fell into the parking lot of the shopping center did a lot of damage.

3. Diane Arbus was a photographer whose work moved and disturbed many people.

4. Judge Ginsberg, whom President Clinton appointed to the Supreme Court, is the second woman to serve on that court.

5. The weather, which had been cold and gloomy all week, improved by the weekend.

EXERCISE 22 Recognizing Adverb Clauses

Underline the adverb clauses in the following sentences. Example:

> <u>Because she can speak Japanese,</u> Ariane found a job easily after college.

1. If a student wants to succeed in college, he or she should study at least two hours for every hour in class.

2. Fired after they had protested some new work rules, the employees picketed the factory.

3. The reporter started writing the story as soon as she had finished interviewing the candidates.

4. Interrupted before he could finish eating breakfast, he felt hungry all morning.

5. Although regular exercise is good for the heart, a low-fat diet is also important.

EXERCISE 23   Recognizing Noun Clauses

Underline the noun clauses in the following sentences. Example:

> That the Yankees did so well this year astonished and pleased their fans.

1. We will choose whichever long-distance plan costs the least.

2. The article in the science section describes how antihistamines work.

3. You never listen to what I am saying.

4. Who erased those important files is a mystery.

5. She told us why she was planning to major in political science.

EXERCISE 24   Using Adjective, Adverb, and Noun Clauses in Writing

Use each of the following clauses in a sentence. Example:

> when and where free flu shots were available
>
> A notice in the newspaper announced when and where free flu shots were available.

1. whose athletic ability astounded the fans

2. because the newspaper was never delivered this morning

3. if you take a full-time job after school

4. how tuberculosis can be prevented

5. which took six hours to finish

EXERCISE 25   Recognizing Basic Sentence Patterns

In the following sentences, underline and label the subjects (S), verbs (V), subject complements (SC), direct objects (DO), indirect objects (IO), and object complements (OC). Example:

```
       S        V              SC
```
Paule Marshall is an interesting writer.

1. Cable television offers viewers an amazing number of programs.

2. Some citizens consider the new tax forms very confusing.

3. Certain kinds of meat are high in calories.

4. The community center runs several youth programs.

5. Elizabeth Cady Stanton was a pioneer in the fight for women's rights.

6. Sears brought us the new washing machine this morning.

7. Jogging can cause shin splints.

8. The commission has designated that house a protected landmark.

9. James Baldwin was versatile writer.

10. A curious noise was coming from the house across the street.

EXERCISE 26 Using Basic Sentence Patterns in Writing

For each topic that follows, write a brief paragraph (of three to five sentences) in which you use each of the basic sentence patterns at least once. (See 13e in the *Workbook* to review the five basic sentence patterns.) Example:

Topic: City life

    Many people consider city life stressful and difficult. They dislike the noise and bustle of urban life. Others, however, give cities high ratings as interesting places to live. They thrive on crowds, noise, and a fast pace. These people are true urbanites.

1. Doing the laundry
2. An interesting movie
3. A popular musician
4. A zoo
5. An annoying incident

6. A television show
7. Watching a sport
8. Playing a sport
9. A difficult task
10. Your favorite author

EXERCISE 27   Recognizing Functional Sentence Types

Identify each sentence as declarative, interrogative, imperative, or exclamatory. Examples:

> Learn to use a computer as soon as possible.   <u>imperative</u>
>
> All post offices will be closed tomorrow.   <u>declarative</u>

1. What a dreadful experience!   _____

2. When will the mayor agree to debate her opponent?   _____

3. Limit your remarks to three minutes.   _____

4. Because he was born and raised in Brazil, he speaks fluent Portuguese.

   _____

5. No one knows when the jury will reach a verdict.   _____

EXERCISE 28   Using Functional Sentence Types in Writing

For each suggested topic, write a sentence using the indicated functional sentence type. Examples:

> Final exams (*declarative*)
>
> The final exam schedule has been posted in Morrison Hall.
>
> Cafeteria food (*interrogative*)
>
> Is the food in the cafeteria any good?

1. Hair (*declarative*)

2. A pair of shoes (*declarative*)

3. An expensive textbook (*interrogative*)

4. Biology lecture notes (*imperative*)

5. Going to the dentist (*exclamatory*)

EXERCISE 29 Recognizing Grammatical Sentence Types

Identify each of the following sentences as simple, compound, complex, or compound-complex. Example:

> Her beautiful black hair was arranged in dozens of braids decorated with small beads. <u>simple</u>

1. The leaves at the top of the maple tree had turned a brilliant red.

   _____

2. Because Sweden enforces its strict drunk-driving laws, in Sweden far fewer motorists are killed in alcohol-related accidents than in America.

   _____

3. Thunder boomed, and the children screamed. _____

4. When this house was built, it was considered daringly contemporary, but now, sixty years later, it seems rather old fashioned. _____

5. In some societies, money is considered the sign of success, but other societies value a close-knit, supportive family structure. _____

EXERCISE 30   Using Grammatical Sentence Types in Writing

For each topic that follows, write a sentence using the indicated grammatical sentence type. Example:

> Being organized (*complex*)
>
> Although being organized is not always easy, it is absolutely essential for a working parent.

1. Losing weight (*simple*)

2. Word processing (*complex*)

3. A math problem (*compound*)

4. A movie you have seen (*compound-complex*)

5. Jury duty (*compound*)

6. Salt (*simple*)

7. Babysitting (*compound-complex*)

8. A sport you like (*complex*)

9. Waiting on line (*compound*)

10. Courtesy (*complex*)

CHAPTER 14

Verbs

Verbs are used to describe actions, ask questions, give commands, express conditions or possibilities, and indicate states of being. The following chart identifies the various features of verbs.

VERB CHARACTERISTICS

Form
    Primary verb forms
    Auxiliary and modal auxiliary forms
    Regular and irregular verb forms
Type
    Linking verbs
    Transitive and intransitive verbs
Tenses
    Simple—present, past, future
    Perfect—present perfect, past perfect, future perfect
    Progressive—present progressive, past progressive, future progressive; present perfect progressive, past perfect progressive, future perfect progressive
Tense sequence
    Verbs and tense sequence
    Infinitives and tense sequence
    Participles and tense sequence
Voice
    Active
    Passive
Mood
    Indicative
    Imperative
    Subjunctive

VERB FORMS

| **14a** | **Primary verb forms** |

All English verbs, except the verb *to be,* have five primary forms.

BASE FORM	PRESENT TENSE	PRESENT PARTICIPLE	PAST TENSE	PAST PARTICIPLE
walk	walk, walks	walking	walked	walked
study	study, studies	studying	studied	studied
keep	keep, keeps	keeping	kept	kept
drink	drink, drinks	drinking	drank	drunk
write	write, writes	writing	wrote	written

The base form is used with the word *to* to form an infinitive, with modal auxiliaries, and with the auxiliaries *do, does,* and *did.*

He wants *to explore* that uncharted cave. [base form used with *to*]

You *could return* the books tomorrow. [base form used with a modal auxiliary]

They *did* not *keep* their promises. [base form used with the auxiliary *did*]

The base form is also used for the present tense when the subject of the verb is *I* or *you* or plural. When the subject is *he, she, it,* or a singular word, the base verb form adds *-s* or *-es.*

I certainly *believe* in luck and coincidences.

You often *speak* about your family.

Mr. Jones and Ms. Suarez usually *arrive* at the office early.

This mother clearly *loves* her children.

He never *laughs* in public.

It rains almost every day.

Everybody on line *wants* the clerk to hurry up.

The present participle is formed by adding *-ing* to the base form. The present participle can be used in a verb with a form of *to be,* as an adjective describing someone or something, or as a gerund (a noun). Look at the following examples:

He *is hoping* for a promotion later this year. [present participle in a verb with *is*]

Looking for the post office, the man wandered up and down the street. [present participle used as an adjective describing *man*]

Swimming does not cause stress fractures. [present participle as gerund (noun)]

In most verbs, the past tense, indicating action that is over, is formed by adding the ending *-d* or *-ed* to the base form. Some verbs, however, form the past tense in other ways.

PRESENT TENSE	PAST TENSE
You call	You called
I hope	I hoped
She notices	She noticed
We keep	We kept

(See 14c in the *Workbook* for more on irregular verbs.)

The past participle is used in two ways: (1) in verbs with forms of *to have* or *to be* and (2) as an adjective to modify nouns and pronouns. In regular verbs, the past participle is identical to the past tense. In irregular verbs, the past participle may have its own form (see 14c in the *Workbook*). Look at the following examples:

The mayor *has appointed* a new police commissioner. [past participle used with a form of *to have*]

The building *will be inspected* by the fire department. [past participle used with a form of *to be*]

Several *exhausted* people were asleep on the train. [past participle used as an adjective to describe *people*]

The mirror has been *broken*. [past participle of an irregular verb]

14b   Auxiliary verb forms

Auxiliary verbs, or helping verbs, combine with base forms of verbs or with present or past participles. Together, the auxiliary verb and the main verb create verb phrases. Following is a list of auxiliary verbs.

have	am	was	be	do
has	is	were	being	does
had	are		been	did
having				

In the sentences that follow, the verb phrases contain auxiliary and main verbs.

His car *was parked* in front of the building.

A lecture on financial planning *is being given* this afternoon.

The movie *had started* at six o'clock.

The paper *has* not *been delivered* yet.

That store *does sell* cowboy boots.

She *did answer* your letter.

Modal auxiliaries never change their form, and they always appear with the base form of the main verb. Here is a list of modal auxiliary verbs:

will	can	shall	may
would	could	should	might
			must

In the following sentences, the verb phrases consist of a modal auxiliary and a base verb form:

I *must return* these books.

The plane *will* not *land* in this snowstorm.

Can you *solve* this math problem?

You *may leave* the room now.

Ms. Torres *might apply* to law school.

Some complicated verb phrases contain a modal auxiliary, a regular auxiliary, and a main verb, as in the following sentences:

We *should have looked* at the map.

The work *can be finished* by this afternoon.

The election results *may have been announced* by now.

The house *will be painted* next week.

By next June, the baby *will have been born.*

They *could have been* badly *injured* in that accident.

It is important to know the forms of the verbs *to be, to have,* and *to do.* These verbs are used often as auxiliaries and as main verbs. Here are their principal forms:

FORMS OF *BE, HAVE,* AND *DO*

BASE FORM	PRESENT TENSE	PRESENT PARTICIPLE	PAST TENSE	PAST PARTICIPLE
be	am	being	was	been
	is		were	
	are			
have	have	having	had	had
	has			
do	do	doing	did	done
	does			

14c Regular and irregular verbs

Regular verbs form the past tense and the past participle by adding *-ed* or *-d* to the base form. Look at the following examples:

BASE FORM	PAST TENSE	PAST PARTICIPLE
reach	reached	reached
hope	hoped	hoped
inform	informed	informed
decrease	decreased	decreased
enjoy	enjoyed	enjoyed

Irregular verbs do not follow the *-ed* or *-d* pattern. Many irregular verbs indicate their past tense and past participle with a spelling change inside the verb. A few irregular verbs do not make any changes at all; their base form, past tense, and past participle are the same. Look at the following examples:

BASE FORM	PAST TENSE	PAST PARTICIPLE
sing	sang	sung
buy	bought	bought
rise	rose	risen
write	wrote	written
cost	cost	cost
hurt	hurt	hurt

All good dictionaries list the base form, the past tense, and past participle of irregular verbs. The following chart gives the principal forms of the most common irregular verbs.

COMMON IRREGULAR VERBS

BASE FORM	PAST TENSE	PAST PARTICIPLE
arise	arose	arisen
awake	awoke	awaked *or* awoken
be	was, were	been
bear	bore	borne *or* born
beat	beat	beaten *or* beat
become	became	become
begin	began	begun
bend	bent	bent
bet	bet	bet
bind	bound	bound
bite	bit	bitten
bleed	bled	bled
blow	blew	blown
break	broke	broken
bring	brought	brought
build	built	built
burn	burned *or* burnt	burned *or* burnt
burst	burst	burst
buy	bought	bought
can	could	could
catch	caught	caught

COMMON IRREGULAR VERBS (*CONTINUED*)

BASE FORM	PAST TENSE	PAST PARTICIPLE
choose	chose	chosen
cling	clung	clung
come	came	come
cost	cost	cost
creep	crept	crept
cut	cut	cut
deal	dealt	dealt
dig	dug	dug
dive	dived *or* dove	dived
do	did	done
draw	drew	drawn
dream	dreamed *or* dreamt	dreamed *or* dreamt
drink	drank	drunk
drive	drove	driven
eat	ate	eaten
fall	fell	fallen
feed	fed	fed
feel	felt	felt
fight	fought	fought
find	found	found
flee	fled	fled
fling	flung	flung
fly	flew	flown
forbid	forbade *or* forbad	forbidden
forget	forgot	forgotten *or* forgot
forgive	forgave	forgiven
freeze	froze	frozen
get	got	gotten *or* got
give	gave	given
go	went	gone
grow	grew	grown
hang (suspend)	hung	hung
hang (execute)	hanged	hanged
have	had	had
hear	heard	heard
hide	hid	hidden
hit	hit	hit
hold	held	held
hurt	hurt	hurt
keep	kept	kept
kneel	knelt *or* kneeled	knelt *or* kneeled
know	knew	known
lay	laid	laid

BASE FORM	PAST TENSE	PAST PARTICIPLE
lead	led	led
leave	left	left
lend	lent	lent
let	let	let
lie	lay	lain
light	lit *or* lighted	lit *or* lighted
lose	lost	lost
make	made	made
mean	meant	meant
meet	met	met
pay	paid	paid
proved	proved	proven *or* proved
put	put	put
quit	quit	quit
read	read	read
rid	rid	rid
ride	rode	ridden
ring	rang	rung
rise	rose	risen
run	ran	run
say	said	said
see	saw	seen
seek	sought	sought
sell	sold	sold
send	sent	sent
set	set	set
shake	shook	shaken
shine (glow)	shone	shone
shine (polish)	shined	shined
shoot	shot	shot
show	showed	shown *or* showed
shut	shut	shut
shrink	shrank	shrunk
sing	sang	sung
sink	sank	sunk
sit	sat	sat
slay	slew *or* slayed	slain *or* slayed
sleep	slept	slept
slide	slid	slid
smell	smelled *or* smelt	smelled *or* smelt
speak	spoke	spoken
spend	spent	spent
spin	spun	spun
spring	sprang	sprung

ASE FORM	PAST TENSE	PAST PARTICIPLE
spread	spread	spread
Bstand	stood	stood
steal	stole	stolen
stick	stuck	stuck
sting	stung	stung
stink	stank *or* stunk	stunk
strike	struck	struck *or* stricken
string	strung	strung
strive	strove	strived *or* striven
swear	swore	sworn
sweep	swept	swept
swim	swam	swum
swing	swung	swung
take	took	taken
teach	taught	taught
tear	tore	torn
tell	told	told
think	thought	thought
throw	threw	thrown
understand	understood	understood
upset	upset	upset
wake	woke *or* waked	waked *or* woken
wear	wore	worn
weave	wove	woven
win	won	won
wind	wound	wound
wring	wrung	wrung
write	wrote	written

14d Other types of verbs

Verbs also can be classified as linking verbs and as transitive or intransitive verbs.

1 Linking verbs

A linking verb joins the subject of a sentence to a subject complement, to an adjective that describes the subject, or to a noun that renames the subject.

The sky *is* cloudy this morning.

You *seem* angry about something.

Mickey Mantle *was* a Yankee.

She *became* a judge in 1993.

Here are some common linking verbs:

to be	to seem
to become	to taste
to remain	to feel
to smell	to appear
to get (to become)	

Note the linking verbs in the following sentences:

The baby *appears* cranky. [subject complement - adjective]

One customer *got* angry at the sales clerk. [subject complement - adjective]

She *will be* the graduation speaker. [subject complement - noun]

This pie *smells* delicious. [subject complement - adjective]

2 | Transitive and intransitive verbs

A transitive verb directs its action toward a noun or a pronoun, the direct object of the verb. In the following sentences, the transitive verbs are italicized and the direct objects are underlined.

Mr. and Mrs. Jenkins *are buying* a house.

The company *promoted* him.

The point guard *passed* the ball.

The committee *will interview* several candidates.

An intransitive verb does not take a direct object. The meaning of an intransitive verb is complete in itself.

He *laughed* uncontrollably.

She *sneezed* three times in a row.

The plane *will arrive* at 5 p.m.

The motor *is running* smoothly.

Some verbs can be used both transitively or intransitively. In the following examples, the transitive verbs have a direct object; the intransitive verbs do not.

TRANSITIVE   The Chicago Bulls *played* the Celtics last night.

INTRANSITIVE   The Chicago Bulls *played* well last night.

TRANSITIVE   She *writes* a column for the local newspaper.

INTRANSITIVE   She *writes* clearly.

TRANSITIVE   You *whispered* some words to your neighbor.

INTRANSITIVE   You *whispered* rather loudly.

TRANSITIVE   He *danced* the role of Oberon in Shakespeare's play.

INTRANSITIVE   He *danced* elegantly.

14e   Using *sit/set, lie/lay,* and *rise/raise*

Three irregular verb pairs, *sit/set, lie/lay,* and *rise/raise,* sometimes cause difficulty. The pairs are often confused, in part because of their similar spellings and in part because of their related meanings. The major difference in each case pair is that one verb is transitive and the other is intransitive.

Sit/set

BASE FORM	PRESENT TENSE	PRESENT PARTICIPLE	PAST TENSE	PAST PARTICIPLE
sit	sit, sits	sitting	sat	sat
set	set, sets	setting	set	set

Sit, which means "to be seated," is an intransitive verb and therefore never takes an object. *Set,* which means "to put" or "to place," is a transitive verb and takes a direct object. Look at the following examples:

The cat *is sitting* on the dining room table. [intransitive verb]

They *sat* together in the cafeteria. [intransitive verb]

We *have sat* here for nearly two hours. [intransitive verb]

She *sets* the table for breakfast the night before. [transitive verb]

I *set* my purse on my desk. [transitive verb]

You *have set* your watch ten minutes ahead. [transitive verb]

Lie/lay

BASE FORM	PRESENT TENSE	PRESENT PARTICIPLE	PAST TENSE	PAST PARTICIPLE
lie	lie, lies	lying	lay	lain
lay	lay, lays	laying	laid	laid

Lie, which means "to recline," is an intransitive verb and therefore never takes an object. *Lay,* which means "to put or place," is a transitive verb and takes a direct object. Look at the following examples:

The dog often *lies* down in the corner. [intransitive verb]

The children *lay* down for their nap. [intransitive verb]

The cat *has lain* in the sun all morning. [intransitive verb]

A skilled worker *lays* bricks evenly and on a level. [transitive verb]

The waitress *laid* both plates in front of me. [transitive verb]

The family *has laid* a big responsibility on your shoulders. [transitive verb]

Rise/raise

BASE FORM	PRESENT TENSE	PRESENT PARTICIPLE	PAST TENSE	PAST PARTICIPLE
rise	rise, rises	rising	rose	risen
raise	raise, raises	raising	raised	raised

Rise, which means "to get up," is an intransitive verb and never takes a direct object. *Raise,* which means "to lift up," is a transitive verb and can take a direct object. Look at the following examples:

She *rises* at five every morning. [intransitive verb]

He *rose* a few minutes before six o'clock. [intransitive verb]

The tide *was rising* rapidly. [intransitive verb]

He *raised* a banner over his head. [transitive verb]

The mayor *will raise* taxes again this year. [transitive verb]

The bake sale *should raise* several hundred dollars. [transitive verb]

VERB TENSES

Tense indicates when the action of a verb occurs, in the past, present, or future. The following chart identifies verb tenses and gives examples of regular and irregular verb tense forms.

VERB TENSES

VERB TENSE	REGULAR VERB	IRREGULAR VERB
Simple present	She walks	She writes
Simple past	She walked	She wrote
Simple future	She will walk	She will write
Present perfect	She has walked	She has written
Past perfect	She had walked	She had written
Future perfect	She will have walked	She will have written
Present progressive	She is walking	She is writing
Past progressive	She was walking	She was writing
Future progressive	She will be walking	She will be writing

VERB TENSE	REGULAR VERB	IRREGULAR VERB
Present perfect progressive	She has been walking	She has been writing
Past perfect progressive	She had been walking	She had been writing
Future perfect progressive	She will have been walking	She will have been writing

14f   Simple tenses

The simple tenses are the past tense, the present tense, and the future tense. These are the most frequently used tenses in speech and writing. They are called simple because each tense consists of a single word, or in the case of the simple future, two words. (In contrast, the perfect, progressive, and perfect progressive tenses use a form of the main verb and one or more auxiliaries. See 14g and 14h in the *Workbook*.)

1   Present tense

The simple present tense is used in the following ways.

1. To designate action occurring at the time of speaking or writing:
   She *lives* in Boston.

2. To indicate habitual actions:
   He *walks* his dog every morning.

3. To express general truths:
   Time *flies*.

4. To express scientific knowledge:
   Blood *circulates* through the body.

5. To refer to (some) future events:
   The concert *begins* at eight o'clock tonight.

6. To discuss literary and artistic works created in the past:
   Shakespeare's Juliet *is* a young girl in her teens.

   The face of Da Vinci's Mona Lisa *appears* serene.

FORMS OF THE SIMPLE PRESENT TENSE

SINGULAR	PLURAL
I help	We help
You help	You help
He helps	They help
She helps	
It helps	

Note that the *-s* ending always appears in the third-person singular form, the one used with *he, she, it*, or a singular word.

2 | Past tense

The simple past tense indicates action occurring in the past and not extending into the present.

The doctor *examined* the baby thoroughly.

A large branch *fell* off the oak tree.

The dog *barked* furiously at the meter reader.

She *wrote* a letter of complaint to the store manager.

FORMS OF THE SIMPLE PAST TENSE

SINGULAR	PLURAL
I walked	We walked
You walked	You walked
He walked	They walked
She walked	
It walked	

Note that in the simple past tense, the verb ending remains the same in all forms.

3 | Future tense

The simple future tense indicates actions that have not yet begun. Verbs in the simple future tense almost always use the auxiliary verb *will*.

He *will clean* his room tomorrow.

The senator *will offer* an alternative tax plan.

FORMS OF THE SIMPLE FUTURE TENSE

SINGULAR	PLURAL
I will work	We will work
You will work	You will work
He will work	They will work
She will work	
It will work	

14g | Perfect tenses

The perfect tenses are the present perfect, the past perfect, and the future perfect. The perfect tenses express more complex time relationships than the simple tenses do. They usually indicate an action finished by a specific time or an action that has been finished before another action begins. Perfect tenses consist of a form of the auxiliary verb *to have* and a past participle.

1   Present perfect tense

The present perfect tense indicates that an action, or the effect of that action, began in the past and continues into the present.

They *have lived* in Montreal for twenty years.

I *have informed* the committee of my decision.

He *has broken* his leg.

FORMS OF THE PRESENT PERFECT TENSE
  (*HAVE* OR *HAS* AND A PAST PARTICIPLE)

SINGULAR	PLURAL
I have decided	We have decided
You have decided	You have decided
He has decided	They have decided
She has decided	
It has decided	

2   Past perfect tense

The past perfect tense indicates an action that has been completed before another action. It indicates a time further back in the past than the simple past tense or the present perfect tense does.

We *had expected* you to arrive long before you did.

He *had left* the office an hour before I called him.

She *had hoped* to retire before she reached sixty-five.

FORMS OF THE PAST PERFECT TENSE
  (*HAD* AND A PAST PARTICIPLE)

SINGULAR	PLURAL
I had followed	We had followed
You had followed	You had followed
He had followed	They had followed
She had followed	
It had followed	

3   Future perfect tense

The future perfect tense indicates an action that began in the past and will be finished in the future.

He *will have finished* the project by the end of the week.

By next June, you *will have graduated*.

By August, the team *will have broken* its previous scoring record.

FORMS OF THE FUTURE PERFECT TENSE
(*WILL HAVE* AND A PAST PARTICIPLE)

SINGULAR	PLURAL
I will have done	We will have done
You will have done	You will have done
He will have done	They will have done
She will have done	
It will have done	

14h Progressive tenses

The progressive tenses indicate action that is ongoing or continuing. They have a form of the verb *to be* and the present participle (the *-ing form*). Each one of the six progressive tenses corresponds to one of the three simple and three perfect tenses.

1 Present progressive tense

The present progressive tense indicates a sense of ongoing action.

We *are hoping* to move soon.

Groups of workers *are picketing* the factory.

Mr. Randall *is teaching* two courses this semester.

FORMS OF THE PRESENT PROGRESSIVE TENSE
(*AM, IS,* OR *ARE* AND A PRESENT PARTICIPLE)

SINGULAR	PLURAL
I am trying	We are trying
You are trying	You are trying
He is trying	They are trying
She is trying	
It is trying	

2 Past progressive tense

The past progressive tense indicates action in the past that was continuing when something else happened.

I *was listening* to the radio when the power failure occurred.

When the smoke detector went off, we *were sleeping*.

She *was writing* a history term paper when I called her.

FORMS OF THE PAST PROGRESSIVE TENSE
  (*WAS* OR *WERE* AND A PRESENT PARTICIPLE)

SINGULAR
I was calling
You were calling
He was calling
She was calling
It was calling

PLURAL
We were calling
You were calling
They were calling

 3   **Future progressive tense**

The future progressive tense indicates continuing action in the future.

He *will be working* in the registrar's office next year.

The team *will be trying* to beat its previous record.

I *will be studying* all week for the chemistry test.

FORMS OF THE FUTURE PROGRESSIVE TENSE
  (*WILL BE* AND A PRESENT PARTICIPLE)

SINGULAR
I will be changing
You will be changing
He will be changing
She will be changing
It will be changing

PLURAL
We will be changing
You will be changing
They will be changing

4   **Present perfect progressive tense**

The present perfect progressive tense indicates that an action has been continuing from the past into the present.

I *have been playing* basketball since I was seven years old.

Ms. Baraka *has been supervising* this department since January.

Mr. Reed *has been delivering* our mail for ten years.

FORMS OF THE PRESENT PERFECT PROGRESSIVE TENSE
  (*HAVE BEEN* OR *HAS BEEN* AND A PRESENT PARTICIPLE)

SINGULAR
I have been working
You have been working

PLURAL
We have been working
You have been working

He has been working
She has been working
It has been working

They have been working

5 | Past perfect progressive tense

The past perfect progressive tense indicates past action that happened before something else occurred. The *-ing* form of the verb indicates that the action was continuing.

He *had been playing* tennis twice a week before his shoulder injury.

She *had been looking* for a better paying job when her boss promoted her.

The guard *had been patrolling* the first floor when he noticed the open door.

FORMS OF THE PAST PERFECT PROGRESSIVE TENSE
   (*HAD BEEN* **AND A PRESENT PARTICIPLE**)

SINGULAR

I had been keeping
You had been keeping
He had been keeping
She had been keeping
It had been keeping

PLURAL

We had been keeping
You had been keeping
They had been keeping

6 | Future perfect progressive tense

The future perfect progressive tense shows actions that began in the past and will continue into a specific future time.

By the time he is forty, he *will have been playing* professional baseball for more than half his life.

At 9 p.m. tonight we *will have been studying* biology for five straight hours.

FORMS OF THE FUTURE PERFECT PROGRESSIVE TENSE
   (*WILL HAVE BEEN* **AND A PRESENT PARTICIPLE**)

SINGULAR

I will have been typing
You will have been typing
He will have been typing
She will have been typing
It will have been typing

PLURAL

We will have been typing
You will have been typing
They will have been typing

14i | Verb tense sequences

Verb tenses indicate time—past, present, and future. In writing, we must choose verb tenses carefully to give an accurate indication of the time relationships of various events. Sequence of tenses refers to the relationship between the verb tense in an independent clause and the verb tense in a dependent clause. The relationship between the verb tenses must make sense. Note the following examples of logical tense sequence:

> When he *sleeps*, he often *snores*. [The two actions happen simultaneously in the present; therefore, both verbs are in the present tense.]

> If you *touch* the stove, you *will burn* your hand. [The two actions happen in sequence, the first in the present, the second in the future; the first verb is in the present tense, the second in the future tense.]

> Nobody *knows* what *happened* to Judge Crater. [The first action is still going on in the present, while the second action concerns a past event; the first verb is in the present, the second in the past.]

> Few people *understood* why he *resigned* his position. [Both verbs are in the past to indicate what people thought at the time the event occurred. Compare this example to the previous one, in which people still do not have understanding of an event to the present day.]

In the following example, the verb tense sequence is not logical:

> He never *exercises* because he *had* no time for it.

If having no time is in the past, why doesn't he exercise now? The two actions do not have a logical relationship. The relationship between the two actions would be clearer and more logical if both verbs were in the present tense or both were in the past tense:

> He never *exercises* because he *has* no time for it.

> He never *exercised* because he *had* no time for it.

1 | Infinitives and verb tense sequences

Present tense infinitives consist of *to* and the base form of the verb—*to think, to reach, to reveal.* Use a present infinitive to indicate a time simultaneous with or later than the time of the main verb.

> They are eager *to meet* you. [The present infinitive, *to meet*, indicates the same time frame as that of the main verb, *are*.]

> They wanted *to travel* during their vacation. [The action of the main verb, *wanted*, occurred before the action indicated by the present tense infinitive, *to travel*.]

> She had decided *to renew* her magazine subscription. [The action of the main verb, *had decided*, occurred before the action indicated by the present tense infinitive, *to renew*.]

The past (or perfect) infinitive consists of *to have* and the past participle of the verb—*to have known, to have answered, to have called.* Use past infinitives to indicate action that happened earlier than the action of the main verb.

> Mr. Flack appears *to have left* the office. [The past infinitive, *to have left*, indicates an earlier time than that of the present tense verb, *appears*.]

2 | Participles and verb tense sequences

The tense of a participle is determined by the tense of the main verb. Use a present participle (the base verb form + *-ing*) to show action occurring at the same time as the action of the main verb, no matter what the tense of the main verb is. Look at the following examples:

Hoping to improve her time, the runner *practices* daily. [The actions of hoping and practicing occur at the same time—in the present tense.]

Keeping far to the right, the novice driver *steered* the car down the road. [The actions of keeping and steering occurred at the same time—in the past tense.]

The past participle (*broken, irritated, angered*) and the present perfect participle (*having broken, having irritated, having angered*) indicate action that happens before the action of the main verb. Look at these examples:

Insulted by the speaker's crude remarks, I *left* the room. [The action of insulting occurs first; then the action of leaving occurs.]

Having locked the car, he *walked* to his apartment building. [The action of locking occurs before the action of walking.]

VOICE

Voice refers to the relationship between the subject and the verb. If the subject performs the action, the verb is in the active voice. If the subject is acted upon, the verb is in the passive voice. A verb in the passive voice always has a form of the verb *to be* immediately before the past participle of the main verb.

ACTIVE AND PASSIVE VOICES

	ACTIVE VOICE	**PASSIVE VOICE**
Present	He helps them.	He is helped.
Past	He helped them.	He was helped.
Future	He will help them.	He will be helped.
Present perfect	He has helped them.	He has been helped.
Past perfect	He had helped them.	He had been helped.
Future perfect	He will have helped them.	He will have been helped.

14j | Uses of the active voice

In active voice verbs, the subject is the agent (doer) of the action, and the direct object is the receiver of the action. Use the active voice to emphasize who or what performs an action.

A bad injury *ended* the football player's career.

The jury *has* not yet *reached* a verdict.

She *writes* a letter to her mother once a week.

Tomorrow, she *will announce* her candidacy for mayor.

Alex *broke* the kitchen window.

Kelly *passed* the physics exam.

Using the active voice makes writing tighter, more vigorous, more directed, and less wordy than writing filled with passive voice verbs. Look here at passive voice versions of the preceding examples:

The kitchen window *was broken* by Alex.

The physics test *was passed* by Kelly.

These versions give more emphasis to the window and the test than to the actions of breaking and passing. When you edit drafts of your writing, convert passive voice verbs to the active voice wherever possible.

14k   Uses of the passive voice

The passive voice indicates that the grammatical subject of a sentence receives the action of the verb. Use the passive voice when the agent (doer) of the action is either unknown or considered relatively unimportant. Passive voice verbs emphasize the fact of an event rather than the cause; descriptions of historical events and scientific developments often use the passive voice.

The election *was decided* by fewer than a thousand votes.

The game *will be delayed* on account of the thunderstorm.

Two crossing guards *have been assigned* to those streets.

The test *has been postponed* until next week.

Electric shock therapy *is* rarely *used* now.

In some cities, the sad process of urban decay *has been reversed*.

MOOD

A verb can be in one of three moods—indicative, imperative, or subjunctive. A verb in the indicative mood states a fact, declares an opinion, or asks a question:

The rain *has stopped*. [states a fact]

The bus *was* twenty minutes early. [states a fact]

He *was* an ineffectual governor. [declares an opinion]

Naylor *is* a better writer than Tyler. [declares an opinion]

Has the football team *had* a winning season recently? [asks a question]

Are scientists close to finding a vaccine against AIDS? [asks a question]

Verbs in the imperative mood give commands, express requests, or give directions. Imperative verbs never change form. The subject of an imperative verb is usually the word *you*, which is implied rather than explicitly stated.

Please *file* these papers as soon as possible. [gives directions]

Stop fighting immediately! [gives a command]

Read over the plans before tomorrow's meeting. [gives directions]

Mr. Kurian, please *tell* me about your recent trip to India. [expresses a request]

Open your books to page 196. [gives directions]

Verbs in the subjunctive mood express wishes, make demands, state requirements, make suggestions, or make statements contrary to fact. Subjunctive verbs often appear in clauses starting with *that* or *if*.

I wish that I *were* taller than I am. [expresses a wish]

The chief executive insists that his assistant *attend* all the important meetings of the board of directors. [states a requirement]

The fund raiser suggested that he *make* a sizable donation to the hospital. [makes a suggestion]

If I *were* the governor, I would pardon him. [states a condition contrary to fact]

USES OF THE SUBJUNCTIVE

- Use the base form of the verb when using the present tense of the subjunctive.

  The first requirement is that the applicant *be* able to use a computer.

  The next requirement is that he or she *speak* Spanish and German.

  Finally, the director insists that the candidate *have* experience dealing with the public.
- The past subjunctive is identical to the past indicative in all verbs except *to be*. When using the past subjunctive of the verb *to be*, always use *were*.

  If you *were* taller, you could reach the top shelf without a ladder.

  If the project *succeeded*, its director would become famous.

  If I *were* you, I would not accept his offer.

  If we *were* mathematicians, we might understand that new proof.

EXERCISE 1   Selecting Standard Verb Forms

Revise the following sentences so that they conform to standard English verb usage. (Some of the sentences may be correct as written.) Examples:

has
Ms. Smith always ~~have~~ good suggestions.

have seen
I ~~seen~~ that movie twice.

1. By the time we arrived at the office, he gone home.

2. As soon as that computer model is on sale, I going to buy one.

3. Every single one of these batteries are dead.

4. Babies often become cranky when they do not get enough sleep.

5. She mail the rent check to the landlord six days ago.

6. I recommends regular exercise as part of a plan to lose weight.

7. The notes you take in physics class is very well organized.

8. He had wrote his brief speech on two index cards.

9. More women today have entered law school and medical school than in the past.

10. In the past she use to be very shy, but now she is very outgoing.

EXERCISE 2   Writing with Standard Verb Forms

For each of the following topics, write a brief paragraph of three to five sentences using the verb forms indicated in parentheses. Example:

Topic: Seeing the dentist (*used to be, have changed*)

Going to the dentist used to be a painful experience years ago, an experience that most people dreaded. Indeed, many people put off seeing the dentist because they feared pain. Today, advances in technology and in pain relief have changed seeing the dentist from a painful experience into a bearable one.

1. Taking an exam (*anticipate, review*)

2. Babysitting (*have explained, have written*)

3. The refrigerator (*is decorated, can see*)

4. My favorite clothing (*have worn, irritates*)

5. A newborn infant (*yawns, sleeps*)

EXERCISE 3   Selecting Auxiliary and Modal Auxiliary Verbs

In each of the following sentences, underline or circle the correct auxiliary or modal auxiliary verb. Example:

Students wishing to change their major (*have/<u>must</u>*) speak to their advisors.

1. A person who (*is/be*) chronically late to work (*do/will*) eventually lose his job.

2. As soon as the rain (*was/had*) stopped, the game (*was/could*) resume.

3. He (*do/did*) not tell me that he (*have/had*) been promoted.

4. A sore throat that (*does/do*) not get better (*do/may*) be a sign of trouble.

5. I (*have/must*) not walked the dog yet this morning.

6. If the course (*must/is*) canceled, you (*do/will*) receive a refund.

7. For best results, the exact directions *(do/must)* be followed.

8. The injured basketball player *(has/might)* miss the next two weeks of play.

9. We *(are/have)* convinced the senator to vote for a tax cut.

10. You *(should/have)* tell your family that you *(have/are)* being transferred to another city.

EXERCISE 4 Writing with Auxiliary and Modal Auxiliary Verbs

For each of the following topics, write a brief paragraph of three to five sentences using the verb forms indicated in parentheses. Example:

Topic: Making breakfast *(must coordinate, may seem)*

Making breakfast is not as simple a task as it may seem. Even a simple menu such as scrambled eggs, toast, and coffee can be a failure if the toast is already cold by the time the eggs are finally cooked. The cook must coordinate the timing of the various foods so that all of them are ready at the same time.

1. One of your hobbies *(will last, am finished)*

2. Waiting in line *(must wait, can irritate)*

3. Snow (*has piled, have experienced*)

4. Choosing a gift for a friend (*may enjoy, should choose*)

5. An animal you dislike (*does [not] look, might happen*)

EXERCISE 5   Selecting Irregular Verb Forms

For each irregular verb, write the appropriate past tense or past participle form in the blank. Example:

(*to stick*)   Tar from the newly paved road had <u>stuck</u> to the tires.

1. (*to spend; to give*)   After all his money had been _____, he _____ up gambling.

2. (*to wear; to shrink*)   This shirt cannot be _____ because it _____ in the wash.

3. (*to win*) In the last election, the incumbent _____ by fewer than one thousand votes.

4. (*to grow*) The child has _____ two inches in the past year.

5. (*to feel; to pay*) She _____ elated after she had _____ the last installment on her loan.

6. (*to think; to shake*) After the accident he _____ he was all right, but he was really quite _____.

7. (*to hide*) The key has been _____ in a very obvious place.

8. (*to eat; to creep; to sleep*) After it had _____, the cat _____ into a corner and _____.

9. (*to fall; to break*) He had _____ down and had _____ his hip.

10. (*to cut*) The toddler's food has to be _____ into very small pieces.

EXERCISE 6 Writing with Irregular Verb Forms

Write two sentences for each of the following verbs. In the first sentence use the verb in the past tense, in the second use it as a past participle (with a form of *to have* or *to be*). Example:

> *Verb:* ride
>
> I *rode* my bike to work.
> I *have ridden* it every day.

1. take

2. buy

3. drink

4. steal

5. become

EXERCISE 7   Recognizing Linking, Transitive, and Intransitive Verbs

Underline the verbs in the following sentences, and identify them as linking, transitive, or intransitive. (Some sentences may contain more than one verb.) Example:

      I often <u>read</u> science fiction.   <u>transitive</u>

1. The movie was lovely, but a little too long.   _____

2. I enjoy hikes in the mountains, but Orrin dislikes them.

    _____

3. When the bus hit a telephone pole, all the passengers screamed.

    _____

4. While he slept, the casserole in the oven burned.

_____

5. He becomes fatigued even after a very short walk. _____

EXERCISE 8   Writing with Linking, Transitive, and Intransitive Verbs

Write a sentence using each verb that follows. Examples:

was (*linking*): She was a judge for fourteen years.

use (*transitive*): We use the fax machine several times a day.

smiled (*intransitive*): He smiled even though my joke wasn't funny.

1. gave (*transitive*)

2. are (*linking*)

3. complain (*intransitive*)

4. sing (*transitive*)

5. sing (*intransitive*)

6. feel (*linking*)

7. annoy (*transitive*)

8. spoke (*intransitive*)

9. have received (*transitive*)

10. had been (*linking*)

EXERCISE 9   Writing with Special Verb Types

Write a sentence for each verb phrase that follows. Example:

Verb phrase: had set

I had set my purse down on this table a minute ago.

1. have been laying

2. could have sat

3. has risen

4. laid

5. may have raised

6. was rising

7. were sitting

8. were setting

9. had lain

10. will rise

EXERCISE 10   Using the Simple Tenses in Writing

For each verb that follows, write three sentences: one in the simple present tense, another in the simple past tense, and the third in the simple future tense. Example:

Verb: to write

Simple present: He *writes* a weekly newspaper for the town's only newspaper.
Simple past: Yesterday I *wrote* a letter of complaint to the Department of Motor Vehicles.
Simple future: If you wish, I *will write* a letter of recommendation for you.

1. to describe

2. to think

3. to study

4. to explain

5. to decide

EXERCISE 11   Using the Perfect Tenses in Writing

For each verb that follows, write three sentences: one in the present perfect tense, another in the past perfect tense, and the third in the future perfect tense. Example:

Verb: to work

Present perfect: She *has worked* at this company for four years.
Past perfect: I *had worked* on that problem for an hour before I found a solution.
Future perfect: By the time we finish, we *will have worked* on this report for five months.

   1. to graduate

   2. to clarify

   3. to compete

   4. to call

   5. to eat

EXERCISE 12   Using the Progressive Tenses in Writing

For each verb that follows, write sentences in these tenses: the present progressive, the past progressive, the future progressive, the present perfect progressive, the past perfect progressive, and the future perfect progressive. Example:

Verb: to read

Present progressive	I *am reading* a novel by Paule Marshall.
Past progressive	He *was reading* the newspaper at breakfast.
Future progressive	The class *will be reading* ten plays this semester.
Present perfect progressive	I *have been reading* his columns for years.
Past perfect progressive	I *had been reading* his columns for years before I actually met him.
Future perfect progressive	At noon, I *will have been reading* for three hours.

1. to dance

2. to work

3. to argue

4. to discuss

5. to play

EXERCISE 13   Recognizing Correct Tense Sequence

The tense sequence in some of the following sentences is incorrect. Correct those sentences. Example:

      graduates
After he ~~will graduate~~ from college, he will go to medical school.

1. When it rains, the highway quickly became flooded.

2. If the governor raises taxes again, he loses the election.

3. Every time Domingo sang in New York, it was a sell-out performance.

4. Having majored in foreign languages, she easily found a job as a translator.

5. That important file seems to have disappeared.

6. Finishing her math homework, she began studying for a biology test.

7. If we do not finish painting the living room today, we will not be able to do it until next weekend.

8. He seems to quit his job without any explanation.

9. People often felt uncomfortable when they speak in public for the first time.

10. Most podiatrists think that high platform shoes are dangerous.

EXERCISE 14   Using Correct Tense Sequence in Writing

For each topic that follows, write a brief paragraph of three to five sentences that uses logical tense sequences. Example:

Topic: Studying

I cannot study efficiently unless I have certain books and materials with me. For example, if I have my textbooks but I have left my class notes in my locker at school, it is impossible for me to study for a quiz. The textbooks are useful, but I also need my notes because they indicate what the teacher thinks is important and they also have summaries of class discussions.

1. A job interview

2. A good vacation

3. Preparing for exams

4. Voting

5. Being sick

EXERCISE 15   Recognizing the Active and Passive Voice

In the following sentences, underline and label the active and passive voice verbs. Example:

active   active   passive

When we <u>arrived</u>, we <u>discovered</u> that the meeting <u>had been canceled.</u>

1. He will not accept any papers that are written by hand.

2. The morning newspaper did not give the score because the game ended well after midnight.

3. Shows that do not earn good ratings are canceled fairly quickly.

4. The taxi hit a telephone pole and overturned.

5. The president has appointed several new federal judges.

EXERCISE 16   Changing the Voice of Verbs

Rewrite the following sentences, changing passive verbs to active ones and active verbs to passive ones. Example:

The window *was broken* yesterday by Carl.

Yesterday Carl *broke* a window.

1. All the flowers were eaten by deer.

2. A person stole Ms. Pantea's car radio last night.

3. Two different newspapers endorsed Senator White for reelection.

4. Workers renovated the apartment building from top to bottom.

5. The game was won by the Giants in the last two minutes of play.

6. A tennis player's eyes are always kept on the ball.

7. The panelists discussed various explanations for the resurgence of tuberculosis.

8. The calculus test was passed by most of the students.

9. A lamp was rewired, a dripping faucet was fixed, and the door hinges were oiled by Marty.

10. The floods in 1993 displaced thousands of people.

EXERCISE 17   Using the Active and Passive Voice in Writing

For each topic that follows write two sentences, one in the active voice and the other in the passive voice. Example:

Topic: Computers

Computers *have changed* the style and the pace of doing business.

A computer *can be used* to do word processing, to keep records, and to prepare income tax returns.

1. Competition

2. A guitar

3. Parallel parking a car

4. A television show you like

5. A television show you dislike

EXERCISE 18   Recognizing the Mood of Verbs

Indicate whether the verb in each sentence is indicative, imperative, or subjunctive. Example:

If I *were* you, I would accept that job offer.   <u>subjunctive</u>

1. At busy airports, a plane *lands* every few seconds.   _____

2. Please *keep* magnets away from the computers.   _____

3. The committee has requested that we *send* our résumés.

   _____

4. He behaved as if he *were* in charge of everything.   _____

5. They have asked that their telephone number *be* changed.

   _____

EXERCISE 19   Using the Subjunctive Mood

In the following sentences, correct the subjunctive verb forms that are used inappropriately. (Some of the sentences may be correct as written.) Example:

> He looks as if he *was* a marathon runner.
>
> He looks as if he *were* a marathon runner.

1. If he was fired, it would cause a great deal of unpleasant publicity.

2. The committee recommended that the tuition remains the same.

3. Mr. Santos insisted that he was allowed to speak at the rally.

4. He would not behave that way if he were not deeply concerned about you.

5. The contestant acted as if she was not at all concerned about winning.

6. The Board of Education suggested that two high schools are closed.

7. If I was in his position, I would resign in protest.

8. His mother treated him as if he was still a rebellious teenager.

9. It is essential that each applicant submits a written statement.

10. If she was in charge of the department, it would run smoothly.

EXERCISE 20   Using the Three Moods in Writing

Write a sentence for each verb that follows. Make sure at least two sentences use verbs in the imperative mood and two other sentences use verbs in the subjunctive mood. Examples:

to be: If I *were* you, I would get more exercise.

to open: Please *open* this jar for me.

to begin: The movie *will begin* at eight o'clock.

1. to answer

2. to be

3. to search

4. to complete

5. to examine

CHAPTER 15

Nouns, Pronouns, and Case

15a | Understanding nouns

A noun is the name of a person, place, thing, concept, or quality. There are different types of nouns—common, proper, abstract, and concrete. The type depends on the person or thing that the noun names. Common nouns refer to classes, to any person, place, thing, concept, or quality in general. Proper nouns name specific people, places, things, concepts, and qualities.

COMMON NOUNS	PROPER NOUNS
writer	Toni Morrison
street	Pennsylvania Avenue
building	Sears Tower
newspaper	*Star Ledger*
high school	Kennedy High School
war	the Civil War

Nouns can also be abstract or concrete. Abstract nouns name concepts, ideas, or qualities, things we can think about but that we do not experience through our senses. An abstract noun is usually not preceded by an article (*a, an, the*) unless the noun is modified. Concrete nouns name things that we know through the senses of sight, hearing, touch, taste, and smell.

ABSTRACT NOUNS	CONCRETE NOUNS
depth	pumpkin pie
intelligence	vegetable garden
heroism	newspaper
happiness	daughter
kindness	subway
strength	books

Nouns can appear in different forms. For example, they can be singular (naming one) or plural (naming more than one). Most plural nouns are formed by adding -*s* or -*es* to the singular form. Some nouns have irregular plural forms; consult your dictionary for information about irregular and foreign language-based plural nouns.

SINGULAR NOUN	PLURAL NOUN
boy	boys
baby	babies
school	schools
brush	brushes
truth	truths
reward	rewards
mouse	mice
man	men
woman	women
curriculum	curricula *or* curriculums

Certain nouns are used, for the most part, only in the singular form. Collective nouns name groups of things yet are often singular. Mass nouns (noncount nouns) name things that cannot be counted one by one and, therefore, cannot be made plural; mass nouns are often preceded by qualifiers such as *some, much,* and *amount.* In contrast, countable nouns can be counted one by one and form the plural in the regular way.

COLLECTIVE NOUNS	MASS NOUNS (NO PLURAL FORM)	COUNTABLE NOUNS (SINGULAR–PLURAL)
family	money	dollar–dollars
jury	furniture	chair–chairs
team	dust	essay–essays
herd	homework	problem–problems
panel (of people)	health	idea–ideas
committee	violence	sale–sales

To show ownership or relationship between the noun and something else, nouns form the possessive in one of the following ways:

—by adding 's to a singular noun (the *boy's* bicycle)
—by adding ', an apostrophe alone, to a plural noun (the *girls'* soccer team)
—by adding 's to a plural noun that does not end in s (the *men's* department, the *women's* decisions)
—by adding 's or ' (an apostrophe alone) to a singular proper noun that already ends in s (*Charles's* book or *Charles'* book)

NOUN (SINGULAR)	NOUN POSSESSIVE (SINGULAR)	NOUN (PLURAL)	NOUN POSSESSIVE (PLURAL)
book	book's title	books	books' titles
boy	boy's shirt	boys	boys' teacher
child	child's room	children	children's room
baby	baby's toys	babies	babies' toys
dog	dog's ears	dogs	dogs' ears
man	man's face	men	men's faces

Nouns and determiners

Nouns are often introduced by determiners, signals that a noun is soon to follow. The most common determiners are the articles *a, an,* and *the.* These articles always precede any adjectives describing the noun. The definite article *the* always refers to a particular noun. The indefinite articles *a* and *an* introduce generalized nouns. Note also that *a* is used before consonants, whereas *an* is used before vowels and vowel sounds. In the following sentences, look at the choice of articles and their placement in the noun phrases:

He stumbled sleepily into *the kitchen.*

The whole family gathered in *the warm, cozy kitchen.*

A year ago he graduated from high school. [No *the* is needed because a specific high school is not named.]

The high school he attended had a good reputation.

He peeled *an onion.*

He peeled *a large onion.*

I waited for you for *an hour.*

I waited for you for *a whole hour.*

He received *an F* in biology.

She received *a C* in the same course.

See Chapter 19 in the *Workbook* for more on articles and other determiners.

15b   Understanding pronouns

Pronouns are words that take the place of nouns. Instead of repeating nouns in sentences and paragraphs, you use pronouns to refer to those nouns. The noun that a pronoun refers to is called the antecedent. In the following examples, the pronouns are *italicized* and their antecedents are underlined.

The <u>cat</u> scratched the furniture with *its* claws.

The <u>baby</u> cried because *he* had dropped *his* toy.

The <u>medicine</u> was not effective because *it* was old and outdated.

The <u>Jacksons</u> are adding a new room to *their* house.

<u>People</u> who are obese are putting great strain on *their* hearts.

The <u>mayor</u> insisted that *she* would not run for reelection.

When using pronouns, make sure the pronouns and their antecedent agree in number (singular or plural) and gender (masculine, feminine, neuter).

Classes of pronouns

Pronouns can be classified as personal, demonstrative, indefinite, relative, interrogative, reflexive, intensive, or reciprocal.

Personal pronouns refer to persons or things; they show distinctions between "first" persons (*I, we*), "second" persons (*you*), and "third" persons (*he, she, it, they*).

PERSONAL PRONOUNS

	SINGULAR	**PLURAL**
First person	I, me, my, mine	we, us, our, ours
Second person	you, your, yours	you, your, yours
Third person	he, him, his	they, them, their,
	she, her, hers	their
	it, its	

Note the personal pronouns in the following examples:

I am very pleased with *my* new job.

Ms. Mercado lost *her* wallet yesterday.

You will have to revise *your* vacation plans.

Demonstrative pronouns point to particular things:

SINGULAR   this, that

PLURAL   these, those

The demonstrative pronouns *this* and *these* are often used to indicate things close to the speaker, whereas *that* and *those* usually indicate things at a distance from the speaker.

This is the most interesting book I have read in years.

Of all the cereals, *these* are the most nutritious and *those* the least.

This is a regular sewing machine needle; *that* is a ballpoint needle.

Indefinite pronouns refer to unspecified persons or things. They also express the concept of quantity.

INDEFINITE PRONOUNS

all	everybody	anybody	somebody	nobody
some	everyone	anyone	someone	no one
few	everything	anything	something	nothing
none				
several				

Look at the indefinite pronouns in these examples:

Everybody came to the tag sale, but hardly *anybody* bought *anything*.

Most people paid attention to the speaker, but a *few* were asleep.

Somebody left an umbrella in the classroom.

Everyone on the block knows my name.

Nobody knows how to turn on that computer.

The customers were angry, and *several* were shouting at the manager.

Does *anyone* have a protractor?

Relative pronouns introduce clauses that modify nouns or pronouns.

RELATIVE PRONOUNS

who	whom	which	that
whoever	whomever	whichever	

In the following sentences, note that the relative pronouns are followed by the clauses they introduce:

The person *who borrowed my leaf blower* has not returned it yet.

The man *whom you just insulted* is my boss.

This house, *which has four bedrooms,* has been on the market for a month.

Cars *that get good gas mileage* have become very popular.

Whoever wins the tennis tournament receives a trophy and a large check.

Interrogative pronouns introduce questions, as in the following examples:

Who chairs the Senate when the vice-president is not there?

What can be done about the problems of hunger and homelessness?

Of all these proposals, *which* is the most practical?

Reflexive pronouns refer to the subject of the clause in which they appear. They are used as direct objects or as objects of a preposition.

REFLEXIVE PRONOUNS

myself	ourselves
yourself	yourselves
himself	themselves
herself	
itself	
oneself	

Look at the reflexive pronouns in these sentences:

He hurt *himself* playing football last weekend.

She surprised *herself* by winning the contest.

They were sitting by *themselves.*

I am never sure of *myself* when I have to speak in public.

Intensive pronouns emphasize their antecedents. Although they take the same form as reflexive pronouns, intensive pronouns do not have a grammatical function in a sentence.

I *myself* built all the bookshelves in the study.

He promised to finish the report *himself.*

Andrea changed the tire *herself.*

Reciprocal pronouns express reciprocity, indicating that each of two things has the same relationship toward the other. Notice the reciprocal pronouns in the following examples:

Mr. Idrovo and Mr. Genfi helped *each other* study for the police exam.

The members of the women's soccer team encouraged *one another.*

15c | Understanding pronoun case

There are three pronoun cases: subjective (nominative), objective, and possessive. Use the subjective case when the pronoun is the subject of a clause. Use the objective case when the pronoun is an object. Use the possessive case to indicate ownership. Note also that possessive personal pronouns never include an apostrophe (*yours, hers, theirs*).

PRONOUN CASE

	SUBJECTIVE	OBJECTIVE	POSSESSIVE
Personal Pronouns			
Singular			
First person	I	me	my, mine
Second person	you	you	your, yours
Third person	he, she, it	him, her, it	his, her, hers, its
Plural			
First person	we	us	our, ours
Second person	you	you	your, yours
Third person	they	them	their, theirs
Relative and Interrogative Pronouns			
	who	whom	whose
	whoever	whomever	
	which	which	
	what	what	
	that	that	

15d Using pronoun case

1 Subjective case

Use the subjective case when a pronoun is the subject of a clause, a subject complement, or an appositive to a subject or a subject complement. (In the *Workbook*, see 13b on complements and 13c on appositives.) In the following examples, the subjective case pronouns perform the functions indicated.

We attended all the town meetings. [subject of a clause]

Ms. Smith was chosen as chair because *she* is both organized and diplomatic. [subject of a clause]

My brother and *I* have not seen each other for weeks. [subject of a clause]

The first people to arrive in the morning were Ms. Brackle and *I*. [subject complement]

The people who should have won the award are *you* and *she*. [subject complement]

Two journalists, Mary Reed and *he*, were granted interviews by the president. [appositive to a subject]

Two of the officers receiving commendations were my former students, Frank Johnson and *she*. [appositive to a subject complement]

2 Objective case

Use the objective case when a pronoun is the direct object or the indirect object of a verb or verbal, the object of a preposition, the subject of an infinitive, or an appositive to an object.

The books were not available in retail stores; I had to order *them* by mail. [direct object of a verb]

You cannot make a person love you by hitting *him*. [direct object of a verbal]

The letter carrier handed *her* a large package. [indirect object of a verb]

I could count on Jane's writing *me* a letter every week. [indirect object of a verbal]

The committee finally had a chance to meet with *us*. [object of a preposition]

The new offices were assigned to Frank and *me*. [object of a preposition]

The bad weather forced *them* to stay indoors. [subject of the infinitive *to stay*, as well as the direct object of the verb *forced*]

The neighbors persuaded *her* to become chair of the block association. [subject of the infinitive *to become*, as well as the direct object of the verb *persuaded*]

The committee interviewed three candidates, Mr. Green, Ms. Andrews, and *her*. [appositive to the object *candidates*]

The movie disturbed us—my husband and *me*—because it was so violent. [appositive to the object *us*]

3 | Possessive case

Use the possessive case when a pronoun indicates ownership. Possessive pronouns appear in two forms: adjective forms that occur before nouns and gerunds, and pronominal (noun) forms that take the place of a noun.

ADJECTIVE FORMS OF POSSESSIVE PRONOUNS

my	our
your	your
his	their
her	
its	

PRONOMINAL (NOUN) FORMS OF POSSESSIVE PRONOUNS

mine	ours
yours	yours
his	theirs
hers	
its	

In the following examples, the possessive pronouns take the form indicated:

Your children are all in grade school. [adjective form]

So are *mine*. [pronominal form; the pronoun takes the place of "my children"]

Mr. and Mrs. Chang have finished painting *their* apartment. [adjective form]

The Joneses have not yet finished painting *theirs*. [pronominal form; the pronoun takes the place of "their apartment"]

I think that *my* job is very difficult. [adjective form]

I think that *yours* is even harder. [pronominal form; the pronoun takes the place of "your job"]

Sometimes you may be unsure whether to use a possessive pronoun or an objective pronoun in front of an *-ing* verbal. The choice of pronoun case depends on whether the *-ing* verbal is a gerund or a participle. If it is a gerund, the verbal is a noun; use the possessive case in front of it. If the verbal is a participle, use the objective case in front of it. Here are some examples:

I enjoyed *his* singing. [*Singing* in this sentence is a noun, so the possessive pronoun *his* is used.]

We heard *him* singing. [*Singing* here is a participle describing *him*.]

The movie critic praised *their* acting. [*Acting* is a noun here, so the possessive pronoun *their* is used.]

It is sad to see *them* acting so foolishly. [*Acting* here is a participle describing *them*.]

15e Using *who* and *whom*

It is sometimes difficult to know whether to use *who* or *whom*. The form you use depends on the word's function in its sentence or clause. Use *who* or *whoever* when the pronoun is the subject. Use *whom* or *whomever* when the pronoun is the direct object, indirect object, or the object of a preposition.

Who delivered the message? [subject of a sentence]

She wondered *who* had sent her flowers. [subject of a clause]

Whoever finishes work first gets a bonus. [subject of a sentence]

I will be grateful to *whoever* can start my car. [subject of a clause]

Whom will the proposed health care plan help most? [direct object of a verb]

To *whom* did you tell the news? [object of the preposition *to*]

I do not want to have to hire *whomever* we interview first. [object of the verb *to hire*]

1 Using *who* and *whom* at the beginning of questions

You can correctly choose between *who* and *whom* at the beginning of a question by answering the question with a personal pronoun. If the answer is a subjective case pronoun, use *who*. If the answer is an objective case pronoun, use *whom*.

Who broke the kitchen window?

He broke the kitchen window. [*He* is a subjective case pronoun, so use *who* in the question.]

Who attended the PTA meeting?

They attended the PTA meeting. [*They* is a subjective case pronoun, so use *who* in the question.]

Who did most of the work on this project?

She did most of the work on this project. [*She* is a subjective case pronoun, so use *who* in the question.]

Whom did you see at the meeting last night?

I saw *her* at the meeting last night. [*Her* is an objective case pronoun, so use *whom* in the question.]

Whom have you invited to the party?

I have invited *them* to the party. [*Them* is an objective case pronoun, so use *whom* in the question.]

Whom did the team elect captain?

The team elected *him* captain. [*Him* is an objective case pronoun, so use *whom* in the question.]

2 | Using *who* and *whom* in dependent clauses

In a dependent clause, the case of a pronoun depends on its function in that clause. Use *who* or *whoever* if the pronoun is the subject of the dependent clause. Use *whom* or *whomever* if the pronoun is an object within the clause. The function of the dependent clause in the whole sentence does not play a role in the choice of *who* or *whom*; rather, that choice depends only on the word's function within the dependent clause.

If you are not sure whether to use *who* or *whom*, turn the dependent clause into a statement using a personal pronoun instead. If your statement contains a subjective personal pronoun, choose *who*. If your statement uses an objective personal pronoun, choose *whom*.

I did not know *who* was calling me.

He was calling me. [*He* is a subjective case pronoun, so choose *who* in the dependent clause.]

Marie Curie was the scientist *who* discovered radium.

She discovered radium. [*She* is a subjective case pronoun, so choose *who* in the dependent clause.]

The reporter asked *who* had seen the accident.

They had seen the accident. [*They* is a subjective case pronoun, so choose *who* in the dependent clause.]

He was the only actor *whom* the critics praised.

The critics praised *him*. [*Him* is an objective case pronoun, so choose *whom* in the dependent clause.]

I will hire *whomever* you recommend.

You recommend *her*. [*Her* is an objective case pronoun, so choose *whomever* in the dependent clause.]

The people *whom* you mistook for loiterers are undercover police officers.

You mistook *them* for loiterers. [*Them* is an objective case pronoun, so use *whom* in the dependent clause.]

15f	**Using personal pronouns with compound structures**

It is not always easy to choose a pronoun in a compound structure. The choice, for example, between *I* and *me*, between *we* and *they*, or between *he* and *him* is not always immediately obvious. To select the correct pronoun, separate the two parts of the compound structure; the pronoun you would use alone is the same pronoun you should use in the compound structure. Here are some examples:

Dolores and (*I, me*) went to a meeting last night.

> Dolores went to a meeting last night.
>
> *I* went to a meeting last night.

Dolores and *I* went to a meeting last night.

The two winners of the scholarships were Nadine and (*he, him*).

> A winner was Nadine.
>
> A winner was *he*. *He* was a winner.

The two winners of the scholarships were Nadine and *he*.

The manager asked Roger, Carlos, and (*she, her*) to work overtime.

> The manager asked Roger to work overtime.
>
> The manager asked Carlos to work overtime.
>
> The manager asked *her* to work overtime.

The manager asked Roger, Carlos, and *her* to work overtime.

The salesperson offered a special price to the Clintons and (*we, us*).

> The salesperson offered a special price to the Clintons.
>
> The salesperson offered a special price to *us*.

The salesperson offered a special price to the Clintons and *us*.

15g	**Using personal pronouns with appositives**

A pronoun appositive should be in the same case, subjective or objective, as the noun that the appositive renames.

> Two members of the jury, Ms. King and *he*, did not think the defendant was guilty. [*Members* is the subject of the sentence, thus the pronoun appositive must be in the subjective case, *he*.]

Three students—Rene, Julissa, and *I*—would like to be yearbook editor. [*Students* is the subject of the sentence, thus the pronoun appositive must be subjective, *I*.]

Bonuses were distributed to two groups, the maintenance workers and *us*. [*Groups* is an object of a preposition, thus the pronoun appositive must be objective, *us*.]

The editorial praised three city officials—the city clerk, the police chief, and *her*. [*Officials* is a direct object, thus the pronoun appositive must be objective, *her*.]

15h Using personal pronouns with elliptical constructions

In elliptical constructions, some words have been omitted, but the meaning of those words is implied. Clauses with elliptical constructions sometimes end in pronouns; it is not always easy to choose the correct pronoun case with such constructions. To decide whether a subjective pronoun or an objective pronoun is needed, mentally fill in the missing words. The pronoun you would use with those words filled in is the pronoun you should use when the words are omitted. Look at the following examples:

I enjoy opera more than (*he, him*).

    I enjoy opera more than *he* does. [*He* is the subject of the omitted verb *does*.]

I enjoy opera more than *he*.

My sister is taller than (*I, me*).

    My sister is taller than *I* am. [*I* is the subject of the omitted verb *am*.]

My sister is taller than *I*.

You have more athletic ability than (*she, her*).

    You have more athletic ability than *she* has. [*She* is the subject of the implied verb *has*.]

You have more athletic ability than *she*.

Loud noises bother you more than (*we, us*).

    Loud noises bother you more than they bother *us*. [*Us* is the object of the unexpressed verb *bother*.]

Loud noises bother you more than *us*.

She likes her three dogs more than (*he, him*).

    She likes her three dogs more than she likes *him*. [*Him* is the object of the implied verb *likes*.]

She likes her three dogs more than *him*.

| 15i | **Using *we* and *us* with a noun** |

Deciding whether to use *we* or *us* with a noun depends on the function of the noun. If the noun is a subject or a subject complement in a clause, use *we*. If the noun is an object, use *us*. The easiest way to see which pronoun is correct is to drop the noun temporarily. The pronoun you would use alone in that sentence is the same pronoun to use with a noun.

(*We, Us*) neighbors should look out for each other.

> *We* should look out for each other. [Use the subjective pronoun *we* because *neighbors* is the subject of the sentence.]

We neighbors should look out for each other.

The block association has invited (*we, us*) neighbors to a special meeting.

> The block association has invited *us* to a special meeting. [Use the objective pronoun *us* because *neighbors* is the object of the verb *invited*.]

The block association has invited *us* neighbors to a special meeting.

EXERCISE 1   Recognizing Common and Proper Nouns

Identify each italicized word as a common noun or a proper noun. Example:

common   common   proper

He graduated ten *years* ago from a *high school* in *Philadelphia.*

1. *Judge Smith* has been a civil court *judge* for nearly a *decade.*

2. Of all the *books* I have read this *semester,* I enjoyed this *book* the most.

3. He works at *Macy's* in the shoe *department.*

4. He wanted to major in *physics* until he took *Physics 101.*

5. It was *time* to visit the *dentist* again.

6. My *doctor* is a capable, caring *person,* but she can't compare with *Dr. Wright.*

7. When her youngest *child* started kindergarten, *Mrs. Cruz* decided to get a part-time *job.*

8. They moved from *Atlanta* to *Rochester;* the *difference* in *climate* between the two *cities* was a big *shock* to them.

9. She can speak three *languages: French, English,* and *Spanish.*

10. Twenty *people* were sitting in the *waiting room* of the maternity *clinic* at *Roosevelt Hospital.*

EXERCISE 2   Recognizing Abstract and Concrete Nouns

Identify each italicized word as an abstract noun or a concrete noun. Example:

        concrete   abstract
    The *editorial* averred that *justice* was not served in this case.

1. Small *children* cannot always distinguish between *truth* and *lies.*

2. Several *deer* were chewing the *bark* off the *apple trees.*

3. *Happiness* means different things to different *people.*

4. The slogan of the French Revolution was *"Liberty, Equality, Fraternity."*

5. Many *people* who like *philosophy* have also had an interest in *mathematics.*

EXERCISE 3   Recognizing Singular, Plural, Collective, and Noncount Nouns

Identify each italicized word as a singular, plural, collective, or noncount noun. Example:

        singular   collective   noncount
    The *woman* on the *jury* said that she had lost her *money.*

1. The *scientist* is doing *research* on *retroviruses.*

2. Some of the *players* on the *team* are holding out for more favorable *contracts.*

3. The *furniture* in this *room* of the *museum* is old and valuable.

4. My *family* is originally from a *country* on the west *coast* of Africa.

5. This *farm* grows *corn*, *pumpkins*, and *soy beans*.

EXERCISE 4   Using Nouns in Writing

Write a sentence using each suggested noun. Then underline and identify the nouns in your sentences as common or proper, abstract or concrete, singular or plural, collective or noncount. Examples:

Noun: beauty

           abstract   common, concrete, plural   common, concrete, plural
The *beauty* of the *mountains* overwhelmed the *hikers*.

Noun: team

          collective   noncount   common, concrete, plural
The *team* will have to raise a lot of *money* to buy new *uniforms*.

1. President Jefferson

2. happiness

3. six babies

4. the jury

5. homework

EXERCISE 5   Using Possessive Forms of Nouns in Writing

Each phrase that follows contains a possessive form of a noun. Write a sentence using each phrase. Example:

Phrase: my son's room

My son's room is usually a mess, with clothes and toys strewn all around.

1. her children's school

2. Charles's boss

3. Ms. Franklin's voice

4. Mr. Gonzalez's job

5. the car's two front tires

EXERCISE 6   Using Articles with Nouns

Fill in each blank with the correct article, *a, an,* or *the*. Example:

> I spoke to Dean Hill, <u>the</u> person in charge of registration.

> To finish this project, we need <u>a</u> protractor and <u>an</u> eraser.

1. _____ large crowd was gathered at _____ corner of Main Street and Broadway.

2. He thought _____ stew he was making needed more taste, so he added _____ pinch of salt and _____ onion.

3. That was easily _____ most exciting movie I have seen all year.

4. It is never _____ easy thing to tell people bad news.

5. He received _____ C in most of his courses but unfortunately _____ F in one of them.

EXERCISE 7   Recognizing Pronouns and Their Antecedents

In each sentence that follows, underline the pronoun once and its antecedent twice. (Some sentences may contain more than one pronoun.) Example:

> <u>Andy</u> drove <u>his</u> cab to the airport.

1. The doctor opened her office in this neighborhood two years ago.

2. All the students were waiting to see their exam results.

3. The dog was wagging its tail furiously.

4. The basketball player had to change his torn uniform.

5. The neighbors usually mow their lawn on weekends.

EXERCISE 8   Identifying Different Types of Pronouns

In the following sentences, underline and identify each pronoun as personal, demonstrative, indefinite, relative, interrogative, reflexive, intensive, or reciprocal. Examples:

> personal   personal   indefinite
> <u>He</u> won't tell <u>his</u> secret to <u>anybody</u>.

> interrogative   personal   intensive
> <u>Who</u> broke this lamp? <u>I</u> will fix it <u>myself</u>.

1. He hurt himself rollerskating.

2. People who do not particularly like each other can still work with each other.

3. What did you think of that movie?

4. Everybody in the bank wanted to know his or her balance.

5. The famous tenor's wife was herself a musician.

6. Nobody knows who misplaced those files.

7. Your car gets much better gas mileage than those do.

8. He woke himself up with his loud snoring.

9. She is an artist whose paintings are popular in South America and Europe.

10. Out of all college athletes, many would like to turn professional but few will actually get the chance to do so.

EXERCISE 9   Using Different Types of Pronouns in Writing

For each of the following items, write a sentence using the pronoun or pronouns indicated. Examples:

Pronoun (relative): who

       Ms. Ebreo, who is majoring in chemistry, is from California.

Pronoun: your, mine

       Your watch is a few minutes fast, and so is mine.

1. yourself (*reflexive or intensive*)

2. our, hers

3. who (*interrogative*)

4. who (*relative*)

5. everybody, nothing

EXERCISE 10 Recognizing Pronoun Case

Identify the italicized pronouns in the following sentences as subjective, objective, or possessive. Example:

> subjective   objective   possessive
> *He* called *me* during *his* lunch hour.

1. *I* was nearly late for work because *my* car wouldn't start right away.

2. *You* should inform *them* if *you* want to change *your* curriculum.

3. Parents *who* wish to talk to *their* children's teachers will have a chance to do so on Parents' Night.

4. *He* is wondering when the jury will announce *its* verdict.

5. The role of Scarpia was sung by a famous baritone, *whose* voice resounded through the huge concert hall.

EXERCISE 11   Choosing Pronoun Case

Underline or circle the correct pronoun or pronouns in each sentence. Example:

> (*We*/*Us*)—my brothers and I—are sending (*our*/*ours*) parents on a trip to Spain.

1. The panelists—Jack, Ben, and (*I*/*me*)—were chosen by lot.

2. I forgot (*my*/*mine*) book. Could I borrow (*you*/*your*/*yours*)?

3. (*They*/*them*) named (*they*/*their*/*theirs*) first child Zoila.

4. All of (*we*/*us*) in this area were affected by the floods.

5. (*They*/*them*) should realize that events happening on the other side of the world can affect (*they*/*them*).

6. The winners of the math prize were Lourdes and (*he*/*him*).

7. The manager sent (*he*/*him*/*his*) a telegram telling (*he*/*him*/*his*) that (*he*/*him*/*his*) contract had been renewed.

8. The twins' mother fed (*they*/*them*/*their*), and then (*she*/*her*/*hers*) bathed (*they*/*them*/*theirs*).

9. (*She*/*Her*/*Hers*) father is a diamond setter; (*she*/*her*/*hers*) has learned the trade from (*she*/*her*/*hers*) father.

10. (*They*/*Them*) buy a new car frequently, but (*we*/*us*) keep (*our*/*ours*) for years.

EXERCISE 12   Using Pronoun Case in Writing

Write one or two sentences using each set of pronouns. Example:

Pronoun set: I, him, his

> I am sorry that the baseball team's owner has traded him because the team really needs his hitting power.

1. we, us, our

2. you (*subjective*), me, your

3. mine, theirs

4. I, your

5. him, them, you (*objective*)

EXERCISE 13   Using *who* and *whom*

Write *who* or *whom* in each blank. Example:

> The students <u>whom</u> you see in the laboratory are doing a chemistry experiment.

1. The astronauts _____ repaired the Hubbell telescope went through years of training.

2. _____ did you vote for in the last election?

3. The gardener wondered _____ had been picking his roses.

4. Ms. Ball, _____ used to work for a bank, is now an X-ray technician.

5. Abraham Lincoln, _____ received little formal schooling, was nevertheless a fine writer.

6. Indira Gandhi, Golda Meir, and Margaret Thatcher are among a small group of women _____ have governed modern nations.

7. To _____ is this package addressed?

8. The person _____ the students select as student government president is usually also elected vice-chairperson of the college senate.

9. Anyone _____ doesn't like children should not become a pediatrician.

10. The computer screen displayed a list of all the people _____ we had interviewed in the past month.

EXERCISE 14   Choosing Appropriate Pronouns

In each of the following sentences, underline or circle the correct pronoun or pronouns. Example:

> Mitch can run a great deal faster than (*she*/her).

1. My father and (*I*/me) enjoy going to baseball games together.

2. Her sarcastic remarks were directed especially at Gloria and (*I*/me).

3. You speak much more clearly than (*he*/him).

4. (*We*/Us) parents have to take an interest in our children's education.

5. She always complains about (*me*/my) talking on the telephone for hours.

6. Two groups—the support staff and (*we*/us)—will receive bonuses at the end of the year.

7. Did you see (*them*/their) playing soccer yesterday?

8. Coincidences happen more often to (*she*/her) than (*I*/me).

9. Some of the candidates are lying to (*we*/us) voters.

10. (*I*/Me) and my sisters arrange a family reunion every summer.

Name _____ Section _____ Date _____

EXERCISE 15 Correcting Pronoun Case Errors

Correct the pronoun case errors in the following sentences. (Some sentences may be correct as written.) Example:

> My brother and I
> ~~Me and my brother~~ both like to play basketball.

1. The citizenship awards went to Erik and she.

2. She is taller than I but shorter than him.

3. This is a very important issue to we students.

4. We enjoyed you singing very much.

5. Me and my partner have opened a new bakery.

EXERCISE 16 Using Pronoun Cases in Writing

Write sentences using the following phrases and the correct pronoun case. Example:

Phrase: My co-workers and I

> My co-workers and I want to make some suggestions about the lighting in these rooms.

1. more quickly than she

2. two people, Karen and he

3. My classmates and I

4. Mr. Espinosa and me

5. we drivers

CHAPTER 16

Adjectives and Adverbs

Adjective and adverbs are modifiers. They describe or modify (limit or qualify) other words. Note the adjectives and adverbs in the following sentences:

The *orange* and *white* cat looked *well fed* and *contented*.

The *thin* man tugged *nervously* at his tie.

The phone rang *shrilly* and woke me from a *deep, much deserved* rest.

He joked *sarcastically* whenever he was *secretly unsure* of himself.

16a | Distinguishing between adjectives and adverbs

Adjectives modify nouns and pronouns. Adjectives answer such questions as: "Which?" "How much?" "How many?" and "What kind?"

Mr. Khan seems *happy*. [The adjective *happy* modifies the noun *Mr. Khan*.]

He is very *suspicious* of strangers. [The adjective *suspicious* modifies the pronoun *He*.]

The *timid* children hid behind their mother. [The adjective *timid* modifies the noun *children*.]

Everybody was *afraid* of the hurricane. [The adjective *afraid* modifies the pronoun *everybody*.]

Adverbs modify verbs, adjectives, and other adverbs. Adverbs answer such questions as "How?" and "To what extent?"

He spoke *quietly* to the class. [The adverb *quietly* modifies the verb *spoke*, answering the question "How did he speak?"]

She glared *angrily* at the other people on line at the grocery store. [The adverb *angrily* modifies the verb *glared*, answering the question "How did she glare?"]

They are *happily* married. [The adverb *happily* modifies the adjective *married*, answering the question "To what extent are they married?"]

I felt *quite* anxious before the sociology exam. [The adverb *quite* modifies the adjective *anxious*, answering the question "How anxious?"]

The police car sped *extremely* quickly toward the scene of the crime. [The adverb *extremely* modifies the adverb *quickly,* answering the question "How quickly?"]

The driver braked the car *very* abruptly. [The adverb *very* modifies the adverb *abruptly,* answering the question "How abruptly?"]

Formation and placement of adjectives

Some adjectives are formed by adding suffixes to nouns and verbs:

NOUN	SUFFIX	ADJECTIVE
charity	-able	charitable
fool	-ish	foolish
dirt	-y	dirty
economy	-ic	economic
season	-al	seasonal
care	-less	careless
courage	-ous	courageous
hope	-ful	hopeful

VERB	SUFFIX	ADJECTIVE
harm	-ful	harmful
hesitate	-ant	hesitant
notice	-able	noticeable
instruct	-ive	instructive

Many common adjectives have no special suffixes:

good	bad	old
evil	light	young
recent	late	yellow
pale	dark	nice

Present participles, past participles, and infinitives can function as adjectives, as in the following examples:

The *irritating* noise from the next apartment finally stopped. [*Irritating* is a present participle used as an adjective to modify the noun *noise.*]

Shocked by the explosion, he could not talk for about an hour. [*Shocked* is a past participle used as an adjective to modify the pronoun *he.*]

We argued about which movie *to see.* [*To see* is an infinitive used as an adjective to modify the noun *movie.*]

Adjectives often precede the nouns or pronouns they modify. Many adjectives, however, follow the words they modify. In the following examples, arrows point to the nouns and pronouns modified by adjectives. Notice that some adjectives precede and some follow the words they modify.

The *yellow taxi* pulled up in front of the hotel.

Smiling at the crowd, *she* walked calmly into the theater.

The senator gave a *thoughtful, informative speech.*

This *food* is *inedible.*

I have *nothing to wear!*

This *building, designed* early in the last century, is still in use.

Formation and placement of adverbs

Most adverbs are formed by adding the suffix *-ly* to adjectives.

ADJECTIVE	ADVERB
careless	carelessly
proud	proudly
angry	angrily
heavy	heavily
thoughtful	thoughtfully
decent	decently
quick	quickly

Some adverbs, often those indicating time and place, do not end in *-ly.*

here	there
now	then
seldom	never
often	very

The *-ly* suffix does not always indicate an adverb, however. Some adjectives end in *-ly.*

timely	homely
lonely	lovely
leisurely	

Like adjectives, adverbs can precede or follow the words they modify. Adverbs can be shifted to the beginning or the end of a sentence, as shown in the following sentences. Notice that changing the placement of an adverb changes the emphasis of a sentence.

The clerk *quickly handed* the customer her change.

Quickly the clerk *handed* the customer her change.

The clerk *handed* the customer her change *quickly.*

The old man *slowly shuffled* along the sidewalk.

The old man *shuffled slowly* along the sidewalk.

The old man *shuffled* along the sidewalk *slowly.*

16b Using adjectives with linking verbs

Adjectives sometimes follow linking verbs, and when they do, the adjectives function as subject complements. The most commonly used linking verbs are forms of the verb *to be.* In addition, sensory verbs and verbs of becoming are linking verbs.

FORMS OF *TO BE*	SENSORY VERBS	VERBS OF BECOMING
am	appear	become
is	feel	get
are	look	grow
was	seem	prove
were	smell	turn
be	sound	
being	taste	
been		

When they function as linking verbs, these verbs are followed by nouns or adjectives, not by adverbs. In the following examples, the linking verbs precede the adjectives (subject complements):

She *is polite.*

The meat *was overcooked.*

The concert *will be wonderful.*

This salad *tastes delicious.*

Mr. Corniel *looked exhausted.*

The speaker's voice *sounded hoarse.*

The runner *became weak* toward the end of the race.

All the charges eventually *proved false.*

The baby *gets irritable* just before bedtime.

Notice also that some of these linking verbs can be used as action verbs. When such verbs express action, they can be followed by adverbs.

The lawyer *proved* her case *admirably.*

The cook *tasted* the sauce *frequently.*

The driver *turned* the corner *quickly.*

16c Using adverbs with two forms

Some adverbs have two acceptable forms.

slow/slowly   quick/quickly
loud/loudly   cheap/cheaply

The *-ly* form is used in academic writing; the short form is generally used only in informal conversation.

INFORMAL   He was speaking as *loud* as he could.

FORMAL   Two people were talking *loudly* in the next room.

In other pairs, the two adverb forms have different meanings.

late = not on time   near = close to
lately = recently   nearly = almost

They arrived at the concert *late.*

Lately, the sprinter's time in the 100-yard dash had improved.

Crowds drew *near* as the juggler performed on the sidewalk.

I had *nearly* forgotten to lock the front door.

16d Using *good/well* and *bad/badly*

Good and *bad* are adjectives; they describe or modify nouns and pronouns. They can be used after linking verbs.

We had a *good* time at the party.

I got a *good* grade on the exam.

Her future looks *good.*

They were in a *bad* accident.

He got a *bad* grade in history.

The milk smells *bad.*

Badly and *well* are adverbs. (See below for an explanation of *well* as an adjective.) Use them to modify verbs, adjectives, and other adverbs. As adverbs, *badly* and *well* follow action verbs.

I did *well* on the test.

He behaved *well* under pressure.

We are *well* paid for our work.

She performed *badly* in the first game.

Two passengers on the train were *badly* injured in the wreck.

That *badly* built fence will have to be replaced.

Well can function as an adjective or an adverb, but its meaning differs in each case. As an adjective, *well* means "healthy"; as an adverb, it means "effectively."

After a long period of recuperation, she looked *well*. [adjective meaning "healthy," modifying *she*]

Despite being rather thin, he seems *well*. [adjective meaning "healthy," modifying *he*]

You did *well* on the exam. [adverb meaning "effectively," modifying the verb *did*]

This floor looks *well* scrubbed. [adverb meaning "effectively," modifying the adjective *scrubbed*]

16e Using comparative and superlative forms

Adjectives and adverbs appear in three forms: positive, comparative, and superlative.

POSITIVE	COMPARATIVE	SUPERLATIVE
angry	angrier	angriest
short	shorter	shortest
courageous	more courageous	most courageous
helpful	more helpful	most helpful
carefully	more carefully	most carefully
quickly	more quickly	most quickly

The positive (or simple) form is the most commonly used. The comparative and superlative forms are used to make comparisons.

The child was *angry* at his brother.

He was *angrier* than I had ever seen him before.

This is the *angriest* editorial I have ever read.

He stepped *carefully* over the puddles.

She works *more carefully* than he does.

Of all the painters on this job, she works *most carefully*.

Most one-syllable and many two-syllable adjectives form the comparative by adding -*er*; they form the superlative by adding -*est*.

	COMPARATIVE	SUPERLATIVE
tall	taller	tallest
pale	paler	palest
happy	happier	happiest
heavy	heavier	heaviest

Some two-syllable adjectives, and adjectives of three or more syllables, form the comparative by adding *more* and the superlative by adding *most*.

	COMPARATIVE	SUPERLATIVE
careless	more careless	most careless
helpful	more helpful	most helpful
worrisome	more worrisome	most worrisome
beautiful	more beautiful	most beautiful

Adverbs form the comparative and superlative with the words *more* and *most*.

	COMPARATIVE	SUPERLATIVE
serenely	more serenely	most serenely
slowly	more slowly	most slowly
carelessly	more carelessly	most carelessly
brightly	more brightly	most brightly
rudely	more rudely	most rudely

There are occasional exceptions to the preceding rules. For example, some adjectives use *more* in the comparative (*more severe*) but add *-est* in the superlative (*severest*). Consult your dictionary for information about comparative and superlative forms.

1 | Distinguishing between comparatives and superlatives

Use the comparative forms of adjectives and adverbs to compare two things. Use the superlative forms of adjectives and adverbs to compare three or more things.

COMPARATIVE ADJECTIVE Rice is *more nutritious* than chocolate.

SUPERLATIVE ADJECTIVE Of all these foods, beans are the *most nutritious*.

COMPARATIVE ADVERB Frank speaks *more quickly* than Joe does.

SUPERLATIVE ADVERB Of all the people in this group, Frank speaks *most quickly*.

2 | Checking for double comparisons

To make a comparison, use only one form of the comparative or one form of the superlative. Do not use double comparisons. Use either *-er* or *more,* but not both. Use either *-est* or *most,* but not both.

FAULTY This paper is *more better* developed than the last one you wrote.

CORRECT This paper is *better* developed than the last one you wrote.

FAULTY   The *most longest* race she ever ran was a 26-mile marathon.

CORRECT   The *longest* race she ever ran was a 26-mile marathon.

3 | Checking for incomplete comparisons

Occasionally, in speaking or writing, we use incomplete comparisons such as "the food was better" or "the weather was worse." In conversation, it might be clear that the speaker meant the food was better at one restaurant than at another, or that the weather was worse on one specific day than it was the day before. In writing, however, the comparison may not be clear. Writers must give enough context to make comparisons clear.

INCOMPLETE   Professional football players, on average, earn lower salaries.

COMPLETE   Professional football players, on average, earn lower salaries than professional basketball players do.

INCOMPLETE   Many people believe Ms. Shalala is the most articulate.

COMPLETE   Many people believe Ms. Shalala is the most articulate member of the president's cabinet.

4 | Using irregular comparatives and superlatives

Some adjectives and adverbs change form to indicate the comparative and superlative. The following chart lists irregular adjectives and adverbs.

IRREGULAR COMPARATIVE AND SUPERLATIVE FORMS OF ADJECTIVES AND ADVERBS

ADJECTIVES

POSITIVE	COMPARATIVE	SUPERLATIVE
good	better	best
bad	worse	worst
little	less	least
many	more	most
some	more	most
much	more	most
ill	worse	worst

ADVERBS

POSITIVE	COMPARATIVE	SUPERLATIVE
badly	worse	worst
well	better	best

Note the irregular adjectives and adverbs in the following examples:

He did a *good* job, she did a *better* job, and you did the *best* job of all.

This computer works *badly*, that computer works *worse*, and the one over here works *worst* of all.

16f   Avoiding double negatives

In many languages, double negatives are used to emphasize the negative, but in modern English double negatives are not acceptable. Using double negatives in English may even give the impression that the speaker or writer is poorly educated.

Two negative words in a clause cancel each other out grammatically (just as, in math, multiplying two negative numbers results in a positive one). To make a clause negative, use only one negative word.

NEGATIVE WORDS

not (n't)	no	never
none	hardly	scarcely
nothing	barely	but (meaning "except")
no one	nobody	seldom

NEGATIVE PREFIXES AND SUFFIXES

un-	-less
dis-	
il-	

| **DOUBLE NEGATIVE** | We *scarcely never* see each other. |
| **REVISED** | We *scarcely ever* see each other. |

| **DOUBLE NEGATIVE** | *Nobody* told the police *nothing.* |
| **REVISED** | *Nobody* told the police *anything.* |

| **DOUBLE NEGATIVE** | I do*n't* have *no* money. |
| **REVISED** | I *don't* have *any* money.
I have *no* money. |

Occasionally, using two negatives in a clause is a way of making a positive understatement:

Her attitude was *not unkind.*

He is *not illiterate.*

16g   Avoiding overuse of nouns as modifiers

A noun can function as an adjective, modifying another noun. Look at the following examples:

movie reviewer	role model	police activity
oat bran	college student	country music
father figure	Christmas carol	holiday plans

These examples have clear meanings, but sometimes using too many nouns as adjectives in one phrase can make a sentence sound awkward. This problem should be revised so that the relationship among the various nouns is clear.

AWKWARD   The college is holding student-mentor relationship sessions.

REVISED   The college is holding sessions to discuss the relationship between students and their mentors.

| **16h** | **Using possessive adjectives** |

Some possessive forms of personal pronouns function as adjectives, modifying nouns and indicating ownership. In the following sentences, the arrows point from the adjectives to the nouns they modify:

Your daughter is in the same grade as *my son.*

Her ambition was to be a tax lawyer.

The jury finally announced *its verdict.*

Possessive forms of personal pronouns do not include an apostrophe. Do not confuse possessive adjectives with words and contractions that sound and sometimes look very similar. Here are some examples:

POSSESSIVE ADJECTIVE   This proposal has *its* flaws, but not many.

SOUND-ALIKE CONTRACTION   We must stay inside because *it's* raining.

POSSESSIVE ADJECTIVE   The Carters are painting *their* house.

SOUND-ALIKE CONTRACTION   *They're* not planning to move.

SOUND-ALIKE ADVERB   *There* is no reason to worry.

EXERCISE 1   Identifying Adjectives and Adverbs

Label each italicized word in the following sentences as an adjective or adverb.
Example:

          adverb   adjective
Traffic moved *slowly* along the *narrow* street.

1. The *timid* man cleared his throat *nervously*.

2. The cats ran *silently* but *swiftly* across the *shadowy* alley.

3. The *loud* buzz of the doorbell *abruptly* broke my concentration.

4. His *polite* demeanor hides his *fierce* determination to succeed.

5. The engine clanked *ominously*, and then with a *loud* bang, it stopped.

EXERCISE 2   Forming Adjectives and Adverbs

Change each of the following words into an adjective and an adverb. Then write two sentences, one using the adjective and the other using the adverb. Example:

irritate

Adjective: irritable
Adverb: irritably

His irritable manner hides a kind heart.
She reacted irritably to being waked at four in the morning.

1. coward

2. hesitate

3. danger

4. infect

5. help

EXERCISE 3   Choosing Modifiers with Linking and Action Verbs

In each sentence that follows, underline the correct modifier, the adjective (if the sentence contains a linking verb), or the adverb (if the sentence contains an action verb). Examples:

The soup tastes (*delicious/deliciously*).

The wisteria vine grew (*quick/quickly*) *up the drain pipe.*

1. That boring movie seemed to be (*endless/endlessly*).

2. The speaker droned on (*endless/endlessly*).

3. The sound of the rain on the roof was (*soothing/soothingly*).

4. Doctors recommend that patients get (*regular/regularly*) check-ups.

5. All those nasty rumors proved (*false/falsely*).

EXERCISE 4   Choosing Adjectives or Adverbs

Underline or circle the correct the appropriate modifiers in the following sentences. Example:

In a (*calm/calmly*) voice, she soothed the (*high/highly*) nervous dog.

1. The driver of the car received (*massive/massively*) injuries.

2. He (*courageous/courageously*) defied his boss in disclosing (*illegal/illegally*) actions by the company.

3. (*Extreme/Extremely*) heavy rains had washed away many of the bridges.

4. A well-known public figure who is (*immediate/immediately*) recognized wherever she goes, she tends to guard her privacy (*fierce/fiercely*).

5. Arriving (*late/lately*) for the class, she missed the most (*important/importantly*) points in the lecture.

EXERCISE 5   Supplying Adjectives and Adverbs

Complete the following sentences. In each blank, provide an adjective or an adverb that you think is appropriate for the sentence. Example:

He spoke <u>softly</u> but with <u>obvious</u> authority.

1. The _____ customer asked a _____ salesperson for help.

2. The _____ child ate her food _____.

3. A _____ student writes _____.

4. My _____ brother has _____ responsibilities.

5. The senator answered my questions _____.

EXERCISE 6   Using Adjectives and Adverbs in Writing

Write a sentence using each adjective and adverb that follows. Example:

pleasant: The conference was pleasant but not really stimulating.

1. intense

2. lately

3. arrogantly

4. immense

5. unpleasantly

EXERCISE 7   Choosing *good/well* and *bad/badly*

Underline or circle the correct modifiers in the following sentences. Example:

He did (*bad/<u>badly</u>*) on the math test but (*good/<u>well</u>*) on the reading test.

1. The game went very (*bad/badly*) in the first half.

2. He scored (*good/well*) on this test, but he did (*bad/badly*) on that one.

3. Even during the flu season, she remained (*good/well*).

4. Their (*bad/badly*) behavior resulted in suspension from school.

5. The supervisor gave you a (*good/well*) evaluation.

EXERCISE 8   Forming Comparatives and Superlatives

Give the comparative and superlative forms of each modifier in the list. Examples:

Modifier

large:	larger	largest
intensely:	more intensely	most intensely
	Comparative	*Superlative*

1. wide   _____   _____

2. repetitious   _____   _____

3. abruptly   _____   _____

4. happy   _____   _____

5. politely   _____   _____

EXERCISE 9   Choosing between Comparatives and Superlatives

Underline or circle the correct adjective or adverb form in each of the following sentences. Example:

She was the (*older*/*oldest*) of three children.

1. His typing speed is (*faster*/*fastest*) than mine.

2. I watch sports on television (*more frequently*/*most frequently*) than he does.

3. Of all the events that year, the end of the Soviet Union was the (*more unexpected*/*most unexpected*).

4. Of the five people on that committee, she works (*harder/hardest*).

5. Of the two cars, this one is the (*more reliable/most reliable*).

EXERCISE 10   Writing with Comparatives and Superlatives

For each topic that follows, write a brief paragraph of three to five sentences in which you use at least one comparative or superlative. Example:

Topic: A ride in a taxi

The funniest but also the most frightening taxi ride I have ever taken was many years ago on St. Croix, one of the Virgin Islands. The driver told jokes as he drove, continually turning around to see our reactions to his stories and thus not paying much attention to the road. Also, the speedometer of his car was broken, but I had the feeling that even if the speedometer had been working, he still would not have paid any attention to it.

1. A gym class

2. A book that entertained you

3. A book that changed one of your ideas

4. Three of your friends

5. Yourself at ten years old and yourself now

EXERCISE 11   Forming Correct Comparisons

Identify the incorrect comparisons in the following sentences. Then rewrite each sentence to make the comparison correct. (Some sentences may be correct as written.) Examples:

For me, swimming is a <u>more safer</u> exercise than jogging because swimming does not give me shin splints.
For me, swimming is a *safer* exercise than jogging because swimming does not give me shin splints.

Sometimes, leasing a car is <u>better.</u>
Sometimes, leasing a car is better *than buying one.*

1. This is the most hardest to solve of all the math problems.

2. Many people think that learning to speak Spanish is easier.

3. The whole wheat bread tastes better.

4. I am more healthier today than I was a year ago.

5. Of the three cars she is considering, this one has the best repair record.

EXERCISE 12 Using Irregular Comparatives and Superlatives

Give the irregular comparative and superlative forms for each word that follows. Then write a sentence using all three forms of the word. Example:

some: more   most

I have *some* money, Caroline has *more* money than I do, and Rosa has the *most* money of the three of us.

	Comparative	Superlative
1. good	_____	_____
2. bad	_____	_____
3. little	_____	_____

4. many _____ _____

5. some _____ _____

EXERCISE 13   Avoiding Double Negatives

Rewrite the following sentences to eliminate double negatives. Example:

I didn't never find the office I was looking for.

I didn't *ever* find the office I was looking for.

1. The concert did not last scarcely an hour.

2. Nobody did not lock the supply closet last night.

3. There was a bad connection, and I couldn't barely hear his voice over the telephone.

4. After that long gym class, he doesn't have no energy left.

5. Small children shouldn't never be left unattended.

EXERCISE 14   Using Nouns as Modifiers in Writing

The following phrases contain nouns modified by other nouns. Use each phrase in a sentence. Example:

Phrase: role model

The usual role models for small children are their parents.

1. college student

2. furniture polish

3. rye bread

4. movie reviewer

5. father figure

EXERCISE 15   Choosing Possessive Adjectives

Underline or circle the correct possessive adjectives in the following sentences.
Example:

Commuters sitting on the train put down (*there*/*their*/*they're*) briefcases.

1. (*Your*/*You're*) proposal was the best of all those submitted.

2. Anyone (*whose*/*who's*) over a certain age has had the measles.

3. The pilot announced that (*there*/*their*/*they're*) would be a slight delay before take-off.

4. (*Its*/*It's*) impossible to tell (*whose*/*who's*) umbrella this is.

5. This painting by Vermeer is admired for both (*its*/*it's*) color and (*its*/*it's*) composition.

6. It is (*there*/*their*/*they're*) own fault that (*there*/*their*/*they're*) not popular with (*there*/*their*/*they're*) neighbors.

7. If (*your*/*you're*) planning to apply to law school, you should see (*your*/*you're*) advisor as soon as possible.

8. Ms. Tran, (*whose*/*who's*) family is originally from Vietnam, put herself through school by working in a bakery.

9. The mayor claimed that (*there*/*their*/*they're*) had been a 10 percent drop in serious crime the previous year.

10. When (*your*/*you're*) feeling dehydrated during exercise, (*its*/*it's*) imperative to drink fluids.

CHAPTER 17

Prepositions, Conjunctions, and Interjections

Prepositions, conjunctions, and interjections are three of the eight parts of speech. Prepositions show the relationship between a noun or pronoun and other words in a sentence. Conjunctions are connecting words; they join together words, phrases, and clauses. Interjections are words that express surprise or emotion. (The other parts of speech are nouns, pronouns, verbs, adjectives, and adverbs.)

17a Recognizing prepositions

Prepositions are words that indicate position, direction, or relationship. Some common prepositions include *of, to, in, for, by,* and *up.* A preposition is often followed by a noun or pronoun called the object of the preposition. The preposition and its object make up a prepositional phrase. Here are some examples of prepositional phrases:

to the city
of my parents
for her
in the room

Following are lists of the most commonly used prepositions and compound prepositions.

COMMON PREPOSITIONS

about	before	from	over
above	behind	in	past
across	beneath	inside	regarding
after	beside	into	since
against	between	like	through
along	beyond	near	toward
among	by	of	under
around	down	off	until
as	during	on	up
at	except	onto	with
below	for	out	without

COMMON COMPOUND PREPOSITIONS

according to	in addition to
along with	in front of
as a result of	in connection with
at the expense of	in place of
because of	in spite of
by means of	instead of
by way of	in view of
due to	next to
out of	on behalf of
with regard to	

Note the prepositional phrases in the following examples:

The view *from the front window* is lovely.

One *of these books* is overdue.

Without a conclusion, your term paper is incomplete.

She is taking astronomy *instead of* geology.

Some prepositions can function as other parts of speech in a sentence. In the following pairs of sentences, the first sentence shows a word used as a preposition, and the second sentence uses the same word as a conjunction.

PREPOSITION   The doors of the electronics store won't open *until* 10 a.m.

CONJUNCTION   We can't enter the store *until* the doors are unlocked.

PREPOSITION   We are going to the cafeteria *after* this class.

CONJUNCTION   *After* you finish your report, send it to the supervisor.

17b Using prepositions in writing

A prepositional phrase almost always functions as an adjective or an adverb in a sentence. Look at the following examples:

He walked *into Mrs. Jerrold's office.* [prepositional phrase functions as an adverb, modifying the verb *walked*]

Ms. Truong worked *as a nurse.* [prepositional phrase functions as an adverb, modifying the verb *worked*]

The briefcase *on the table* belongs to Mr. Rosario. [prepositional phrase functions as an adjective, modifying the noun *briefcase*]

Athletic shoes *with twinkling lights* were popular for a while. [prepositional phrase functions as an adjective, modifying the noun *shoes*]

Excessive use of prepositional phrases can make writing awkward and wordy. In the following pairs of sentences, notice how the wordiness of the first sentence is improved in the second by using adjectives, verbs, and gerunds.

WORDY   It was an evening of gloom and clouds.

IMPROVED   It was a gloomy, cloudy evening.

WORDY   We can provide a solution to this problem.

IMPROVED   We can solve this problem.

WORDY   The biology professor began a period of review of blood types.

IMPROVED   The biology professor began reviewing blood types.

Note also that extra prepositions are not usually necessary:

WORDY   The dog was sleeping *inside of* the house.

IMPROVED   The dog was sleeping *inside* the house.

WORDY   She told me where the maternity clinic was *at.*

IMPROVED   She told me where the maternity clinic was.

17c   Recognizing conjunctions

Conjunctions join words, phrases, and clauses to one another. There are four types of conjunctions: coordinating conjunctions, correlative conjunctions, subordinating conjunctions, and conjunctive adverbs.

1   Coordinating conjunctions

There are seven coordinating conjunctions:

and (indicates addition)	She is taking biology *and* chemistry.
but (indicates contrast)	He was rather slim *but* not weak.
yet (indicates contrast)	She was cautious *yet* hopeful.
or (indicates choice)	Should I take history *or* sociology next term?
nor (indicates negative choice)	They do not smoke, *nor* do they eat red meat.
for (indicates cause or reason)	I fell asleep, *for* I was very tired.
so (indicates a result)	It was raining, *so* the baseball game was canceled.

Use coordinating conjunctions to link items that are equal grammatically. In the following examples, the coordinating conjunctions connect nouns, verbs, phrases, or clauses that are equal to each other.

CONNECTED NOUNS	James Baldwin wrote *essays, novels,* <u>and</u> *plays.*
CONNECTED VERBS	He *turned* on the news <u>and</u> *sat* down in his easy chair.
CONNECTED PHRASES	The singer is popular *in South America* <u>but</u> *not in Europe.*
CONNECTED CLAUSES	*Vegetables like carrots do well in cool weather,* <u>but</u> *frost will kill cucumbers and string beans.*

2 Correlative conjunctions

Like coordinating conjunctions, correlative conjunctions join nouns, verbs, phrases, and clauses. However, correlative conjunctions occur in pairs.

both . . . and	not only . . . but also
either . . . or	whether . . . or
neither . . . nor	just as . . . so

CONNECTED NOUNS	She studied <u>both</u> *political science* <u>and</u> *history.*
CONNECTED VERBS	For two days he <u>neither</u> *ate* <u>nor</u> *slept.*
CONNECTED PHRASES	I couldn't decide <u>whether</u> *to repair my old car* <u>or</u> *to buy a new one.*
CONNECTED CLAUSES	<u>Not only</u> *did the hurricane cause flooding,* <u>but also</u> *it destroyed many houses.*

3 Subordinating conjunctions

Subordinating conjunctions introduce subordinate (dependent) clauses and indicate the relationship of the subordinate clause to the main (independent clause). Here is a list of common subordinating conjunctions and their uses:

Cause	as, because, now that, since
Concession	although, even if, though, even though
Comparison	as if, more than, rather than
Place	where, wherever
Purpose	in order that, that
Time	after, before, ever since, since, until, when, whenever, while
Manner	as, as if
Condition	but that, except that, if, if only, unless, provided that

Note that subordinate clauses can be placed either before or after the independent (main) clause. In the following examples, the subordinate clauses are italicized and the subordinating conjunctions are underlined:

<u>When</u> *the first computers were invented,* they were large and bulky.

He could not play soccer last year *<u>because</u> he had injured his back.*

<u>If</u> the day care center closes, many parents will have trouble finding child care during their working hours.

Although Ms. Rienzi is a very demanding boss, her employees like her very much.

Ms. Rienzi's employees like her very much *although she is a very demanding boss.*

4 | Conjunctive adverbs

Conjunctive adverbs are not true conjunctions because they do not indicate a grammatical relationship between two independent clauses. Instead, conjunctive adverbs emphasize the close relationship of the subject matter of the two independent clauses. Here is a list of common conjunctive adverbs and phrases that function as conjunctive adverbs:

accordingly	furthermore	moreover	similarly
also	hence	namely	still
anyway	however	nevertheless	then
besides	incidentally	next	thereafter
certainly	indeed	nonetheless	therefore
consequently	instead	now	thus
finally	likewise	otherwise	undoubtedly
further	meanwhile		
as a result	in fact	in other words	in addition
in any event	for example	on the other hand	for instance

Because they are adverbs, conjunctive adverbs do not have a fixed place in a clause but can be shifted to different places in order to create emphasis and provide variety. Regardless of its position in a sentence, a conjunctive adverb is always followed by a comma. If the conjunctive adverb appears in the middle of a clause, it is marked off by two commas, one before and another after the adverb. Notice both the position and the punctuation of the conjunctive adverbs in these examples:

The computer was not working. *Therefore,* registration had to be postponed.

The computer was not working. Registration, *therefore,* had to be postponed.

The computer was not working; *therefore,* registration had to be postponed.

The computer was not working; registration, *therefore,* had to be postponed.

Beginning too many sentences with conjunctive adverbs can create a monotonous tone. Occasionally moving the conjunctive adverb into the middle of an independent clause provides variety. Notice the placement of the conjunctive adverbs in the following examples:

I would like to take a vacation; *however,* I cannot afford it at the moment.

The students want an open-book exam; the professor, *however,* has a different sort of exam in mind.

Fred is very organized. Pete, *on the other hand,* is totally disorganized.

All the flights to Philadelphia are full. *Moreover,* no rental cars are available.

It is a lovely day; *indeed,* it is the most pleasant day so far this spring.

17d Using interjections

Interjections express surprise or strong emotion. They do not have a grammatical relationship to the other parts of a sentence; rather, they tend to stand alone as fragments. Interjections are most commonly used in speech and dialogue; for the most part, they are not appropriate in formal and academic writing.

Heavens! I can't possibly finish the report by tomorrow.

Hah! You finally got what you deserved!

EXERCISE 1   Recognizing Prepositions and Prepositional Phrases

Put parentheses around each prepositional phrase and underline each preposition. Example:

The skater slipped and fell (<u>on</u> the ice).

1. One of these children has not been immunized.

2. Over the last three years, sixteen accidents have occurred at this corner.

3. Without a backward glance, his small daughter walked into the kindergarten classroom.

4. He kicked the football between the goalposts.

5. I found my watch underneath the morning newspaper.

EXERCISE 2   Recognizing the Difference between Prepositions and Conjunctions

Identify each italicized word as a preposition or a conjunction. Examples:

I have been here *since* early morning.   <u>preposition</u>

I have not seen you *since* we graduated.   <u>conjunction</u>

1. *Before* the game began, the coach reviewed some important plays.
   _____

2. She worked *as* a translator for several years.   _____

3. On the day *after* Thanksgiving, many people begin diets.
   _____

4. Several significant holidays occur *in* the spring. _____

5. Offensive hockey players should not cross the blue line *until* the puck has crossed the line. _____

EXERCISE 3   Eliminating Excessive Prepositions and Prepositional Phrases

Rewrite each sentence to eliminate the excessive use of prepositions and prepositional phrases. Examples:

Ron was a man of cheerful disposition with many friends.
Ron was a cheerful man with many friends.

The child rolled off of the bed.
The child rolled off the bed.

1. She spoke to the committee in an angry way.

2. The suspect was last seen walking in the direction of the bus stop.

3. He does not know where the telephone directory is at.

4. Several pairs of shoes were lying outside of the front door.

5. The football field is near to the gym.

EXERCISE 4   Using Prepositional Phrases in Writing

Write a brief paragraph of three to five sentences for each topic that follows. Underline the prepositions in your paragraphs. Example:

Topic: Rumors

People often pass along information they have heard <u>without</u> first verifying the facts. <u>In</u> this way, rumors get started. <u>Before</u> long, the facts are distorted <u>out of</u> proportion.

1. A telephone book

2. Gossip

3. Cooking scrambled eggs

4. Taking notes in class

5. A country road

EXERCISE 5 Identifying Coordinating, Correlative, and Subordinating Conjunctions

Identify each italicized conjunction as coordinating, correlative, or subordinating. Example:

You cannot register *until* you bring proof of immunization.   <u>subordinating</u>

1. *Both* physics *and* chemistry require some knowledge of math.

   _____

2. He can drive a car with an automatic transmission, *but* he does not know how to drive a stick shift.   _____

3. *After* he stopped smoking and lost weight, his blood pressure went down.

   _____

4. *Neither* Florida *nor* Texas was one of the thirteen original states.

   _____

5. No one could hear him *because* he spoke so softly.   _____

EXERCISE 6 Identifying Conjunctions and Conjunctive Adverbs

Identify each italicized word as a conjunction or a conjunctive adverb. Examples:

I tried to call you, *but* your line was busy all evening.   <u>conjunction</u>

I tried to call you; your line, *however,* was busy all evening.   <u>conjunctive adverb</u>

1. Ms. Barnes does not allow her children to watch television on school nights; *indeed,* she had a special lock put on the family's only television.   _____

2. My doctor told me I had to lose weight; *otherwise,* my health is apt to be affected in the future.   _____

3. He is allergic to certain over-the-counter medicines, *so* he reads labels on such medicines very carefully. _____

4. The city's tax revenues have decreased; police, fire, and sanitation services, *therefore,* have been affected. _____

5. Judith Jamison did not fit the image of a traditional ballerina, *yet* she became one of the most exciting dancers of the late twentieth century. _____

EXERCISE 7 Punctuating Conjunctive Adverbs

Place commas where necessary in the following sentences. Example:

This book incidentally is now out of print.

This book, incidentally, is now out of print.

1. I would like to attend the meeting; however I have another appointment.

2. Heavy rain fell for days. Consequently many roads were flooded.

3. Jack is very shy; his twin brother on the other hand is a real extrovert.

4. Exercise seems very popular in America; nevertheless there are more overweight Americans today than there were ten years ago.

5. The candidate vowed to lower taxes; also he promised to improve city services.

EXERCISE 8   Using Conjunctions and Conjunctive Adverbs in Writing

Write a sentence using each word in the list. Example:

consequently

The election results were contested; consequently, a recount had to be taken.

1. for

2. both . . . and

3. whenever

4. therefore

5. so

6. not only . . . but also

7. even though

8. however

9. because

10. on the other hand

CHAPTER 18

Maintaining Agreement

In grammar there are two kinds of agreement: subject–verb agreement and pronoun–antecedent agreement.

SUBJECT–VERB AGREEMENT

A verb must agree with its subject in number and in person. *Number* refers to whether the subject is singular or plural. *Person* refers to the way that pronouns and verbs identify who is speaking (first person), who is spoken to (second person), and who or what is spoken about (third person). Most verbs in the present tense (and one verb in the past tense) change form to match the number and person of their subjects.

The *director wants* to start rehearsing right now. [third-person singular]

Several *customers* in the store *want* their money back. [third-person plural]

18a Making a verb agree with a third-person singular subject

In the present tense, regular verbs take the same form in the first- and second-person singular and in the first-, second-, and third-person plural. The only form that is different is the third-person singular. With a third-person singular subject, a regular verb in the present tense adds *-s* or *-es*.

	SINGULAR	PLURAL
First person	I write	We write
Second person	You write	You write
Third person	He writes	They write
	She writes	
	It writes	

	SINGULAR	PLURAL
First person	I rush	We rush
Second person	You rush	You rush
Third person	He rushes	They rush
	She rushes	
	It rushes	

Note the matching subjects and verbs in the following examples:

She always *reads* the financial news first.

I insist on our meeting as soon as possible.

They never *answer* my letters.

He rushes to work every morning.

The irregular verbs *to be* and *to have* are exceptions to this rule:

TO HAVE	SINGULAR	PLURAL
First person	I have	We have
Second person	You have	You have
Third person	He has	They have
	She has	
	It has	

You obviously *have* a bad cold.

He has some good news for you.

They have two children.

TO BE	SINGULAR	PLURAL
First person	I am	We are
Second person	You are	You are
Third person	He is	They are
	She is	
	It is	

I am delighted with your progress.

You are usually on time.

He is a conductor.

Past tense verbs do not change in number, with the exception of the irregular verb *to be*:

TO BE	SINGULAR	PLURAL
First person	I was	We were
Second person	You were	You were
Third person	He was	They were
	She was	
	It was	

I thought *you were* absent today.

We were fast asleep.

She was very helpful.

Nouns used as subjects are in the third person. If the subject is a singular noun, use a verb in the third-person singular. If the subject is a plural noun, use a verb in the third-person plural.

This *car is* very expensive.

These *cars are* very expensive.

The *technician works* carefully and precisely.

The *technicians work* carefully and precisely.

The *customer was* rather angry.

The *customers were* rather angry.

18b Making separated subjects and verbs agree

Agreement between subject and verb in a sentence must be maintained even when the subject and verb are separated. Sometimes writers mistakenly assume that the verb should agree with the word nearest to it. You can avoid this error by ensuring that the verb agrees with its subject, not with an intervening word. In the following examples, note that a subject and verb can be separated by a short prepositional phrase, a descriptive phrase, or even an entire clause:

A *carton* of books *is* on your desk. [singular subject and verb]

The *goalie,* along with her teammates, *wants* to practice this afternoon. [singular subject and verb]

The *carpet,* worn out by hard use in the last ten years, *has* to be replaced. [singular subject and verb]

The reference *book* that I need to consult *is* on the top shelf. [singular subject and verb]

The *people* on this chartered bus *are* retired schoolteachers. [plural subject and verb]

18c Making subject and verb agree with a compound subject

Two or more subjects joined by a conjunction form a compound subject. Compound subjects joined by *and* usually take a plural verb.

An oak tree *and* a maple tree *were* hit by lightning.

Small children *and* teenagers *have* different needs.

Mr. *and* Mrs. Lamkay *work* for the same company.

Protein, fiber, *and* vitamins *are* found in healthy foods.

When parts of a compound subject refer to the same person or thing or function as a single unit, the subject is considered singular and should take a singular verb.

Ham and eggs was her favorite meal.

Smith, Bean, and Grill is an influential law firm.

Her best friend and advisor was her brother Frank.

When a compound subject is preceded by the adjectives *each* or *every,* use a singular verb form.

Each infant, child, and teenager *deserves* adequate health care.

Every nook and cranny *was* thoroughly searched.

When compound subjects are joined by *or, nor, either. . . or,* and *neither. . . nor,* the verb should agree with the subject nearest to it.

No smoking or drinking *is* permitted. [The singular verb *is* agrees with *drinking.*]

Either medics or emergency medical technicians *are* on call. [The plural verb *are* agrees with *technicians.*]

Neither the players nor the manager *knows* where the coach is. [The singular verb *knows* agrees with *manager.*]

Neither the manager nor the players *know* where the coach is. [The plural verb *know* agrees with *players.*]

If one of the subjects joined by *or* or *nor* is singular and the other is plural, place the plural subject second to avoid awkwardness:

AWKWARD   Either his neighbors or *he is* going to have to move.

REVISED   Either he or his *neighbors are* going to have to move.

When the joined subjects are pronouns that take different verb forms, rephrase the sentence to avoid making an awkward choice:

AWKWARD   Neither he nor I is willing to compromise.

REVISED   Neither of us is willing to compromise.

| **18d** | **Making a verb agree with an indefinite pronoun subject** |

Although some indefinite pronouns such as *everybody* and *everyone* seem plural because they refer to people in general, most indefinite pronouns are singular and must take a singular verb.

INDEFINITE PRONOUNS TAKING SINGULAR VERB FORMS

anybody	everybody	somebody	nobody
anyone	everyone	someone	no one
anything	everything	something	nothing

another	each
one	either
	neither

In the following examples, note that each indefinite singular pronoun takes a singular verb:

Everybody on line *wants* to buy play-off tickets.

Nobody in the store *knows* the price of this item.

Each of the students *has* a lab notebook.

Somebody is knocking on the door.

Some indefinite pronouns, however, take plural verb forms:

both	few	many
others	several	

In the following examples, note the agreement between plural subject and plural verb:

She is taking history and sociology; *both require* a lot of reading.

He is reading the help-wanted ads; *several look* promising.

Some indefinite pronouns can be singular *or* plural, depending on the noun or pronoun to which they refer:

all	more	some	enough
any	most	none	

In the following examples, note the agreement between subject and verb:

SINGULAR   *All* of my money *was* stolen. [*All* refers to the singular noun *money*.]

PLURAL   *All* of these coats *are* on sale. [*All* refers to the plural noun *coats*.]

SINGULAR   *Enough* snow *has* fallen to clog the highways. [*Enough* refers to the singular noun *snow*.]

PLURAL   There *were enough* people to form two volleyball teams. [*Enough* refers to the plural noun *people*.]

18e Making a verb agree with a collective noun subject

Collective nouns name a group or a class. Because the group or class is considered a single unit, the collective noun subject is usually singular and takes a singular verb.

COLLECTIVE NOUNS

group	class	committee
jury	crowd	audience
family	team	

In the following examples, the emphasis is on the group rather than on individual members of the group. Each collective noun subject, therefore, takes a singular verb.

The *jury is* not in the courtroom.

An *audience* of two hundred people *is* waiting to hear your speech.

The *class has* done its work well.

When you wish to emphasize individual members of a group, do not use a collective noun as your subject.

The *members* of the jury *were* not in agreement.

Several *people* in my family *do* not attend family reunions.

Players on the team *have* differing opinions about the coach.

18f   Making a verb agree with its subject rather than a complement

Sometimes a subject and its complement are different in number, one singular and the other plural. The verb should always agree with the subject, not the complement.

Her frequent *absences were* one reason for her low grade. [The plural verb *were* agrees with the plural subject *absences*, not with the singular complement *reason*.]

A significant *factor* in population shifts *is* job opportunities. [The singular verb *is* agrees with the singular subject *factor*, not with the plural complement *opportunities*.]

18g   Making a verb agree with relative pronoun subjects

When the relative pronoun *who, which,* or *that* introduces a dependent (subordinate) clause, the verb in the dependent clause must agree in number with the pronoun's antecedent.

Penicillin, *which has* been in use for decades, causes allergic reactions in some people. [The singular verb *has* is used because *which* refers to the singular word *penicillin*.]

Cow's milk and cheese, *which are* sometimes considered basic foods, cause digestive problems for many people. [The plural verb *are* is used because *which* refers to the plural *cow's milk and cheese*.]

Sometimes the antecedent of the relative pronoun is not easy to spot, especially in sentences containing the phrase *one of the*. In these cases, you must decide whether your sentence is making a statement about people in general or about one person in particular.

> Ms. Ramos is one of the students who always *hand* in assignments on time. [Here *who* refers to many students, including Ms. Ramos, and so takes the plural verb *hand*.]

> Harold is one of those people who never *arrive* on time. [*Who* refers to many people, including Harold, and so takes the plural verb *arrive*.]

> Ariane is the only one of my friends who *speaks* Japanese. [*Who* refers to the singular word *one* and so takes the singular verb *speaks*.]

18h Making subject and verb agree in inverted sentences

In an inverted sentence, the usual word order is turned around; the verb appears first, and the subject follows later. Subject and verb still must agree. Make sure the verb agrees with the subject, not with a nearby noun. Note the subject–verb agreement in the following sentences:

Speeding through the streets *was* an *ambulance*.

Among the clutter on the kitchen table *were* my history *notebook* and my *watch*.

There *is* always a long *line* at the supermarket.

There *was* one important *item* on the agenda.

There *are* two *prerequisites* for this advanced course.

Here *is* the committee's *report* on retention rates.

Here *are* the latest unemployment *figures*.

There's a *deer* in the backyard. ['s stands for the singular verb *is*]

There're six *people* waiting to see the dentist. ['re stands for the plural verb *are*]

18i Maintaining agreement with singular words that appear plural

Some nouns ending in *s* look plural but are actually singular. When one of these words is a subject, it must take a singular verb.

Mathematics is a popular major at this college.

Mumps was a common childhood disease until a vaccine became available.

Astrophysics has fascinated Greg for years.

Other such nouns, such as *politics* and *statistics,* can be singular or plural.

Politics is a complex area of study. [Here *politics* means a single subject area.]

Your *politics do* not agree with mine. [Here *politics* means beliefs or views.]

The word *data* means "facts" and thus often takes a plural verb. Some writers, however, think of *data* as referring to a single collection of information, in which case *data* can take a singular verb.

Here *is* the *data* you requested.

We cannot come to a conclusion until all the *data have* been analyzed.

18j   Making verbs agree in titles and with words used as words

Titles of books, articles, movies, and so on take a singular verb, even when the titles look plural or contain plural words.

The Women of Brewster Street <u>is</u> one of Gloria Naylor's early books.

Down These Mean Streets <u>was</u> the autobiography of Piri Thomas.

Similarly, a word referred to as a word takes a singular verb, even though the word may be plural.

When used to refer to ordinary human beings, the word "people" *is* considered plural.

The word "desks" *is* difficult for some people to pronounce because of the consonant cluster.

PRONOUN–ANTECEDENT AGREEMENT

In writing, we use pronouns to stand in for nouns (see 15b in the *Workbook*). A pronoun must agree with its antecedent in person, number, and gender. Look at the following examples:

In the last marathon, the *runner* achieved the best time of *her* career. [The pronoun *her* agrees with the antecedent *runner*; the pronoun is third person, singular, and feminine.]

Mr. Jett tries to spend as much time as *he* can with *his* children. [The pronouns *he* and *his* agree with the antecedent *Mr. Jett* and are third person, singular, and masculine.]

The *clinic* is easy to reach because *it* is conveniently located near all major forms of transportation. [The pronoun *it* agrees with the antecedent *clinic*; the pronoun is third person, singular, and neuter.]

| 18k | **Making a pronoun agree with an indefinite pronoun antecedent** |

Most indefinite pronouns refer to people or things in general, thus they seem plural; grammatically, however, they are singular. Here is a list of common indefinite pronouns:

anybody	everybody	somebody	nobody
anyone	everyone	someone	no one
anything	everything	something	nothing

Each word in the list is singular, so it takes a singular verb. Furthermore, the pronouns used to refer to a singular indefinite pronoun should also be singular. Look at the following examples:

Everybody has *his or her* opinion.

If *someone* has my notebook, *he or she* should give it back.

Nobody knows what *he or she* will be doing next year.

It has become common to hear people use a plural pronoun to refer to a singular antecedent, as in "*Everybody* has *their* own opinion." Grammatically, however, the singular antecedent and the plural pronoun do not match. In academic and professional writing, use a singular pronoun, or rewrite the sentence to avoid the agreement problem. Often, using plural words instead of indefinite singular pronouns can help you avoid the tedious repetition of *he or she* and *his or her* (see 18n in the *Workbook*).

Everybody has an opinion.

All people have *their* opinions.

If *someone* has my notebook, *that person* should give it back.

The *people* here do not know what *they* will be doing next year.

| 18l | **Making a pronoun agree with a collective noun antecedent** |

When a collective noun refers to a group as a single unit, the collective noun takes a singular pronoun.

The *committee* decided to hold *its* next meeting on Tuesday morning.

The *team* is preparing for *its* next game.

When a collective noun refers to the individual members of the group, it can take a plural pronoun. However, for grammatical accuracy, it is best to rewrite the sentence to include a plural antecedent that names the individual members of the group.

The *members* of the committee are consulting *their* calendars to schedule the next meeting.

At the end of the season, *players* on the team go *their* separate ways.

18m   Making a pronoun agree with a compound antecedent

A compound antecedent has two antecedents joined by a conjunction. Compound antecedents may be singular or plural, depending on the conjunction used to join the two. Compounds joined by *and* are plural and require a plural pronoun.

My cousin *and* her husband are selling *their* house.

Use a singular pronoun when the compound antecedent is preceded by *each* or *every*, or when the sense of the compound is clearly singular because it refers to one person.

Every town or village in this area has *its* own elementary school.

The heart and soul of this college is *its* core curriculum.

The breadwinner and sole support of the family exhausted *herself* working eighty hours a week.

When compound antecedents are connected by *or, nor, either. . . or*, or *neither. . . nor*, the pronoun should agree with the closer of the two antecedents.

Either Mr. Cruz or Mr. and Mrs. Johnson will allow the committee to meet in *their* apartment.

Neither Ginny nor Diane can find *her* car keys.

If one of the antecedents is singular and the other is plural, avoid awkwardness by putting the plural antecedent second.

AWKWARD   Neither the children nor the teacher could keep *herself* from laughing.

REVISED   Neither the teacher nor the children could keep *themselves* from laughing.

18n   Checking for gender-specific pronouns

Generic nouns and indefinite pronouns refer to people in general, to both men and women, not to one or the other. Traditionally in English, the third-person, singular, masculine pronouns *he, him*, and *his* were used to refer to generic nouns and indefinite pronouns. Look at the following examples:

A police officer is required to wear *his* cap in most circumstances.

Does everybody here have *his* textbook?

If anyone has a problem, *he* should see the dean.

Use of the generic pronouns *he* and *his* in these examples can be considered sexist because the pronouns are masculine. The first sentence seems to imply that all police officers are men; the other two sentences suggest that all students are men.

You can avoid the appearance of sexism by using one of the following alternatives:

1. Use masculine and feminine pronouns together.

    A police officer is required to wear *his or her* cap in most circumstances.

    Does everybody here have *his or her* textbook?

    If anyone has a problem, *he or she* should see the dean.

However, using both masculine and feminine pronouns can create awkwardness when numerous references to *he or she* and *his or her* occur.

2. Use a plural antecedent and plural pronouns.

    Police officers are required to wear *their* caps in most circumstances.

    Do all of you have *your* textbooks?

    If any students have a problem, *they* should see the dean.

3. Rewrite the sentence to eliminate the pronoun.

    A police officer is required to wear a cap in most circumstances.

    Police officers are required to wear caps in most circumstances.

    Does everybody here have a textbook?

    Any student with a problem should see the dean.

For additional discussion of sexist and other forms of biased language, see 32b in the *Workbook.*

EXERCISE 1   Subject–Verb Agreement

Underline or circle the correct verbs in the following sentences. Example:

A football game (*lasts*/*last*) sixty minutes.

1. A microwave oven (*heats*/*heat*) food very quickly.

2. It (*has*/*have*) been raining for two days.

3. I thought you (*was*/*were*) working late tonight.

4. They (*is*/*are*) widening the highway; the work (*is*/*are*) taking longer than expected.

5. The national debt (*seems*/*seem*) to increase every year.

6. The Carters (*has*/*have*) a bigger house than we (*does*/*do*).

7. The new tax laws (*allows*/*allow*) certain deductions; these deductions (*was*/*were*) not allowed before.

8. Every single child (*is*/*are*) born with curiosity; a parent's job (*is*/*are*) to encourage that trait.

9. Radial tires (*sounds*/*sound*) very different on pavement than conventional tires (*does*/*do*).

10. All those television advertisements (*makes*/*make*) me irritated, especially when they (*interrupts*/*interrupt*) a good movie.

Name _____ Section _____ Date _____

EXERCISE 2   Using Verb Agreement in Writing

For each topic that follows, write a brief paragraph of three to five sentences using the present tense. Then underline the singular verbs in all of your paragraphs. Example:

Topic: Owning a pet

Owning a pet <u>seems</u> like a wonderful idea, but the reality <u>is</u> very different from the abstract idea of companionship and love. A dog or a cat, for example, <u>has</u> to be fed, brushed, and occasionally bathed; in addition, a dog <u>has</u> to be walked several times a day. A pet owner <u>spends</u> a great deal of time every day looking after the animal, so a person whose free time <u>is</u> limited may feel that owning a pet <u>is</u> not such a good idea.

1. Your favorite sport

2. A hobby

3. A favorite recipe

4. A food you dislike

5. Exercise

EXERCISE 3   Verb Agreement When Subjects and Verbs Are Separated

Underline or circle the correct verbs in the following sentences. Example:

One of the headlights (*is*/*are*) burned out.

1. One of my shoes (*has*/*have*) a small hole in the sole.

2. Knitting sweaters in complicated patterns (*was*/*were*) my grandmother's hobby.

3. Quite a few people waiting in the emergency room (*does*/*do*) not have any health insurance.

4. The client, accompanied by her lawyer, (*was*/*were*) sitting at the defense table.

5. Grounds from the coffee pot (*has*/*have*) clogged the drain.

EXERCISE 4   Verb Agreement with Compound Subjects

Underline or circle the correct verbs in the following sentences. Example:

Moe, Larry, and Curly (*was*/*were*) the names of the Three Stooges.

1. Books and newspapers (*was*/*were*) strewn all over her desk.

2. Ross, Angelo, and Strickland (*is*/*are*) the biggest law firm in this town.

3. Every sentence and paragraph in your essay (*has*/*have*) to be carefully checked.

4. No beer or alcohol (*was*/*were*) served.

5. Neither the taxi driver nor the dispatcher (*is*/*are*) familiar with that address.

EXERCISE 5   Verb Agreement with Indefinite Pronouns

Underline or circle the correct verbs in the following sentences. Example:

Everybody living on this block (<u>*knows*</u>/*know*) Mr. Gates.

1. If anybody (*wants*/*want*) tutoring in physics, see Ms. Ramos.

2. Some of these cookies (*was*/*were*) baked with peanut oil.

3. Enough paint (*is*/*are*) left to give the kitchen a second coat.

4. Nothing in the senator's remarks (*seems*/*seem*) unusual.

5. Amazingly, out of millions of snowflakes, each (*is*/*are*) unique.

EXERCISE 6   Verb Agreement with Collective Nouns

Underline or circle the correct verbs in the following sentences. Example:

The team (<u>*has*</u>/*have*) had its fifth winning season in a row.

1. A group of tourists from Spain (*is*/*are*) visiting Seattle.

2. The Zavin family (*has*/*have*) a huge reunion every five years.

3. Some members of the committee (*wants*/*want*) to change the date of the next meeting.

4. The block association (*sponsors*/*sponsor*) a big party every summer.

5. During the first two speeches, the audience (*was*/*were*) restless and inattentive.

EXERCISE 7   Verb Agreement with Subjects and Relative Pronouns

Underline or circle the correct verbs in the following sentences. Example:

An important factor in the last two elections (*was*/*were*) women, who now (*makes*/*make*) up 51 percent of all registered voters in the city.

1. An important source of income for many colleges (*is*/*are*) sports events.

2. A driver who never (*checks*/*check*) the oil will have engine trouble sooner or later.

3. Toys that (*has*/*have*) small parts should not be given to very young children.

4. Greek and Latin, which (*was*/*were*) part of the curriculum at many colleges years ago, are no longer required at most universities.

5. Eric is the only one of the soccer players who also (*plays*/*play*) on the basketball team.

EXERCISE 8   Verb Agreement in Inverted Sentences

Underline or circle the correct verbs in the following sentences. Example:

There (*is*/*are*) only two sections of History 201 being given this term.

1. Standing outside the courtroom (*was*/*were*) several police officers.

2. I am not sure if there (*is*/*are*) any registration guides left.

3. The reporter is saying that there (*has*/*have*) been a serious accident on the interstate highway.

4. Because of distribution problems, there (*was*/*were*) practically no food in the grocery stores.

5. On the top shelf practically out of sight (*was*/*were*) the Spanish-English dictionary I needed.

EXERCISE 9 Verb Agreement in Special Cases

Underline or circle the correct verbs in the following sentences. Example:

Little Women (<u>*was*</u>/*were*) for many years a popular book, especially with young girls.

1. Mathematics (*is*/*are*) useful in many careers, even those not directly involved in engineering or science.

2. "Themselves" (*is*/*are*) a plural pronoun.

3. All the data (*indicates*/*indicate*) that the ozone layer is thinning.

4. *Mules and Men* by Zora Neale Hurston (*was*/*were*) published in 1945.

5. Ms. Albert's politics (*is*/*are*) very different from mine, but we are still friends.

6. Years ago, unlike today, statistics (*was*/*were*) not a required part of a major in economics.

7. "Seven Brides for Seven Brothers" (*features*/*feature*) Jacques D'Amboise, a dancer from the New York City Ballet.

8. "Possesses" (*is*/*are*) not easy to spell or to pronounce.

9. Either biology, chemistry, or physics (*is*/*are*) required for all students.

10. Athletics (*provides*/*provide*) the college with much needed revenue.

EXERCISE 10   Using Verb Agreement in Writing

Write a sentence using each word or phrase that follows. Wherever possible, use the word or phrase as a subject. Then underline the subjects and verbs in your sentences. Example:

Phrase: One of my neighbors

I recently found out that <u>one</u> of my neighbors <u>is</u> a former football player with the Dallas Cowboys.

1. My father and I

2. Everyone

3. The publicity committee

4. The person who

5. There was

6. *The Age of Innocence*

7. Measles

8. Some of the contributions

9. Some of the money

10. Neither Ms. Khan nor the other bank officers

EXERCISE 11 Pronoun–Antecedent Agreement

In each sentence that follows, underline the antecedent once and the pronoun (that refers to the antecedent) twice. Example:

The marathon <u>runner</u> is pacing <u>herself</u> so that <u>she</u> will have some strength left by the end of the race.

1. Ms. DeJesus is head of the PTA at her children's school.

2. This house is less expensive than others on the block because it needs a lot of work.

3. Mr. Sollis worked for most of his life in his brother's construction business.

4. Dr. Tan joined a group of other doctors right after she finished her residency in neurology.

5. Gardeners grow peas and beans not only for food but also because they fix nitrogen in the soil.

EXERCISE 12   Pronoun Agreement with Indefinite Pronoun Antecedents

Underline or circle the correct pronouns in the following sentences. Example:

Everybody wants the best for (*his or her*/*their*) family.

1. Something is missing, but I can't think what (*it*/*they*) could be.

2. Everyone on the boys' soccer team has to get permission from (*his*/*their*) parents to attend weekend practice.

3. The consumer magazine recommends these two cars; both have minor flaws, but (*it*/*they*) are very reliable.

4. Large numbers of people never vote; many do not realize that (*he or she*/*they*) are losing a chance to make (*his or her*/*their*) preferences known.

5. Somebody on the women's lacrosse team left (*their*) shoes in the locker room.

EXERCISE 13   Pronoun Agreement with Collective Noun Antecedents

Underline or circle the correct pronouns in the following sentences. Examples:

The team was very loyal to (*his or her*/*its*/*their*) coach.

The members of the team were very loyal to (*his or her*/*its*/*their*) coach.

1. He thanked the Parents' Association for (*his or her*/*its*/*their*) hard work raising funds for the student orchestra.

2. The basketball team has (*its*/*their*) last game of the season next Friday.

3. The people in this group have already bought (*its*/*their*) tickets.

4. The jury has not yet announced (*its/their*) verdict.

5. The crowd voiced (*its/their*) disapproval of the candidate's views with boos and catcalls.

EXERCISE 14   Pronoun Agreement with Compound Antecedents

Underline or circle the correct pronouns in the following sentences. Example:

Both Ann and Cathi hope (*she/they*) get into the nursing program.

1. The president and the vice-president of the student government gave (*his or her/their*) support to the proposed governance amendment.

2. Every store and house on the block had holiday decorations in (*its/their*) windows.

3. Each avenue and street in the city should have (*its/their*) potholes filled in.

4. Neither I nor my brothers were informed of (*my/our*) mother's illness until yesterday.

5. Pines and firs, unlike the larch, do not shed (*its/their*) needles in the fall.

EXERCISE 15   Avoiding Gender-Specific Pronouns

Rewrite each of the following sentences to eliminate the use of gender-specific pronouns. Examples:

Everyone on line to register was holding his transcript.
Everyone on line to register was holding a transcript.

A doctor should keep his files up to date.
Doctors should keep their files up to date.

1. Did anyone forget his textbook?

2. Somebody left his umbrella near the coat rack.

3. A cashier should count the change carefully before she gives it to the customer.

4. A driver should signal before he changes lanes.

5. Every athlete should warm up and stretch before he begins to play.

6. Does everybody know what he wants to major in?

7. Nobody knows what he will do in an emergency until an actual emergency happens.

8. Every person who rents space in this mall is worried that his rent will go up.

9. It is easy to tell when a child is two years old; his favorite word is "No!"

10. Each applicant must send in his forms by June 10; otherwise, he will not be considered for the job.

EXERCISE 16   Using Pronoun–Antecedent Agreement in Writing

For each topic that follows, write a brief paragraph of three to five sentences. Then carefully check your paragraphs for errors in pronoun–antecedent agreement.

Topic: Gardening

Many people take up gardening as a hobby and then find that it brings unexpected benefits. For example, it gets people outdoors and provides some exercise. In addition, vegetable gardening often results in better tasting meals and lower food bills.

1. Writing a term paper

2. Fashion

3. Learning a new language

4. Dancing

5. Washing a dog

CHAPTER 19

Grammar for ESL Writers

Certain grammatical structures in English can cause difficulties for some non-native speakers of English. This chapter provides explanations and extra practice in the following areas.

Count nouns and noncount nouns

Determiners

Articles (indefinite and definite)

Quantifiers for count and noncount nouns

Demonstratives

Possessive pronouns

Word order for adjectives and other noun modifiers

Present and past participles as adjectives

Forms of *be, have,* and *do*

Auxiliary verbs

Modal auxiliaries

Gerunds and infinitives

Phrasal verbs

Prepositions

Adverbs

Indirect discourse

Conditional sentences

Idiomatic expressions

19a Learning to distinguish count nouns from mass nouns

1. Count nouns refer to people, places, or things that can be counted separately, one by one. A count noun may be singular or plural. You may use *a* or *an* with a singular count noun.

Sixteen *students* want to see the dean.

He gave the parking lot attendant a *dollar.*

Several of my *relatives* are visiting me this month.

He ordered two *hamburgers* and a *milkshake*.

One *salesperson* cannot help all these *customers*.

2. Mass, or noncount, nouns refer to things that cannot be counted separately one by one. Do not use *a* or *an* before noncount nouns. A noncount noun is always singular; it cannot be made plural. When a noncount noun is a subject, it takes a singular verb, and any pronouns referring to it are also singular.

Swimming is beneficial because *it* strengthens the heart.

Patience certainly *is* a necessary quality in teachers.

Last night he cooked *pasta* for dinner. *It was* very good.

She never drinks *coffee* because *it* makes her nervous.

I was doing my *homework* instead of polishing the *furniture*.

When you travel, keep *money* in your wallet, not in your *luggage*.

Noncount nouns often fall into the following categories:

Abstract words	courage, greed, knowledge, patience, peace, time
Activities	business, tennis, reading, talking, work
Fields of study	biology, engineering, history, sociology, zoology
Foods	bread, fruit, meat, pasta, rice, spaghetti
Gases	air, helium, oxygen, smoke, steam
Languages	English, Italian, Korean, Spanish
Liquids	blood, coffee, gasoline, milk, water
Materials	cotton, iron, linen, polyester, rayon, tin, wood
Particles	air, dust, sugar, salt, pepper
Natural phenomena	cold, electricity, heat, light, rain, sleet, snow, thunder

3. Some noncount nouns do not fit into the categories just mentioned. You must memorize these nouns. Here are some examples:

advice	housework	money
information	jewelry	news (singular)
furniture	luggage	work
garbage	makeup	
homework	mail	

4. Many nouns can be countable or uncountable, depending on their use.

COUNTABLE	UNCOUNTABLE
He made two *cakes* for the party.	He really enjoys eating *cake*.
I have two *irons*, but I never use them.	The window guard is made of *iron*.
She has seen that movie three *times*.	I have no *time* for myself these busy days.

All the *papers* have photographs of the railroad accident.	This painting was done on *paper,* not canvas.
There were several *hairs* in the soup.	Jacques has bright red *hair.*
Only two *spaces* were left in the parking lot.	Is there life in outer *space?*
The *light* in the kitchen has burned out.	There is plenty of *light* in the office.

19b   Recognizing and using determiners

Determiners, or noun markers, precede nouns. There are three types of determiners: articles, demonstratives, and possessive adjectives.

- Articles (the indefinite *a* and *an* and the definite *the*)

  I need *a* new *umbrella.*

  She is *an officer* in the Navy.

  The car you bought gets very good gas mileage.

- Demonstratives

  This chair is comfortable.

  That store is open until midnight.

- Possessive adjectives

  My apartment has two bedrooms.

  Are you visiting *your family* this weekend?

Remember these rules for determiners:

1. Use singular determiners for singular nouns. Use plural determiners for plural nouns.

   He is writing *an essay* about James Baldwin.

   I have read *several books* by Paule Marshall.

   This tree was planted by my grandmother.

   Those buildings are for sale.

2. We usually do not use more than one determiner in each noun phrase.

INCORRECT   *The your* essay was well written.

CORRECT   *Your* essay was well written.

INCORRECT   *The* essay was well written.

19c   Using the articles *a, and,* and *the* correctly

An indefinite article is often used when no particular person, place, or thing is specified. A definite article is often used when a specific person, place, or thing is mentioned. Use the following guidelines to select the correct article.

1. First decide whether the noun is definite or indefinite. A noun is indefinite if the writer or speaker does not specify a particular person, place, or thing.

Speaking in public makes some people nervous.

The copier is out of *paper.*

I have to put on *a sweater.*

A noun is definite when both the writer/speaker and the reader/listener know which specific thing is referred to. This shared knowledge occurs in the following situations:

- When the noun is mentioned a second or subsequent time after its first introduction:

  A taxi was involved in a head-on collision. *The taxi* was totally wrecked.

- When the person, place, or thing is unique in the world, in society, or in the relationship:

  The ozone layer is getting thinner.

  I have to defrost *the refrigerator.*

- When the context makes clear which one is meant:

  The radio is not working. Does it need new batteries?

- When a clause or an adjective such as *right, wrong, first, best, last,* or *only* identifies which one:

  She is sitting in *the first row.*

  I liked *the birthday card you sent me.*

2. If the noun is indefinite, see if it is a count or noncount noun. Use *a* or *an* before singular count nouns. Use *a* before a consonant sound. Use *an* before a vowel sound. (Note that it is the sound, not the letter, that determines whether to use *a* or *an.*)

A new shoe store has opened in town.

A calculator is *a* useful gift.

An enormous package stood outside the door.

She gave *an* unusual speech.

Do not use an article or a quantifier (such as *some*) with an indefinite noncount noun or a plural indefinite count noun when not specifying a particular person, place, or thing.

I am preparing *turkey* and *rice.*

Would you like *some soup?*

He found *several coins* in the pockets of his jeans.

Do not use an article before both noncount nouns or plural count nouns to make generalizations:

Truth is stranger than *fiction.*

The widow was consoled by *friends* and *neighbors.*

3. Use *the* with definite nouns. You can use *the* with most nouns, singular and plural, count and noncount.

I like all *the* jewelry in this display, especially *the* necklace and *the* rings.

19d Choosing the correct quantifier for countable and uncountable nouns

Quantifiers indicate the amount or quantity of a noun. Some quantifiers can be used only with noncount nouns, some only with count nouns, and some with both types of nouns. Use the following guidelines to choose quantifiers correctly.

1. Use the correct quantifier for each type of noun.

NONCOUNT	COUNT	BOTH	
a little money	*a few* dollars	*enough* work	*enough* jobs
too much work	*too many* tasks	*some* furniture	*some* tables
a great deal of time	*two* hours	*a lot of* homework	*a lot of* assignments

2. Use *much* with noncount nouns. Use *many* with count nouns. Use *any* with both noncount and count nouns in negative sentences.

They don't have *much* money.

Our children have brought us *much* happiness.

Many students are majoring in business.

This cookbook contains *many* recipes for chicken.

There isn't *any* milk in the refrigerator.

There weren't *any* lights on in the house.

3. Use *how much* to ask about the quantity of noncount nouns. Use *how many* to ask about the quantity of count nouns.

How much time do we have left?

How much money do you spend on entertainment each month?

How many miles have we driven so far?

How many children are in this class?

19e Using demonstratives correctly

The words *this, that, these,* and *those* are demonstratives. These words are determiners that indicate the distance of a noun from the speaker or writer.

1. To show that a noun is close to you in either space or time, use *this* and *these.* Use *this* with mass nouns and with singular count nouns. Use *these* with plural count nouns.

INCORRECT	*These furniture* is very expensive.
CORRECT	*This furniture* is very expensive.

INCORRECT	*These newspaper* has a good sports section.
CORRECT	*This newspaper* has a good sports section.

INCORRECT	*This children* are studying earth science.
CORRECT	*These children* are studying earth science.

2. To indicate that a noun is distant in either space or time, use *that* and *those*. Use *that* with mass nouns and singular count nouns. Use *those* with plural count nouns.

INCORRECT	*Those jewelry* is really lovely.
CORRECT	*That jewelry* is really lovely.

INCORRECT	*Those classroom* has a good view of the baseball field.
CORRECT	*That classroom* has a good view of the baseball field.

INCORRECT	At *those time* women were not accepted by law schools.
CORRECT	At *that time* women were not accepted by law schools.

19f   Using possessive forms of pronouns correctly

Possessive adjectives and possessive pronouns look very similar, but they have different functions. A possessive adjective precedes the noun it modifies and indicates ownership. A possessive pronoun does not precede a noun; rather, it substitutes for a noun phrase. Use possessive adjectives, not possessive pronouns, to modify nouns.

> *Your* daughter is younger than *mine*. [*Your*, a possessive adjective, modifies the noun *daughter*; *mine*, a possessive pronoun, substitutes for the noun phrase *my daughter*.]

1. Note the different forms of possessive adjectives and possessive pronouns.

POSSESSIVE ADJECTIVES	**POSSESSIVE PRONOUNS**
It was *my* idea.	It was *mine*.
your	*yours.*
his	*his.*
her	*hers.*
its	*its.*
our	*ours.*
their	*theirs.*

2. Use the question word *whose* to ask about possession.

Whose coat is this?	It is *my* coat.

Note: Do not confuse the question word *whose* with *who's*, the contraction for "who is."

Who's absent?   Sonia is absent.

3. Do not use an apostrophe with possessive adjectives, possessive pronouns, or the question word *whose*.

The dog has lost *its* collar.

Whose boyfriend is at the door?

I think this notebook is *yours*.

4. The possessive forms of indefinite pronouns have apostrophes, like the possessive forms of nouns.

One's eyesight tends to get worse with age.

Professor Cohen is *everybody's* favorite teacher.

Is this *anybody's* business?

I found *someone's* wallet on the sidewalk.

19g   Using correct word order for adjectives and other noun modifiers

Noun modifiers are words added to nouns to make a noun phrase. Such modifiers include determiners (articles, demonstratives, and personal pronouns), quantifiers, and adjectives. Usually, a noun phrase includes no more than three or four noun modifiers.

an extremely interesting book

several large ripe apples

the first really modern opera

his new green and blue striped jacket

too much noisy music

too many really boring movies

Noun modifiers occur in the following order:

QUANTIFIERS	DETERMINERS	WORDS SHOWING ORDER	INTENSIFIERS	DESCRIPTIVE ADJECTIVES	NOUNS USED AS MODIFIERS	HEAD NOUN
many	a/an/the	first	very	good/small	student	government
a few	these/those	next	too	big/yellow	family	dinner
a little	your/their	last	really	interesting	summer	vacation
too much	Dave's	second	extremely	intense	business	contract

In the following noun phrases, note the word order of the noun modifiers:

determiner	word showing order	intensifier	descriptive adjective	head noun
the	first	really	modern	opera

quantifier	intensifier	descriptive adjective	noun used as adjective	head noun
many	very	bright	college	students

determiner	word showing order	noun used as adjective	head noun
your	first	childhood	memory

quantifier	intensifier	descriptive adjective	head noun
some	extremely	interesting	books

Adjectives modify nouns and pronouns. An adjective can precede the noun or pronoun it modifies, or it can follow the noun or pronoun and a linking verb.

He gave a *fascinating* speech. [The adjective *fascinating* precedes the noun *speech*.]

It was *unusual*. [The adjective *unusual* follows the pronoun *It* and the linking verb *was*.]

The audience seemed *mesmerized*. [The adjective *mesmerized* follows the noun *audience* and the linking verb *seemed*.]

A long string of adjectives describing one noun would be awkward, even difficult for a reader to follow. Instead, choose the most important features of the noun, and then pick two or three adjectives to describe it. Here are some rules for word order and punctuation when you use descriptive adjectives in a series.

1. Use the following word order for descriptive adjectives:

JUDGMENT	SIZE/ LENGTH	SHAPE/ WIDTH	CONDITION	AGE	COLOR	NATIONALITY/ RELIGION	MATERIAL	NOUNS AS ADJECTIVES	HEAD NOUN
pretty	large	square	broken	new	red	Spanish	tin	photograph	album
good	short	oval	renovated	old	purple	Muslim	wood	kitchen	counter
bad	gigantic	square	dusty	young	blue	Jewish	polyester	stamp	collection
strange	tiny	round	neglected	modern	green	Korean	cotton	summer	sweater

Note the adjective word order in the following phrases:

the first three student essays

several old, wooden salad bowls

a challenging, narrow trail

an unattractive, round plastic table

a beautiful, old Flemish painting

2. Use a comma between adjectives that are equally important:

She was a *relaxed, friendly* person.

It is a *long, fascinating* movie.

If you are not sure whether to use a comma, try substituting *and* for the comma. If the phrase makes sense, use the comma. If the phrase does not make sense with *and*, it does not need the comma.

POSSIBLE   a *long and difficult* exam
              a *long, difficult* exam

NOT POSSIBLE   several silver and soup spoons

3. When two adjectives follow the noun they describe, join them with *and*.

His hair is *black and curly.*

4. Do not use a comma between the last adjective in a series and the noun.

comma   no comma
adjective adjective   noun

The police conducted a *lengthy, thorough investigation.*

19h | Distinguishing between the present participle and past participle used as adjectives

The present and past participles of verbs can be used as adjectives. Although the present participle and the past participle of a verb may look similar, they have very different meanings. Following are guidelines for using participles as adjectives.

1. Use present participles to describe people, places, or things that *cause* a feeling or state of mind.

The movie was *boring.* [The movie *caused* this feeling.]

Our vacation was *exciting.* [The vacation *caused* this state.]

That noise is *irritating.* [The noise *causes* this state.]

Your paper is *interesting.* [The paper *causes* this feeling.]

2. Use past participles to describe people, places, or things that *experience* a feeling or state of mind.

Peter was *bored* by the movie. [He *experienced* that feeling.]

We are *excited* about our vacation. [We *experience* that feeling.]

I am *irritated* by that noise. [I *experience* that state of mind.]

They are *interested* in your paper. [They *experience* that state of mind.]

Note: Participles used as adjectives do not show tense. The *-ed* ending on the past participle does not indicate past tense, and the *-ing* ending on the present participle does not indicate present tense.

Right now I am *exhausted.*

Yesterday I had an *annoying* experience.

3. Be careful when using the following participles:

PRESENT PARTICIPLE	PAST PARTICIPLE
amazing	amazed
annoying	annoyed
boring	bored
depressing	depressed
exciting	excited
exhausting	exhausted
fascinating	fascinated
interesting	interested
satisfying	satisfied
surprising	surprised

19i Learning the forms of *be, have,* and *do*

The verbs *be, have,* and *do* are used frequently, both as main verbs and as auxiliary verbs. Because they are irregular verbs, you must memorize their forms.

FORMS OF *BE, HAVE,* AND *DO*

be
Base form: *be*
   Present participle: *being*
   Past participle: *been*

Present Tense	*Singular*	*Plural*
First person	I am	we are
Second person	you are	you are
Third person	he is	they are
	she is	
	it is	

Past Tense	*Singular*	*Plural*
First person	I was	we were
Second person	you were	you were
Third person	he was	they were
	she was	
	it was	

have
Base form: *have*
   Present participle: *having*
   Past participle: *had*

Present Tense	*Singular*	*Plural*
First person	I have	we have
Second person	you have	you have
Third person	he has	they have
	she has	
	it has	

Past Tense	*Singular*	*Plural*
First person	I had	we had
Second person	you had	you had
Third person	he had	they had
	she had	
	it had	

do

Base form: *do*
   Present participle: *doing*
   Past participle: *done*

Present Tense	*Singular*	*Plural*
First person	I do	we do
Second person	you do	you do
Third person	he does	they do
	she does	
	it does	

Past Tense	*Singular*	*Plural*
First person	I did	we did
Second person	you did	you did
Third person	he did	they did
	she did	
	it did	

19j Using the auxiliary verbs *be*, *have*, and *do* correctly

Auxiliary (helping) verbs combine with a base verb form or a participle to create a verb phrase. The progressive and perfect tenses, the passive voice, negatives, and questions are all formed with auxiliary verbs. Look at the following examples:

auxiliary   past participle
She *has* just *finished* her report.

auxiliary   base form of verb
I *do* not *recognize* the person in the photograph.

 auxiliary   present participle
He *is* now *living* in Wisconsin.

Progressive tenses

Progressive tenses have a form of *be* and the present participle. The form of *be* must agree with its subject. Do not use the present participle alone as a verb; remember to include the form of *be*. Note too that the forms of *be* are sometimes contracted.

I *am cooking* dinner right now.

We *are discussing* the novels of Gabriel García Marquez.

He *was sleeping* when I called.

The team *will be playing* its last game tomorrow.

She*'s moving* to North Dakota.

They*'re planning* to visit us soon.

Note: Some verbs are seldom used in the progressive tense. Do not use the progressive for verbs in the following categories:

Linking verbs: be, become, exist, seem

Verbs that show possession: belong, have, own, possess

Verbs that show perception: feel, hear, see, taste, smell

Verbs that show feelings, preferences, or intellectual states: believe, forget, hate, imagine, intend, know, like, love, need, pity, prefer, remember, suppose, understand, want, wish

Perfect tenses

Perfect tenses combine a form of *have* with the past participle. The form of *have* in the present tense must agree with its subject. Do not use the past participle alone in a verb. Note too that forms of *have* are sometimes contracted. If you are not sure of the past participle of a verb, consult your dictionary. If the past participle and the past tense have different forms, the dictionary will give both forms.

My cousin *has worked* as a nurse for ten years.

The children *have gone* to the zoo.

I *have been* here since ten this morning.

She *had* never *seen* snow until she visited Vermont.

He*'s been* absent only once before this.

We*'ve known* the Wyatts for about a year.

By the time I got to the party, you*'d gone.*

Passive voice

In the passive voice, the subject receives the action of the verb. The passive voice has a form of *be* and a past participle. The past participle does not change, but the form of *be* must agree with the subject.

The new mayor *was elected* by a small margin.

Spanish *is spoken* throughout most of South America.

Holiday decorations *were displayed* in all the store windows.

Use only transitive verbs in the passive voice. Transitive verbs take an object.

ACTIVE   He *cleaned* the kitchen floor yesterday.

PASSIVE   The kitchen floor *was cleaned* yesterday.

ACTIVE   Loud noises *startle* the baby.

PASSIVE   The baby *is startled* by loud noises.

Intransitive verbs, such as *happen* and *occur,* do not take an object. They cannot be used in the passive voice. They are used only in the active voice in which the subject does the action.

ACTIVE   Thunderstorms often *occur* in late summer.

PASSIVE   [None]

ACTIVE   They *arrived* at the party late.

PASSIVE   [None]

Negative sentences and questions

Negative sentences and many questions use a form of *do* and the base form of a verb. In the present tense, use *does* with a third-person singular subject.

I *do not have* any time to waste.

She *doesn't speak* Portuguese.

They *don't watch* much television.

We *didn't know* his name.

Does this bus *go* downtown?

Do your upstairs neighbors *make* a lot of noise?

Did the plane *arrive* on time?

Dialect forms of verbs

Some dialects of nonstandard English use verb forms that are different from the verb forms of standard English. For example, in some dialects the base form of *be* is used as an auxiliary, no auxiliary is used with a participle, and *don't* is used with a third-person singular subject. However, you must use standard English in both college and your career.

DIALECT   They *be standing* around in the hall.

STANDARD   They *are standing* around in the hall.

DIALECT   I *seen* that movie already.

STANDARD   I *have seen* that movie already.

DIALECT   The baby *don't* have any teeth yet.

STANDARD   The baby *doesn't* have any teeth yet.

19k | Recognizing and using modal auxiliaries

Modals are auxiliaries that combine with the base form of a verb. A modal gives information about the speaker's or writer's attitude toward that verb. For example, a modal can express whether an action is likely to happen or whether an action is a good idea. Modals convey the following information:

ability:	can, could
advisability:	should
necessity:	must, have to
prohibition:	must not
intention:	shall, will, would
possibility:	may, might, could

Note the following rules for modals.
1. Do not add *-s* to a modal, no matter what the subject is:

He *must* rewrite this memo.

An emergency *may* occur at any moment.

She *can* speak Serbo-Croatian.

2. Do not use an infinitive or the past tense after a modal. Use the base form of the verb.

You *can speak* English better now than before.

We *could see* the ocean from our house.

He *would* not *take* my advice.

3. When the modal is followed by *be* or *have*, use a present participle or a past participle, depending on the meaning of the sentence.

The doctor *could be talking* to another patient.

The work *cannot be completed* today.

I *will be driving* to New Hampshire tonight.

I hope the letter *will be delivered* tomorrow.

I *should have called* you sooner.

It is possible that he *might have gone* home.

You *may have noticed* the new furniture in the office.

They *should have been paying* attention.

4. Do not use more than one modal with any main verb. To convey the same meaning, use one of these phrases:

MODAL	SIMILAR MEANING
can	be able to
must	have to
should	be supposed to, be obliged to

INCORRECT The dean *might can* see you tomorrow.

CORRECT The dean *might be able to* see you tomorrow.

INCORRECT You *will must* finish your term paper.

CORRECT You *will have to finish* your term paper.
You *must finish* your term paper.

19I   Using gerunds and infinitives

A gerund is a verb form ending in *-ing*. Gerunds function as nouns. An infinitive is the base form of a verb preceded by the word *to.*

GERUNDS

Swimming is excellent aerobic exercise.

The committee discussed *changing* the date of the next meeting.

They do not allow *smoking* in their house.

INFINITIVES

The candidates agreed *to debate* each other just before the election.

I promise *to call* you as soon as I can.

Mr. and Mrs. Eng decided *to open* a bookstore.

Gerunds and infinitives often follow verbs as objects. Some verbs and phrases may be followed by an infinitive, a gerund, or both.

1. The verbs in this list are followed by an infinitive with *to.*

agree	come	have	mean	refuse
arrange	decide	hope	offer	wait
beg	deserve	intend	plan	want
claim	expect	manage	promise	wish

Jose *expects to graduate* in June.

I *decided not to take* that job.

She *plans to retire* next year.

2. The following verbs require a noun or pronoun object before the infinitive.

advise	convince	invite	persuade	tell
allow	forbid	order	remind	urge
cause	instruct	permit	require	warn

We *persuaded him to attend* the town meeting.

I *convinced Ms. Santos to apply* for the job.

The editorial *urges people to vote* on Election Day.

3. Some verbs may be followed by a noun or pronoun object and an infinitive, or by only an infinitive.

allow	expect	help	want
ask	force	need	would like
cause	get	permit	

The boss *wants us to work* overtime.

Ms. Truong *wants to major* in business administration.

The chemistry teacher *expects her students to follow* directions.

The team did not *expect to win* the game by such a wide margin.

Note: When *allow* and *permit* do not have a noun or pronoun object, they are followed by a gerund:

The town does not *allow parking* on these streets after 2 a.m.

4. The verbs *let, make,* and *have* are followed by a noun or pronoun object and the base form of a verb. (The base form is sometimes called the "bare infinitive" because the word *to* is understood but not used.)

My mother would not *let us play* with toy guns.

Too much coffee *makes her heart race.*

The coach *has the players practice* certain plays repeatedly.

5. When you want to use a verb form after one of the following verbs, you must use a gerund.

admit	discontinue	mention	report
allow	discuss	mind	resent
appreciate	dislike	miss	resist
avoid	enjoy	postpone	risk
celebrate	finish	practice	stop
consider	forgive	prevent	suggest
delay	imagine	regret	tolerate
deny	keep	remember	understand

The suspect *denied stealing* the money.

We cannot *finish painting* the kitchen today.

Would you *consider changing* your work schedule?

Many of the verbs in the preceding list can be followed by a possessive and then a gerund.

I really *appreciate your working* overtime this week.

The fans *resented the owner's firing* yet another coach.

She *dislikes his answering* a question with another question.

6. Many phrases made up of a verb and a preposition are followed by a gerund.

accuse (someone) of	be responsible for	feel like
apologize for	be tired of	insist on
approve of	be used to	look forward to
be afraid of	believe in	object to
be capable of	depend on	talk about
be interested in	dream of	think about

I *apologize for keeping* you waiting.

Each person *is responsible for finishing* his or her own work.

We *look forward to talking* with you again.

7. A few verbs may be followed by either an infinitive or a gerund with no change in meaning.

attempt	hate	omit
begin	like	prefer
continue	love	start

Mariella *started to work* in the pharmacy last month.

Mariella *started working* in the pharmacy last month.

Note: Use the infinitive after progressive forms to avoid the awkward combination of two *-ing* forms in a row.

AWKWARD   She was *beginning understanding* English better than she had before.

REVISED   She was *beginning to understand* English better than she had before.

8. Certain verbs may be followed by a noun or pronoun object and then either the base form or a gerund. However, the meaning changes slightly depending on whether the base form or a gerund is used.

feel	look	see
hear	notice	smell
listen	observe	watch

We *saw a man change* a flat tire. [We watched the whole event from beginning to end.]

We *saw a man changing* a flat tire. [The action was in progress when we noticed it.]

9. When used after the following verbs, the infinitives and gerunds have very different meanings.

forget	stop
go on	try
remember	

I *stopped to talk* to my supervisor. [I talked to the supervisor.]

I *stopped talking* to my supervisor. [I no longer talk to the supervisor.]

I *remembered to mail* that letter. [I mailed the letter.]

I *remembered mailing* that letter. [I have a memory of doing so.]

19m | Recognizing phrasal verbs and correctly placing their objects

Phrasal verbs consist of a verb and one or two particles (prepositions or adverbs). They often express an idiomatic or nonliteral meaning; the phrasal verb means something different from each of its parts separately. For example, when the words *look* and *up* are used separately, they mean to look in a particular direction:

The audience *looked up* at the speaker on the platform.

However, the phrasal verb *look up* can mean to improve, to get better, or to admire (someone).

The economy is definitely *looking up*. [getting better, improving]

Children often *look up* to famous athletes as role models. [admire]

1. Not every combination of a verb plus preposition or adverb is a phrasal verb. You can test whether a word combination is a phrasal verb by substituting a similar phrase. If the combination is a true phrasal verb, substitution is not possible.

POSSIBLE   Each graduate ~~stepped up~~ [climbed up] onto the platform to get a diploma.

NOT POSSIBLE   Two weeks before exams, she ~~stepped up~~ [climbed up] her review and study. [Because *step up* is a phrasal verb meaning "to increase," substitution is not possible.]

2. Phrasal verbs may be either intransitive or transitive. Intransitive verbs do not take a direct object.

After his outburst, he *calmed down* quickly.

Transitive verbs may take a direct object.

She *turned down* that job offer.

3. There are two types of transitive phrasal verbs—inseparable and separable. Inseparable transitive verbs must always keep the verb and the particle together; the object cannot be placed between the verb and the particle.

We must *get off* the bus here.

The police are *looking for* him.

Please *watch out for* that broken step.

With separable transitive verbs, you may place a noun object either after the verb and its particle or in between the verb and its particle.

She *handed in her term paper* on time.

She *handed her term paper in* on time.

However, if the object is a pronoun, you must place it between the verb and the particle.

She *handed it in* on time.

4. Many phrasal verbs are colloquial and, therefore, inappropriate in academic writing. If the word is marked *slang* in your dictionary, use a one-word verb instead of the phrasal verb.

> associating
They moved because they didn't want their children ~~hanging out~~ with drug dealers.

5. Many phrasal verbs are idiomatic; as a result, you must make sure they convey the meaning you really intend. In the following list of phrasal verbs, note that the inseparable transitive phrasal verbs are marked with an asterisk (*).

COMMON PHRASAL VERBS

INTRANSITIVE

act up	cut in	pay off
add up	cut out	run out
break down	get off	slow down
calm down	get up	stay up
catch on	give in	step in
come off	grow up	wear off
cough up	hang on	work out

TRANSITIVE

call back	give up	tear up
call on*	grow up*	throw away
do over	hand in	turn off
figure out	look up	turn on
get off*	pay back	turn down
get on*	put away	turn up
get in*	run into*	watch out for*
get over*	take off	
get along with*	tear down	

19n Using prepositions to express time, place, or motion

A preposition shows the relationship between a noun or pronoun and another word or group of words in a sentence. The prepositions that indicate relationships of time, place, or motion can be confusing. The following chart will help you use these prepositions correctly.

A GUIDE TO USING PREPOSITIONS TO INDICATE TIME, PLACE, OR MOTION

TIME

To indicate time, use the preposition *in, on,* or *at.*

in October	on Thanksgiving Day	at 5:45 a.m.
in the 1950s	on Saturday	at noon
in a minute	on my birthday	at dinnertime

PLACE

To indicate place, use the preposition *in, on,* or *at.*

in Cambodia	on the bus	at the grocery store
in the kitchen	on the Hudson River	at my cousin's house
in Nevada	on television	at work

MOTION

To indicate motion, use the preposition *into.*

in the street	into the room	into a fight
into her briefcase	into the dark, scary cave	into bed

19o Placing adverbs

Adverbs modify verbs, adjectives, or other adverbs in sentences. Adverbs can be placed at the beginning, the middle, or the end of a sentence. They can appear before or after a verb or between an auxiliary verb and a main verb. Note the placement of adverbs in the following examples (verbs are italicized and adverbs are underlined).

<u>Nervously,</u> he *waited* for the phone to ring.

She *has* <u>always</u> *encouraged* me to do my best.

I *ironed* each piece of clothing <u>carefully.</u>

That store *is* <u>always</u> open; it <u>never</u> *closes.*

He *complained* <u>irritably</u> at the delay.

Many variations are possible, but the basic word order of a sentence that is not a question or a command is as follows:

SUBJECT	VERB	OBJECT	ADVERBS OF MANNER	PLACE	TIME
The snow	fell		steadily		all day.
We	ate	breakfast	quickly	in the kitchen.	

Note: Never place an adverb between a verb and its direct object.

Adverbs that describe how often something is done usually occur midsentence.

- In front of verbs (except *be*):

We <u>seldom</u> *go* to baseball games anymore.

- After *be:*

We *are* <u>always</u> happy to see you.

- Between the auxiliary and the main verb:

I *have* <u>always</u> *wanted* to visit Hawaii.

- In questions, after the subject:

Have *they* <u>ever</u> met a professional basketball player?

- In negative statements, after the negative word:

My car *doesn't* <u>always</u> start on very cold mornings.

Other adverbs often are placed in the following positions:

- Adverbs telling how much or to what extent are placed immediately before the modified word (or words):

I was <u>quite</u> *shocked* by his behavior.

The burned building was <u>completely</u> *destroyed.*

- Adverbs indicating sequence may come first or last in a sentence:

<u>Next,</u> we will study pediatric nursing.

We will study pediatric nursing <u>next.</u>

- Adverbs indicating the writer's viewpoint are usually placed first in a sentence:

<u>Luckily,</u> the tree fell in the yard, not on the house.

<u>Unfortunately,</u> all the flights to Jamaica are full.

19p | Changing forms with indirect discourse

When you quote direct speech, you reproduce the writer's or speaker's exact words and enclose them in quotation marks. When you report someone's speech, you state it indirectly, without quotation marks. Look at the following examples:

DIRECT   "I will not run for reelection," said the governor.

INDIRECT   The governor said that she would not run for reelection.

In addition to the removal of quotation marks in indirect discourse, there are other changes. The most important change is a shift in verb tense. Pronouns also change to show the different point of view. Notice the various changes in the following examples:

- Change the simple present tense to the simple past tense.

DIRECT	INDIRECT
"The house *is* for sale," she said.	She said that the house *was* for sale.

- Change the present progressive to the past progressive.

DIRECT	INDIRECT
"The flood *is receding*," he said.	He said that the flood *was receding*.

- Change the present perfect and simple past to the past perfect.

DIRECT	INDIRECT
"We *have noticed* a change," he said.	He said that they *had noticed* a change.
"I *answered* his letter last week," she said.	She said that she *had answered* his letter last week.

- Change *will* to *would, may* to *might,* and *can* to *could.*

DIRECT	INDIRECT
"Snow *will* fall tonight," she said.	She said that snow *would* fall tonight.
"He *may* improve," the doctor said.	The doctor said that he *might* improve.
"I *can* speak Spanish," she said.	She said that she *could* speak Spanish.

- Change *have to* and *must* to *had to.*

DIRECT	INDIRECT
"We *have to* go," they said.	They said that they *had to* go.
"I *must* leave," she said.	She said that she *had to* leave.

- Report *yes/no* questions with *if* or *whether.* Use sentence word order, not question word order, with reported questions. Do not use *do, does,* or *did* as you would with a direct question.

DIRECT	INDIRECT
"Did you mail the letter?" I asked.	I asked *if* he had mailed the letter.
"Can you speak Danish?" she asked.	She asked *whether* he could speak Danish.

- Report information questions with a question word (*who, what, when, where, how, why*).

DIRECT	**INDIRECT**
"When does the bus leave?" I asked.	I asked *when* the bus would leave.
"Who took my dictionary?" he asked.	He asked *who* had taken his dictionary.

• Report invitations and commands with the infinitive.

DIRECT	**INDIRECT**
"Please come to the holiday party," we asked her.	We asked her *to come* to the holiday party.
"Don't leave the key in the lock," he reminded me.	He reminded me *not to leave* the key in the lock.

Note: Direct questions often become part of declarative sentences. When changing a direct question to an indirect question inside another sentence, follow the same rules for verb tenses, word order, and auxiliaries.

DIRECT QUESTION	**INDIRECT QUESTION (IN ANOTHER SENTENCE)**
Is it going to rain?	I wondered if it was going to rain.

19q Using verb tenses in conditional sentences

When one fact depends on the existence of another fact, the situation is often expressed in a conditional sentence.

> More accidents occur when the roads are slippery. [The increase in accidents is caused by the slippery conditions.]

> If the weather is good, we will go hiking. [Going hiking depends on the weather being good.]

A conditional sentence usually has a main clause and a subordinate (dependent) clause that starts with *if, when, whenever,* or *unless.* In a conditional sentence, the verb tenses used in the main clause and the subordinate clause follow a formula. Following are the verb tenses and the meanings of the most commonly used conditional sentences.

Present and past real conditions

In these sentences, the conditions mentioned in the main clause and the subordinate clause actually exist or did exist. Use the same tense in the main clause and the subordinate clause.

main clause, present tense subordinate clause, present tense
I *get* very nervous whenever I *drink* too much coffee.

subordinate clause, past tense main clause, past tense
Whenever the dog *heard* a siren, he *began* to bark.

Future real conditions

These sentences predict situations that are likely to occur. Use *will, may, can, should,* or *might* in the main clause and *if* or *unless* with the present tense in the subordinate clause.

subordinate clause   main clause
If you *leave* the headlights on, your car battery *will* need recharging.

       main clause   subordinate clause
You *can't* lose weight *unless* you *eat* sensibly.

Present and future unreal conditions

These sentences discuss situations that are probably not going to happen in the present or the future. Use *would, could,* or *might* with a base verb form in the main clause and *if* with the past tense in the subordinate clause.

       subordinate clause   main clause
If we *had* lots of money, we *would* retire. [We don't have lots of money, so we can't retire.]

           main clause   subordinate clause
Frank *would* be a fine musician if he *practiced.* [Frank is not a fine musician because he does not practice.]

Past unreal conditions

These sentences tell about situations that could have occurred but that did not occur in the past. Use *would have, could have,* or *might have* with a past participle in the main clause and *if* with the past perfect in the subordinate clause.

       subordinate clause   main clause
If you *had registered* early, you *would have avoided* these crowds.

           main clause   subordinate clause
You *could have passed* the test *if* you *had studied* harder.

Hope and *wish*

Sentences using the verb *hope* or *wish* are like conditional sentences because they discuss situations that may not happen.

Use the past tense to express a wish about the present or the future.

I *wish* I *had* a million dollars. [I don't have a million dollars.]

I *wish* I *were going* home tomorrow. [I am not going home tomorrow.]

Use the past perfect to express wishes about the past.

Laura *wishes* that she *had studied* biology. [She did not study biology.]

Jim *wishes* that he *had* not *dropped* out of school. [He did drop out of school.]

Use the present tense or the future tense to express hopes for things that could possibly happen.

I *hope* I *pass* my driver's test.

I *hope* you *will come* to our anniversary party.

19r | Learning idiomatic expressions

Idiomatic expressions, or idioms, are phrases that mean something different than the literal meaning of the individual words in the expressions. For example, the idiom *to make ends meet* means to take care of all one's financial obligations, but with some difficulty and no surplus money. The expression does not mean literally to put two ends of something next to each other.

Each language has its own idiomatic expressions, which usually do not translate well into other languages. If you want to speak and write good English, you need to understand and use its idioms.

EXERCISE 1   Choosing Count and Noncount Nouns

Underline or circle the correct count and noncount nouns in the following sentences. Example:

He does not eat (*bread*/*breads*) because he is allergic to wheat.

1. You are putting too much (*butter*/*butters*) on your (*toast*/*toasts*).

2. All these (*bowl*/*bowls*) are made of (*wood*/*woods*).

3. I can't take your photograph because there is not enough (*light*/*lights*).

4. I cleaned the bookcase three (*time*/*times*) to get all the (*dust*/*dusts*) off.

5. A month after I got a cat, all my (*furniture*/*furnitures*) was covered with cat (*hair*/*hairs*).

EXERCISE 2   Writing with Count and Noncount Nouns

Use each of the following words or phrases in a sentence. Example:

all my luggage

By mistake, all my luggage was sent to Dallas instead of to Fort Smith.

1. a lot of makeup

2. knowledge

3. very little time

4. some of the jewelry

5. the furniture in their living room

EXERCISE 3   Choosing Definite and Indefinite Articles

Complete the following sentences by adding the appropriate articles (*a, an, the*) in the space provided. If no article is needed, leave the space blank. Example:

<u>The</u> woman next door likes to give me _____ advice.

1. _____ soup you made for me was _____ best I have ever tasted.

2. Bernice has _____ unusual voice.

3. I walked around in _____ museum for about _____ hour.

4. I think that _____ patience is necessary when working with _____ children.

5. _____ man sitting in _____ row of _____ auditorium wants to ask _____ speaker _____ question.

EXERCISE 4   Writing with Definite and Indefinite Articles

Use each of the following phrases in a sentence. Example:

honesty and loyalty

Two qualities that I value in people are honesty and loyalty.

1. the red sweater

2. an onion and a clove of garlic

3. tell the truth

4. ambition and hard work

5. modern furniture

EXERCISE 5 Choosing Quantifiers

Underline or circle the correct quantifiers in the following sentences. Example:

You have put (*too much*/*too many*) furniture in this little room.

1. This coat costs only (*a little*/*a few*) dollars more than the other one.

2. They studied biology for (*many*/*a great deal of*) hours.

3. I cannot go out because I have (*too much*/*too many*) homework to do.

4. (*How much*/*How many*) eggs do you need for the pumpkin pie?

5. The doctor asked him (*how much*/*how many*) cups of coffee he drank each day.

Name _____ Section _____ Date _____

EXERCISE 6   Writing with Quantifiers

Use each suggested phrase that follows in a sentence. Example:

a lot of good advice

My parents always gave me a lot of good advice, but I didn't always follow it.

1. a lot of jewelry

2. some fruit

3. very little furniture

4. too much dust

5. too many people

EXERCISE 7   Choosing Demonstratives

Underline or circle the correct demonstratives in the following sentences. Example:

(*That*/*Those*) cereal contains a lot of sodium and sugar.

1. I can't leave until I have finished (*this*/*these*) work.

2. All of (*this*/*these*) dirty dishes in the kitchen sink must be washed.

3. Several of (*that/those*) books are overdue at the library.

4. Put your packages over here on (*this/these*) table.

5. The Diaz family lives in (*that/those*) house with the green door.

EXERCISE 8 Choosing Possessive Adjectives and Possessive Pronouns

Underline or circle the correct possessive pronouns and possessive adjectives in the following sentences. Example:

That umbrella is (*my/<u>mine</u>/mines*), not (*your/your's/<u>yours</u>*).

1. (*My/mine*) house is a bit smaller than (*their/theirs/their's*).

2. The firm is relocating (*its/it's*) executive offices in Connecticut.

3. When I won the lottery, suddenly I was (*everybodys/everybody's*) best friend.

4. There is no name on this paper, so I can't tell (*who's/whose*) it is.

5. (*Our/Ours*) apartment is across the hall from (*her/her's/hers*).

EXERCISE 9 Writing with Possessive Adjectives and Possessive Pronouns

Use each of the following phrases in a sentence. Example:

her responsibility, not yours

Walking the dog is her responsibility, not yours.

1. their jobs

2. his idea, not mine

3. everyone's favorite singer

4. whose briefcase

5. the team and all its coaches

EXERCISE 10   Using Correct Word Order in Writing

For each word set that follows, first give the correct word order, and then use the phrase in a sentence. Example:

interesting/some/very/books

some very interesting books

I have just borrowed some very interesting books from the library.

1. first/job/serious/my

2. living room/not much /furniture/comfortable

3. important/a/very/interview

4. first/doctor/the/female

5. vacation/summer/your/last

EXERCISE 11   Ordering and Punctuating Series of Adjectives

Rewrite and punctuate each word set that follows, using *and* where necessary. Then use each phrase in a sentence. Example:

elegant/an/actor/sophisticated/polished

an elegant, sophisticated, polished actor

This role calls for an actor who is polished, elegant, and sophisticated.

1. a/woman/Vietnamese/young

2. somebody's/notebook/gray/tattered

3. yellow/some/pears/ripe

4. energetic/grandmother/healthy/your

5. brat/whining/spoiled/selfish/a

EXERCISE 12   Choosing Present and Past Participles as Adjectives

Underline or circle the correct adjectives in the following sentences. Example:

I am (*interesting*/*interested*) in astronomy.

1. The last movie we went to see was (*boring/bored*), but I am not at all (*boring/bored*) by this one.

2. My daughter was really (*surprising/surprised*) when she first saw snow.

3. A (*satisfying/satisfied*) customer will return to the store again; a (*dissatisfying/dissatisfied*) customer will not.

4. The six-day geology field trip was (*exhausting/exhausted*), but we did learn some (*fascinating/fascinated*) things.

5. The air conditioner was making an (*irritating/irritated*) noise.

EXERCISE 13   Writing with Present and Past Participles as Adjectives

Use each suggested phrase that follows in a sentence. Example:

a frightening experience

Riding that rollercoaster was a frightening experience, at least for me.

1. an exhilarating experience

2. an irritated yet somewhat pleased expression

3. worried and alarmed

4. a very depressing sight

5. delighted with your work

EXERCISE 14   Choosing Forms of *be, have,* and *do*

Underline or circle the correct form of *be, have,* or *do* in the following sentences. Example:

We (*was/were*) just about to eat dinner when you called.

1. Seventeen people (*is/are/be*) in line at the bus stop.

2. I (*am/be*) surprised to see you; I thought you (*was/were*) out of town.

3. The Cuevas family has lived in Rhode Island longer than we (*has/have*).

4. I can type a lot faster than Alice (*does/do*).

5. We (*have/had*) to take the dog to the veterinarian yesterday because he (*was/were/be*) attacked by a porcupine.

EXERCISE 15   Writing with forms of *be, have,* and *do*

Use each phrase or set of phrases that follows in a sentence. Example:

I am, he is

I am a little bit taller than he is.

1. they did

2. we have

3. I was, they were

4. he is, they are

5. she does, they do

EXERCISE 16   Forming Progressive Verb Tenses

Rewrite each sentence that follows using the suggested progressive verb tense and changing other words as necessary to maintain clarity and sense. Example:

I go to work at seven-thirty each morning.

Present progressive: I am going to work right now.

1. We will start our project soon.
   Future progressive:

2. He typed his term paper yesterday.

   Past progressive:

3. She watches the news at six every evening.

   Present progressive:

4. He drove a taxi for a living.

   Past progressive:

5. He irons his shirts and even his jeans.

   Present progressive:

EXERCISE 17   Forming Perfect Verb Tenses

Rewrite each sentence that follows using the indicated perfect tense and changing other words as necessary to maintain clarity and sense. Example:

I saw that movie last week.

Present progressive: I have seen that movie three times.

1. She ran in the New York marathon last year.

   Present perfect:

2. On our vacation, we went to Australia.

   Past perfect:

3. He will graduate from business school next June.

   Future perfect:

4. They live in Arizona.

   Present perfect progressive:

5. You worked at the restaurant for three years.

   Past perfect progressive:

EXERCISE 18   Forming the Passive Voice

Rewrite the following sentences in the passive voice without changing the tense of verbs. Example:

After the snowstorm, they plowed the streets.

After the snowstorm, the streets were plowed.

1. Voters reelected the congresswoman by a large margin.

2. They speak French in Haiti.

3. By tomorrow, the judge will have decided on the case.

4. They will announce the winners of the contest tonight.

5. They have released a new *Star Trek* movie.

EXERCISE 19   Writing with Progressive and Perfect Verb Tenses

Use each verb phrase that follows in a sentence. Example:

have lived

They have lived in Portland all their lives.

1. has known

2. are working

3. have been driving

4. had discovered

5. were frowning

EXERCISE 20   Writing with Modal Auxiliaries

Use each verb phrase that follows in a sentence. Example:

could not speak

When she first came to New York, she could not speak English.

1. should tell

2. should have called

3. must pass

4. would finish

5. might have found

EXERCISE 21   Choosing Infinitives and Gerunds

Underline or circle the correct infinitives and gerunds in the following sentences. Example:

She intends (*to go*/*going*) to law school after college.

1. He expected (*to find*/*finding*) the kitchen in a mess, but the children had cleaned it.

2. Every winter, I look forward to (*watch*/*watching*) baseball again in the spring.

3. She regretted (*to drop/dropping*) out of college after three semesters.

4. Their boss won't let them (*to take/take/taking*) their vacation now.

5. During snow emergencies, the city does not allow (*to park/parking*) on major streets.

6. We convinced her not (*to quit/quit/quitting*) her job.

7. I had no milk at home, so this afternoon I stopped (*to buy/buying*) some.

8. The candidate denied (*to spend/spending*) campaign money for personal use.

9. We offered (*to lend/lending*) him some money, but he refused (*to accept/accepting*) it.

10. He apologized for (*to forget/forget/forgetting*) my birthday.

EXERCISE 22   Writing with Infinitives

Use each infinitive phrase that follows in a sentence. Example:

persuaded (someone) to take

After many discussions, I finally persuaded Elena to take the job.

1. forgot to call

2. asked (someone) to paint

3. told (someone) to study

4. arrange to babysit

5. deserve to win

EXERCISE 23   Writing with Gerunds

Use each gerund phrase that follows in a sentence. Example:

appreciate your helping

We really appreciate your helping us change the flat tire.

1. accuse (someone) of shoplifting

2. began looking

3. stopped playing golf

4. do not believe in spending

5. wouldn't dream of hurting

EXERCISE 24   Writing with Phrasal Verbs

Use each phrasal verb that follows in a sentence. Example:

calm down

After she won the race, it took her awhile to calm down.

1. get along with

2. look for

3. cut out

4. add up

5. throw away

EXERCISE 25   Choosing Prepositions

Underline or circle the correct prepositions in the following sentences. Example:

I will pick you up (*in/on/at*) the airport.

1. A short course in first aid will be given (*in/on/at*) Saturday morning.

2. She is a science teacher (*in/on/at*) North Adams, Massachusetts.

3. There were two kittens playing (*in/on/at/into*) the pet store window.

4. The ball rolled along the sidewalk and (*in/on/at/into*) the street.

5. My first class starts (*in/on/at/into*) 8:15 a.m.

EXERCISE 26   Choosing Adverb Placement

Rewrite each sentence using the italicized adverb or adverbial phrase. Example:

(*never*)   I have spoken to him.

I have never spoken to him.

1. (*always*)   Kendra was an attentive student.

2. (*in the office lobby*)   I waited for a few minutes before the elevator arrived.

3. (*nervously*)   He waited in the dentist's office.

4. (*completely*)   She was surprised when she received the promotion.

5. (*almost never*)   They have been sick.

EXERCISE 27   Writing with Adverbs

Use each adverb or adverbial phrase that follows in a sentence. Example:

totally

The car was totally wrecked in the accident, but nobody was hurt.

1. anxiously

2. in the rearview mirror

3. always

4. seldom

5. quickly

EXERCISE 28   Changing Direct Speech to Indirect Discourse

Rewrite the following sentences, changing direct speech (including questions, invitations, and commands) to indirect discourse. Example:

"The hurricane will hit Florida by midmorning," she said.

She said that the hurricane would hit Florida by midmorning.

1. "I'm hungry," the little boy complained.

2. "We are going to change registration procedures," said the dean.

3. "The repairs on the bridge have been completed," said the engineer.

4. "With these improvements, air pollution will decrease," she reported.

5. "She can speak German and Spanish," he insisted.

6. "When will the lecture start?" they asked.

7. "Date each set of lab notes," the professor said.

8. "Was the medication tested in double-blind experiments?" the reporter asked.

9. "The graduation rate in the high schools must be improved," the chancellor said.

10. "Please join the debating team," we told her.

EXERCISE 29   Working with Conditional Sentences

Rewrite each set of sentences that follows as a conditional sentence. Example:

I suggest you start your term paper early. That way, you will have time to make revisions.

If you start your term paper early, you will have time to make revisions.

1. The weather is hot and dry. Crops do not grow well.

2. You did not turn off your headlights. Your car battery needs recharging.

3. I suggest we leave for the movie theater now. That way, we will get there before the movie starts.

4. I am not athletic, so I will not be a professional baseball player.

5. She saw the Goodyear blimp. She got very nervous.

6. You get seasick. You cannot go sailing with us.

7. He dropped out of school. He did not graduate with the rest of his friends.

8. I suggest you make up a budget and stick to it. That way, you will not run out of money before the end of the month.

9. Alice probably won't learn to play the piano. She does not have the time.

10. They lost the directions to my house. They were late to the party.

EXERCISE 30 Using *hope* and *wish* in Sentences

Rewrite each of the following sentences using *hope* or *wish* and changing other words as needed. Example:

Andrew quit his job.

Andrew wishes that he had not quit his job.

1. Xiomara did not major in political science.

2. I may not be able to find a job after graduation.

3. We are not going on vacation this summer.

4. I probably can't get a football scholarship.

5. You might not find your wallet.

PART SEVEN

Clear and Effective Sentences

CHAPTER 20

Sentence Fragments

A sentence fragment often looks like a sentence, beginning with a capital letter and ending with a period. The fragment, however, is not a sentence because it is incomplete. A fragment may lack a subject or a complete verb; it may lack a complete idea. A dependent clause standing by itself is a fragment because the idea in the dependent clause is not complete.

20a Correcting sentence fragments

Many fragments can be corrected by supplying the missing sentence part. Look at the following examples:

FRAGMENT   Insisted on doing what he had planned to do in the first place. [The subject is missing: *Who* insisted?]

REVISED   Mr. Weston insisted on doing what he had planned to do in the first place.

FRAGMENT   Two consecutive years of declining sales. [There is no verb: what did those two years *do*?]

REVISED   Two consecutive years of declining sales brought the company close to bankruptcy.

FRAGMENT   The audience cheering enthusiastically. [The verb is incomplete; *-ing* verb forms need a helping verb.]

REVISED   The audience was cheering enthusiastically.

FRAGMENT   Since Audrey entered medical school. [The idea is incomplete. One way to revise the fragment is to omit the word *since*, but that would result in a short, abrupt sentence. A better revision would be to add an independent clause to complete the idea.]

REVISED   Audrey entered medical school.

REVISED   Since Audrey entered medical school, she has had practically no free time.

Consult the following checklist to make sure you find and revise the fragments in your writing.

CHECKING FOR SENTENCE FRAGMENTS

1. Locate the subject. If the subject is missing, there is no sentence.
2. Locate the verb. Make sure the verb is complete. A participle, gerund, or infinitive alone cannot function as the main verb in a sentence.
3. Look for subordinate conjunctions at the start of clauses. Make sure every sentence has at least one independent clause.
4. Look for relative pronouns (*who, whom, which, that*) at the start of clauses. If a relative pronoun introduces a clause, that clause cannot stand alone as a complete sentence, unless the clause is a question.

Revising fragments

You can revise a fragment by making it an independent clause or by combining it with an independent clause.

FRAGMENT   The flood waters rising over the riverbanks.

REVISED   The flood waters were rising over the riverbanks.

REVISED   The flood waters rose over the riverbanks.

REVISED   The townspeople fearfully watched the flood waters rising over the riverbanks.

REVISED   The flood waters, rising over the riverbanks, carried away fences, cars, and even houses.

Often, the fragment can be combined with the complete sentence that comes before or after it, as in the following examples:

FAULTY   The roads were impassable. *Because the blizzard had dropped fifteen inches of snow.*

REVISED   The roads were impassable because the blizzard had dropped fifteen inches of snow.

FAULTY   *As soon as the contractions are ten minutes apart.* A woman in labor should call her doctor.

REVISED   As soon as the contractions are ten minutes apart, a woman in labor should call her doctor.

| 20b | Revising phrase fragments |

Phrases (groups of related words lacking a subject and predicate) sometimes appear as sentence fragments. Verbal phrases and prepositional phrases often are set apart, thus creating fragments.

| 1 | Verbal phrase fragments |

A verbal phrase consists of an infinitive, a present participle, a past participle, or a gerund, and any objects or modifiers. Verbal phrase fragments can usually be combined with the independent clause they are related to. They can also be rewritten as independent clauses. Note the verbal phrase fragments in the following examples:

FRAGMENT   She drove very slowly down the steep, icy road. *Keeping the truck in first gear.*

REVISED   She drove very slowly down the steep, icy road, keeping the truck in first gear.

FRAGMENT   Displayed on the table was a piece of beautiful, old embroidery. *Protected by a glass cover.*

REVISED   Displayed on the table was a piece of beautiful, old embroidery, protected by a glass cover.

FRAGMENT   The runner had one goal. *To beat his own record in the mile run.*

REVISED   The runner had one goal, to beat his own record in the mile run.

FRAGMENT   The family shared various activities during the holidays. *Making ornaments for the Christmas tree.*

REVISED   The family shared various activities during the holidays. Making ornaments for the Christmas tree was a traditional activity.

| 2 | Prepositional phrase fragments |

A prepositional phrase consists of a preposition and its object and any modifiers. Prepositional phrases are not complete ideas and, therefore, should not be punctuated as separate sentences. A prepositional phrase fragment can be corrected by combining it with the previous sentence or by adding a subject and a verb. Note the prepositional phrase fragments in the following examples:

FRAGMENT   All residents received a pamphlet describing voter registration. *In Spanish as well as English.*

REVISED   All residents received a pamphlet describing voter registration in Spanish as well as English.

FRAGMENT   The mayor proposed giving free immunizations. *To all children, not just those in public school.*

REVISED   The mayor proposed giving free immunizations. All children, not just those in public school, would receive them.

3 | Noun phrase fragments

A noun phrase consists of a noun along with any words, phrases, or clauses that modify it. Noun phrase fragments have a subject but that subject lacks a verb. Such fragments can be corrected by adding a verb and other words. Some noun phrase fragments are followed by another fragment containing a verb but no subject. These fragments can be revised by joining the noun phrase fragment and the verb fragment. Note the noun phrase fragments in the following examples:

FRAGMENT   *An old station wagon with a large dog sitting in the backseat.*

REVISED   Parked in front of the coffee shop was an old station wagon with a large dog sitting in the back seat.

FRAGMENT   *A person thinking about going to medical school. Must take many science courses, beginning in the first year.*

REVISED   A person thinking about going to medical school must take many science courses, beginning in the freshman year.

4 | Appositive phrase fragments

Appositives are nouns, or nouns and their modifiers, that rename or describe other nouns. An appositive is not a complete idea and cannot stand alone as a sentence. It should be combined with the word it describes or renames. Note the appositive phrase fragment in the following example:

FRAGMENT   I admire Buster Keaton's *The General. A movie set during the Civil War.*

REVISED   I admire Buster Keaton's *The General*, a movie set during the Civil War.

20c | Revising compound predicate fragments

Compound predicates contain two or more verbs and their objects. Compound predicate fragments occur when the second predicate is set off as a separate sentence even though it does not have a subject. To correct a compound predicate fragment, join it to the preceding independent clause, as in this example:

FRAGMENT   The jury deliberated for three days. *And found the defendant guilty.*

REVISED   The jury deliberated for three days and found the defendant guilty.

| **20d** | **Revising dependent clause fragments** |

A dependent clause has a subject and a verb, but it cannot stand alone as a sentence because it does not express a complete idea. A dependent clause must be accompanied by at least one independent clause to complete its meaning.

Dependent clauses begin with a subordinating conjunction, such as *because, if, when,* or *unless,* or with a relative pronoun, such as *who, which,* or *that.* You can correct a dependent clause fragment by combining it with the independent clause that precedes or follows the fragment. Alternatively, you can change the fragment into an independent clause. Note the dependent clause fragments in the following examples:

FRAGMENT   The letter offering a scholarship finally arrived. *Just as Elsa was about to give up hope.*

REVISED   The letter offering a scholarship finally arrived, just as Elsa was about to give up hope.

FRAGMENT   *After graduating from college in 1967.* Bob spent two years in the Peace Corps.

REVISED   Bob graduated from college in 1967. He then spent two years in the Peace Corps.

One way to tell if a clause is dependent or independent is to try changing it into a question that can be answered with *yes* or *no.* If the clause can be changed easily into a *yes/no* question, it is probably an independent clause. Dependent clauses often cannot be changed into questions that make sense. Here are some examples:

My sister-in-law is a geologist. [The sentence can be easily changed into the question "Is my sister-in-law a geologist?"; therefore, the sentence is an independent clause.]

Whenever we go hiking in the mountains. [The question "Are whenever we go hiking in the mountains?" does not make sense; therefore, this example is a dependent clause—and a fragment.]

Situations that can lead to sentence fragments

Certain writing choices can occasionally lead to fragments. Be alert for constructions that can lead to fragments. Use the following guidelines to assess your writing for sentence fragments.

1.   When using subordinating words to begin a sentence, make sure the sentence also has an independent clause. Here are some common subordinating words:

after	even if	so that	whether
although	even though	that	which
as	how	though	while
as if	if	unless	who
as soon as	in order that	until	whose
as though	now that	when	
because	since	where	

Note how fragments have been revised in the following examples:

FRAGMENT   *Although he is relatively small.* He is a great football player.

REVISED   Although he is relatively small, he is a great football player.

FRAGMENT   Many people are buying the book *The Age of Innocence. Which was made into a movie in 1993.*

REVISED   Many people are buying the book *The Age of Innocence,* which was made into a movie in 1993.

2.   When using transitional words or phrases to introduce examples or a list, make sure those words are combined with an independent clause. The following list contains some commonly used transitional words and phrases:

also	especially	in addition	namely	such as
and	for example	like	that is	as well as
but	for instance	mainly		

Note how the fragment has been revised in this example:

FRAGMENT   Many people are unhappy with the new tax proposals. *Especially people whose taxes will go up.*

REVISED   Many people are unhappy with the new tax proposals, especially people whose taxes will go up.

3.   When using an infinitive to begin a sentence, make sure the sentence also contains a complete verb. An infinitive phrase fragment can be combined with an independent clause, or it can be rewritten as a separate, complete thought. Note how the fragment has been revised in the following example:

FRAGMENT   A city ordinance requires tenants to cover most of the floor in each room with a rug. *To keep noise from disturbing neighbors.*

REVISED   A city ordinance requires tenants to cover most of the floor in each room with a rug to keep noise from disturbing neighbors.

REVISED   A city ordinance requires tenants to cover most of the floor in each room with a rug. A rug keeps noise from disturbing neighbors.

4.   When using present or past participles as modifiers to begin a sentence, make sure the sentence also has an independent clause. Present and past participle fragments can be corrected by combining them with an independent clause. Note how these fragments have been revised:

FRAGMENT   *Crashing into a teammate on the soccer team.* She sprained her wrist.

REVISED   Crashing into a teammate on the soccer team, she sprained her wrist.

FRAGMENT   *Angered by the lack of a new contract.* The hockey players voted to go on strike.

REVISED   Angered by the lack of a new contract, the hockey players voted to go on strike.

20e | Using acceptable fragments

Sentence fragments are only rarely used in academic and formal writing. However, fragments are occasionally acceptable in informal writing. Experienced writers sometimes use them to achieve special effects, particularly for emphasis. Articles in popular magazines sometimes use fragments; advertisements often contain sentence fragments. Unless you want to give your writing an informal style or you wish to use a fragment for emphasis, avoid sentence fragments in your academic and professional writing.

EXERCISE 1 Identifying Fragments

Identify each sentence that follows as a fragment or a complete thought. Example:

The weather forecast predicts sleet.   complete thought

As soon as the dry cleaning store is open.   fragment

1. Before anyone can take physics.   _____

2. Even though I had a fever and a bad cold.   _____

3. In the top drawer of the bureau at the end of the hall.   _____

4. Nobody came to the party.   _____

5. Extremely tired after working double shifts for a week.   _____

EXERCISE 2 Revising Fragments

Rewrite each fragment that follows so that it contains a complete thought. Example:

Because my son needed a decongestant.

I went out last night at 11 p.m. to the all-night drugstore because my son needed a decongestant.

1. When the football team finally had a winning season.

2. Told the employees that they would have to work overtime all week.

3. A well-researched, well-written article about genetic diseases.

4. Responsibilities along with privileges.

5. Raising money for the new wing of the hospital.

EXERCISE 3   Revising Fragments in Paragraphs

Each paragraph that follows contains one or more fragments. Rewrite the paragraphs to eliminate the fragments. Example:

As technology has advanced. Computers have become smaller and smaller. Many companies now make portable, battery-operated computers. Some as light as six pounds.

As technology has advanced, computers have become smaller and smaller. Many companies now make portable, battery-operated computers, some as light as six pounds.

1.   Some American educators have suggested that children in public school should wear uniforms. As is done in many other countries. Uniforms, these educators feel, would give children a sense of school pride. And make it easier to identify which school children attend.

2.   In the movie *Jurassic Park,* based on the novel of the same name. Scientists create dinosaurs from scraps of dinosaur DNA found preserved in amber. Currently, such genetic engineering is not possible. Although the movie made it seem quite plausible.

3.   Years ago, Americans were taught that a balanced diet included equal portions from the four food groups. Milk and dairy products, meat and fish, grains and breads, and fruits and vegetables. Today, because the first two groups are high in fat and low in fiber. A diet based on the old four food groups is considered dangerous.

4.   Although many people think that the verb *to discriminate* means to treat someone unfairly on the basis of race, gender, or religion. The verb also means to perceive the distinguishing features of someone or something. It can also mean to tell the difference between things. Or to show good judgment.

5.   In Italy recently, a 59-year-old English woman gave birth to twins. After she received treatment to reverse the effects of menopause. Donated eggs fertilized in a test tube by her husband's sperm were inserted into her uterus. Two of the implanted eggs developed. Resulting in the birth of normal twins.

EXERCISE 4   Correcting Phrase Fragments

Rewrite the following as needed to eliminate phrase fragments. Note that some are correct as written. Example:

Universal health care would include all citizens. Not just those who can afford health insurance.

Universal health care would include all citizens, not just those who can afford health insurance.

1. Several important letters that I had been expecting. Never were delivered to me.

2. Trying to reach a bowl on the top shelf of the cabinet. I accidentally knocked a glass to the floor.

3. The town swimming pool, athletic fields, and tennis courts are open. Only to town residents and their guests.

4. The most interesting movie I saw that year was *The Piano*. A movie that was directed by Jane Campion, an Australian.

5. The election was very close. Neither candidate, however, has asked for a recount.

EXERCISE 5 Revising Phrase Fragments

Rewrite each phrase fragment that follows so that it contains a complete thought. Example:

Fragment: without thinking about the consequences

We cannot plan a new dam without thinking about the consequences to the environment.

1. a coach who never shouted at or humiliated the players

2. vaccines for mumps, measles, and rubella

3. on the walls as well as all over the floor

4. knowing that his parents wouldn't be back before midnight

5. delayed by heavy traffic on Route 280

EXERCISE 6   Revising Compound Predicate Fragments

Rewrite the following as needed to eliminate compound predicate fragments. Note that some are correct as written. Example:

He locked the car doors. But forgot to roll up the windows.

He locked the car doors but forgot to roll up the windows.

1. The preacher spoke for nearly an hour. And then took a short break before beginning again.

2. The deer was caught in some ice in the river. It couldn't get free.

3. She learned American Sign Language as a child. And later worked for a television station as a translator for the deaf.

4. They have never had a bank account. Or used a credit card in all their lives.

5. The office building was put up two years ago. But not occupied until last month.

EXERCISE 7   Revising Dependent Clause Fragments

Rewrite the following as needed to eliminate dependent clause fragments. Note that some are correct as written. Example:

When he turned on the microwave oven. A fuse blew.

When he turned on the microwave oven, a fuse blew.

1. However hard the child tried. She couldn't open the refrigerator.

2. Although they bought a CD player a few weeks ago. They still have not figured out how to use it.

3. Often, a patient's blood pressure will go down. When the patient pets a dog or a cat.

4. If you do not send in your application this week. You will miss the deadline.

5. I cannot read the return address on this letter. That I received this morning.

EXERCISE 8   Revising Fragments in Paragraphs

Rewrite each of the following paragraphs to eliminate fragments. Example:

Athletes seem to get bigger every year. An obvious statement to make about basketball and football players, but also true in professional tennis. Lately, the tennis players with most consistent success seem to be those. Who are above average in height.

Athletes seem to get bigger every year. That is an obvious statement to make about basketball and football players, but also true in professional tennis. Lately, the tennis players with most consistent success seem to be those who are about average in height.

1.   Although some people have trouble balancing their checkbooks. It really is not such a difficult task. Of course, if people have forgotten to enter some of the checks they have written. Balancing the checkbook may be nearly impossible.

2.   Some people think that wearing the skins and furs of animals is a barbaric practice. While others don't find it barbaric, just unnecessary. On the other hand, still others point out that many people would be out of work. If the fur industry did not exist.

3.   The standards for acceptable public behavior. Have changed a great deal over the years. Nowhere is this change seen more than at stadiums and hockey arenas. Where fans now routinely jeer, curse, and throw objects at the players.

4.   For a baseball fan, it is astonishing to realize. That Hank Aaron was born in 1934. In fact, he began his major league career in 1954. And didn't retire until 1976. Two years after breaking Babe Ruth's home-run record.

5.   Although the sandwich was not invented by John Montagu, the first earl of Sandwich. It was named after him. The earl was a gambler who was so reluctant to leave the gambling tables. That he preferred to eat food placed between slices of bread rather than sitting down to a formal meal.

EXERCISE 9   Using Complete Sentences in Writing

For each topic that follows, write a brief paragraph of three to five sentences. Make sure each sentence in the paragraph expresses a complete idea.

Topic: Television home shopping programs

Home shopping programs on television are obviously popular, but the merchandise sold on them is not always a bargain. In fact, people who check flyers and advertisements in newspapers can often get the same products for much lower prices than those charged by the home shopping shows. On the other hand, shopping by TV and telephone does not take a lot of time or energy.

1. Athletes as role models

2. Television cameras in courtrooms

3. The best age to get married

4. Choosing a major

5. Your most memorable birthday

EXERCISE 10   Considering Intentional Fragments

Choose two advertisements from magazines or newspapers and look for fragments in the text. What effects do the fragments have? Rewrite the advertisements to eliminate the fragments. Then describe how the advertisements have changed and why they are more or less effective than before.

CHAPTER 21

Comma Splices and Fused Sentences

A sentence that continues past its logical stopping point and into the next sentence with no end punctuation can confuse and irritate readers. Often, these run-on sentences are ambiguous because they can be interpreted in more than one way, leaving the reader uncertain of which meaning the writer intends. It is not the reader's job to figure out which of several possible meanings the writer really intends; rather, it is the writer's job to communicate that meaning clearly.

There are two kinds of run-on sentences: comma splices and fused sentences. In a comma splice, the comma is the only punctuation between independent clauses. In a fused sentence, there is no punctuation between the two complete ideas. Look at the following examples:

COMMA SPLICE   The train is delayed, we will be late for work.

FUSED SENTENCE   The train is delayed we will be late for work.

COMMA SPLICE   I made breakfast, after walking the dog, I went to work.

FUSED SENTENCE   I made breakfast after walking the dog I went to work.

The last example shows just how confusing a run-on can be: Did I walk the dog before or after making breakfast? The meaning is unclear. As you will see, there are six ways to fix comma splices and fused sentences.

21a Dividing clauses into separate sentences

Often, the quickest and most convenient way to correct run-on sentences is to put a period after each independent clause.

COMMA SPLICE   Although the dancer is thin, he is very strong, his looks are deceiving.

FUSED SENTENCE   Although the dancer is thin he is very strong his looks are deceiving.

REVISED   Although the dancer is thin, he is very strong. His looks are deceiving.

21b Joining clauses with a semicolon

Sometimes a fused sentence or a comma splice occurs because the writer wants to emphasize that the two independent clauses are closely related and of equal importance. The comma, however, is not a sufficiently strong punctuation mark to signal the end of one complete idea. In this case, then, use a semicolon to join the independent clauses.

COMMA SPLICE	For weight loss, exercise is not enough, dieting is also necessary.
FUSED SENTENCE	For weight loss exercise is not enough dieting is also necessary.
REVISED	For weight loss, exercise is not enough; dieting is also necessary.

21c Joining clauses with a semicolon and a conjunctive adverb

Comma splices and fused sentences can be corrected with a semicolon and a conjunctive adverb. Conjunctive adverbs (e.g., *however, therefore, moreover, consequently,* and *furthermore*) are signal words but not conjunctions; thus they are not punctuated in the same way as coordinating conjunctions. A clause containing a conjunctive adverb must always follow a period or a semicolon.

COMMA SPLICE	The meeting starts at ten, however, I will be a little late.
FUSED SENTENCE	The meeting starts at ten however I will be a little late.
REVISED	The meeting starts at ten; however, I will be a little late.

A conjunctive adverb is not always placed at the beginning of a clause; it may instead be placed in the middle or at the end of a clause. Wherever it is placed, the conjunctive adverb is always marked off by one or two commas.

COMMA SPLICE	The telephone system has not yet been installed, the office therefore is not usable.
FUSED SENTENCE	The telephone system has not yet been installed the office therefore is not usable.
REVISED	The telephone system has not yet been installed; the office, therefore, is not usable.
COMMA SPLICE	This old truck seems useless, its spare parts may come in handy however.
FUSED SENTENCE	This old truck seems useless its spare parts may come in handy however.
REVISED	This old truck seems useless; its spare parts may come in handy, however.

As you will notice in the preceding examples, conjunctive adverbs can be placed in different positions in a clause.

21d Joining clauses with a comma and a coordinating conjunction

If two independent clauses are of equal importance, you can join them with a comma and a coordinating conjunction—*and, or, but, for, nor, yet,* or *so.* Be sure to put the comma before, not after, the coordinating conjunction.

COMMA SPLICE	The weather was always warm, it never rained during the day.
FUSED SENTENCE	The weather was always warm it never rained during the day.
REVISED	The weather was always warm, *and* it never rained during the day.
COMMA SPLICE	I am majoring in history, I had considered political science.
FUSED SENTENCE	I am majoring in history I had considered political science.
REVISED	I am majoring in history, *but* I had considered political science.
COMMA SPLICE	It was raining hard, the game was canceled.
FUSED SENTENCE	It was raining hard the game was canceled.
REVISED	It was raining hard, *so* the game was canceled.

21e Converting two clauses into a single independent clause

If the two clauses of a run-on sentence are somewhat repetitious, the best way to revise is to combine the ideas into one independent clause.

COMMA SPLICE	The soft feet of a camel do not scuff up topsoil, the topsoil does not blow away.
FUSED SENTENCE	The soft feet of a camel do not scuff up topsoil the topsoil does not blow away.
REVISED	The soft feet of a camel do not scuff up topsoil, *causing it to blow away.*

The revised sentence is more precise and less repetitious than the other two versions.

21f Converting one of two independent clauses into a dependent clause

Often in a comma splice or a fused sentence, one idea is more important than the other. In such a case, you can turn the less important idea into a dependent clause by beginning it with a subordinating conjunction. Some common subordinating conjunctions are *because, when, since, although, if,* and *while.*

COMMA SPLICE	Basketball has become very popular in Italy, soccer is still the national craze.
FUSED SENTENCE	Basketball has become very popular in Italy soccer is still the national craze.
REVISED	*Although* basketball has become very popular in Italy, soccer is still the national craze.
COMMA SPLICE	Elizabeth Cady Stanton could not become a lawyer, the law profession did not admit women in her day.
FUSED SENTENCE	Elizabeth Cady Stanton could not become a lawyer the law profession did not admit women in her day.
REVISED	Elizabeth Cady Stanton could not become a lawyer *because* the law profession did not admit women in her day.

21g   Using comma splices and fused sentences appropriately

Some writers use run-on sentences deliberately to create a particular effect. Many comma splices in a row, for example, create an effect of confusion and disorientation. In his novel *The Autumn of the Patriarch,* Gabriel García Marquez uses no periods or other end punctuation except at the end of every chapter. This technique mirrors very effectively the bewilderment and tangled memories of the novel's central character, an aging dictator. Poets may use fused sentences to give an effect of speed and connection; regular punctuation might slow down and separate the ideas. However, in your academic and professional writing, avoid comma splices and fused sentences. The purpose of such writing is to clarify, not to confuse.

EXERCISE 1   Identifying Comma Splices and Fused Sentences

Identify each run-on as a comma splice or a fused sentence. (Some sentences may be correct as written.) Example:

The city was practically deserted it was easy to find a parking space.   <u>fused sentence</u>

1. I lost my lab notes they are somewhere in this messy room. _____

2. Aleksandr Pushkin was a Russian writer, his great grandfather was the black general Abram Hannibal. _____

3. Harpo Marx was one of the famous comic Marx Brothers, he got his nickname because he played the harp. _____

4. Certain seals are born with white fur, then over time their coat slowly darkens to gray. _____

5. Hope, Arkansas, is the childhood home of President Clinton in 1990 its population was nearly ten thousand. _____

EXERCISE 2   Dividing Run-ons into Separate Sentences

Correct the run-ons as needed by separating the two independent clauses with a period. (Some of the sentences may be correct as written.) Example:

Disney Studios has produced many movies based on fairytales some examples are *Beauty and the Beast, Aladdin,* and *Snow White.*

Disney Studios has produced many movies based on fairytales. Some examples are *Beauty and the Beast, Aladdin,* and *Snow White.*

1. Beethoven showed great musical talent at an early age his father hoped that his son would be a child prodigy.

2. The people who are called the Pennsylvania Dutch are not Dutch at all, but of German ancestry.

3. Goose down is an excellent insulator used in jackets and comforters, the down sometimes does shift.

4. John came to my college graduation that was the last time I saw him.

5. Somebody left the window open all the papers blew off my desk.

EXERCISE 3   Correcting Run-ons with Semicolons

Correct the run-ons as needed by joining the two independent clauses with a semicolon. (Some of the sentences may be correct as written.) Example:

Max was looking forward to his tenth high school reunion, he had not attended any of the earlier ones.

Max was looking forward to his tenth high school reunion; he had not attended any of the earlier ones.

1. Certain kinds of leaf lettuce are almost never found in grocery stores their delicate leaves do not stand up well in shipment.

2. Tuberculosis was rarely found in the United States until recently, unfortunately, the disease has been spreading rapidly in the last few years.

3. She read three papers every day, one of them is the *Investor's Business Daily*.

4. A bus crashed into a telephone pole on Walton Avenue six people received minor injuries.

5. Looking out her window in the morning, she could see joggers and dog walkers in the park.

EXERCISE 4 Correcting Run-ons with Semicolons and Conjunctive Adverbs

Correct the run-ons as needed using a semicolon and a conjunctive adverb. (Some of the sentences may be correct as written.) Example:

Laura took up new projects with enthusiasm, she seldom completed them.

Laura took up new projects with enthusiasm; however, she seldom completed them.

1. Frank does not know how to play bridge he is an expert poker player.

2. Several of the toll lanes are not operational, traffic is backed up for miles.

3. Since many members of the baseball team are sophomores, the team can anticipate at least two more winning seasons.

4. I would like to spend my vacation in Arizona I have always wanted to see Scotland.

5. Many two-year-old children are stubborn, they can also be rather charming.

EXERCISE 5   Correcting Run-ons with Coordinating Conjunctions

Correct the run-ons as needed by joining the two independent clauses with a comma and an appropriate coordinating conjunction. (Some of the sentences may be correct as written.) Example:

He could not roller skate he could not ride a bike.
He could not roller skate, nor could he ride a bike.

She wanted to learn to speak Spanish, she did not have the time.
She wanted to learn to speak Spanish, but she did not have the time.

1. The front door was open, I walked into the house.

2. Ms. Andrews had never met Mr. Jackson before, his face was familiar.

3. My favorite television show never was taped I had forgotten to program the VCR.

4. Before you lose your temper over something trivial, ask yourself if it will still be important in a week.

5. Mr. Elkins was not a registered voter his telephone number was not listed.

EXERCISE 6 Converting Run-ons to a Single Independent Clause

Rewrite the run-ons as needed to convert to a single independent clause. (Some of the sentences may be correct as written.) Example:

After the accident he could not see, he could not hear.

After the accident, he could neither see nor hear.

1. It will be difficult to prosecute him there are no witnesses.

2. The cat crept through the living room, she made a big circle around the sleeping dog.

3. Even though children are a big expense and responsibility, most parents are glad they had them.

4. I called Ben after the sales meeting, I told him about the new director's suggestions.

5. She's going to the block party tonight you should go with her.

EXERCISE 7   Correcting Run-ons with Subordinating Conjunctions

Correct the run-ons as needed by using a subordinating conjunction to change one of the two independent clauses into a dependent clause. Reword the sentences if necessary. Example:

The quarterback's arm was very sore he had to stop playing.

The quarterback's arm was so sore that he had to stop playing.

1. Tom never drinks coffee it makes his heart race.

2. She flipped the switch to turn on the lights nothing happened.

3. Elsa was mowing the lawn, Lee was cleaning the gutters.

4. I never knew your mother, I am sure I would have liked her.

5. The neighbors don't stop their dog from barking all day, I am calling the police.

EXERCISE 8   Correcting Run-ons in Paragraphs

Correct the run-ons in the following paragraphs. Example:

Most Americans eat far too much protein, they get much of that protein from animal sources. Unfortunately, the body turns excess protein to fat. Meat protein already may have a lot of fat, it is also low in fiber.

Most Americans eat far too much protein, *and* they get much of that protein from animal sources. Unfortunately, the body turns excess protein to fat. Meat protein may already have a lot of fat; it is also low in fiber.

1. Abigail Adams was the wife of President John Adams she was the mother of President John Quincy Adams. She was intelligent, she had strong opinions about the issues of her times. The many letters she wrote to her relatives supply vivid, interesting pictures of the people and customs of eighteenth- and nineteenth-century America.

2. Sequoias may have originated over 100 million years ago. They were widespread in the Northern Hemisphere, the glaciers of ice nearly exterminated them. In the twentieth century only two species of sequoia survive both grow on the Pacific Coast of the United States.

3. During the holiday season in fall and early winter, millions of catalogs arrive on the doorsteps of potential customers, some people receive as many as five or six a day in November and December. Most of these catalogs are never glanced at, they are immediately thrown in the trash.

4.   Years ago, cigarettes were advertised on television. Some cigarette commercials tried to associate the product with youth and springtime those ads featured young people smoking near lovely meadows or running brooks. Other commercials tried to link certain brands of cigarettes with rugged manhood the actors in those commercials were often dressed as cowboys.

5.   Like other languages, American Sign Language (ASL) is not static, new signs are created for recently invented technology or concepts. Lately, new signs have been replacing older signs designating some ethnic groups. The older signs are considered offensive, they often emphasize a physical characteristic of an ethnic group.

EXERCISE 9   Writing with Correct Punctuation

For each topic that follows, write a paragraph of three to five sentences. Then check and revise your paragraphs for comma splices and fused sentences. Example:

Topic: The first day at college

Even though it is many years ago, I remember my first day at college quite well. My father was trying very hard to hide his emotions, but it was obvious that he was both pleased and sad that his first child was starting college. As for me, although I was a little nervous about living away from home for the first time, the excitement of moving into the dorm and meeting new people exhilarated me.

1. Your first college class

2. A pleasant surprise

3. An unpleasant surprise

4. Lending clothes

5. A food you detest

CHAPTER 22

Misplaced, Interrupting, and Dangling Modifiers

Modifiers are single words, phrases, or clauses that function as adjectives or adverbs. Modifiers should point clearly to the words they modify. If they do not, your readers may be confused and your meaning will not be clear. Misplaced, interrupting, and dangling modifiers may hinder the clear communication of your ideas.

MISPLACED MODIFIERS

22a Revising misplaced words

The most basic kind of misplaced modifier is the awkward placement of a single word, usually an adverb. Look at the following examples:

CONFUSING He *only* ate yogurt for breakfast.

CONFUSING She *almost* spoke for twenty minutes.

In the first example, *only* is next to the verb *ate,* suggesting that he did not do anything else to the yogurt except eat it. That is probably not what the writer wants to convey. Similarly, in the second example, *almost* is next to the verb *spoke,* suggesting that she did not speak at all for twenty minutes. Again, the writer probably does not mean that. Now look at the revised versions of these two sentences:

REVISED He ate *only* yogurt for breakfast.

REVISED She spoke for *almost* twenty minutes.

Notice that the modifiers have been moved next to words they are intended to modify. In the first revised sentence, it is clear he ate yogurt and nothing else for breakfast. In the second, it is clear that her speech lasted close to twenty minutes.

Be especially careful about where you place limiting modifiers. Here is a short list of the most commonly used limiting modifiers:

almost	just	only
even	merely	scarcely
hardly	nearly	simply

Limiting modifiers should be placed directly before the words they modify. In the following examples, notice how the placement of an adverb can either confuse or clarify meaning:

CONFUSING   Children *only* can look at the animals. [Are children but not adults allowed to look? Can the children look but not touch? The meaning is not clear.]

CLEAR   *Only* children can look at the animals. [Adults are excluded.]

CLEAR   Children can *only* look at the animals. [They may look but not touch.]

22b   Revising misplaced phrases

1   Misplaced prepositional phrases

Revise misplaced phrases the same way you revise misplaced words. Put modifying phrases as close as possible to the words they modify. In particular, prepositional phrases should usually be placed directly before or immediately after the words they modify. Notice in these examples how prepositional phrases in the wrong place can cause confusion:

CONFUSING   I watched a woman changing a flat tire from the kitchen window. [This sentence suggests that the tire was changed from the window.]

CLEAR   From the kitchen window, I watched a woman changing a flat tire.

CONFUSING   He was disappointed that he failed to win the election by a large margin. [Did he win by a small margin, or did he lose?]

CLEAR   He was disappointed that he failed by a large margin to win the election.

CLEAR   He was disappointed that his margin of victory was not larger.

Even when a misplaced phrase does not cause confusion, it may make a sentence awkward. Try to place phrases that modify nouns as close as possible to those nouns. In the following examples, notice how much smoother each revised version is:

MISPLACED   The frequency of accidents is appalling *at that intersection.*

REVISED   The frequency of accidents *at that intersection* is appalling.

MISPLACED   I prefer a vehicle for my trip in the mountains *with a stick shift.*

REVISED   I prefer a vehicle *with a stick shift* for my trip in the mountains.

Unlike phrases that modify nouns, phrases that are used as adverbs are often movable. An adverb phrase can be placed within a sentence near the word it modifies (usually a verb), or it may be placed at the beginning or end of the sentence. Notice in these examples the various placements of the adverb phrase:

In her most recent book, Gloria Naylor has created several mysterious and disturbing characters.

Gloria Naylor has created *in her most recent book* several mysterious and disturbing characters.

Gloria Naylor has created several mysterious and disturbing characters *in her most recent book.*

2 | Misplaced participial phrases

Misplaced participial phrases can also cause confusion. Place such phrases directly before or immediately after the words they modify. In the following examples, notice how misplacement of participial phrases causes confusion about meaning:

CONFUSING	*Lying by the side of the road,* I saw an opossum. [Was the speaker lying by the side of the road? It is not likely.]
CLEAR	I saw an opossum *lying by the side of the road.*
CONFUSING	I showed photographs of the new baby to my friends *wrapped in a pink blanket.* [Is the blanket around the baby or the friends?]
CLEAR	I showed photographs of the new baby *wrapped in a pink blanket* to my friends.

22c | Revising misplaced clauses

The guidelines for revising misplaced words and phrases apply also to misplaced clauses. Place dependent clause modifiers as close as possible to the words they modify. Sometimes, the sentence must be rewritten in order to avoid confusion.

CONFUSING	Daniel Ellsworth released documents *that disturbed the staff at the White House.* [What disturbed the staff—the documents or the fact that they were released?]
REVISED	The release by Daniel Ellsworth of certain documents disturbed the staff at the White House.
CONFUSING	Rita hoped that her daughter would become a doctor *before the child was eight years old.* [This sentence suggests that the mother expects the child to be a doctor by the age of eight.]
REVISED	*Before the child was eight years old,* Rita hoped that her daughter would become a doctor.

22d | Revising squinting modifiers

A modifier should refer to only one word or sentence element. Squinting modifiers are confusing because they seem to modify the words before them and the words after them. Readers are unable to determine which meaning the writer intends. Revise sentences with squinting modifiers so that the modifiers refer clearly to only one word or sentence element. Sometimes the modifier can be moved to a more logical position; in other cases, the sentence must be rewritten.

SQUINTING	People who work at video terminals *occasionally* should take a break. [Do the people work only occasionally, or should they take an occasional break?]
SQUINTING	People who *occasionally* work at video terminals should take a break.
REVISED	People who work at video terminals should take *an occasional break.*

INTERRUPTING MODIFIERS

Interrupting modifiers break the continuity of thought in a sentence. They cause confusion and awkwardness, making it difficult for readers to understand the meaning intended by the writer. Try not to put a modifier in between the two parts of an infinitive, in the middle of a verb phrase, or in between a subject and its predicate.

22e Revising lengthy modifiers that separate a verb from its subject

Awkwardness or confusion can result when modifying phrases and clauses come between a subject and a verb.

AWKWARD	Several tree branches, *because they were loaded down with heavy snow,* broke off.
REVISED	Several tree branches broke off *because they were loaded down with heavy snow.*
AWKWARD	The kitten, *abandoned in an alley and shivering in the subfreezing weather,* was mewing piteously.
REVISED	*Abandoned in an alley and shivering in the subfreezing weather,* the kitten was mewing piteously.

22f Revising modifiers that separate a verb from its direct object or a subject complement

When modifiers separate a verb from a direct object or from a subject complement, readers may have difficulty following the writer's train of thought. Place modifiers so that objects or subject complements directly follow the verbs.

AWKWARD	Helen Hayes played, *in the course of a long and illustrious career filled with honors,* many memorable roles.
REVISED	*In the course of a long and illustrious career filled with honors,* Helen Hayes played many memorable roles.

22g   Revising modifiers that split an infinitive

There is nothing ungrammatical about splitting an infinitive. However, it is common practice not to place an adverbial modifier between *to* and the verb.

AWKWARD   Jack asked his children to *not* make so much noise.

REVISED   Jack asked his children *not* to make so much noise.

AWKWARD   He asked me to *briefly and succinctly* explain the new schedule.

REVISED   He asked me to explain the new schedule *briefly and succinctly.*

Sometimes, to avoid splitting an infinitive, you may decide to rewrite the sentence without the infinitive.

AWKWARD   The Committee for Safe Schools hoped *to* significantly *influence* the school board elections. [The infinitive is split.]

REVISED   The Committee for Safe Schools hoped to have a significant influence on the school board elections. [The infinitive is eliminated.]

22h   Revising modifiers that separate parts of a verb phrase

A verb phrase contains a main verb and one or more auxiliary verbs (e.g., *must find, should have seen, will have been delivered).* A single adverb or two consecutive adverbs can usually be inserted into a verb phrase without causing awkwardness or confusion. However, in other cases, do not separate the parts of a verb phrase.

ACCEPTABLE   He *has* very seldom *disapproved* of any of my suggestions.

AWKWARD   The assertions of fact in this article *should have,* considering its shocking content and the allegations against the governor, *been checked* more carefully than they were.

REVISED   Considering its shocking content and the author's allegations against the governor, the assertions of fact in this article *should have been checked* more carefully than they were.

DANGLING MODIFIERS

Dangling modifiers are words, phrases, or clauses that do not modify anything in a sentence. In such cases, a modifier *dangles* because it is next to a word that it cannot logically modify; in fact, it cannot logically modify *any* word in the sentence. Consider the following example:

DANGLING   *Walking along the trail,* a thick stand of maples came into view.

The phrase *Walking along the trail* cannot logically modify the maples, so who or what was doing the walking? The answer is in the writer's mind but not on paper. Correct the dangling modifier by adding a word or words that the modifier can describe or by changing the dangling modifier into a phrase or clause that clearly modifies another part of the sentence.

REVISED   Walking along the trail, we saw a thick stand of maples.

REVISED   As we were walking along the trail, a thick stand of maples came into view.

22i | Revising dangling word and phrase modifiers

Dangling words are often adverbs; dangling phrases are frequently prepositional phrases or participial phrases.

ADVERB

DANGLING   Irritably, the paper was rewritten. [The paper was not irritable; a person probably was.]

REVISED   Irritably, Fred rewrote the paper.

PARTICIPIAL PHRASE

DANGLING   Assessing the results of the new curriculum, significant gains in test scores were found.

REVISED   When the committee assessed the results of the new curriculum, significant gains in test scores were found.

REVISED   Assessing the results of the new curriculum, the committee found significant gains in test scores.

PREPOSITIONAL PHRASE

DANGLING   *After a hard day at work, playing with the children is relaxing.* [Who had a hard day at work?]

REVISED   After a hard day at work, I find that playing with the children is relaxing.

DANGLING   At the age of eight, my mother taught me to knit. [The mother would not have been eight years old when she taught her child to knit.]

REVISED   When I was eight years old, my mother taught me to knit.

22j | Revising dangling elliptical clauses

An elliptical clause is a dependent clause that lacks all or part of the subject or predicate. To revise a dangling elliptical clause, supply the words that are implied by the clause.

DANGLING   Although weak and feverish, the ambitious father made his daughter play in a tennis tournament. [implied subject and verb: *his daughter was*]

REVISED   Although his daughter was weak and feverish, the ambitious father made her play in a tennis tournament.

DANGLING   Although argumentative and opinionated, Gerald enjoyed Aurelia's company. [implied subject and verb: *Aurelia was.*]

REVISED   Although Aurelia was argumentative and opinionated, Gerald enjoyed her company.

Name _____ Section _____ Date _____

EXERCISE 1   Correcting Misplaced Adverbs

Rewrite each sentence that follows to correct the misplaced adverb. Example:

I almost ate the whole pizza by myself.

I ate almost the whole pizza by myself.

1. We are not sure what he spent the money on exactly.

2. The mayor said that taxes would not be raised simply.

3. I can hardly see any mistakes in your math homework.

4. She was a little late, but she almost saw the whole movie.

5. The children only use the playground during the day.

EXERCISE 2   Writing with Limiting Modifiers

For each limiting modifier that follows, write two sentences whose meaning differs according to the placement of the limiting modifier. Example:

Modifier: just

Just Margaret touched the computer.

Margaret just touched the computer.

1. almost

2. even

3. exactly

4. just

5. only

EXERCISE 3   Correcting Misplaced Phrases

Rewrite the following sentences to correct misplaced phrases. Example:

We watched the players practice in seats behind third base.

In seats behind third base, we watched the players practice.

1. Already tired from a hard day at work, the traffic delay irritated Clara.

2. Stretching and loosening up, the reporters observed the football players.

3. Ms. Chinea noticed two men having an argument from the window of her office.

4. I met an interesting man who spoke Korean in the cafeteria.

5. Irene spoke to the boss about the chance of getting a promotion before the meeting.

EXERCISE 4   Writing with Modifying Phrases

Write a sentence using each modifying phrase that follows. Be sure to place the phrases near the word or words they modify. Example:

Phrase: from a seat in the front row

From a seat in the front row, he watched Domingo sing the role of Othello.

1. pleased with her new job

2. with air bags and side-impact panels

3. walking with a slight limp

4. in most hotels and restaurants

5. stretching across the entire length of the gym

EXERCISE 5   Revising Misplaced Clauses

Rewrite the following sentences to correct misplaced clauses. Example:

The term paper was already late that he was finishing.

The term paper that he was finishing was already late.

1. When he was five years old, Mr. Gwin gave his son Alex a baseball and bat.

2. Mr. Gould gave a lecture with music and slides that we liked.

3. Ms. Liston bought a radio from a department store that can also play tapes and CDs.

4. In San Francisco, he took a ride in a trolley car that he enjoyed very much.

5. The coach thought Ramon could be a professional baseball player before the boy was twelve years old.

EXERCISE 6   Writing with Dependent Clause Modifiers

Write a sentence using each dependent clause that follows as a modifier. Place the modifiers close to the word or words they modify. Example:

Clause: that we saw last night

The movie that we saw last night was good but rather sentimental.

1. when she was four years old

2. as soon as he grew up

3. who have become professional athletes

4. that can be removed from the car

5. that she threw away

EXERCISE 7 Correcting Squinting Modifiers

Rewrite the following sentences to correct squinting modifiers that do not clearly refer to one word or one sentence element. Example:

The commissioner said at noon she would hold a press conference.

At noon, the commissioner said she would hold a press conference.

Or: The commissioner said she would hold a press conference at noon.

1. He stood up suddenly saying that he had to leave.

2. Parents always tell children when they are older they will receive more privileges.

3. People who drive through red lights often do not get ticketed.

4. Going swimming often reduces stress.

5. The program he wanted to apply to last year was eliminated.

EXERCISE 8   Correcting Interrupting Modifiers

Rewrite the following sentences to correct modifiers that separate sentence parts. (Some sentences may be correct as written.) Example:

They wanted to eventually move to Portland.

They wanted to move to Portland eventually.

1. The river, because heavy rains fell for nearly a week, overflowed.

2. The children in the audience, as the Christmas tree in *The Nutcracker* grew larger and larger, sat spellbound.

3. The ranger warned tourists to not feed any animals, especially bears.

4. You really ought to carefully and thoroughly proofread your paper.

5. In the past ten years, the two cousins had rarely seen each other.

EXERCISE 9   Correcting Dangling Modifiers

Rewrite the following sentences to eliminate dangling modifiers. Example:

To enter the lab, the right code must be entered on this panel.

To enter the lab, you must enter the right code on this panel.

1. Muscles aching from a long workout, a warm shower was welcome.

2. Studying your proposal, several questions come to mind.

3. Delighted by the performance, there was a standing ovation.

4. To become a lawyer, three years of law school are required, and the state bar exam must be passed.

5. As a young boy, my father went to all my Little League games.

EXERCISE 10   Writing with Modifiers

Write a sentence using each modifier that follows. Example:

when he returned from vacation

When he returned from vacation, Mr. Gibbs said he had gone scuba diving.

1. very seldom

2. after ten years in the National League

3. often

4. as soon as the election results were in

5. annoyed at not receiving an invitation

6. looking intently at the graph

7. only

8. when she was fifteen years old

9. from the fifth floor

10. jogging on the track surrounding the football field

CHAPTER 23

Avoiding Shifts and Maintaining Consistency

Shifts that are unnecessary or illogical can confuse readers. Try to aim for consistency in your use of pronoun person and number, verb tenses, mood of verbs, voice of verbs, direct and indirect quotation, and diction and tone.

23a | Maintaining consistency of person and number

Do not shift unnecessarily among pronouns that are in the first person (*I, we*), second person (*you*), or third person (*he, she, it, one, they*). Similarly, do not shift between pronouns that are singular (*I, you, he, she, it, one*) and pronouns that are plural (*we, you, they*).

INCONSISTENT   When *one* is looking for a new job, *you* should update *your* resume.

REVISED   When *one* is looking for a new job, *one* should update *one's* resume.

REVISED   When *you* are looking for a new job, *you* should update *your* resume.

INCONSISTENT   When *one* wants a raise or a promotion, *they* must earn it.

REVISED   When *one* wants a raise or a promotion, *one* must earn it.

In addition, avoid shifting between singular nouns and plural nouns unless the meaning requires such a change. Unnecessary shifts in number sometimes occur in discussions of people in general; they are less apt to happen when writing about specific people. To prevent awkward shifts in number when writing about people in general, avoid using singular words; try to use plural words as the antecedents so that plural pronouns may then be used in the rest of the sentence (or paragraph).

INCONSISTENT   As children, *boys* may play more sports than girls do, although *a girl* may be encouraged by parents to develop athletic skills.

REVISED   As children, *boys* may play more sports than girls do, although some *girls* may be encouraged by parents to develop athletic skills.

Shifts in number from singular to plural often cause lack of agreement between pronouns and their antecedents.

INCONSISTENT	When *a person* wants to buy a house, *they* usually have to get a mortgage.
REVISED	When *people* want to buy a house, *they* usually have to get a mortgage.
INCONSISTENT	When *a lawyer* is preparing a case, *they* often have to do a lot of research.
REVISED	When *lawyers* are preparing a case, *they* often have to do a lot of research.

(See 18k–18n in the *Workbook* for more on pronoun–antecedent agreement.)

23b Maintaining consistency in verb tenses

Consistent verb tenses establish clearly the time of the action. Unnecessary shifts in verb tenses can confuse readers as to the exact time of the action.

INCONSISTENT	Reporters *asked* questions after the deputy mayor *finishes* her opening statement.
REVISED	Reporters *ask* questions after the deputy mayor *finishes* her opening statement.
REVISED	Reporters *asked* questions after the deputy mayor *finished* her opening statement.

Use the present tense to describe the action in works of literature and in films.

INCONSISTENT	The novel *follows* the young hero as he *grew* from a naive child to a confident adult.
REVISED	The novel *follows* the young hero as he *grows* from a naive child to a confident adult.

Use the present tense to describe general truths:

Most people *know* that a diet high in fat *is* dangerous.

Combining tenses

Maintaining consistency in verb tenses does not mean that you are limited to just one tense in a sentence, paragraph, or essay. Obviously, actions that occur at the same time should be described in the same verb tense. However, you can use more than one verb tense in a sentence or paragraph when describing actions occurring at different times. In the following paragraph, note that verb tenses change to indicate actions performed at different times:

As the next presidential election *draws* near, political reporters *speculate* about which candidates *will fade* early in the campaign and which *will gain* support as various state primaries *are held*. Some people *wonder* if any candidate *will be* able to duplicate the success of Ronald Reagan, who *won* reelection in 1984 by a huge majority.

(For more on verb tenses, see 14f–14i in the *Workbook*.)

23c   Maintaining consistency in mood

Verbs can be in one of three moods: indicative, imperative, or subjunctive. A verb in the indicative mood makes a statement or asks a question: *The book is overdue. Is the book overdue?* A verb in the imperative mood gives a command or offers advice: *Shut the window. Don't worry about tomorrow.* A verb in the subjunctive mood expresses a wish, a condition, or a statement contrary to fact: *I wish they were here.* Do not shift from one verb mood to another.

INCONSISTENT   Always *watch* the ball and you *should keep* the tennis racket up.

REVISED   Always *watch* the ball and *keep* the tennis racket up.

INCONSISTENT   If I *won* the lottery, I probably *spend* all the money immediately.

REVISED   If I *won* the lottery, I *would* probably *spend* all the money immediately.

(For more on the mood of verbs, see Chapter 14 in the *Workbook*.)

23d   Maintaining consistency in voice

Verbs may be in the active or passive voice. When a verb is in the active voice, the subject of the verb does the action: *Fernando broke the window.* When a verb is in the passive voice, the subject receives the action: *The window was broken this morning.* Do not shift unnecessarily between one voice and the other.

INCONSISTENT   The car *grazed* a fire hydrant, and then a telephone pole *was hit* by it.

REVISED   The car *grazed* a fire hydrant and then *hit* a telephone pole.

INCONSISTENT   The candidate *made* personal appearances, and many speeches *were given* by her.

REVISED   The candidate *made* personal appearances and *gave* many speeches.

Sometimes, shifting between the active and the passive voice is logical in that it focuses the sentence on its subject.

LOGICAL SHIFT   Members of the chorus *sang* magnificently and *were rewarded* by thunderous applause.

(For more on the voice of verbs, see 14j and 14k in the *Workbook*.)

23e   Avoiding shifts between direct and indirect quotations

A direct quotation reproduces a person's exact words. When you use direct discourse in your writing, put the quoted words within quotation marks.

When reporters asked Mr. Smith why he had embezzled money from his employer, he replied, "I needed the money so I could retire."

Indirect quotation, or indirect discourse, reports or summarizes what someone has said or written without reproducing the original words exactly. Some (or all) of the words may change, and no quotation marks are used.

When reporters asked Mr. Smith why he had embezzled money from his employer, he answered that he needed the money for his retirement.

Shifts between direct and indirect discourse cause awkwardness and confusion. Avoid such shifts, especially in research essays, which are likely to incorporate quotations from secondary sources.

INCONSISTENT	In *The Philosophy of History*, G. W. F. Hegel states, "Peoples and government have never learned anything from history," and he also insists that they have never acted on principles that can be deduced from history.
REVISED (INDIRECT)	In *The Philosophy of History*, G. W. F. Hegel states people and government have learned no lessons from history and have never acted on principles that can be deduced from history.
REVISED (DIRECT)	In *The Philosophy of History*, G. W. F. Hegel states, "Peoples and government have never learned anything from history, or acted on principles deducible from it."

23f | Maintaining consistency in diction and tone

In academic writing, do not shift from one type of diction (word selection) or tone to another. If you are using formal language, try to avoid the use of contractions, colloquialisms, and slang expressions.

INCONSISTENT	The late Thomas P. O'Neill, Jr., who was Speaker of the House of Representatives from 1977 to 1987, began his political career in the wards of Boston. His loyalty to his liberal views and his mastery of the political process earned him much respect, even from his opponents. Some Republicans, however, smeared him as a bloated old pol with broken-down views.
REVISED	The late Thomas P. O'Neill, Jr., who was Speaker of the House of Representatives from 1977 to 1987, began his political career in the wards of Boston. His loyalty to his liberal views and his mastery of the political process earned him much respect, even from his opponents. Some Republicans, however, tried to portray him as an anachronistic, self-aggrandizing politician with outdated views.

EXERCISE 1 Consistency of Person and Number

Rewrite the following sentences to correct unnecessary shifts in pronoun person and number. Example:

If one plans to travel abroad, you should take traveler's checks, not cash.

If one plans to travel abroad, one should take traveler's checks, not cash.

1. A working parent has to schedule their days carefully or they will soon be over-whelmed.

2. When one feels a bit sad and lonely, you should call up some friends and go to the movies.

3. Deborah Tannen has noted that boys and girls communicate differently and that a little girl is usually more verbal than little boys.

4. When a student has to take several exams in just a few days, you have to be very organized.

5. As soon as one walks into that store, salespeople ask if you want to sample various perfumes.

EXERCISE 2   Consistency in Verb Tenses

Rewrite the following sentences to correct unnecessary or illogical shifts in verb tenses. Example:

Shoppers stream into the store the minute the doors were opened.

Shoppers streamed into the store the minute the doors were opened.

1. All the people in the courtroom rose when the judge enters.

2. Just before the phone rang, he picks it up.

3. The college Senate begins its meeting when the chair called for order.

4. The novel concerns a young woman who felt that she was destined for greatness.

5. Doctors now know that alcohol had deleterious effects on fetuses.

EXERCISE 3   Consistency in the Mood of Verbs

Rewrite the following sentences as needed to correct unnecessary shifts in the mood of verbs. (Some sentences may be correct as written.) Example:

If she were my boss, she fires me.

If she were my boss, she would fire me.

1. Wear several layers of clothing, and you should always wear a hat when it is very cold.

2. If he won a lot of money, he probably does not quit his job.

3. I wish that I am three inches taller.

4. If you lost your glasses, it would take two weeks to get a replacement pair.

5. If the star center were traded, the team has a losing season.

EXERCISE 4   Consistency in the Voice of Verbs

Rewrite the following sentences as needed to correct unnecessary shifts in the voice of verbs. (Some sentences may be correct as written.) Example:

I like broccoli, but turtle soup is not enjoyed by me.

I like broccoli, but I don't enjoy turtle soup.

1. While she was standing outside the front door, two people inside the house could be heard arguing.

2. She danced in many classic ballets, and several new ballets were choreographed by her.

3. Although models often wear expensive designer clothes, those clothes are rarely owned by the models.

4. Many leading roles in opera were sung by him, and he could also play the piano.

5. As we hiked in the woods in the early spring, several trillium plants could be seen.

EXERCISE 5 Consistency in Direct and Indirect Quotations

Use each of the following excerpts first in a direct quotation and then in an indirect quotation. Example:

Excerpt: He that is down can fall no lower. —Samuel Butler

Direct: Samuel Butler states, "He that is down can fall no lower."

Indirect: Samuel Butler states that a person who is down cannot fall any farther down.

1. Of a compliment only a third is meant. —Welsh proverb

2. Life is like drunkenness; the pleasure passes away, but the headache remains. —Persian proverb

3. A man in debt is so far a slave. —Ralph Waldo Emerson

4. It is part of the cure to wish to be cured. —Seneca

5. Curiosity is ill manners in another's house. —Thomas Fuller

EXERCISE 6   Consistency in Diction and Tone

Rewrite the following sentences to eliminate contractions, colloquialisms, and slang expressions. Example:

The English commander and the American general touched base with each other frequently.

The English commander and the American general communicated with each other frequently.

1. Caesar is said to have reproached one of his assassins just before kicking the bucket.

2. Edgar Allan Poe didn't have a stable personality; he'd repeatedly undermine his friends' attempts to help him.

3. Marquez's sentences are pretty long; they're difficult to follow but fascinating.

4. Patton hit the roof and slapped a soldier.

5. The defendant's mouthpiece is about to give a news conference.

EXERCISE 7   Avoiding Shifts and Maintaining Consistency in Writing

For each topic that follows, write a brief paragraph of three to five sentences. Then check and correct the paragraphs for inconsistencies in pronoun person and number, verb tenses, mood and voice of verbs, and diction and tone.

Topic: Neighbors who are different from you

   The neighbors who live across the hall are very different from me. They are in their late forties; I am in my mid-twenties. They speak English and some French; I usually speak Spanish at home. In one very important way we are similar—in our love for our children. They have a son in college and another in high school; I have a one-year-old daughter.

1. An opinion you once had but have no longer

2. An emergency and your reaction to it

3. Directions for changing a flat tire

4. A friend very unlike yourself

5. A person you admire

CHAPTER 24

Pronoun Reference

A pronoun refers to a noun that it substitutes or stands in for; that noun is the antecedent of the pronoun. Using pronouns in place of nouns helps us avoid repetition and awkwardness.

REPETITIOUS Ed asked *Ed's* sister to help *Ed* out in *Ed's* store for a few days.

REVISED Ed asked *his* sister to help *him* out in *his* store for a few days.

The revised sentence is clear. However, the meaning of a sentence can be unclear when a pronoun's antecedent is ambiguous—that is, when a pronoun can refer to more than one antecdent. Look at the following example:

UNCLEAR Yvette asked Doreen if she could stay for lunch. [Did Yvette ask Doreen to stay for lunch at Yvette's house, or did Yvette ask to have lunch at Doreen's?]

REVISED Yvette invited Doreen to come for lunch.

REVISED Yvette asked if Doreen would let her stay for lunch.

To avoid ambiguity, make sure that a pronoun clearly refers to only one antecedent. (See 18k–18m in the *Workbook*.)

24a Making sure a pronoun refers to a single antecedent

Antecedents of pronouns must be clear. If a pronoun appears to have two possible antecedents, rewrite the sentence so that the pronoun refers to a single, clear antecedent.

CONFUSING Andy told William that he needed a vacation. [Who needs the vacation, Andy or William?]

REVISED Andy thought that William needed a vacation and told him so.

REVISED Andy felt he needed a vacation and spoke to William about it.

When you write sentences reporting what someone has said, those sentences often have verbs such as *said* and *told*. If it is difficult to write a clear sentence using indirect quotation, use direct quotation to avoid confusion:

CONFUSING   Alice told Carol that she should retire.

CLEAR   Alice said, "Carol, I think you should retire."

CLEAR   Alice said, "Carol, I think I should retire."

24b | Keeping pronouns and antecedents close together

When a pronoun is too far away from its antecedent, it may be difficult for the reader to determine the actual antecedent. A noun may appear in the first sentence of a paragraph, and a pronoun referring to that noun may appear several sentences later. If the antecedent and pronoun are widely separated, the reader may forget what the pronoun refers to, or there may be intervening nouns to which the pronoun could possibly refer. To avoid confusion, keep the antecedent and the pronoun as close together as possible. If it is not possible to move them closer to each other, you can repeat the noun or use a synonym.

CONFUSING   Mr. and Mrs. Carter live outside of Reading, Pennsylvania. Mr. and Mrs. Smith live in Rochester, New York. In some ways, they are similar.

REVISED   Mr. and Mrs. Carter live outside of Reading, Pennsylvania. Mr. and Mrs. Smith live in Rochester, New York. In some ways, the two couples are similar.

24c | Clarifying confusing references with particular pronouns

1 | Using *this, that, which,* and *it*

Sometimes writers use the word *this, that, which,* or *it* to refer to an idea or a situation mentioned in a previous clause, sentence, or paragraph. Using these words in such a way can be confusing for readers because the words could refer to various preceding nouns, and readers cannot be sure which noun the writer intends as the antecedent. In such cases, do not use a pronoun; instead, use a noun or a noun phrase. Consider the following examples:

CONFUSING   Fat on the upper body is more dangerous than fat on the lower body. People with fat on their hips and thighs are less likely to have heart attacks than people with fat on their upper torso. *This* was not determined until recently.

REVISED   Fat on the upper body is more dangerous than fat on the lower body. People with fat on their hips and thighs are less likely to have heart attacks than people with fat on their upper torso. *The connection between the position of fat and heart attacks* was not determined until recently.

CONFUSING   Eric thought that he was a great driver and that the traffic rules did not apply to him. *That* got him into a lot of trouble.

REVISED   Eric thought that he was a great driver and that the traffic rules did not apply to him. *His attitude* got him into a lot of trouble.

To avoid too broad a use of *this* and *that,* do not use these two words by themselves. Instead, ask yourself the question: This *what?* That *what?* Then, use your answer in the paragraph: *this theory, that attitude, this plan,* and so on.

2 Avoiding indefinite use of *it, they,* and *you*

In everyday conversation, people often use expressions like the following: "*It* said in the paper," "*They* say he's not well," and "*You* always hear." In these examples of conversation, the words *it, they,* and *you* are being used indefinitely. Academic writing, however, must be more precise. Therefore, use *you* to refer only to "you, the reader." Use *it* and *they* to refer only to clear antecedents.

INFORMAL   *It* said in the paper that the unemployment rate is falling.

FORMAL   *An article in the paper stated that* the unemployment rate is falling.

INFORMAL   In that neighborhood *they* put up special decorations for every holiday.

FORMAL   *Many people living* in that neighborhood put up special decorations for every holiday.

INFORMAL   The ads try to get *you* to equate smoking with popularity.

FORMAL   The ads *imply that smoking will bring one popularity.*

3 Using *who, which,* and *that* with appropriate antecedents

The pronouns *who, which,* and *that* are not interchangeable. The following guidelines specify which pronouns to use with various antecedents.

—Use *who* to refer to people and to animals with names.

—Use *which* to refer to animals and things.

—Use *that* to refer to animals, things, and anonymous or collective references to people.

Note the uses of *who, which,* and *that* in the following examples:

Maya Angelou, *who* read a poem at President Clinton's inauguration, is a woman of many talents.

Our dog Cato, *who* is a golden retriever, loves attention.

Mount Graylock, *which* is in western Massachusetts, has a lodge, a radio tower, and a war memorial at its summit.

Last winter we had a problem with mice, *which* gnawed at our telephone wires.

He is wearing a sweater *that* his sister knit for him.

This world is a comedy to those *that* think, a tragedy to those *that* feel. —Horace Walpole

(For a discussion of *that* and *which* in restrictive and nonrestrictive clauses, see 36c in the *Workbook*.)

4 | Avoiding pronouns with adjectives and possessives as antecedents

A pronoun can substitute only for a noun, not for an adjective or a possessive. For example, the pronoun *it* cannot correctly refer to the adjective *delicious,* nor can the pronoun *she* correctly refer to a possessive form such as *Carmen's.* Sentences containing such incorrect references should be rewritten to eliminate the pronoun or to provide a noun antecedent.

INAPPROPRIATE   In Emily Dickinson's poetry, *she* often writes about time, death, and God.

REVISED   Emily Dickinson's poetry emphasizes the themes of time, death, and God.

REVISED   In her poetry, Emily Dickinson often writes about time, death, and God.

EXERCISE 1   Avoiding Ambiguous Pronoun Reference

Rewrite the following sentences to make pronoun reference clear. Example:

My children told their friends that they had to go home.

My children had to go home and told their friends so.

Or: My children's friends had to go home and said so.

1. Mr. Andrews met Mr. Ojeda when he was interviewed for a job.

2. Fred told Gabe that he had made a serious mistake.

3. When he set the bowl on the glass shelf, it broke.

4. Ms. Miranda called Ms. Goldman when she got home from work.

5. When the center crashed into the goalie, he was taken out of the game.

EXERCISE 2 Avoiding Remote Pronoun Reference

Revise the following sentences to eliminate remote pronoun reference. Example:

Penny is a landscape gardener with many clients, among them Rosa Jenkins, the president of Jenkins Enterprises, Inc. She is also an excellent mechanic.

Penny is a landscape gardener with many clients, among them Rosa Jenkins, the president of Jenkins Enterprises, Inc. Penny is also an excellent mechanic.

1. Japanese teachers work in conditions that are very different from those of American teachers. They teach fewer classes and have time to meet with colleagues.

2. I had used a gas stove for years before I moved to an area where gas was not available so I had to use an electric stove. It definitely was better for cooking foods that required stir-frying.

3. Jimmy Carter was from Plains, Georgia; Bill Clinton grew up in Hope, Arkansas. They have certain similarities but also crucial differences.

4. Her home office is equipped with a computer, a modem, a printer, and a fax machine. It is always in use.

5. The committee decided to hold a meeting to plan the annual company picnic. Unfortunately, it had to be postponed.

EXERCISE 3   Avoiding the Confusing Use of *this, that, which,* and *it*

Rewrite the following sentences to eliminate the overly broad use of *this, that, which,* and *it*. Example:

I read an article about the budget deficit, which I found confusing.

I read an article about the budget deficit, a topic which has always confused me.

1. He told her that she had to rewrite her report. It irritated her.

2. A photograph of the lottery winner appeared in the newspaper. This resulted in hundreds of letters and phone calls to the winner.

3. Doctors once thought that the placenta was a barrier protecting a fetus from drugs and alcohol. That proved to be untrue.

4. He was constantly chewing gum and popping bubbles, which distracted his classmates.

5. The house was run down and in need of repairs. That changed when the new owners moved in.

EXERCISE 4   Avoiding Indefinite Use of *it, they,* and *you*

Rewrite the following sentences to eliminate the indefinite use of *it, they,* and *you.* Example:

In the conclusion, it offers suggestions for improvement.

The conclusion offers suggestions for improvement.

1. In this town they do not allow parking on the streets overnight.

2. It said in the newspaper that the city clerk is going to resign.

3. The salespeople at that store treat you with courtesy.

4. They grow a lot of rice in Japan but not enough to meet the demand.

5. It says in this article that last year in Sweden there were fewer than twenty shooting deaths.

EXERCISE 5   Using *who, which,* and *that* with Appropriate Antecedents

Fill in each blank with *who, which,* or *that.* Example:

Ms. Banks, <u>who</u> once taught chemistry, is now dean of students.

1. The videotape _____ you ordered has arrived.

2. Nobody _____ heard Rosa Ponselle sing will ever forget it.

3. The salmon _____ used to spawn in this river no longer do so because a dam has prevented them from swimming upstream.

4. *The Adventures of Huckleberry Finn,* _____ was once banned in Boston, has become a classic of American literature.

5. Ms. Hartman's cat Kleine, _____ is about a year old, is part Siamese.

EXERCISE 6   Avoiding the Use of Adjectives and Possessives as Antecedents

Rewrite the following sentences to eliminate pronoun references to an adjective or a possessive. Example:

In Ms. Bailey's speech, she emphasizes hard work and dedication.

In her speech, Ms. Bailey emphasizes hard work and dedication.

1. In Piri Thomas's autobiography, he describes his turbulent childhood.

2. Your spelling is Elizabethan; they did not worry about consistency!

3. I try to serve food that is both tasty and nutritious; they are my two guidelines.

4. In Ms. Brown's report, she criticizes lax security at the municipal jail.

5. He is asleep; it will do him good.

CHAPTER 25

Mixed and Incomplete Sentences

Mixed and incomplete sentences do not convey clear, comprehensible messages to readers. Such sentences are caused by incompatible grammatical patterns, faulty predication, confusing elliptical constructions, missing words, or incomplete comparisons.

MIXED SENTENCES

25a Revising mixed sentences with incompatible grammatical patterns

A mixed sentence often begins with one grammatical pattern and then switches to another that is incompatible with the first. Consider the following example:

MIXED After spraining her ankle was the reason she could not play soccer.

This sentence begins with the prepositional phrase *After spraining her ankle,* which the reader expects to be followed by an independent clause. Instead, the prepositional phrase is followed by a verb, *was,* and a subject complement, *the reason.* As a result, the sentence has no subject. The word *spraining* cannot function as the subject because it is already the object of the preposition *after. One word can never function as two different sentence elements.* The example sentence has three grammatical parts—modifying phrase + verb + subject complement—that do not fit together to form one of the five basic sentence patterns (see 13e in the *Workbook*). The sentence can be corrected in various ways, as the following revisions show. Note in each revised sentence the clear and logical relationship between subject and predicate.

REVISED After spraining her ankle, she could not play soccer.

REVISED Her sprained ankle was the reason she could not play soccer.

REVISED She could not play soccer because of her sprained ankle.

The careless use of an introductory clause or phrase sometimes results in a mixed sentence. Adverb clauses and prepositional phrases are modifiers; they cannot be the subject of a sentence.

MIXED	*Because the roads were icy* was the reason for so many accidents.
REVISED	Because the roads were icy, many accidents occurred.
REVISED	The icy roads was the reason for so many accidents.

MIXED	*By walking four miles a day* is how she keeps in shape.
REVISED	Walking four miles a day is how she keeps in shape.
REVISED	By walking four miles a day, she keeps in shape.

MIXED	*Because of his shyness* makes him nervous about meeting people.
REVISED	His shyness makes him nervous about meeting people.
REVISED	Because of his shyness, he is nervous about meeting people.

25b Revising mixed sentences with faulty predication

When the subject and predicate do not fit together logically, the result is known as faulty predication. In mixed sentences with faulty predication, the subject is described as being or doing something that it cannot logically be or do. Faulty predication often occurs with forms of the verb *to be,* especially with *is, are, was,* and *were,* though other verbs can also lead to inconsistent predication. Whatever the verb, make sure the subject and the complete predicate are logically related. Look at the following examples:

FAULTY	The *purpose* of this meeting *was intended* to give community residents a chance to express their views. [The subject *purpose* is illogically matched to the predicate *was intended;* a purpose already suggests an intention.]
REVISED	The purpose of this meeting was to give community residents a chance to express their views.
REVISED	This meeting was intended to give community residents a chance to express their views.

FAULTY	The *result* of the hockey game *ended* in a 2–2 tie. [The subject *result* does not fit logically with the predicate *ended;* a result already suggests an ending, so the predicate *ended* is redundant.]
REVISED	The result of the hockey game was a 2–2 tie.
REVISED	The hockey game ended in a 2–2 tie.

FAULTY   The *sales* of athletic shoes containing air pumps *were* very popular. [The sales were not popular, but the shoes were.]

REVISED   Athletic shoes containing air pumps were very popular.

1 | *When* and *where* used with *be*

Faulty predication often results when the adverb *when* or *where* is used after the verb *to be*, especially in the combination *is when*. Do not use *is when* or *is where* to explain a term or an idea.

FAULTY   A consensus *is when* all the members of a group are in agreement.

REVISED   A consensus results when all the members of a group are in agreement.

REVISED   A consensus is general agreement among members of a group.

FAULTY   An ace *is where* a tennis ball is served so that the opponent cannot return it.

REVISED   An ace occurs when a tennis ball is served so that the opponent cannot return it.

REVISED   An ace is a serve of a tennis ball hit so well that the opponent cannot return it.

2 | *The reason . . . is because*

Faulty predication also results from using the construction *the reason is because*. When giving an explanation, use either *reason* or *because*, but not both words together. The word *because* always begins a phrase or clause containing a reason; using the two words together is redundant. Like *is when* and *is where*, the construction *the reason is because* is often heard in everyday conversation; however, this kind of phrasing is not acceptable in standard written English. (Grammatically, a clause beginning with *because* is an adverbial clause. After a linking verb, only a noun clause can function as a subject complement.) Consider the following examples:

FAULTY   The *reason* the team loses so often *is because* the defense is weak.

REVISED   The reason the team loses so often is that the defense is weak.

REVISED   The team loses so often because the defense is weak.

FAULTY   The *reason* for his decision to retire *was because* he wanted to spend more time with his family.

REVISED   The reason for his decision to retire was that he wanted to spend more time with his family.

REVISED   He decided to retire because he wanted to spend more time with his family.

INCOMPLETE SENTENCES

| **25c** | **Revising confusing elliptical constructions** |

Elliptical structures are compound structures in which words are left out or implied rather than explicitly stated. In an elliptical construction, the omitted words must match the words that have not been omitted. Look at the following examples:

ACCEPTABLE   The first act of the play was slow, but the second was quite exciting. [The words *act of the play* are omitted after *second*.]

ACCEPTABLE   The Romanian gymnastics team won the gold medal, and the Americans the silver. [The words *won* and *medal* are omitted from the second half of the sentence.]

In these examples of correct elliptical constructions, exactly the same nouns, verbs, or phrases that occur in the first part of each sentence are omitted in the second part.

Now look at the following example. Here the elliptical construction causes confusion because the omitted word does not exactly match any word in the first part of the sentence.

FAULTY   The first act *is* slow, the second and third acts forceful and exciting. [The first verb, *is*, is singular, but the omitted verb, *are*, is plural to agree with its subject.]

REVISED   The first act *is* slow; the second and third acts *are* forceful and exciting.

| **25d** | **Revising sentences to include missing words** |

It is not unusual for writers to omit words in their eagerness to get thoughts down on the page. Articles, pronouns, and prepositions are often left out in such situations. Careful proofreading, including reading your sentences aloud, will help you find and supply the unintended omissions. Some omissions are acceptable—those that are intentional and that do not obscure meaning. Look at the following example:

Ms. Jones said [that] it was raining.

In this case, the meaning of the sentence is clear whether the word *that* is included or omitted; therefore, omitting *that* is acceptable.

In other cases, however, omitting the word *that* can lead to confusion because a sentence could be interpreted in more than one way, causing readers to be uncertain about which way the writer intended. Here is an example:

FAULTY   Ms. Elders heard several speeches were boring. [Because *that* has been omitted, it is unclear whether Ms. Elders actually listened to several boring speeches or whether someone else had told her about several boring speeches.]

REVISED   Ms. Elders heard that several speeches were boring. [She heard this opinion from someone else.]

REVISED   Ms. Elders heard several speeches that were boring. [She listened to the speeches herself.]

In your writing, do not omit important prepositions, especially those that follow verbs. Many phrasal verbs include prepositions, and those prepositions are needed to complete the meaning.

FAULTY   He not only learned but also profited by this experience. [The verbs *learned* and *profited* are parallel, each introduced by part of the correlative conjunction *not only . . . but also.* Therefore, a preposition governing one verb applies also to the other. However, the phrase *learned by* is not correct idiomatic English; the correct phrasal verb is *learned from.*]

REVISED   He not only learned from but also profited by this experience.

(If English is not your native language, you may wish to consult Chapter 19 for a discussion of phrasal verbs, and guidelines on using the articles *a*, *an*, and *the*.)

25e Revising incomplete comparisons

Comparisons are statements expressing a relationship between two or more things. To make your meaning certain, be sure that comparisons are complete, clear, and logically consistent.

1 Complete comparisons

To be complete, a comparison must specifically mention the two (or more) things being compared.

INCOMPLETE   His temper was more controlled. [More controlled than what or whose?]

REVISED   His temper was more controlled than mine was.

REVISED   His temper was more controlled than it had been in the past.

2 Clear comparisons

Unclear comparisons can be interpreted in more than one way, leaving readers unsure of which interpretation the writer intended. Revise an unclear comparison so that it conveys only one meaning.

UNCLEAR   The math tutor helped Carlos more than Jim. [Did the tutor help Carlos more than the tutor helped Jim, or did the tutor help Carlos more than Jim helped Carlos?]

CLEAR   The math tutor gave more help to Carlos than to Jim.

CLEAR   The math tutor helped Carlos more than Jim did.

3 | Logically consistent comparisons

To be logically consistent, a comparison must make sense. The words in one part of the comparison should not contradict the words in another part.

ILLOGICAL President Reagan's time in office was longer than President Bush. [It is not logical to compare a person's time in office to a person. It is logical to compare the time each person spent in office.]

LOGICAL President Reagan's time in office was longer than President Bush's.

ILLOGICAL Manute Bol is taller than any basketball player. [Bol cannot be taller than himself.]

LOGICAL Manute Bol is taller than any other basketball player.

EXERCISE 1 Correcting Incompatible Grammatical Constructions

Rewrite the following sentences to eliminate incompatible grammatical constructions. Example:

By taking local roads is how to avoid delays on the highway.

By taking local roads, you can avoid delays on the highway.

1. Because she writes science fiction is one reason why she is not regarded as a serious writer.

2. After seeing Judith Jamison perform was the main reason Olivia wanted to become a dancer.

3. By cutting his intake of fat is the way he lowered his dangerously high cholesterol.

4. Because of his frequent lies made the villagers distrust anything the little boy said.

5. After tutoring young children helped her realize that she wanted to be a teacher.

EXERCISE 2 Correcting Faulty Predication

Rewrite the following sentences to correct faulty predicaion. Example:

A ground rule double is where a baseball bounces into te stands in fair territory.

A ground rule double occurs when a baseball bounces ito the stands in fair territory.

1. The conclusion of the soccer game ended in a tie.

2. A political debate is when two or more candidates present their views on various issues.

3. The reason I called you is because I need some advice.

4. A free throw is where a basketball player gets to make an unopposed shot from the foul line.

5. The target of the investigation aimed at government corruption.

EXERCISE 3   Writing with Consistent Grammatical Patterns

Use consistent grammatical patterns to complete each of the following incomplete sentences. Example:

After hearing conflicting reports about X-rays

After hearing conflicting reports about X-rays, I was not sure if dental X-rays could cause any harm.

1. The reason registration takes so long is

2. By double majoring in history and political science

3. Because of his dedication and courage

4. The end of 1994

5. After watching the evening news

EXERCISE 4   Avoiding Confusing Elliptical Constructions, Missing Words, and Incomplete Comparisons

Rewrite the following sentences to eliminate confusing elliptical constructions, missing words, and incomplete comparisons. Example:

The review class helped me more than Frank.

The review class helped me more than it helped Frank.

1. The first chapter of the book was confusing, the others clear.

2. She discovered many valuable manuscripts had been lost.

3. Mr. Brown's resume is more complete than Ms. Weldon.

4. The captain is stronger than any member of the wrestling team.

5. Parents should listen, not just lecture their children.

EXERCISE 5   Writing with Complete Constructions and Comparisons

For each topic that follows, write a brief paragraph of three to five sentences. Check your paragraphs for incomplete constructions and comparisons, and then revise to correct those errors.

Topic: Two friends

In high school, I had two close friends, Ann and Cindy, who played with me on the lacrosse team. Ann's skills were more advanced than Cindy's, yet I enjoyed the game more with Cindy than with Ann. While not as fast or as strong as Ann, Cindy had a better sense of team play than Ann did.

1. Two courses you have taken

2. Three classmates

3. Two close relatives

4. Team sports

5. Two books by the same author

PART EIGHT

Sentence Style

CHAPTER 26

Writing Coordinate and Subordinate Sentences

Writers use coordination and subordination to show the relative importance of ideas and actions. Writers use coordination to emphasize that two or more ideas are equal in importance. They use subordination to show the relationship between unequal ideas. Look at the following examples:

COORDINATION   They wanted to go to Utah, but they ended up going to Florida. [Both halves of the sentence are equal in importance, so they are joined by a coordinating conjunction.]

SUBORDINATION   Although they wanted to go to Utah, they ended up going to Florida. [The halves of the sentence are related, but the writer stresses the second half by making the first half a subordinate clause.]

26a   Using coordination to relate equal ideas

To express a relationship between ideas of equal importance, use coordination. Coordination can be established in several ways. One way is to use a coordinating conjunction—*and, or, but, for, nor, yet,* or *so.* (See 17c-1 in the *Workbook.*)

The play was written in 1978, *but* it was not produced until 1992.

You can also coordinate with a semicolon and a conjunctive adverb such as *therefore, however,* or *moreover.* (See 37b and 17c-4 in the *Workbook.*)

The play was written in 1978; *however,* it was not produced until 1992.

Similarly, you can coordinate the two related ideas with a semicolon. (See 37a in the *Workbook*.)

> The play was written in 1978; it was not produced until 1992.

1 Writing sentences with coordination

Indicating coordinating relationships

When you coordinate two ideas, use a coordinating conjunction that is logical. For example, the coordinating conjunction *but* expresses contrast, so it would not be appropriate in a sentence expressing consequence. Look at the following examples:

EQUIVALENCE   The nurse weighed the patient, *and* then she took his blood pressure.

CONTRAST   She can't read Korean, *but* she can speak it.

ALTERNATIVES   The company must improve sales, *or* it will go bankrupt.

EXPLANATION   The baby was a little cranky, *for* he had just waked from a nap.

CONSEQUENCE   The roads had not been sanded, *so* they were quite icy.

DISTINCTION   He and I had never met, *yet* he seemed familiar.

Notice in the preceding sentences that a comma precedes the coordinating conjunction when that conjunction joins two independent clauses. When the two independent clauses are very short, however, you may choose to omit the comma.

> A shot rang out and he screamed.

In addition, a comma is unnecessary between two coordinate words, phrases, or dependent clauses.

> She likes broccoli *but* not kale.

> He has relatives in Germany *and* in Denmark.

> If there is fog *or* when pollutants fill the air, the visibility can be close to zero.

A conjunction is not always necessary to indicate coordination. You can use a semicolon between two independent clauses, especially those that are parallel in structure.

> She enjoyed operas by Wagner; he preferred operettas by Gilbert and Sullivan.

> Liberal arts majors spend a lot of time in the library; science majors spend hours in their laboratories.

When using a semicolon to join coordinate clauses, you may sometimes use a conjunctive adverb.

> The temperature was only ten degrees; *however,* the football game was played as scheduled.

> Ticket sales were excellent; the manager, *therefore,* extended the movie's run for three more weeks.

Another way to create coordinate structures is with the correlative conjunctions *either . . . or, neither . . . nor, both . . . and,* and *not only . . . but also.* (See 17c-2 in the *Workbook.*)

This semester I must take *either* math *or* biology.

Your decision was *neither* wise *nor* fair.

She was *both* surprised *and* pleased by her promotion.

When *not only . . . but also* is used to coordinate two sentences, an auxiliary verb is placed in front of the subject in the first independent clause, and the word *also* is placed near the verb in the second independent clause.

Not only did the attack leave Monica Seles physically injured, *but* the incident *also* caused emotional trauma.

Not only has the mail been delivered late every day, *but* some of it has *also* been torn.

Both . . . and is not used to coordinate two independent clauses, just elements within a sentence.

He is allergic to *both* ragweed *and* dust.

Both physics *and* chemistry require knowledge of math.

Coordination and revision

Coordinating conjunctions and conjunctive adverbs link ideas and give readers clear signals about the relationships among ideas. Without coordination, writing may seem choppy, rough, and disjointed. Compare the following two paragraphs:

WITHOUT COORDINATION

The various schools and departments in a big university may not bring in equal amounts of money in tuition and grants. Those schools and departments are equally important. A university's business school, for example, may have many students. The school generates a lot of income for the university. The Department of Slavic Languages may not have many undergraduate majors and graduate students. The tuition charged those few students may not cover the salaries of the professors in the department. Nevertheless, the function of a university is to foster education and scholarship. Both the business school and the small department must be considered equally necessary. They should not be regarded as successful or unsuccessful subsidiaries of a large company.

WITH COORDINATION

The various schools and departments in a big university may not bring in equal amounts of money in tuition and grants; *those* schools and departments, *however,* are equally important. *On the one hand,* a university's business school, for example, may have many students; *therefore,* the school generates a lot of income for the university. *On the other hand,* the Department of Slavic Languages may not have many undergraduate majors and graduate students; the tuition charged those few students may not cover the salaries of the professors in the department. Nevertheless, the function of a university is to foster education and scholarship, *so* both the business school and the small department must be considered equally necessary *and* not regarded as successful or unsuccessful subsidiaries of a large company.

Coordination makes the revised version much smoother than the original version. Coordination indicates equivalence, contrast, and explanation, thus signaling to the reader the relative importance of each idea.

2 | Avoiding excessive coordination

Coordination can be overused. Do not use coordination as the only way, or the primary way, to link ideas. Excessive coordination results in monotonous, stiff, unnatural-sounding writing. Look at the following example:

EXCESSIVE COORDINATION

> Some people use credit cards excessively, *and* they run up huge bills. The bills arrive at the end of the month, *and* they are unable to pay those bills. They pay a portion of the bill, *and* then interest charges start to accumulate. They get deeper into debt, *but* there seems to be no way out. Their problem lies in their attitude toward credit cards, *for* they seem to regard the cards as unlimited money. A more sensible attitude is to think of a credit card as a way of borrowing money until the end of the month, *and* then people would not charge more than they can pay for at the end of that month.

REVISED

> Some people use credit cards excessively, running up huge bills. When the bills arrive at the end of the month, they are unable to pay them. If they pay only a portion of the bill, interest charges start to accumulate. They get deeper into debt, seeing no way out. Their problem lies in their attitude toward credit cards; they seem to regard the cards as unlimited money. A more sensible attitude is to think of a credit card as a way of borrowing money until the end of the month; then people would not charge more than they can pay for at the end of that month.

The revised version is more effective than the excessively coordinated version. The revision more accurately describes the relationship among ideas, and it is far less monotonous.

3 | Avoiding illogical coordination

Illogical coordination occurs when the ideas in two joined clauses are not related or when the coordinating word expresses an inaccurate relationship between the clauses.

ILLOGICAL   Ms. Truong had a slight fever, and she went to work anyway. [The *and* is illogical because the two clauses suggest contrast.]

REVISED   Ms. Truong had a slight fever, *but* she went to work anyway.

ILLOGICAL   Diabetes mellitus is a disease, and it is usually caused by a deficient secretion of insulin. [Its classification as a disease and its cause are not two separate entities.]

REVISED   Diabetes mellitus is a disease that is usually caused by a deficient secretion of insulin.

To check coordination in your writing, first look at coordinating conjunctions join-ing independent clauses and determine if these conjunctions are used logically. Then check for excessive coordination; if you find heavy use of *and* and *but*, change some of your coordinate structures to subordinate structures. You might replace some coordi-nating conjunctions with conjunctive adverbs. If many of your sentences contain two independent clauses joined with just a semicolon, consider subordinating one of the clauses in some of the sentences.

26b   Using subordination to distinguish main ideas

1   Writing sentences with subordination

Subordination helps readers to distinguish the main idea in a sentence from ideas that qualify or expand the main idea. Usually the main idea appears in an independent clause; related ideas and details appear in phrases or in dependent clauses. By using subordination, you can signal the relative importance of the ideas. In the following example, the independent clause is italicized, and the dependent clause is underlined:

Ms. Smith was a dedicated biologist who loved to ice skate and ski.

In this sentence, the dependent clause adds information about Ms. Smith. The main point of the sentence is expressed in the independent clause: *Ms. Smith was a dedicated biologist.* To emphasize Ms. Smith's love of skating and skiing, the sentence could be rewritten to subordinate her career as a biologist:

Ms. Smith, who was a dedicated biologist, *loved to ice skate and ski.*

Although Ms. Smith was a dedicated biologist, *she loved to ice skate and ski.*

Each revision results in a slightly different meaning; one idea is emphasized and the other becomes secondary. Subordination, therefore, offers you choices. You decide which idea dominates and which idea supports.

The placement of a subordinate construction is also important. Look at the follow-ing two examples:

If you do not stop smoking, *you may get lung cancer.*

You may get lung cancer if you do not stop smoking.

Because of its placement at the end of the sentence in the first example, the independent clause is the more emphatic clause. In the second example, emphasis shifts to the depen-dent clause because it appears at the end.

Subordination has other uses as well. It signals logical relationships among facts and details. The uses of some commonly used subordinating conjunctions are explained and illustrated in the following chart:

To show cause or explain why
   because, since

Because the road was washed out, the ambulance could not get through.

To express concession
   although, as if, though, even though

Although I started late, I will arrive in time.

To indicate a condition
   even if, provided, since, unless

Unless the snow stops, no flights will be able to leave.

To establish time
   as soon as, after, before, since, when, whenever, while, until

We went for coffee *after* the concert ended.

To indicate location
   where, wherever

Michael Jordan is recognized *wherever* he goes.

To indicate choice
   rather than, whether

Whether it snows or not, our ski trip will be fun.

To show purpose
   that, in order that, so that

He changed his work schedule *so that* he could spend more time with his children.

In addition to using subordinating conjunctions, you can subordinate with adjective clauses introduced by relative pronouns—*who, whom, which, that, when,* and *where.*

I admired the opinions *that* you expressed at the meeting.

We enjoy the times *when* the whole family gets together.

He hid the letter in a place *where* no one could find it.

2 | Avoiding excessive subordination

Writers sometimes use too many dependent clauses, and the result is excessive subordination. Sentences with excessive subordination tend to run so long that the relationship between ideas becomes confused and hard for readers to follow. Rewriting such sentences as several shorter ones gives writing more clarity and emphasis. Consider the following example:

EXCESSIVE SUBORDINATION

If the semester is shortened from fourteen to thirteen weeks, most people at the college will be pleased, as long as students feel that they have enough time to study and faculty members feel that they have enough time to present all the course material, because otherwise the shortened semester could have deleterious effects.

REVISED TO ELIMINATE EXCESSIVE SUBORDINATION

If the semester is shortened from fourteen to thirteen weeks, most people at the college will be pleased. However, if students feel that they do not have enough time to study and faculty members feel that they do not have enough time to present all the course material, the shortened semester could have deleterious effects.

3	Avoiding illogical subordination

Illogical subordination happens when the most important idea in a sentence is put in a dependent clause or when the subordinating conjunction does not accurately reflect the relationship between two clauses.

ILLOGICAL   Because he referred to his script, the actor forgot his lines during rehearsal. [The expected relationship between clauses is mistakenly reversed; referring to a script cannot make the actor forget his lines.]

REVISED   Because the actor forgot his lines during rehearsal, he referred to his script.

ILLOGICAL   Bill Gates is not yet forty, although he has been running an incredibly successful business for nearly twenty years.

REVISED   Although Bill Gates is not yet forty, he has been running an incredibly successful business for nearly twenty years.

EXERCISE 1   Combining Sentences to Coordinate Related Ideas

Use coordination to combine the following sentence pairs. Write two versions for each pair of sentences. Example:

I can hear his voice. I cannot understand what he is saying.

I can hear his voice, but I cannot understand what he is saying.

I can hear his voice; however, I cannot understand what he is saying.

1. Some people cannot work under pressure. Others seem to thrive on it.

2. Mr. Santos is a diamond cutter. He is teaching the trade to his son.

3. The math problem looked easy. It took me forty minutes to do it.

4. The hurricane may reach land by midday. It may veer out over the ocean.

5. He did not look at the district attorney. He did not raise his voice above a whisper.

EXERCISE 2   Eliminating Excessive and Illogical Coordination

Rewrite the following sentences to eliminate excessive and illogical coordination. Example:

He was full of anger, and he did not show it.

He was full of anger, but he did not show it.

1. I called her three times, and she was never home.

2. Judy was worried about her history class, and she talked to Professor Gotkin, and Professor Gotkin told Judy that tutoring might help, and Judy decided to try it.

3. She does regular aerobic exercise, but she works out with weights.

4. Mark remembered to lock the car doors, so he forgot to roll up all the windows.

5. He needed to buy cheese, vegetables, and pasta, and he went to the grocery store, but he had forgotten his wallet, and he had to go home to get it, and then he went back to the store, but it was late, and the store was closed.

EXERCISE 3 Combining Sentences to Achieve Subordination

Use subordinate structures to combine each set of short sentences into one longer sentence. Example:

Rick is a great shortstop. He seldom makes an error. He may never play in the major leagues. He needs to become a better hitter.

Rick is a great shortstop who seldom makes an error. However, unless he can become a better hitter, he may never play in the major leagues.

1. Every morning a woodpecker awakened us. It was always six in the morning. The bird pecked at the chimney pipe. The chimney pipe is made of metal. The noise echoed throughout the house.

2. Years ago, there were few food co-ops. Now, there are more. Individuals usually pay high retail prices for groceries. Groups of people can arrange to buy in bulk at wholesale prices.

3. Record players are no longer very popular. It is easy to see the reasons. Many people prefer the sound of CD players over record players. Record players are neither convenient nor portable.

4. Sara worked very hard writing her college application essay. She was not happy with it. She reread it carefully. She decided to change its focus.

5. In January I was shopping for a winter coat. I noticed that bathing suits were on sale. I would not need a bathing suit until June. I bought one anyway.

EXERCISE 4   Eliminating Excessive and Illogical Subordination

Rewrite the following sentences to eliminate excessive and illogical subordination. Example:

Ruth was ninety years old even though she continued to play golf.

Even though Ruth was ninety years old, she continued to play golf.

1. The building would not be occupied although all the asbestos could be removed.

2. By next June, since Christine has completed almost all the necessary courses, and if the college accepts some credits taken years ago at another institution, she will have graduated, unless some unforeseen emergency occurs.

3. The museum has a magnificent collection of Amish quilts even though they contain bright primary colors.

4. Alicia Alonso became nearly blind even though she continued to dance.

5. Because new television shows appear every season, certain old favorites continue to appeal to viewers.

EXERCISE 5   Revising with Coordination and Subordination

Use coordination and subordination to revise the following sets of short sentences. Example:

My car was stuck on some ice. The wheels were spinning. I poured some cat litter around each wheel. I was able to move the car.

My car was stuck on some ice, and the wheels were spinning. After I poured some cat litter around each wheel, I was able to move the car.

1. Karen had tried to lose weight. She was not successful. She got a treadmill. She used it for half an hour, five or six times a week. Slowly but surely the weight came off.

2. All the ornaments on our Christmas tree are homemade. They are unbreakable. We own two dogs and a cat. They are rambunctious. They could knock the tree down. Nothing on the tree would break. The animals would not be hurt.

3. Some people find opera exceedingly boring. Others think it is thrilling. Some people are bored by geology. Others are fascinated by it. There is an old saying, "One man's meat is another man's poison."

4. Mr. and Mrs. Thurmond's dog Rover did not like staying in the yard. He dug out under the fence at least twice a week. The Thurmonds would fix the fence. They thought Rover would not be able to get out again. They were always wrong.

5. A study method works for one student. It may not work for another. Each person learns in a different way. Every student needs to find the way that works best for him or her.

EXERCISE 6   Writing with Coordination and Subordination

For each topic that follows, write two sentences, one using coordination and the other using subordination.

Topic: A recent news event

I liked Tip O'Neill's loyalty to his unabashedly liberal views, and I was saddened by his death.

I was saddened by the death of Tip O'Neill, who was an old-fashioned politician with unabashedly liberal views.

1. Your favorite hobby

2. Why you chose your college

3. A memorable movie

4. The food you dislike most

5. A clothing fashion you consider inappropriate

CHAPTER 27

Using Parallelism in Sentences

Parallelism consists of using similar grammatical forms for two or more coordinate elements. Note the parallel elements in the following sentences:

They spent their vacation *golfing, swimming,* and *hiking.*

She *made* breakfast, *walked* the dog, and *drove* to work.

He looked for his keys *under the sofa, on top of the refrigerator,* and *in his briefcase.*

Parallelism is used with elements in a series, with paired elements, to enhance coherence, and to organize lists and outlines.

27a Using parallelism to coordinate elements in a series

Use parallel structure for all items in a series. That series may consist of single words, phrases, or clauses.

NOUNS	His good qualities include *patience, trust,* and *humor.*
VERBS	As the wind changed, the flag *fluttered, flapped,* and then *drooped.*
PHRASES	I can't remember whether I left that file *at home* or *at the office.*
CLAUSES	He wants to know *where we went, what we did,* and *when we came back.*

A break in parallel structure often creates awkwardness in writing:

NONPARALLEL	She is loyal, trustworthy, and *has discretion.*
REVISED	She is loyal, trustworthy, and *discreet.*
NONPARALLEL	The course guide sets out attendance regulations, reading assignments, and *when you have to take* the midterm and final exams.
REVISED	The course guide sets out attendance regulations, reading assignments, and *the dates of* the midterm and final exams.

27b Using parallelism with pairs

A common use of parallelism is the pairing of two ideas. To compare or contrast ideas, use a coordinating conjunction, a correlative conjunction, or the subordinating conjunction *as* or *then,* and state the two ideas in parallel grammatical form.

1 | Parallelism with coordinate conjunctions

To create a parallel structure, use similar grammatical structures on both sides of a coordinating conjunction—*and, or, but, for, nor, yet, so.*

He was delighted one minute *and* depressed the next.

Any male can be a father, *but* only a real man can be a daddy.

When sentence elements do not appear in similar grammatical form, the relationship between them may not be clear. In addition, the sentence will be awkward or confusing.

NONPARALLEL   Their clothing was *torn* and *in a mess.* [The adjective *torn* and the prepositional phrase *in a mess* are not parallel structures.]

REVISED   Their clothing was *torn* and *messy.* [The clothing is now described by two single-word adjectives, *torn* and *messy.*]

NONPARALLEL   Two things to consider when buying a house are the *taxes* and *if the local schools are good.* [The noun *taxes* and the clause *if the local schools are good* are not parallel structures.]

REVISED   Two things to consider when buying a house are the *taxes* and the *quality* of the local schools. [The nouns *taxes* and *quality* are parallel.]

2 | Parallelism with correlative conjunctions

Use parallel forms with correlative conjunctions—*either . . . or, neither . . . nor, both . . . and, not only . . . but also.*

He *not only cooked* a great meal *but also cleaned* up afterwards.

At best, the team can achieve *either third place or a tie* for second.

The same grammatical structure must be used after each part of the correlative conjunction.

NONPARALLEL   They read neither *newspapers* nor *watch news on television.* [The noun *newspapers* follows *neither,* but the verb phrase *watch news on television* follows *nor.*]

REVISED   They neither *read newspapers* nor *watch news* on television. [Here both parts of the correlative conjunction are followed by verb phrases.]

3 | Parallelism with the subordinate conjunctions *than* and *as*

When you compare or contrast two things using the word *than* or *as,* use a similar grammatical structure in both parts of the comparison or contrast.

It is better to be *safe than sorry.*

She was *as generous as* she was *kindhearted.*

A sentence lacking parallel structure may sound awkward.

NONPARALLEL   The coach always motivated the players with *praise* rather than *criticizing them.*

REVISED   The coach always motivated the players with *praise* rather than *criticism.*

NONPARALLEL   She always dreamed of becoming *a doctor* rather than *to go to law school.*

REVISED   She always dreamed of becoming *a doctor* rather than *a lawyer.*

27c Using parallelism to enhance coherence

Parallelism emphasizes the connections between related elements in sentences and paragraphs, thereby helping readers see how those elements are related. Look at this example:

NONPARALLEL   Before a long automobile trip, one ought to check the oil and other fluids, fill the tires to the recommended pressure, and *making sure* that the brakes work well. [*Check, fill,* and *making sure* are not parallel in structure.]

REVISED   Before a long automobile trip, one ought to check the oil and other fluids, fill the tires to the recommended pressure, and *make sure* that the brakes work well.

27d Using parallelism to organize lists and outlines

Lists and outlines are most effective and most useful when the elements within them appear in parallel grammatical form. Consider the following list:

NONPARALLEL   The town board will discuss three things:
  1. the need for more street lights
  2. increasing numbers of burglaries
  3. a raise in the salary of municipal employees

Each item in the preceding list has a different grammatical structure. For clearer presentation, all three items should be similar. Here are two possible revisions:

PARALLEL   The town board will discuss three issues:
  1. street lights
  2. recent burglaries
  3. municipal salaries

PARALLEL   The town board will discuss three issues:
  1. requests for more street lights
  2. increases in recent burglaries
  3. raises for municipal employees

EXERCISE 1   Identifying Parallel Elements

Underline the parallel elements in the following sentences. Example:

She has worked as a <u>waitress,</u> a <u>salesperson,</u> and a <u>painter.</u>

1. Finches, cardinals, and chickadees visit the bird feeder.

2. We cleaned the house, threw out all the old food, and brought out the special dishes and cups for the holiday.

3. There was cat fur on the sofa, on the chairs, and on all the rugs.

4. When we walked in, we saw that paintings of ducks hung on the walls, duck decoys adorned the shelves, and photographs of our host going duck hunting sat on the coffee table.

5. I may have lost my gloves in the restaurant, in the cab, or in the theater.

EXERCISE 2   Revising for Parallelism

Rewrite the following sentences to correct nonparallel structures. Example:

Before the play-offs, the team was both excited and had anxiety.

Before the play-offs, the team was both excited and anxious.

1. This is a time for joy; it is not a time that you should be sad.

2. He wants to own a pet store because the idea of being his own boss pleases him and his love of animals.

3. He worked as a gardener, a bike messenger, and cooking on a freighter.

4. He drinks neither alcohol nor smokes cigarettes.

5. It is wiser to check the oil now than risking trouble later on the road.

EXERCISE 3   Using Parallel Elements in Writing

Write a sentence using each set of parallel elements that follows. Example:

Parallel elements: to see or to hear

After the accident, he was temporarily unable to see or to hear.

1. in the classroom, in the lab, and in the library

2. saying nothing or talking to the professor

3. listened . . . wrote . . . asked

4. studying either biology or chemistry

5. well educated but not snobbish

EXERCISE 4   Using Parallelism in Writing

For each topic that follows, write a sentence using parallel structure. Example:

Topic: Jobs you have done

I have worked as a camp counselor, a waitress, and a cook.

1. Good traits in a friend

2. An interesting course

3. A perfect vacation

4. Skills a parent needs

5. A dilemma you once experienced

CHAPTER 28

Achieving Sentence Variety

Sentence variety can make your writing readable and interesting. A lack of variety leads to monotony and boredom in writing. You can achieve variety in sentence length, sentence openings, sentence type, and sentence structure.

28a Varying sentence length

A paper in which all the sentences were the same length would be monotonous and boring. Varying sentence length gives strength to your writing. Short sentences give emphasis; longer sentences demonstrate the connections between ideas.

1 Avoiding strings of short sentences

Using too many short sentences in a row usually produces monotony. In addition, a series of short sentences cannot indicate the relationship among ideas or their relative importance. Further effects are choppiness and a lack of sophistication. Look at the following example:

UNVARIED SHORT SENTENCES

Many junior and senior high school students are volunteers. They tutor children in the elementary grades. The teenagers help the children with reading and math. The children certainly benefit from the extra help. The teenage volunteers also gain. Their academic skills increase. They have more self-esteem.

REVISED

Many junior and senior high school students volunteer to tutor children in the elementary grades, helping them with reading and math. While the children certainly benefit from the extra help, the teenage volunteers also gain in both academic skills and self-esteem.

The revised version eliminates the choppiness and childlike tone of the unrevised version. It also makes clear the relationship among the various ideas.

2 Avoiding strings of long sentences

A string of long sentences can confuse readers about which ideas the writer wishes to emphasize. Here is an example:

UNVARIED LONG SENTENCES

The term "bourgeoisie" was originally the name for people who lived in walled towns in medieval France, people who worked as artisans and craftspeople and thus occupied a social and economic position between the peasants and the landlords of the countryside. The term was extended to include the French middle class and then the middle classes of all nations, and in time the bourgeoisie was instrumental in the decline of feudalism and the expansion of political rights.

REVISED

The term "bourgeoisie" was originally the name for people who lived in walled towns in medieval France. These people worked as artisans and craftspeople and thus occupied a social and economic position between the peasants and the landlords of the countryside. The term was extended to include the French middle class and then the middle class of all nations. In time the bourgeoisie was instrumental in the decline of feudalism and the expansion of political rights.

The unrevised version places too many important concepts in each sentence, thus diluting the significance of each idea. The revised version gives emphasis to each important characteristic of the subject.

3 | Mixing long and short sentences

Blending long sentences with short ones allows you to use short sentences for emphasis, while employing longer ones to express relationships among ideas. Consider the following example:

Many of my experiences on the subway have been painful. During one trip downtown to report for jury duty, my wallet was stolen, a fact I did not discover until I arrived at the courthouse. On another occasion, the train was stuck between stations, and one of my fellow passengers went into insulin shock. Yet another time, two men stumbled into the car, grappling with each other and shouting incomprehensible but disturbing words at each other and then at other passengers. I never take naps on the subway.

The opening sentence in this paragraph is neither short nor long; it introduces the topic. The second, third, and fourth sentences average about twenty words apiece, each describing a particular experience. The final short sentence concludes the paragraph unexpectedly and emphatically. In your writing, you do not have to limit yourself to placing short sentences only at the end of a paragraph. A brief, emphatic sentence can be just as effective at the beginning or in the middle of a paragraph.

28b | Varying sentence openings

Another way to make your writing more interesting is to vary the beginnings of your sentences. If almost every sentence in a paragraph begins the same way, the result will be monotony even if sentence length varies. In the following example, notice how every sentence begins with the subject:

UNVARIED SENTENCE OPENINGS

Exercise brings benefits of many kinds, in physical health, appearance, athletic performance, endurance, and emotional health. Aerobic exercise can improve the cardiovascular system. It can strengthen the heart and increase the capacity of the lungs. Regular exercise can lead to weight loss. Of course, it should be combined with a sensible diet. Exercise can also improve muscle tone and enhance the appearance. It builds strength and endurance for better athletic performance. Regular exercise gives people energy to perform well in all areas of their lives. It can provide more than physical benefits. Exercise also can relieve stress and tension. Regular exercise should be part of everyone's life.

VARIED SENTENCE OPENINGS

Exercise brings benefits of many kinds, in physical health, athletic performance, endurance, and emotional health. Aerobic exercise can improve the cardiovascular system, strengthening the heart and increasing the capacity of the lungs. Combined with a sensible diet, regular exercise can lead to weight loss while improving muscle tone and enhancing the appearance. Greater strength and endurance result in both better athletic performance and higher energy levels so that people can function well in all areas of their lives. Providing more than physical benefits, exercise can also relieve stress and tension. Exercise should be part of everyone's life.

1 | Using transitions to create sentence variety

Transitions, whether single words or phrases, link one sentence to another. Transitional words and phrases signal to the reader the relationship between two sentences. Words denoting time (*now, then, later, afterwards*) indicate chronological relationship. Words and phrases of contrast (*however, on the other hand, on the contrary*) indicate a shift of opinion or emphasis. Words signaling result (*therefore, as a result*) indicate that a consequence or an effect will be described.

In the 1940s, many law schools did not admit women. *Now* women comprise half of all the students in law school.

My supervisor is demanding and irritable. *On the other hand*, she is also scrupulously fair.

The mountain road had been blocked by an avalanche. *Therefore*, the trapped motorists had to be rescued by helicopters.

2 | Using dependent clauses to create sentence variety

For variety, begin some of your sentences with dependent clauses (see 13d in the *Workbook*). Notice the difference between these two examples:

Some people fantasize about an endless vacation. They might find unlimited free time more of a burden than a boon.

Although some people fantasize about an endless vacation, they might find unlimited free time more of a burden than a boon.

In the second example, beginning with a dependent clause breaks the monotonous pattern of starting each sentence with the subject. In addition, placing a dependent clause first puts strong emphasis on the idea in the independent clause.

Put a dependent clause first in a sentence when you want to clarify the relationship between ideas or to emphasize the independent clause.

Because construction had slowed traffic to a standstill, we missed our flight to New Mexico.

While my back was turned, the cat swiped a drumstick off my plate.

Although he took up the game only two years ago, he is already a skilled tennis player.

3 | Using phrases to create sentence variety

Beginning some sentences with phrases can add variety to your writing. You may use prepositional phrases and verbal phrases, including participial, infinitive, and absolute phrases (see 13c in the *Workbook*). Here are some examples:

PREPOSITIONAL PHRASE	*In the catalog* you will find short descriptions of all course offerings.
PARTICIPIAL PHRASE	*Worried about a persistent cough,* he made an appointment with his doctor.
PARTICIPIAL PHRASE	*Holding a large package in one hand,* she tried to pick up her purse and briefcase with the other hand.
INFINITIVE PHRASE	*To increase flexibility,* the athlete follows a regular program of stretching.
ABSOLUTE PHRASE	*The flat tire having been fixed,* we continued our trip.

Adverbs can be effective sentence openers. Overuse of opening adverbs, as with any other frequently repeated element, can cause monotony; however, occasional use increases variety. Note the opening adverbs in the following sentences:

Eventually, the long speech came to an end.

Unfortunately, a broken leg was the least of his injuries.

28c | Varying sentence types

You can achieve sentence variety by using different sentence types. Sentences can be classified as simple, compound, complex, or compound-complex (see 13f in the *Workbook*). Give your writing variety and interest by using different grammatical structures. In addition, sentences can be varied according to function. Declarative sentences assert, interrogative sentences question, imperative sentences command, and exclamatory sentences express strong feelings. Most of your sentences will be declarative, but occasional use of the other kinds will add variety to your writing. Notice that the sentences in the following paragraph are varied both in grammatical structure and in function:

> Why has Davy Crockett had such a hold on the American imagination? Perhaps one reason is his image as an unsophisticated yet crafty backwoodsman, for Americans often like to think of themselves as both unpretentious and astute. Although Crockett was indeed a frontiersman from Tennessee, he served in the Tennessee state legislature, and in 1827 he was elected to the first of three terms in Congress. The incongruity between Crockett's frontier background and his service in government may be another factor contributing to his popularity. Imagine a buckskin-clad frontiersman making naive but shrewd comments about politics in Washington, D.C.! Crockett's heroic death in the defense of the Alamo has added to his legend; he has become almost a mythic figure of American history.

Sentences are also classified, according to their rhetorical effects, as cumulative (loose) or periodic (climactic). Cumulative sentences state the subject and predicate at the start and then add details. Periodic sentences delay the main idea until the end. Using these sentence types can also add variety to your writing.

1 | Cumulative sentences

A cumulative sentence states its subject and predicate first, then develops by adding details—modifying phrases and clauses. Use a cumulative sentence when you want to set forth the main point of a sentence right away, when you have much detail to include, or when you wish to emphasize an image at the end of a sentence. Notice the effect produced in the following cumulative sentence:

> My aunt Petra was an efficient cook, reading a recipe in advance, making sure she had all the required ingredients, stirring the simmering food briskly, and cleaning pots and utensils immediately after use.

2 | Periodic sentences

A periodic sentence delays the verb and sometimes the subject until the end of the sentence. Readers must reach the end to find the main idea of a periodic sentence. Such a structure builds anticipation and suspense; it also gives emphasis to the main idea. Notice the placement of subject and verb in this periodic sentence:

> When teenagers regularly take weapons to school, when many children are often awakened by the sound of gunfire, and when huge numbers of grade school students have not had routine immunizations, clearly society has failed its most vulnerable members.

EXERCISE 1   Varying Sentence Length

Rewrite the following sets of sentences to vary sentence length. Example:

Snow had been falling steadily for six hours. Houses, lawns, and streets were blanketed in white. The effect was ghostly. It was also beautiful.

Snow had been falling steadily for hours, blanketing houses, lawns, and streets in white. The effect was ghostly, yet beautiful.

1. Bertha likes gardening. She feels it relieves tension. She goes into her garden. Soon she has forgotten all the day's worries.

2. Ella is never around when an emergency happens, and this is not a coincidence because she dislikes trouble and makes herself scarce when trouble arises.

3. Doctors have some contact with individual patients. Nurses have more. Nurses may be with particular patients for many hours. Nurses often notice changes in a patient's condition first. Doctors may notice the change later.

4. Movies whose plots have been taken from novels are sometimes successful, but, interestingly, really great novels do not always result in great movies, perhaps in part because a novel may have rich interior monologues that do not translate easily into a cinematic medium.

5. Car phones have become status symbols. Having a car phone indicates wealth. It could also indicate power. Certain stores sell fake, nonworking car phones. These fake car phones give their owners the appearance of status.

EXERCISE 2   Varying Sentence Openings

Combine each set of sentences that follows into a single sentence. Use transitional words, dependent clauses, prepositional phrases, and verbal phrases as openings. Example:

My car radio broke. I couldn't listen to the traffic and news.

After my car radio broke, I couldn't listen to the traffic and news.

1. He loves to eat eggplant. He had never seen an unpeeled, uncooked eggplant.

2. One can get help with computer software problems. One can call the manufacturer's toll-free "800" number.

3. The concert had ended. We went out for a late dinner.

4. Mr. Allen was waiting for his daughter's bus to arrive. He was reading the sports pages.

5. The project was finally finished. She took a much-needed vacation.

EXERCISE 3   Using Various Sentence Openings in Writing

Write a sentence using each suggested opening. Example:

Opening: Before your presentation

Before your presentation, review your notes and try to relax.

1. On the other hand

2. Although he could not speak Vietnamese

3. During the entire semester

4. Watching the dial carefully

5. Fascinated yet horrified

EXERCISE 4   Sentence Combining for Variety

Combine each set of simple sentences to create one compound, complex, or compound-complex sentence. Example:

We admired the wedding cake. It was four tiers high.

We admired the wedding cake, which was four tiers high.

1. The harpsichord and the piano look alike. Their sounds are not produced in the same way.

2. It rained only once during our trip. We were able to play golf every day.

3. The drought has lasted for months. The fields are dry. The crops are stunted.

4. She can't go to work. She has a cold. I will have to fill in for her.

5. My father just got a new VCR. He does not know how to program it.

EXERCISE 5   Using Cumulative and Periodic Sentences

Combine each set of short sentences two different ways: first as a long cumulative sentence, and then as a long periodic sentence. Example:

The driveway was steep. The surface was icy. Visibility was limited. I got my car into the garage.

I got my car into the garage even though the driveway was steep, the surface was icy, and visibility was limited.

Even though the driveway was steep, the surface was icy, and visibility was limited, I got my car into the garage.

1. He was not happy. The sun was shining. The weather was warm. The fish were biting.

2. The people on the tour visited four countries in six days. They went to the theater in London. They walked through the Louvre in Paris. They admired tulips in Holland. They saw the Little Mermaid in Denmark.

3. I got several bills in today's mail. There were two offers of credit cards. An entry form for a contest arrived. There was nothing I wanted to read.

4. The front of the fruit and vegetable store looked like a jeweler's shop. Piles of red apples looked like garnets and rubies. Green apples, avocados, and honeydew melons glowed like emeralds or jade.

5. Her desk looks as if a cyclone had hit it. Books are piled up haphazardly. Pieces of paper lie crumpled on the blotter. Some rather old flowers droop in a plastic vase.

EXERCISE 6 Sentence Variety in Writing

For each topic that follows, write a brief paragraph of three to five sentences in which you vary the length of sentences. Example:

Topic: Speaking in public

I may get used to speaking in public, but I will probably never be relaxed about it. Being the center of attention makes me uncomfortable. Aware that people's eyes are on me and that some of them are even taking notes, I become very nervous and begin to talk too fast.

1. Starting a new job

2. The first day at college

3. Tutoring someone

4. Regional accents

5. Attitudes toward money

CHAPTER 29

Achieving Emphasis and Conciseness

Two aspects of effective writing reinforce one another: emphasis and conciseness. Emphasis involves stressing key words and ideas; conciseness involves expressing ideas directly and succinctly.

29a Writing with emphasis

1 Achieving emphasis with parallel structures

Parallel structures contain similar words, phrases, or clauses. Look at the following examples:

PARALLEL WORDS   The day was *damp, dark,* and *cold.*

PARALLEL PHRASES   There were books everywhere—*on the shelves, on the chairs,* and *on the floor.*

PARALLEL CLAUSES   We did not know *how the incident happened* or *how it would end.*

To use parallel structures emphatically, place them in order of increasing importance. In a series of three or more items, place the most important item last.

UNEMPHATIC   The experience robbed him of his time, all his self-esteem, and his money.

EMPHATIC   The experience robbed him of his time, his money, and all his self-esteem.

In order to emphasize one of two related statements, subordinate the less important one, and put the more important statement last.

UNEMPHATIC   The tenor's voice is still magnificent even though he may be past his prime.

EMPHATIC   Even though the tenor may be past his prime, his voice is still magnificent.

The most emphatic position in a sentence or a paragraph is the end. The next most emphatic spot is the beginning; the least emphatic is the middle.

2 Achieving emphasis with short sentences

Short sentences can give writing emphasis when placed at the beginning of a paragraph or when placed after a series of longer sentences. Short sentences in such positions command attention. In the following paragraph, a short sentence is used emphatically after two longer ones:

> Karl's parents were worried that the eleven-year-old was dangerously thin, so he was given a special, high-calorie diet and was not allowed to play or exercise for two hours after every meal. This weight-gaining routine was followed meticulously for over a month, at the end of which the child was weighed. Karl had lost two pounds.

3 Achieving emphasis with repetition

Words repeated within a sentence can be emphatic, as in the following example:

> It had something to do with his blackness, I think—he was very black—with his blackness and his beauty, and the fact that he knew he was black but did not know he was beautiful.

> —James Baldwin, "Notes of a Native Son"

In this example, the purposeful repetition of important words gives emphasis to the writing.

Be careful, however, of careless repetition. Do not place words near each other if they sound the same or almost the same:

CLUMSY   New graduates are *finding* it more and more difficult to *find* jobs.

REVISED   New graduates have more and more difficulties finding jobs.

CLUMSY   The *reporter* for Channel 3 *reported* that a major water main had burst.

REVISED   The reporter for Channel 3 said that a major water main had burst.

4 Achieving emphasis by placing important elements in key positions

Although placing words first in a sentence or paragraph can give those words importance, the *most* emphatic place in a sentence or a paragraph is *last*. Notice the slight differences in emphasis in the following sentences:

> She achieved her goals because of her ambition, persistence, and intelligence.

> She achieved her goals because of her intelligence, persistence, and ambition.

In the first example, placing the word *intelligence* last suggests that it is the most important of the three qualities. The arrangement of words in the second example suggests that ambition is the most important quality.

5 Achieving emphasis with inversion

In standard word order, the subject comes first and the predicate follows. An inverted sentence puts part or all of the predicate before the subject. In the following examples, the simple predicate (verb) is italicized and the simple subject is underlined:

STANDARD   An <u>ambulance</u> *raced* down the street.

INVERTED   Down the street *raced* an <u>ambulance</u>.

The inverted sentence keeps the reader waiting a bit and thus creates suspense. Use inverted sentences occasionally for variety and emphasis; too many inverted sentences cause awkwardness in and slow down the pace of writing.

6 Achieving emphasis with short paragraphs

Short paragraphs are most commonly used in journalism. However, an occasional short paragraph can effectively give emphasis to academic writing as well. Look at the following example:

> Every year, between 80,000 and 100,000 babies in China are born with neural tube defects, including spina bifida and anencephaly. Chinese rates of neural tube defects are nearly ten times greater than those in the West. These kinds of birth defects occur when there are problems in the first month of pregnancy, problems that interfere with the normal formation of the brain and spinal column. Because of the lack of special hospitals and surgical techniques to treat neural tube defects, most of the Chinese babies born with these conditions die.
> Taking .04 miligrams of folic acid during early pregnancy prevents more than half of all neural tube defects.

After the longer first paragraph describing the problem of neural tube defects, the short, one-sentence paragraph flatly stating a solution appears quite emphatic.

29b Writing with conciseness

Concise writing gets to the point. Whether sentences are long or short, they should deliver ideas efficiently, using no unnecessary words.

1 Eliminate unnecessary intensifiers

An intensifier is a word, usually an adjective or an adverb, that tries to reinforce the effect of the word it modifies. Intensifiers such as *very* and *really* are often unnecessary. Instead of an intensifier, use a word that more exactly conveys your meaning.

UNNECESSARY   She was *very, very angry.*

REVISED   She was *furious.*

UNNECESSARY   His job is *really boring*.

REVISED   His job is *tedious and monotonous*.

2 | Replace wordy phrases

Wordy phrases take up room on the page but do not add substance. Replace wordy phrases with single words or concise phrases. Look at the following examples:

WORDY   I cannot join you *due to the fact that* I have to finish some work.

CONCISE   I cannot join you *because* I have to finish some work.

Here is a list of wordy phrases and concise alternatives:

WORDY	CONCISE
at this point in time	now
at all times	always
in this day and age	today
by means of	by
for the most part	mostly
in order to	to
give consideration to	consider
in view of the fact that	since
a large number of	many
few in number	few
lend assistance to	assist, help
make contact with	contact
past experience	experience
persons of the Catholic faith	Catholics
sufficient amount of	enough
ideas of a serious nature	serious ideas
remarks of a humorous nature	humorous remarks
until such time as	until
in light of the fact that	since, because
regardless of the fact that	although
for the purpose of	to
in close proximity to	near
aware of the fact that	know
in the event that	if
in the nature of	like
in the final analysis	finally
has the capacity for	can
disappear from view	disappear
destroy by fire	burn

3 | Avoid negating words

To reduce wordiness, eliminate negating words such as *no* and *not*. Use a more exact word instead.

WORDY   I *do not approve* of the way you handled that situation.

CONCISE   I *disapprove* of the way you handled that situation.

WORDY   He was *not present* all week.

CONCISE   He was *absent* all week.

4 | Eliminate redundancy

Redundancy is the needless repetition of words, phrases, sentences, or paragraphs. Redundant expressions add nothing to what has already been said but simply take up space.

Redundant word pairs

Redundant word pairs have three words where only one is needed. Eliminate the implied word and the coordinating conjunction.

REDUNDANT   *Each and every* proposal will be carefully considered.

REVISED   *Each* proposal will be carefully considered.

Redundant modifiers

Redundant modifiers are implied by the nouns they modify and are therefore unnecessary.

REDUNDANT   Her *future hope* is to be a respiratory therapist. [The noun *hope* implies a wish for the future.]

REVISED   Her *hope* is to be a respiratory therapist.

Redundant categories

Redundant categories are implied by the adjectives that illustrate those categories. Use the adjectives alone, without the extraneous words.

REDUNDANT   Everyone thinks he plays basketball because he is *tall in size*. [The adjective *tall* implies size.]

REVISED   Everyone thinks he plays basketball because he is *tall*.

Redundancies are often difficult to recognize in writing because we hear or read them often—in conversation, on television, at the movies, in speeches, in newspapers, in advertisements, and in books. Try to be alert to the redundancies you encounter. When a sportscaster says, "This athlete has a great future ahead of him," you might wonder where else a future might be except ahead, since a future cannot lie behind someone. Here is a list of common redundancies:

basic fundamentals	expensive in price
circle around	important essentials
component parts	join together
continue on	past history
cooperate together	positive benefits
negative drawbacks	crisis situation
refer back	repeat again
the future ahead	small (or large) in size
red in color	good advantages

5   Avoid excessive use of the verb *be*

While the verb *to be* is important, excessive use of its forms, especially *is, was, are,* and *were,* makes writing flat. Using too many phrases like *it is, there is, there was,* and *there were* dilutes the impact of your sentences. Eliminate such phrases wherever possible.

WEAK   It is important for all children to be immunized against polio.

REVISED   All children should receive polio immunizations.

6   Prefer verbs to nouns

The tendency to use nouns instead of verbs to convey a sentence's meaning is called nominalization. Nominalization results when a verb form is changed to a noun; such as when the verb *intend* becomes the noun *intention*. In the following examples, notice how nominalization lessens the impact of writing:

NOMINALIZATION   The committee held a *discussion* of possible funding cutbacks.

REVISED   The committee *discussed* possible funding cutbacks.

To strengthen writing, check for overuse of nouns ending in *-ment, -tion,* or *-ance*. These sorts of nouns are often accompanied by such verbs as *make, take,* and *give*. Whenever possible, eliminate such verbs and change the noun to a verb. Look at these examples:

NOMINALIZATION   He gave an accurate assessment of the situation.

REVISED   He assessed the situation accurately.

7   Use the active rather than the passive poice

Using too many verbs in the passive voice results in wordiness and lessens the impact of writing. Whenever possible, use the active voice. Sometimes the passive voice best expresses your idea, and trying to shift to the active voice would result in awkwardness. In most cases, however, the active voice is appropriate.

PASSIVE VOICE   Sam *was bitten* by your dog Spot.

ACTIVE VOICE   Your dog Spot *bit* Sam.

In the preceding example, the active voice version is less wordy and more direct than the passive voice version.

In addition to wordiness, passive constructions can present another problem—the concealing of important information. Look at these examples:

PASSIVE VOICE   The files were misplaced.

PASSIVE VOICE   The tape was accidentally erased.

Use of the passive voice allows the writer or speaker to evade, perhaps purposely, naming those responsible for the actions. Use of the active voice does not permit such evasion:

ACTIVE VOICE   Mr. Roberts misplaced the files.

ACTIVE VOICE   Ms. Wood accidentally erased the tape.

8 | Avoid the excessive use of prepositional phrases

Excessive use of prepositional phrases contributes to wordiness and dilutes the impact of writing. Revise for conciseness by eliminating some prepositional phrases.

WORDY   *In* the event *of* an emergency *of* great seriousness, people *in* the vicinity *of* the situation should begin the administration *of* first aid and initiate notification *of* the police.

REVISED   In a serious emergency, the nearest people should administer first aid and call the police.

EXERCISE 1   Identifying Techniques of Emphasis

Identify the technique of emphasis used in each sentence that follows. Example:

To get his way, he whined, complained, and begged.   <u>parallel structure</u>

1. Pots and dishes were piled everywhere—on the kitchen counters, in the sink, and under the table. _____

2. They tried planting various vegetables in their little urban garden: squash, broccoli, corn, string beans, and even, one daring season, okra and peanuts. Nothing ever succeeded. _____

3. If her sad love affair taught her nothing else, it taught her caution. _____
   _____

4. He found himself out of doors, out of money, and out of luck. _____
   _____

5. I found myself in a strange city, unable to speak the language, and surrounded by a group of menacing people carrying ax handles and clubs. Then I woke up.
   _____

EXERCISE 2   Writing Sentences with Emphasis

Write two sentences for each phrase that follows—one with the phrase in an emphatic position and the other with the phrase in a less emphatic position. Example:

Phrase: every morning

Every morning she walks her dog in the park. (*emphatic*)

She walks her dog every morning in the park. (*less emphatic*)

1. as soon as possible

2. intentionally

3. slowly and painfully

4. in a loud voice

5. without a doubt

EXERCISE 3 Identifying Additional Techniques of Emphasis

Identify the technique of emphasis used in each of the following items. Examples:

Over the sea wall burst an unstoppable flood of water.   <u>inversion</u>

We have wasted our energy, our time, and, worst of all, our money.   <u>placement at end</u>

1. In "The Case of the Purloined Letter," an important document was hidden where no one would think to look for it—in plain sight. _____

2. In 1993 in this city, there were fifty-two murders of cab drivers. _____
   _____

3. The telephone was ringing, the doorbell was ringing, and my head was ringing.
   _____

4. On our high school basketball team that year, the center was rather short, the forwards had little experience, and our best guard was out for most of the season with an injury. The team won every game. _____

5. Quickly and efficiently, the cook sliced the onions, peeled the potatoes, diced the carrots, and minced the parsley. _____

EXERCISE 4   Using Techniques of Emphasis

For each topic that follows, write one or two sentences using the suggested technique of emphasis. Example:

Topic: An unfulfilled wish (*parallel structure*)

Even though he cannot read music, even though he cannot sing, he would have loved to be a great opera star.

1. An interesting neighbor (*short sentence after longer ones*)

2. An ambition (*placement of most important idea last*)

3. An item in the news (*parallel structure*)

4. A writer whose work you admire (*repetition*)

5. A valued possession (*inversion*)

EXERCISE 5 Revising for Conciseness

Revise the following sentences to eliminate unnecessary intensifiers, wordy phrases, and unnecessary negative words. Example:

The accident happened in close proximity to the fire station.

The accident happened near the fire station.

1. They do not have a sufficient amount of money to take a vacation this year.

2. I am not at all optimistic about the team's chances in the play-offs.

3. It is very likely possible that it will rain again tomorrow.

4. Her remarks of a critical nature discouraged me.

5. We want to make contact with him to see if he will lend assistance to us.

EXERCISE 6   Revising for Conciseness

Rewrite the following sentences to stress verbs and to eliminate the overuse of prepositional phrases and of the verb *to be*. Example:

It is essential for the company to find a larger office.

The company must find a larger office.

1. There is a new registration procedure that is much more efficient than the old one.

2. The use of an ATM card for many people is a matter of convenience, especially at night or in times of emergency.

3. The intention of the owner is to move the baseball team to another state.

4. In today's paper, there is a lead editorial that is very critical of the police department.

5. The union's acceptance of the new contract is a certainty.

EXERCISE 7   Using the Active Voice

Change each sentence from the passive to the active voice. Example:

Irene was bitten by the dog.

The dog bit Irene.

1. A verdict has been reached by the jury.

2. The history exam was failed by Fred and Irma.

3. I was startled by a loud noise from the street.

4. The house was bought by Mr. and Mrs. Cardozo.

5. The garage roof was crushed by a fallen tree.

EXERCISE 8   Writing with Emphasis and Conciseness

For each topic that follows, write a brief paragraph of three to five sentences in which you follow the guidelines for achieving emphasis and conciseness discussed in this chapter. Example:

Topic: Handling a difficult situation

    People react to difficult situations in different ways. Some people face them, some people run away from them, and others deny that they exist. Running away or denial never solves a problem; it merely delays its resolution. The problem still remains.

1. A book you would recommend to friends

2. How to study for exams

3. A skill you recently acquired

4. Your most boring job

5. Your most interesting job

PART NINE
Words

CHAPTER 30

Using a Dictionary

The dictionary is often regarded as an authority. People frequently say "Look it up in the dictionary" or "The dictionary says . . . ." The assumption is that there is one dictionary, known as *the* dictionary, and that it is the final, certain judge of correct spelling and usage.

Dictionaries record agreed-upon spellings, meanings, and pronunciations of words, but dictionaries do not present universal, unchanging rules about spelling, meaning, and pronunciation. With time, language and meanings of words change, and dictionaries change to reflect current usage. A dictionary is a reference work that documents how language is used today; it is not a rulebook of unvarying, eternal regulations about words. There are different kinds of dictionaries; one essential tool, for example, is the abridged college dictionary.

30a Exploring a dictionary

In addition to the meanings of words, dictionaries provide other useful information. For example, look at the accompanying entry for the word *cordial* from the *American Heritage Dictionary of the English Language* (third edition).

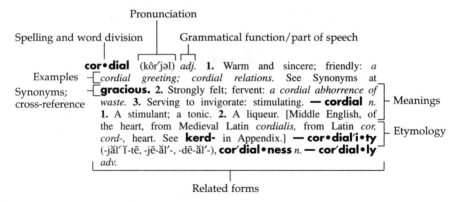

As you can see, a dictionary entry contains much information. Generally, most good dictionaries provide at least the following information about a word:

- *Spelling.* A dictionary entry begin with the word's spelling. If more than one spelling is indicated, the first version is preferred but the others are acceptable.

- *Word division.* Dots, bars, or spaces separate a word into syllables, and a hyphen indicates where the word can be divided at the end of a line.

- *Pronunciation.* An accent mark over or immediately after a syllable indicates that the stress is placed on that syllable. Other such marks indicate the pronunciation of various letters or letter combinations. You can find a key explaining the pronunciation marks at the beginning or end of your dictionary. In addition, a brief version of the pronunciation key is at the top or bottom of your dictionary's pages.

- *Part of speech.* Dictionaries classify words according to their grammatical functions as parts of speech. In addition, verbs are labeled transitive or intransitive, and adjectives and adverbs are shown with comparative and superlative forms.

- *Etymology or origin.* Dictionaries indicate the derivation or history of words. Often, the languages from which words derive are abbreviated. All abbreviations are explained in the front or back of the dictionary.

- *Meanings.* A word's meanings are numbered according to historical order (the oldest meaning given first) or according to frequency of use.

Some dictionaries provide other kinds of information as well.

- *Related words* or varied forms of a word.

- *Examples.* Many dictionaries provide examples of a word's use in the context of a phrase or sentence.

- *Usage labels.* Some words may have labels indicating the context in which a word is or is not acceptable. Here are some common usage labels:

    obsolete (no longer used)

    archaic (rarely used anymore)

colloquial (informal or conversational)

slang (extremely informal)

dialect (used regionally)

- *Field labels.*   Field labels, such as *astron., econ.,* and *mus.,* indicate when a word has a specific meaning in a particular field.
- *Synonyms and antonyms.*   Some dictionaries include synonyms, words similar in meaning, and antonyms, words opposite in meaning.
- *Idioms.*   Dictionaries sometimes list idiomatic uses of words. Many idiomatic uses are listed in entries for verbs with multiple meanings as phrasal verbs.

Your dictionary may provide still other resources, depending on its size and scope. It may include, for example, a preface describing how to use the dictionary, explanations of abbreviations and symbols, a history of the English language, a style manual, tables of weights and measures, geographical and biographical information, keys to pronunciation and spelling, and an index.

Dictionaries are also valuable because they provide information about morphemes, the smallest meaningful units of words. In addition to giving the meanings of words, dictionaries break down words into their component parts. Consider, for example, the word *transmitted,* which has three morphemes—the prefix *trans-,* meaning "across"; the suffix *-ed,* indicating the past tense or a past participle; and the root *mit,* meaning "to send." Each morpheme tells you something different about the word. Thus, by looking at a word's morphemes, you learn not only what the word means but also why it means what it does.

30b   Using different types of dictionaries

1   Abridged dictionaries

Abridged dictionaries, sometimes called desk dictionaries, are the kind most often consulted by students, teachers, and writers. They lack the completeness of unabridged dictionaries, but their scope is sufficient for most writing situations. The following dictionaries are of this type.

Random House Webster's College Dictionary, 1991.

Webster's New World Dictionary of the English Language, Third College Edition, 1988.

American Heritage Dictionary of the English Language, Third Edition, 1992.

2   Unabridged dictionaries

The unabridged or unabbreviated dictionary is the most comprehensive, most scholarly, and most historically minded of all dictionary types. The best known and most highly respected of unabridged dictionaries include the following:

Webster's Third New International Dictionary of the English Language, 1986.

The Oxford English Dictionary, Second Edition, 20 volumes, 1989. (An abridged form of the *OED* is available in two-volume and single-volume formats.)

3 | Specialized dictionaries

Specialized dictionaries do what their name suggests: they specialize in a particular category of word (e.g., slang or idioms), a single type of information (etymology), or a single subject (art, music, engineering). You may find three types of specialized dictionaries useful: dictionaries of usage, dictionaries of synonyms, and thesauruses.

EXERCISE 1   Checking Spelling

Look up the preferred dictionary spellings for the following words and underline the preferred forms. Example:

<u>crystallize</u> *or* crystalize

1. aerie *or* aery

2. dextrous *or* dexterous

3. honour *or* honor

4. marshal *or* marshall

5. judgment *or* judgement

EXERCISE 2   Checking Word Division

For each word the follows, show where it may be divided at the end of a line by inserting a hyphen or hyphens. Note that some words may be divided in more than one place; other words may not be divided at all. Examples:

carbon   <u>car-bon</u>

matador   <u>mat-a-dor</u>

schism   <u>no division possible</u>

1. decide   _____

2. national   _____

3. pleasure   _____

4. embellish   _____

5. roast   _____

EXERCISE 3   Determining Correct Pronunciation

Use your dictionary to identify the pronunciation of the following words. Example:

mnemonic   <u>ni-mon′ik</u>

1. colonel   _____

2. aunt   _____

3. rook   _____

4. masseuse   _____

5. lieutenant   _____

EXERCISE 4   Determining Parts of Speech

Use your dictionary to determine the part of speech for each word that follows. Note that some words may function as more than one part of speech. Example:

angry   <u>adjective</u>

release   <u>noun, verb</u>

1. pantheism   _____

2. quilt   _____

3. experience   _____

4. bureaucratic   _____

5. effluent   _____

EXERCISE 5   Investigating Word Origins

Use your dictionary to describe the etymologies of the following words. Example:

assassin

From French; before that, from medieval Latin; and before that, from Arabic

1. fabric

2. eugenics

3. regular

4. skirt

5. icon

EXERCISE 6   Finding Synonyms and Antonyms

Use your dictionary to find at least one synonym and one antonym for each of the following words. Example:

advanced

Synonym: forward, precocious

Antonym: backward, retrogressive

1. adventurous

2. reticent

3. explicit

4. sincere

5. desultory

CHAPTER 31

Using Appropriate Words

To use words appropriately, you need to understand the various characteristics of words: denotation and connotation; general and specific words; abstract and concrete words; formal and informal language; colloquialisms and slang; jargon, archaisms, neologisms, and acronyms; regionalisms and dialect expressions; euphemisms and clichés; and similes and metaphors.

31a Understanding denotation and connotation

Denotation is the dictionary meaning of a word; it is usually neutral and objective. Connotation, however, involves a word's associations beyond the strict dictionary definition; it is often subjective and personal, evoking strong feelings and reactions.

Consider, for example, the word *shark*. The denotative meaning of the word *shark* is "any of numerous chiefly marine fishes of the order *Squaliformes* (or *Selachii*), which are sometimes large and voracious and have a cartilaginous skeleton and tough skin covered with small, toothlike scales." The denotation of *shark* is objective and unemotional. The connotations, however, are quite different. On hearing or reading the word *shark*, one may feel horror, fascination, or fear as one recalls the movie *Jaws* or remembers a news account of swimmers attacked by sharks; or one might think of greedy, rapacious people, as in the phrase *loan shark*.

As a writer, you need to be aware of the connotations of the words you use. You cannot, of course, predict how various readers will react to certain words that may have particular, private meanings related to their individual experiences. However, you should be aware of generally shared connotations so that you can communicate effectively.

31b Using general and specific, abstract and concrete words

General words identify broad categories; specific words identify narrower categories within the wider, more general ones. For example, the word *recreation* identifies a broad category; the word *sports* is more specific than *recreation*; and the word *tennis* is more specific than *sports*.

General words can also be described as abstract and specific words as concrete. Abstract words refer to ideas, ideals, emotions, concepts, or qualities. Some examples are *faith, ambition, perspicacity, gravity, vigor,* and *pity.* Concrete words identify things we know through our senses. Examples are *newspaper, turnips, children, bicycle,* and *dimes.*

Writers need both abstract and concrete words. General words convey ideas, attitudes, and relationships; specific words explain and illustrate the abstract concepts. Notice the blend of general and specific statements in the following paragraph:

> On January 17, 1994, a violent earthquake hit the Los Angeles area. The quake, measuring 6.6 on the Richter scale, crumpled highway overpasses, damaged hundreds of buildings, broke water mains, and ignited many fires. Three freeway overpasses collapsed, and roads across the area buckled and cracked. Hundreds of private houses, apartment buildings, commercial properties, and public buildings were badly damaged. Scores of dwellings in a trailer park were destroyed. Anaheim Stadium sustained over $3 million in damage. The earthquake was not the strongest to hit the area in recent years, but it was certainly the most devastating because it occurred in a heavily populated area.

Notice that the first and last sentences of the paragraph are general, whereas the other sentences are more specific.

31c Using formal and informal language

Formal language represents the level of discourse appropriate for academic and business writing. Formal language uses a serious tone and adheres to the conventions of standard English, including rules of grammar, sentence structure, and punctuation. Contractions are seldom used. Informal language, in contrast, is more conversational and personal. When writing informally, you may address the reader as "you," you may refer to yourself as "I," and you may use some contractions.

The formality or informality of language is a matter of degree. Highly formal language is rare, traditionally used for ceremonial occasions. Highly informal language (slang and jargon) is used within intimate groups, such as among family and friends.

1 Colloquialisms

Colloquialisms are informal expressions appropriate to ordinary spoken language. Examples include *hang out, step on it,* and *bail.* Such expressions may be common in casual conversation, but they should be avoided in academic writing. In your professional and academic writing, replace colloquialisms with standard English expressions, such as *spend time, hurry,* and *leave.*

Colloquialisms also include clipped forms of words—*dorm* for *dormitory* or *vet* for *veterinarian.* Do not use clipped word forms in professional or academic writing, except when you intend to create an informal tone.

2 Slang

Informal language also includes slang. Although some slang words eventually become part of standard English, most go out of fashion within a few years or even a few months (e.g., *far out, awesome, rad, nerd, grind,* and *geek*). You may use current slang in creative writing with the intention of conveying an informal tone. However, you should avoid slang in professional and academic writing.

31d Avoiding jargon

Jargon is the specialized or technical language of a trade, profession, or other group. Jargon can be a sort of shorthand that is precise and efficient, eliminating the need for lengthy explanations. Lawyers, doctors, scientists, engineers, and other groups use specialized jargon that is easily understood by members of the same group. One specialized word takes the place of many words. Physicians, for example, use the term *pericarditis* to refer to an inflammation of the membranous sac surrounding the heart. The law term *estoppel* indicates a bar against an allegation or denial that is contrary to one's previous allegation or denial of a fact.

Among members of the same group jargon is efficient and useful. However, using jargon in communication with people outside the group can cause confusion and misunderstanding, even incomprehension. Patients told by a doctor that they have *viral rhinorrhea* might feel quite worried, when in fact they have merely a common cold. Jargon is also sometimes used to make an idea sound more significant than it really is. For example, *collocation* and *conflation* may sound like formidable activities, but they merely mean "a gathering" and "a combination," respectively.

Sometimes technical words have both a standard meaning and a specialized one. The word *absolute,* for instance, has different meanings to lawyers, mathematicians, and the public. The words *crash, boot, mouse,* and *virus* each has both a standard meaning and a specialized meaning for computer users. Using jargon when you communicate with people outside a specialized group impedes rather than promotes understanding. Avoid jargon except when you are writing for specialized groups; even then, it is best to use more familiar words. You can usually make your point more clearly with familiar words.

31e Using archaisms, neologisms, and acronyms

Archaisms are words that have become obsolete and are no longer in current usage. Dictionaries still include archaisms because they are found in historical documents and in older literary works. Examples include *quotha* (an exclamation of surprise) and *bespake* (past tense of *bespeak*). Knowing the meanings of archaisms helps you understand older writings; however, do not use archaisms in your own writing.

Neologisms are newly created words that have not come into common usage and are not yet recorded in dictionaries. The following words were once neologisms but have since come into established usage: *brunch, gridlock,* and *surrogate mother*. Until newly created words have become widely used, avoid them in your academic writing.

However, one form of neologism that you can use in all kinds of writing is the acronym. An acronym is an abbreviation that is used as an ordinary word. One example is *NATO,* which stands for North Atlantic Treaty Organization. Another is *AIDS,* standing for *Acquired Immune Deficiency Syndrome.* Both *NATO* and *AIDS* are acronyms because they are pronounced as words, unlike the non-acronym *HIV* (*Human Immunodeficiency Virus*) in which each letter is pronounced separately. Abbreviations such as *IRA* and *HIV* are called initialisms. When spelling acronyms, use all capital letters without periods. In uncertain cases, consult your dictionary to check if a word is an acronym or a word (e.g., *radar,* once an acronym, is now considered a word). In addition, clipped words such as *sitcom* are neologisms, but not true acronyms because they combine shortened forms of words rather than being composed of first letters of a series of words.

You have two choices when using acronyms in writing. You can spell out the words the acronym represents on first occurrence and then use the acronym for each subsequent mention. Or you can use the acronym throughout and at its first appearance give a parenthetical explanation—as in *FAX (facsimile transmission).*

31f   Avoiding regionalisms and dialect expressions

Pronunciation, accent, and word choice vary widely in different parts of the United States. For example, in various parts of the country you can order a *hero, hoagie,* or *submarine* and be given the same kind of sandwich. Regionalisms extend beyond the borders of the United States. Though both the British and Americans speak English, their vocabulary can differ greatly. The American *elevator* is the British *lift.* American *apartments* are British *flats.* The game that Americans call *soccer* is called *football* in Europe.

As a writer you need to be aware of regionalisms that may be unfamiliar to your audience. Consult your dictionary's usage labels for words that may be regionalisms. Avoid using regionalisms in academic writing; they are appropriate in conversation and in informal writing. Avoid dialect as well in academic and professional writing. While dialect is neither substandard nor wrong, it is nonstandard, and its use in academic and professional writing can impede communication with your audience.

31g   Avoiding euphemisms

A euphemism is an inoffensive, pleasant-sounding term used as a substitute for a more direct and possibly offensive term. For example, the words *corpse* and *died* may seem too harsh and blunt for some people; thus they may use instead *the deceased* and *passed on.* Occasionally, euphemisms are useful, especially when you want to avoid blunt terms and spare people's feelings. In academic writing, however, avoid euphemisms; express yourself directly and honestly. Look at the following example:

EUPHEMISM   When the company is downsized, some workers will be nonretained.

REVISED   When the size of the company is reduced, some workers will be fired.

Euphemisms are common in political discourse to evade giving a straight answer or, as with doublespeak, to make something seem like what it is not. The burning of villages may be called "pacification," or the slaughter of civilians may be described as a "battle with rebel guerrillas." Doublespeak uses euphemism to obscure truth and evade responsibility. Avoid it in your writing.

31h Avoiding clichés

Clichés are expressions that have become worn out through overuse. Some examples are *Blind as a bat, Between a rock and a hard place,* and *Sadder but wiser.* Clichés are so familiar that, after hearing the beginning of one, you can accurately predict the rest of the expression. You can find clichés everywhere—on television, in newspapers, in the movies, in advertisements, in ordinary speech. It might be interesting (and revealing) to keep a log of all the clichés you read or hear in the course of one day.

The use of many clichés makes writing stale and boring, lacking in surprise and freshness. Consider the following expressions:

steady as a rock

spread like wildfire

cool as a cucumber

red as a beet

These expressions do not pique our interest; they do not add to our understanding of a situation; they tell us nothing we did not know before. Avoid clichés in academic writing. Using clichés implies that you have no ideas of your own, and, therefore, must fall back on the overused expressions of others.

31i Using figurative language

Language can be classified as literal or figurative. When you speak literally, you mean exactly what each word conveys. When you use figures of speech, you mean something other than the exact meaning of each word. Taken literally, the expression *tied up at the office* would mean being tied, perhaps by ropes, to a piece of furniture or equipment in one's office. Figuratively, of course, the expression means being too busy with work to leave early.

Rhetoricians have catalogued more than 250 figures of speech. Two of them, metaphor and simile, are used frequently and are important to reading and writing. Metaphors and similes are types of comparisons; they make connections between dissimilar things.

1 Metaphor

Metaphor involves a transfer from one area of meaning to another. Metaphors describe one thing in terms of another; they identify one thing with a second apparently unrelated thing. You use metaphor, perhaps without realizing it, in daily conversation, describing feelings and explaining things to others who did not experience them. Look at the following metaphorical expressions:

She has a very dry wit.

He has a will of iron.

Florence Nightingale was an angel of mercy.

He is a wolf in sheep's clothing.

When she finally spoke, a flood of words poured out.

Someone's will cannot literally be made of iron; the metaphor transfers the hard, unyielding quality of iron to a human characteristic. Words cannot literally pour out in a flood; the metaphor transfers the gushing nature of a river or flood to a person's speech.

2 | Simile

When the metaphorical connection is made with the word *like* or *as,* or the expression *as though,* the comparison is called a simile. *My son eats like a pig* is a simile; *My son is a pig* is a metaphor. However, the difference between a simile and metaphor involves more than the use of the word *like* or *as;* the comparison is more restricted in a simile than in a metaphor. In the preceding simile, the son has only one piglike quality—the way he eats. In the metaphor, he possesses many piglike qualities.

Using metaphor is natural and, when done carefully, can enhance writing. However, you should be aware of two problems with metaphor. First, some metaphors have been used so often that they have become clichés. Avoid using familiar sayings; they have little impact on readers. Second, be careful not to use mixed metaphors, which combine two or more incompatible metaphors in a single description. Look at the following example:

MIXED   His words sowed seeds of doubt, leaving me adrift in a sea of confusion. [The writer mixes metaphors of agriculture and sailing.]

REVISED   His words sowed seeds of doubt and left me confused.

REVISED   His words made me lose my bearings, leaving me adrift in a sea of confusion.

EXERCISE 1   Determining a Word's Connotations

Identify as many connotations as you can for each of the following words. Example:

snake

a legless reptile; a plumber's tool used to clear clogged drains; a dangerous beast; a treacherous person

1. freak

2. vulture

3. eagle

4. lottery

5. prejudice

EXERCISE 2   Determining Positive and Negative Connotations

For each word in the list, identify one synonym with negative connotations and another synonym with positive connotations. Example:

well known

Negative: infamous

Positive: celebrated

1. courageous

2. ambition

3. animal

4. sing

5. different

EXERCISE 3   Writing with Denotative and Connotative Language

For each topic that follows write two sentences, one using words with positive connotations and another using words with negative connotations. Example:

Topic: A snowfall

Positive: Large, puffy snowflakes floated down for hours, covering the landscape in a soft white blanket.

Negative: Large, heavy snowflakes fell unceasingly for hours, burying everything in a thick, white shroud.

1. A shopper during a sale

2. An automobile salesperson

3. Lines at the Motor Vehicle Bureau

4. A large dog

5. A job interview

EXERCISE 4   Expanding General Statements with Concrete Details

Expand the following sentences by using specific and concrete words. Example:

Camels can survive in extremely hot and dry climates.

One reason camels can survive in extremely hot and dry climates is that their body temperature fluctuates with the changes in environmental temperature. At night, a camel's temperature may fall to 93°F, and during the heat of the day it may rise to 106°F. Because the difference between environmental temperature and a camel's body temperature is not great, the transfer of heat from the air to the camel's body is reduced.

1. Registration was a long, frustrating experience.

2. Exercise is good for the health.

3. Parents must be patient with small children.

4. A job applicant should try to make a good impression.

5. Food is more appetizing when it looks attractive.

EXERCISE 5   Revising for Concreteness and Specificity

Rewrite the following sentences to make them more concrete and specific. Example:

The puppy caused a lot of damage.

The puppy knocked over lamps and gnawed the legs of the dining room chairs.

1. That professor always makes her lectures interesting.

2. Keep your car in good working order, especially in winter.

3. One of my classmates is very opinionated.

4. If you want to lose weight, you must diet.

5. Use only essential electrical appliances during an energy crisis.

6. The freezing temperatures caused many problems.

7. Cleaning up after the party took a long time.

8. I got quite nervous just before the exam.

9. He is a very good cook.

10. This chair is uncomfortable.

EXERCISE 6   Writing at Different Levels of Formality

For each topic that follows, write two sentences, one with informal language, and the other with formal language. Example:

Topic: A thunderstorm

The thunderstorm made the dog freak out.
The thunderstorm made the dog extremely nervous.

1. Studying for exams

2. Swimming at the beach

3. A nosy neighbor

4. A hair style you dislike

5. A course you enjoy

EXERCISE 7 Understanding Acronyms

Spell out what the following acronyms stand for. Example:

FAX: facsimile transmission

1. ERA

2. OPEC

3. SALT

4. UNICEF

5. SAT

EXERCISE 8 Considering the Social Acceptability of Words

Use your dictionary to determine the social acceptability of the following words. Example:

scram: *slang*

1. ain't

2. hillbilly

3. the creeps

4. reckon

5. to scrag

EXERCISE 9   Comparing American English and British English

Identify the common American English equivalents for the following British words. Example:

barrister: lawyer

1. bonnet

2. lift (*noun*)

3. pram

4. bonny

5. flat (*noun*)

EXERCISE 10   Playing with Euphemism

Create euphemistic terms for the following words and phrases. Example:

a failing student: underachiever

1. drunk

2. to get fired

3. rude

4. pregnancy

5. pushy

EXERCISE 11 Freshening Stale Clichés

For each cliché in the list, write a comic version or a fresh version. Example:

dressed to kill: dressed to stun

1. hit below the belt

2. last but not least

3. face the music

4. stubborn as a mule

5. green with envy

EXERCISE 12   Revising Mixed Metaphors

Rewrite the following sentences to eliminate mixed metaphors and to make similes and metaphors consistent. Example:

He fired insults at us like bullets, trampling our hopes into the dust.

He fired insults at us like bullets, shattering our hopes.

1. The prosecutor presented mountains of evidence flowing from a parade of witnesses.

2. You can't expect to change horses in midstream and make a safe landing.

3. Her argument flooded over him and left him feeling caged.

4. The candidate's speech struck a chord with voters and turned the tide of the election.

5. Moving like lemmings, fans surrounded the rock star like moths around a candle.

CHAPTER 32

Avoiding Biased Language

Biased or prejudiced language disparages, stereotypes, or patronizes others. Not only does biased language interfere with the clear communication of ideas, but it can also impair a writer's effort at persuasion. Biased language should be avoided because it hurts people.

32a Avoiding racially and ethnically biased language

Racially and ethnically prejudiced language contains unfair stereotypes of members of a racial or ethnic group. The assumption behind such language is that all members of a particular group are alike and can be identified by one or two broad characteristics. This stereotypical thinking is inaccurate, simplistic, and unfair. The stereotypes are often negative, but even when they are benign or seemingly complimentary, biased language insults the person or group to which it is applied.

Choosing appropriate language

In referring to race and ethnicity, take care to choose your language carefully. Doing so is not always easy, for you may not be aware that a phrase reveals bias. The meanings of words often change, and words that were once acceptable to refer to racial or ethnic groups may now be unacceptable. In recent years, for example, the term *Asian American* has replaced *Oriental*. Many people, who now prefer to be called *African American*, some years ago preferred the term *black*, and before that, *negro*. Spanish-speaking Americans use a variety of terms to refer to themselves, among them *Hispanic* and *Latino/Latina*. The same is true of people once called *American Indians;* some prefer the term *Native American*, whereas others use their original tribal names.

If you are unsure how to refer to a group or to any of your acquaintances, you should ask if possible. Also be alert to the preferred terminology used in newspapers, in magazines, in movies, and on television. However, remember that most people like to be thought of as individuals first.

32b Avoiding sexually biased language

Sexually biased (sexist) language consists of words that emphasize one sex and ignore the other. For example, if a writer discussing people in general uses the word *man* or *mankind,* half the human race is excluded by such language. More inclusive terms are *human beings, humanity, people,* and *individuals.*

1 | Sexist pronouns

Choosing pronouns can be difficult when writers try to use inclusive language. To avoid sounding sexist, do not use masculine pronouns (*he, his, him*) when referring to an individual who might be either male or female. If the hypothetical person represents a group of people, use plural forms that are inclusive (*we, us, our, you, your, they, them, their*). Look at these examples:

SEXIST   A doctor must undergo years of training before *he* can start practicing medicine.

REVISED   Doctors must undergo years of training before *they* can start practicing medicine.

SEXIST   A good first-grade teacher knows how to motivate all of *her* students.

REVISED   Good first-grade teachers know how to motivate all of *their* students.

The indefinite pronouns, especially *everybody, everyone, anyone,* and *nobody,* can be troublesome. Grammatically, indefinite pronouns are singular and must take singular pronouns.

Everybody has *his* own ideas about health care reform.

By using the word *his,* however, this sentence excludes women. To include both men and women, you can use the dual form *his or her:*

Everybody has *his or her* own ideas about health care reform.

However, this solution can make writing sound awkward when overused, resulting in too many references to *he or she, his or her, him or her,* or *his or hers.* A better solution is to change to plural forms when writing about people in general.

AWKWARD   *Nobody* wants to have *his or her* taxes raised.

INCLUSIVE   *People* do not want to have *their* taxes raised.

AWKWARD   *Everybody* has *his or her* own ideas about health care reform.

INCLUSIVE   People have *their* own ideas about health care reform.

2 | Occupational stereotypes

An occupational stereotype conveys the assumption that only men or only women can perform certain kinds of jobs. For example, the term *policeman* excludes a great many people on police forces, which in recent years have hired significant numbers of women. A better term, therefore, is *police officer.* As in other instances of gender-specific language, do not mention an individual's gender unless it is relevant to your point. Here is a list of gender-specific occupational terms and the preferred inclusive versions.

GENDER SPECIFIC	INCLUSIVE
anchorman	anchor
businessman	business executive, manager
chairman, chairwoman	chair
cleaning lady	housecleaner, domestic worker
clergyman	priest, rabbi, minister
congressman, congresswoman	legislator, member of Congress
fireman	fire fighter
foreman	supervisor
insurance man	insurance agent
mailman	mail carrier, postal worker
salesman, saleswoman	sales representative
steward, stewardess	flight attendant
weatherman	weather reporter, meteorologist
workman	worker

32c Avoiding other kinds of biased language

Language can convey still other types of bias. Choose language carefully so as not to show insensitivity toward age, social class, religion, geographical location, physical and mental qualities, and sexual orientation.

1 Age

Certain words referring to a person's age may be taken as derogatory, even when you have no such intention. Some young people do not like being called *kids*, *adolescents*, or *teenagers*. Some older people dislike the terms *senior citizens* and *the elderly*. Calling an individual "old" may seem descriptive, but it may also be unflattering.

2 Social class

In all your writing, avoid using negative and unfairly biased class terms. For example, referring to some people as part of *the lower classes* is patronizing and demeaning. Referring to some as part of *the upper class* or *the leisure class* may convey feelings of envy or dislike. Avoid any terms, including slang, that stereotype by social class.

3 Religion

Most words used to designate religious groups do not convey bias. Examples are *Protestant, Catholic, Jew, Muslim, Christian*, and *Buddhist*. However, without realizing it, some writers assume that their own religious beliefs are the norm by which all others are measured. Just as you would avoid any other kind of stereotype, do not make broad assumptions about *all* people of a certain religious faith.

4   Geographical area

Some expressions not only denote the geographical area from which people come, but also connote opinions, emotions, and attitudes about those people. Two examples are *city slickers* and *country bumpkins.* Other geographical references may not be denigrating, but they may reveal ignorance and oversimplification. For example, not all New Yorkers are rude and aggressive, not all Californians are sybaritic, and not all New Englanders are reserved and unemotional. Avoid all such sweeping generalizations.

5   Physical and mental characteristics

Avoid language that calls unnecessary attention to an individual's or a group's physical or mental characteristics. When such references are necessary, take care to use language that does not offend. The best guide is to choose words that the individuals or groups use to describe themselves. For example, some but not all people who use wheelchairs object to the terms *crippled* and *disabled* because of their negative connotations. Do not refer to people with hearing impairments as *deaf mutes* or as *deaf and dumb. Mute* and *dumb* mean "unable to speak," and most deaf people can speak. In addition, though the word *dumb* originally meant "unable to speak," it has taken on the secondary meaning of "stupid." Refer to people with such hearing impairments as "deaf."

When referring to people who have mental retardation, always avoid denigrating terms such as *idiots, retards,* and *defectives.* These terms are derogatory and cruel. Do not mention a mental condition at all if it is not relevant to your point. When references to the condition are germane, use terms that convey factual information rather than judgmental attitudes.

Avoid labeling people as victims—as leukemia victims, AIDS victims, victims of Tourette's syndrome or of Down's syndrome. Refer to them as people—people with leukemia, people with Tourette's syndrome, people with Down's syndrome. A person's condition is not that person's whole identity. In general, give the person priority over the condition.

6   Sexual orientation

Just as you would not use denigrating language in referring to people's race, religion, gender, and so on, be careful when making references to sexual orientation. Do not assume that your readers share your sexual orientation. In fact, sexual orientation may have no relevance whatsoever to a person's achievements in business, sports, medicine, acting, law, and so on; therefore, references to sexual orientation are often not necessary.

EXERCISE 1   Eliminating Gender-Biased Language

Revise the following sentences to eliminate gender bias. Example:

The girls' basketball team has a better record than the men's team.

The women's basketball team has a better record than the men's team.

1. Because of allergies to cotton and wool, I have to wear only man-made fabrics.

2. The great American poetess Emily Dickinson wrote over 1,700 poems.

3. Many universities that were once limited to men are now admitting coeds.

4. That company hires only salesmen with at least two years of experience.

5. Every parent should attend PTA meetings at her child's school.

EXERCISE 2   Considering Sexist Connotations

Describe the connotations of the following pairs of words. Example:

mankind/womankind

Despite the prefix *man,* the term *mankind* has traditionally been used to refer to all of humanity, the human species, all people of both genders. It has been regarded as an inclusive term. *Womankind,* on the other hand, simply refers to women in general; it does not encompass all people.

1. bachelor/spinster

2. handsome/pretty

3. potent/fertile

4. physique/figure

5. master/mistress

6. manly/womanly

7. patron/matron

8. lord/lady

9. to father/to mother

10. sorcerer/sorceress

EXERCISE 3   Stereotypes in Advertisements

In the following excerpts from advertisements, identify words, phrases, and situations that are stereotypically feminine or masculine or that project stereotypical attitudes toward race, ethnicity, age, social class, religion, geographical location, appearance, or sexual orientation. Example:

Excerpt: "You've come a long way, baby." (from an ad for cigarettes supposedly designed just for women)

The word *baby* reflects an attitude regarding women as children or sexual playthings rather than as independent adults.

1. "Banish Wrinkles Without Surgery." (ad for facial cream)

2. "Men—Improve Your Athletic Performance! Women—Fit in Those New Fashions!" (ad for a health club)

3. "California Dreaming (Still)." (ad explaining an oil company's views of emissions rules)

4. "Gal/Guy Friday." (heading in a classified job advertisement)

5. "Holiday Madness—One Week Only." (ad for an electronics store)

EXERCISE 4   Revising Biased Language

Revise the following sentences to eliminate biased language. Example:

He looked like a real hick.

He seemed to be inexperienced and naive.

1. The old crone who lived in the apartment upstairs constantly complained about my stereo.

2. A judge must not allow his personal opinions to affect his decisions.

3. We worked like peons to get the project finished.

4. The hefty soprano sang the title role of "Manon Lescaut" with feeling and sensitivity.

5. The network executives did not believe the provocative TV series would play in Peoria.

6. Martina Navratilova, who admitted some years ago that she is gay, won more important tennis championships than any other professional tennis player.

7. He is more repressed than a Methodist minister.

8. "You can learn to speak like royalty—even if you grew up in the Bronx."

9. They teach at a school for mentally defective children.

10. The late flight is usually full of tired businessmen.

CHAPTER 33

Enriching Your Vocabulary

The most effective strategies for increasing your reading and writing vocabularies include learning about the history of the English language, recognizing the roots of words, understanding the meanings of prefixes and suffixes, learning the stories behind words, and using context clues.

33a Learning about the history of the English language

English contains many words that derive from other languages. Learning the roots of English will increase your ability to use it well. Like many other languages, English descends from a 5,000-year-old language that scholars call Indo-European. The people who spoke Indo-European eventually migrated throughout what is now known as Europe, and out of Indo-European there eventually developed many languages, including English, German, Dutch, Swedish, Danish, and Norwegian. The earliest form of English, known both as Anglo-Saxon and as early English, was spoken from about A.D. 400 to 1100. Around A.D. 600, Latin and Greek began to influence English because of the reintroduction into England of Christianity by the Catholic church. The Christian influence gave English such words as *altar, apostle, chalice, litany,* and *martyr.* Around A.D. 700, the Viking invasions introduced such words as *keg, knife,* and *trust.* Early English was followed by Middle English (A.D. 1100–1500); Modern English, the language used throughout the world today, became established by about 1600.

The Norman invasion of England in 1066 brought the most dramatic changes in the English language. The Normans, who spoke French, controlled the political and legal systems. Eventually, hundreds of French words entered English; among them *majesty, royal, cathedral, mercy, saint, jury, verdict, lieutenant, pearl, romance, beauty, appetite, veal,* and *beef.*

Although the French influence is predominant, English has also borrowed from many other languages, including Italian (*cameo, macaroni*), Spanish and Portuguese (*cannibal, guitar*), Persian (*bazaar*), Turkish (*coffee*), Dutch (*landscape*), Arabic (*alcohol*), and Algonquin (*wampum*).

33b   Recognizing the roots of words

A word's root is the unchanging part that is related to other words. The root of the word *pedal*, for example, is *ped*, a Latin root meaning "foot." This root is evident in other words: *quadruped* (four-footed), *pedestrian* (a person who travels on foot), and *centipede* (a many-legged creature). Be careful, however, with roots; the words *pediatrician*, *pedigree*, and *pedantry*, for instance, may seem to include the root *ped*, but they actually derive from the Greek root *pedi*, meaning "child." In learning word roots, remember that not every word that looks the same derives from the same root, and that you should consult your dictionary to learn the meanings and origins of words.

Here is a list of common Greek and Latin roots, their meanings, and related English words:

COMMON ROOTS AND THEIR MEANINGS

ROOT	MEANING	EXAMPLES
-aster-, -astr- (Greek)	star	astronomy, astrology
-audi- (Latin)	to hear	audiology, audience
-auto- (Greek)	self	automobile, autoimmune
-bene- (Latin)	good, well	benefactor, benefit
-bio- (Greek)	life	biology, biosphere
-chrono- (Greek)	time	chronology, chronometer
-dict- (Latin)	speak	dictation, dictaphone
-fer- (Greek)	bear, carry	ferry, infer, conifer
-gen- (Greek)	give birth, race	genealogy, genesis
-geo- (Greek)	earth	geography, geology
-graph- (Greek)	write	graphic, pictograph
-greg- (Latin)	herd, flock	gregarious, segregate
-jur-, -jus- (Latin)	law	justice, jury
-log-, -logue- (Greek)	thought, word	monologue, loquacious
-luc- (Latin)	light	lucid, elucidate
-manu- (Latin)	hand	manufacture, manual
-meter-, -metr- (Greek)	measure	thermometer, metrical
-mit-, -mis- (Latin)	send	missile, missive
-omni- (Latin)	all	omnipotent, omnivorous
-op-, -oper- (Latin)	work	opera, inoperable
-path- (Greek)	feel, suffer	pathetic, sympathy
-phil- (Greek)	love	philosophy, philanthropy
-phon- (Greek)	sound	phonograph, phonics
-photo- (Greek)	light	photosynthesis, photon
-port- (Latin)	carry, bear	transport, transpose
-psych- (Greek)	soul	psychic, psychology
-scrib-, -script- (Latin)	write	transcript, scripture
-sent-, -sens- (Latin)	feel	sensation, insensate
-tele- (Greek)	far off	telegraph, telepathy

-ter-, -terr- (Latin)	earth	terrestrial, terrain
-therm- (Greek)	heat	thermal, thermometer
-vac- (Latin)	empty	vacation, vacate
-verb- (Latin)	word	verbose, verbal
-vic-, -vin- (Latin)	conquer	victor, invincible
-vid-, -vis- (Latin)	see	invisible, vista

33c   Understanding the meanings of prefixes and suffixes

In addition to roots, prefixes and suffixes contribute to the meanings of words. A prefix is a letter or a group of letters attached to the beginning of a word. A suffix is a letter or a group of letters attached to the end of a word. Both prefixes and suffixes are known as affixes or attachments.

1   Prefixes

By looking at a word's prefix, root, and suffix, you have a good chance of determining its meaning. In the following list, the prefixes are arranged by meaning. For each prefix, try to think of at least one more word that could be added to the examples given.

COMMON PREFIXES AND THEIR MEANINGS

PREFIXES OF NUMBER AND QUANTITY

PREFIX	MEANING	EXAMPLES
uni-, mono-	one	unicycle, monopoly
du-, bi-, dis-, dy-, di-	two	dual, bipolar, disparate
tri-	three	trilogy, triangular
quadr-, tetra-	four	quadrangle, tetrameter
quint-, penta-	five	quintet, pentagon
sex-, hexa-	six	sextuplets, hexagonal
sept-, hepta-	seven	September, hebdomadal
octo-	eight	octet, octagon
nov-, non-, ena-	nine	novena, nonagenarian
decim-, deca-	ten	decimal, decathlon

PREFIXES OF NEGATION

PREFIX	MEANING	EXAMPLES
a-, an-	without, not	asexual, amoral
anti-	against	antipathetic
contra-	against	contradict
de-	from, remove, take away	detoxify, devalue
dis-	apart, away	disappear, disconnect

il-, im-, in-, ir-	not	illegal, immoral, innocuous, irreparable
mal-	bad, wrong	malevolent, malicious
mis-	wrong, bad	mistake, miscue
non-	not	noncompliant
un-	not	unbearable

PREFIXES OF TIME

PREFIX	MEANING	EXAMPLES
ante-	before	antecedent, anterior
fore-	before	foretell
pre-, pro-	before	precede, project
post-	after	posterior
re-	again	revision
syn-	the same time	synchronize

PREFIXES OF SPACE, DIRECTION, AND POSITION

PREFIX	MEANING	EXAMPLES
ad-	to, for	adverb, adhere
circum-	around	circumstantial
co-, col-, com-, con-, cor-	with	coequal, collude, communicate, contact, correspond
e-, ex-	out of	extract, eject
hetero-	other	heterodox
homo-	same	homoerotic
hypo-	under, less	hypoallergenic
hyper-	over, more	hyperkinetic
inter-	between	interview, internecine
intra-	within	intramural
sub-	under	subterranean
super-	above	supersonic
trans-	across	transcontinental

Note that the spelling of some prefixes varies, usually to make pronunciation easier. For instance, *ad-* becomes *ac-* in *accuse* and *ag-* in *aggregate*.

2 | Suffixes

Suffixes provide clues to the meanings of words; they also change the grammatical function of words from one part of speech to another. Adding the suffix *-ful* or *-less* to the noun *care* changes it to the adjective *careful* or *careless*. The verb *irritate* can be changed to a noun (*irritation*), an adjective (*irritable*), and an adverb (*irritably*). The following chart lists verb, noun, and adjective suffixes along with their meanings and some examples.

COMMON SUFFIXES AND THEIR MEANINGS

VERB SUFFIXES	MEANING	EXAMPLES
-ate	cause to become	eradicate, regulate
-en	cause to become	whiten, enlighten
-ify	cause to become	deify, codify
-ize	cause to become	synthesize, organize

NOUN SUFFIXES	MEANING	EXAMPLES
-acy	state or quality	democracy
-al	process of	portrayal
-ant	one who	participant
-er, -or	one who	trainer, protector
-ion	process of	addition
-ism	doctrine, belief	Confucianism
-ist	one who	chemist
-ity, -ty	quality	capacity, cruelty
-ment	condition of	deportment
-ness	state of being	heaviness
-sion, -tion	state of being	concession, perdition

ADJECTIVE SUFFIXES	MEANING	EXAMPLES
-able, -ible	capable of being	presentable, edible
-al	pertaining	consequential
-esque	reminiscent of	statuesque, grotesque
-ful	notable for	fanciful, wonderful
-ic, -ical	pertaining to	poetic, gigantic, musical, economical
-ish	the quality of	womanish, standoffish
-ive	having the nature of	festive, restive
-less	without	regardless, helpless
-ous, -ious	characterized by	portentous, surreptitious
-y	characterized by	dirty, sleazy

Using the suffixes you know

You can use your knowledge of word meanings and of familiar suffixes to figure out the meanings of other words. Suppose, for example, that you had never heard of the word *matricide*. Knowing that the suffix *-cide* means "kill" and that *matri* means *mother* (as in the words *maternity* and *maternal*), you can deduce that *matricide* involves killing a mother.

33d   Learning the stories behind words

Another way to develop your reading and writing vocabulary is to learn the stories associated with words. Many English words derive from historical figures, fictional characters, geography, and mythology. The adjective *Machiavellian,* for instance, means "suggestive of or characterized by the principles of expedience, deceit, and cunning"—the same qualities advocated by Niccolò Machiavelli (1469–1527) as necessary for political leaders to gain and retain power. The adjective *quixotic,* meaning "idealistic without regard to practicality," derives from the title character of *Don Quixote* by Miguel de Cervantes (1547–1616). The verb *meander,* meaning "to wander aimlessly," comes from the name of a river in Asia Minor known for its winding course. The meaning of the adjective *mercurial*—"having the characteristics of eloquence, shrewdness, swiftness, and thievishness"—comes from the qualities attributed to the Latin god Mercury.

33e │ Using context clues

An excellent way to develop your vocabulary is to use the context in which a word appears to figure out its meaning. The words appearing before and after an unfamiliar word provide important clues to the meaning of the unfamiliar word. They are thus called context clues.

Occasionally writers may define an unusual or unfamiliar word for readers in the sentence in which it appears. When, in most cases, no such definition is provided, you can still get a general sense of a word's meaning by recognizing its grammatical function, by considering the writer's subject, and by noticing the writer's tone. Sometimes an unfamiliar word is contrasted with a word you do know. Often, an unfamiliar word is followed by an example that gives you a general idea of the word's meaning. Look at the following examples of context clues:

When astronauts first brought back rock samples from the moon, scientists gained a fuller understanding of *lunar* geology. [The meaning of *lunar* can be determined from its inclusion in a sentence about the moon.]

I thought your vacation would refresh and strengthen you, but instead you look *enervated.* [The meaning of *enervated* can be determined as being the opposite of "refreshed" and "strengthened."]

EXERCISE 1   Identifying Word Origins

Look up the following words in a dictionary to identify their country of origin. (If your dictionary does not provide this information, consult an unabridged dictionary in your school library.) Example:

cyst: Greece

1. sauna

2. easel

3. trek

4. voodoo

5. chowder

6. algebra

7. zebra

8. plaza

9. squash

10. shawl

EXERCISE 2   Determining the Derivation of Synonyms

Determine whether the following words derive from French, from Latin, from Old English, or from another language. Examples:

beer: Old English

wine: Latin

sangria: Spanish, Latin

1. bad, malevolent

2. good, benevolent

3. shun, avoid

4. wind, turbulence, airflow

5. build, erect

6. road, street, avenue

7. jaunty, animated

8. spur, urge, encourage

9. mad, insane

10. haste, dispatch

EXERCISE 3   Identifying Word Roots

For each word that follows, identify the word's root and determine its meaning. Then list one or more words containing the same root. Example:

audible

Root: *audi*

Meaning: capable of being heard
Other words: audience, audiology

1. telemetry

2. transference

3. psychiatry

4. vacuous

5. chronological

6. graphology

7. operation

8. prescription

9. visible

10. emphatic

EXERCISE 4   Identifying Prefixes of Number in Words

For each word that follows, identify the number prefix and determine the word's meaning. Example:

bicycle

Number prefix: *bi*

Word's meaning: vehicle with two wheels, one wheel behind the other

1. pentathlon

2. trivial

3. unanimous

4. quintuplets

5. bifurcate

6. octagonal

7. dichotomy

8. duplicitous

9. December

10. quadrant

EXERCISE 5   Working with Prefixes

First give the meaning of each word in the list. Then, using the list of prefixes in 33c-1 of the *Workbook,* find a word with an opposite meaning and give that word's meaning. Example:

prenatal: before birth

postnatal: after birth

1. homogeneous

2. exclude

3. antemeridian

4. progressive

5. export

6. benevolent

7. hyposensitive

8. exterior

9. malign (*adjective*)

10. posterior

EXERCISE 6   Working with Negative Prefixes

Provide the negative or reverse counterparts of the following words by using prefixes of negation. Example:

functional: dysfunctional

1. aerobic:

2. appear:

3. viable:

4. healthy:

5. responsible:

6. movable:

7. sane:

8. please:

9. repair:

10. accelerate:

EXERCISE 7   Working with Verb Suffixes

For each verb suffix, list five verbs that end in that suffix. Here is one example for each suffix:

-ate: eradicate

-en: whiten

-ify: intensify

-ize: organize

1.*-ate:*

2.*-en:*

3.*-ify:*

4.*-ize:*

EXERCISE 8   Working with Adjective Suffixes

For each adjective suffix, list two adjectives that end in that suffix. Example:

-less: careless, selfless

1. *-able, -ible:*

2. *-al:*

3. *-esque:*

4. *-ful:*

5. *-ic, -ical:*

6. *-ish:*

7. *-ous, -ious:*

8. *-ive:*

9. *-less:*

10. *-y:*

EXERCISE 9   Using Suffixes to Alter Grammatical Function

By adding and changing suffixes, convert verbs to nouns and nouns to verbs. Examples:

initiate: initiation

validity: validate

1. assess:

2. participant:

3. inscribe:

4. qualification:

5. portray:

6. analysis:

7. explain:

8. organization:

9. encourage:

10. operation:

EXERCISE 10   Working from Suffixes to Roots

For each suffix that follows, first give a word that ends in that suffix. Then identify the root of your word and find another word containing that root. Example:

-cide: fratricide, fraternal

1. *-ologist*

2. *-gamy*

3. *-tropic*

4. -cide

5. -trophy

6. -phobia

7. -anthropy

8. -phil

9. -cracy

10. -ology

EXERCISE 11   Learning Words Based on People and Places

Use your dictionary to identify the people, places, or literary characters from which the following words are derived. Example:

samaritan: from the parable of the Good Samaritan

1. mesmerize:

2. sadism:

3. utopian:

4. galvanize:

5. billingsgate:

6. sandwich:

7. bowdlerize:

8. bloomers:

9. masochism:

10. sideburns:

EXERCISE 12 Learning Words Based on Stories

Using your dictionary as a resource, explain the story behind each word that follows. Example:

narcissism: Narcissus was a youth in Greek myth who pined away in love for his own image in a pool or water and was transformed into the flower that bears his name.

1. protean

2. Homeric

3. tantalize

4. Achilles' heel

5. lilliputian

6. gargantuan

7. a doubting Thomas

8. yahoo

9. junoesque

10. odyssey

EXERCISE 13   Discovering the Mythical Origins of Words

Use your dictionary to give the meaning and explain the mythical origin of each word that follows. Example:

amazon: a strong woman.

In Greek myth, Amazons were a tribe of female warriors.

1. the Midas touch

2. procrustean

3. chimera

4. Sisyphean

5. siren

6. satyric

7. jovial

8. cereal

9. echo

10. vulcanize

EXERCISE 14   Using Context Clues

Determine the meaning of each italicized word by using the context clues within the sentence. Example:

The quiet defendant remained *impassive* during both the trial and his sentencing.

impassive: unchanged, showing no emotion

1. Until the president visited the site of the earthquake, he had not realized the *gravity* of the situation.

2. *Scree* all over the trail made walking difficult because our feet kept slipping.

3. Years of overindulgence in food and liquor had a *deleterious* effect on his liver.

4. Her *garish* dress contrasted sharply with her brother's conservative dark suit.

5. Because we have not been able to raise the required funds, our plan to expand the clinic is in *abeyance*.

6. They went through the doors and then stopped for a moment in the *narthex* before entering the church.

7. *Burdocks* and other weeds had taken over the abandoned garden.

8. If the temperature falls below a certain point, *thermophilic* bacteria die.

9. Breadfruit was not *indigenous* to the Americas; it was imported from Polynesia.

10. Those nosy neighbors constantly *impinge* upon my privacy.

CHAPTER 34

Improving Your Spelling

English is a complex language that derives from many other languages, including Old German, Old Norse, Danish, Norman French, Latin, and Greek. In addition, English has borrowed many words from other languages, such as Italian, Spanish, and Arabic. As a result, English spelling can sometimes be troublesome. However, most English words are spelled the way they sound; despite exceptions, therefore, spelling rules are helpful. This chapter provides both rules and practical hints for improving your spelling.

34a Using word meanings to aid spellings

Knowing the meanings of words can help you with their spelling. Learning the meanings of words in groups or clusters can both increase your vocabulary and aid you with spelling. For example, if you know that the word *copyright* has something to do with the right of legal protection for creative work, you will not misspell it as *copywrite* because the meaning of the word *right* will guide you. (There is no real verb *copywrite*, although the noun *copywriter* indicates a person who writes the text of advertisements.)

Some people have trouble choosing between *site* and *sight;* others have difficulty remembering which words contain *ie* and which *ei.* In both these cases, knowing word clusters can help. For example, *sight* implies vision, and can be remembered as one of a group of words concerning vision: *sight, insight, insightful.* If you cannot remember whether to use *ie* or *ei* in *receive,* connect the word *receive* with the related word *reception;* the first four letters of *receive* and *reception* are the same.

34b Recognizing homonyms

Homonyms are words that sound alike but are spelled differently and have different meanings. Examples are *complement/compliment, plane/plain,* and *allude/elude.* Since homonyms are similar in sound and share many letters, they can be confusing.

Following are two lists of homonyms that create confusion. The first, shorter list contains words that appear frequently in writing. The second list includes other commonly confused homonyms.

FREQUENTLY CONFUSED HOMONYMS

its (possessive form of *it*)
it's (contraction of *it is*)

whose (possessive form of *who*)
who's (contraction of *who is*)

their (possessive form of *they*)
they're (contraction of *they are*)
there (in that place)

your (possessive form of *you*)
you're (contraction of *you are*)

to (toward)
too (also, very)
two (number after one)

than (as compared with)
then (at that time; therefore)

OTHER COMMONLY CONFUSED HOMONYMS

accept (to receive)
except (to leave out)

conscience (feelings of right and wrong)
conscious (aware)

advice (recommendation)
advise (to recommend)

council (*noun*, an assembly)
counsel (*verb*, to advise)

affect (*verb*, to influence; *noun*, an emotion)
effect (*verb*, to make happen; *noun*, a result)

desert (*noun*, dry, sandy terrain)
desert (*verb*, to abandon)
dessert (last part of a meal)

all ready (prepared)
already (by this time)

elicit (to draw out)
illicit (illegal)

allude (to refer)
elude (to avoid)

eminent (distinguished)
immanent (inherent)
imminent (impending)

allusion (indirect reference)
illusion (false idea or appearance)

fair (just; light complexioned)
fare (a charge for transportation)

ascent (movement up)
assent (agreement)

gorilla (an ape)
guerrilla (a soldier)

bare (naked)
bear (to carry, endure; an animal)

hear (to perceive by ear)
here (in this place)

board (piece of lumber)
bored (uninterested)

heard (past tense of *hear*)
herd (a group of animals)

brake (to stop)
break (to smash)

hole (an opening)
whole (entire)

capital (seat of government)
capitol (government building)

lead (a metal; to go before)
led (past tense of *to lead*)

complement (to make complete)
compliment (to praise)

loose (not tight)
lose (to fail to win; misplace)

passed (past tense of *to pass*)

past (after, beyond)

patience (forbearance)

patients (persons under medical care)

peace (absence of war)

piece (a part of something)

presence (attendance)

presents (gifts)

principal (school administrator)

principle (a basic truth or law)

scene (setting, part of a play)

seen (past participle of *to see*)

stationary (standing still)

stationery (writing paper)

threw (past tense of *to throw*)

through (finished; by means of)

waist (part of the body)

waste (to squander)

weather (climactic conditions)

whether (which of two)

weak (feeble, not strong)

week (seven-day period)

which (what; that)

witch (female sorcerer)

1 | Recognizing homonyms with more than one form

Homonyms sometimes appear as a single word and sometimes as two words. Their meanings differ in each case. Use your dictionary to check forms of which you are unsure. The following sentences illustrate correct use of certain homonyms whose different forms can cause confusion.

always, all ways

He *always* [invariably] drinks tea at breakfast.

She studied the problem *all ways* [every way] in order to find a solution.

every day, everyday

He feeds the fish in that aquarium *every day.* [each day]

She never varies her *everyday* [usual] routine.

may be, maybe

I *may be* [might be] able to help you.

Maybe [perhaps] we will win the lottery.

altogether, all together

I am not *altogether* [entirely] convinced that you are telling the truth.

Gathering the children *all together* [in a group], the park ranger showed them how to read trail markers.

all ready, already

By the end of the day, the apartment was *all ready* [completely prepared] for us to move in.

I have *already* [previously] seen that movie.

Other variable-form homonyms include the following:

anybody [any one]
any body [any single person]

anymore [ever]
any more [more of something]

somebody [someone]
some body [some individual person]

sometimes [occasionally]
some times [certain times]

Also, remember that *cannot* is always one word, whereas *a lot* and *all right* are always two words.

2   Distinguishing between American versus British (and Canadian) spellings

AMERICAN	BRITISH AND CANADIAN
honor, color	honour, colour
judgment	judgement
connection	connexion
center, theater	centre, theatre
criticize, realize	criticise, realise
traveled	travelled

34c   Applying common spelling rules

1   Distinguishing between *ie* and *ei*

The *ie/ei* rule is set to a rhyme: *i* before *e* except after *c*, or when sounded like "ay," as in *neighbor* or *weigh*. This rule yields the following spellings:

I BEFORE E

belief	bier	hygiene
grief	field	relieve

E BEFORE I AFTER C

receive	deceive	perceive
conceive	ceiling	conceit

EI PRONOUNCED "AY"

weight	eight	sleigh
freight	vein	beige

However, the *ie/ei* rule carries you only so far.

EXCEPTIONS:

caffeine	seize	sovereign	foreign
either	species	forfeit	their
leisure	weird	financier	conscience

2 | Dropping or retaining the final *e*

When adding a suffix to a word ending in a silent *e,* drop the *e* if the suffix begins with a vowel.

EXAMPLES:

eas [e] + ing = easing
inhal [e] + ation = inhalation
sens [e] + ible = sensible

EXCEPTIONS:

To avoid homonym confusion:
dye (to stain with a color) + ing = dyeing (*not* dying)
singe (to burn slightly) + ing = singeing (*not* singing)

Keep the *e* when the suffix begins with a consonant.

EXAMPLES:

intens*e* + ly = intensely
induc*e* + ment = inducement
hop*e* + ful = hopeful

EXCEPTIONS:

argu[e] + ment = argument
judg[e] + ment = judgment
acknowledg[e] + ment = acknowledgment
aw[e] + ful = awful
tru[e] + ly = truly
whol[e] + ly = wholly
nin[e] + th = ninth

3 | Spelling words ending in *-cede, -ceed, -sede*

With the exception of *supersede,* all words ending in a suffix pronounced *seed* end either in *-ceed* or in *-cede.*
Only three words end in *-ceed: exceed, proceed,* and *succeed.* All others end in *-cede: intercede, precede, secede, concede, recede,* among others.

4 | Distinguishing *-ally* from *-ly*

Use the suffix *-ally* for words ending in *ic.*

logic + ally = logically
magic + ally = magically

An exception is *publicly.*

Use the suffix *-ly* for words that do not end in *ic.*

slow + ly = slowly
glorious + ly = gloriously
candid + ly = candidly

5 Retaining the final *y* or changing it to *i*

When adding a suffix to a word that ends in *y,* change the *y* to *i* when the letter before the *y* is a consonant.

harmony + ous = harmonious
pity + ful = pitiful
fifty + eth = fiftieth
happy + ness = happiness

defy + ed = defied
comply + ance = compliance
angry + ly = angrily
merry + ment = merriment

Exceptions

Keep the *y* before the suffix *-ing.*

hurry + ing = hurrying
cry + ing = crying

study + ing = studying
defy + ing = defying

Note that the word *skiing* is an exception to the exception.

Keep the *y* in some one-syllable words.

wry + ly = wryly
dry + ly = dryly
fry + er = fryer

If a word ends in *y* preceded by a vowel, keep the *y* when adding a suffix.

employ + er = employer
stay + ed = stayed
annoy + ance = annoyance

In addition, proper names keep the *y* when adding a suffix.

Mr. and Mrs. Hardy = the Hardys

6 Doubling consonants

Doubling consonants when adding prefixes

When adding a prefix ending in a consonant to a word beginning with one, combine the two consonants.

dis + similar = dissimilar

mis + step = misstep

under + rate = underrate

When the word starts with a vowel, simply combine the prefix and the word.

dis + agree = disagree

mis + align = misalign

de + emphasize = deemphasize

Sometimes the prefix must be changed slightly when combining it with a word beginning with a consonant. Look at the following examples using *in*, meaning "not":

in   im + mobile = *imm*obile

in   il + legible = *ill*egible

in   ir + reverent = *irr*everent

This prefix change is called assimilation; the last letter of the prefix is assimilated by the root of the word.

Doubling the final consonant when adding suffixes

For one-syllable words ending in a consonant, double the consonant when adding a suffix.

stop + ing = sto*pp*ing

flop + y = flo*pp*y

bar + ed = ba*rr*ed

For two-syllable words, double the consonant when the accent falls on the second syllable.

control' + able = contro*ll*able

begin' + ing = begi*nn*ing

occur' + ed = occu*rr*ed

Exceptions

Words ending in *d* and *y* never double the consonant.

reward + ed = rewarded	obey + ing = obeying
rotund + ity = rotundity	allay + ed = allayed

When not to double consonants

Do not double the consonant when the accent falls on the first syllable of a two-syllable word.

pro' fit + able = profitable

hap' pen + ed = happened

This rule of accent holds true when a word has more than two syllables.

encum' ber + ed = encumbered

dismem' ber + ing = dismembering

Do not double the consonant when the suffix begins with a consonant.

commit + ment = commitment

adroit + ly = adroitly

Do not double the consonant when the ending consonant is preceded by more than one vowel or by another consonant.

confident + ial = confidential

alert + ed = alerted

keep + ing = keeping

Do not double the consonant when a word's accent shifts to the first syllable with the addition of the suffix.

refer' + ence = re' ference

When the accent does not shift, double the consonant.

deter' + ent = deterr' ent

Note: Be careful not to confuse words with short vowel sounds and words with long vowel sounds. Look at the difference in the way the following words are spelled and pronounced:

| pine—pined | cone—coned | scare—scared | tube—tubing | hope—hoped |
| pin—pinned | con—conned | scar—scarred | tub—tubbing | hop—hopped |

34d | Forming plurals

1 | Regular plurals

The most common way to form the plural of nouns is to add -s.

| chair—chairs | message—messages |
| reaction—reactions | worker—workers |

Nouns ending in s, sh, z, x or ch form their plurals by adding -es.

| dress—dresses | dish—dishes | buzz—buzzes |
| tax—taxes | church—churches | |

For words ending in o, add either -s or -es. If the final o is preceded by a vowel, add -s. If the final o is preceded by a consonant, add -es.

| patio—patios | tomato—tomatoes |
| video—videos | potato—potatoes |

EXCEPTIONS

piano—pianos	pro—pros
memo—memos	solo—solos

For words ending in *y*, change the *y* to *i* and add *-es*, but only if the *y* is preceded by a consonant.

history—histories	eulogy—eulogies
story—stories	baby—babies

If the *y* is preceded by a vowel, keep the *y* and add *-s*.

monkey—monkeys	attorney—attorneys
replay—replays	boy—boys

Exception: Proper names ending in *y* are an exception: There are two *Sallys* in the first grade.

For most words that end in *-f* or *-fe*, change the *-f* or *-fe* to *v* and add *-es*.

shelf—shelves	knife—knives
wife—wives	yourself—yourselves

EXCEPTIONS

safe—safes	scarf—scarfs *or* scarves
hoof—hoofs *or* hooves	dwarf—dwarfs *or* dwarves
roof—roofs *or* rooves	

2   Irregular plurals

Some nouns have irregular plural forms, and some nouns use the same form for both singular and plural. Familiarize yourself with the following irregular forms:

man—men	locus—loci	deer—deer
woman—women	alga—algae	sheep—sheep
child—children	basis—bases	moose—moose
foot—feet	alumna—alumnae	series—series
tooth—teeth	alumnus—alumni	species—species

3   Plurals of compound nouns

When compound nouns are written as one word, form the plural by making the last part of the word plural.

streetcar—streetcars	bookshelf—bookshelves

When compound words are separated or hyphenated, make the most important part of the compound plural.

father-in-law—fathers-in-law

lieutenant governor—lieutenant governors

hospital ward—hospital wards

34e Spelling words with unstressed vowels and consonants

Although it is not a letter of the alphabet, the schwa is the most common sound in the English language. Meaning "emptiness" in Hebrew, *schwa* is the term designating an unstressed vowel, the "uh" sound pronounced in many words. The schwa is designated by an upside down *e* (ə). You can find the schwa in the pronunciation guide of your dictionary. Listen and look for the unstressed vowel as you pronounce the following words:

acad[*e*]my	emph[*a*]sis	mir[*a*]cle
hist[*o*]ry	wom[*a*]n	med[*i*]cine
hum[*a*]n	comp[*e*]tent	ill[*u*]strate

The "uh" sound in these examples is spelled with five different vowels: *a, e, i, o,* and *u.* The lack of consistent spelling for the "uh" sound is the reason that unstressed vowels sometimes cause spelling problems. Should you write *democracy* or *demacracy? histery* or *history? definite* or *definate?*

Spelling words with unstressed vowels

To spell a word with an unstressed vowel, follow these steps:

1. Isolate the unstressed vowel (the schwa) of the word you want to spell: *defin[ ]te.*
2. Think of a related word with a similar form: *definition.*
3. Isolate the stressed vowel that matches the schwa: *definition.*
4. The stressed vowel in the related word is the same vowel you should use in the word with an unstressed vowel: *definite.*

Spelling words with silent consonants

You can use the same four-step process to figure out the spelling of words with silent consonants:

1. Isolate the silent consonant in the word you are trying to spell: *mus[ ]le.*
2. Think of a related word with a similar form: *muscular.*
3. Isolate the sounded consonant: *muscular.*
4. The sounded consonant in the related word is the same consonant to use in the original word: *muscle.*

34f Spelling words with the hyphen

Some compound words are written as single words *(needlework),* some are written as two words *(home run),* and some are joined with a hyphen *(walk-on).* When you are not sure how to spell compound words, consult an up-to-date dictionary.

WHEN TO HYPHENATE COMPOUND WORDS

1. When two or more words serve as a single modifier before a noun:

   She is a *well-regarded* spokesperson for the community.

   He claimed to have had an *out-of-body* experience.

Note: When the modifier appears after the noun, no hyphen is needed.

   The senator is *well respected* by his peers.

2. When a compound adjective appears as part of a series:

   The program is open to *seventh-, eighth-,* and *ninth-grade* students.

3. With fractions and compound numbers:

   one-third

   forty-two

4. With whole numbers between twenty-one and ninety-nine.

5. With coined compounds (words not usually linked):

   He made a great *behind-the-back* pass.

6. When attaching prefixes to words beginning with a capital letter:

   He was accused of being *un-American.*

7. When attaching suffixes to capital letters:

   the *A*-train

   an *X*-ray

For more on hyphens, consult Chapter 45 in the *Workbook.*

34g Six steps to better spelling

1 Keep a list of your misspelled words

Are there some words that you repeatedly misspell? In your list of words that give you trouble, are there patterns of misspelling? Try to discover the reason for the trouble: Is it mispronunciation, or confusion over homonyms?

2 Develop the habit of observing words

In addition to remembering how words sound, visualize how words *look* on the page. The more you read, the more opportunities you have to observe the correct spellings of words.

3   Use your dictionary

Keep your dictionary at hand when studying or writing. Keep a list of words to look up after finishing the task at hand.

4   Edit and proofread your writing carefully

Sometimes misspellings occur because of carelessness. Plan ahead so that you have enough time to edit and proofread your writing. If you use a word processor, do preliminary editing and proofreading on the screen, but print out a non-final copy for further editing and proofreading. It is easier to spot mistakes on a white sheet of paper with the text double spaced than it is to spot them on a computer screen.

5   Use a spell checker with caution

A spell checker is very useful, but it cannot tell you if you have used words incorrectly. For example, if you use *their* where you need *there,* the spell checker cannot detect the error.

6   Study lists of spelling words

In addition to making a list of your own spelling demons, you can study the following list of frequently misspelled words.

FREQUENTLY MISSPELLED WORDS

absence	attendance	deceive	exceed	height
acceptable	bargain	decision	exercise	humorous
accessible	basically	descendant	existence	hurriedly
accidentally	believe	desperate	experience	hypocrite
accommodate	beneficial	develop	extremely	imaginary
achieve	bureaucracy	dictionary	familiar	immediately
acknowledge	business	disastrous	fascinate	immigrant
acquire	cemetery	discipline	favorite	incidentally
address	choose	dissatisfied	foreign	incredible
adolescent	column	doctor	forty	independence
aggravate	commitment	ecstasy	friend	influential
aggressive	committee	efficient	frightening	initiate
amateur	competent	eighth	gauge	insistence
analysis	conceive	embarrass	generally	intelligence
angel	condemn	enemy	ghost	irrelevant
annual	controversial	entirely	government	irresistible
ascend	convenience	environment	grief	island
assassinate	courteous	especially	guarantee	jealousy
athlete	criticize	exaggerate	harass	jeopardy

FREQUENTLY MISSPELLED WORDS (*continued*)

judgment	nuisance	quiet	strategy	vegetable
knowledge	obstacle	rebel	strict	vengeance
laboratory	occasion	receipt	summary	verbal
leisure	occurrence	recommend	supersede	verify
length	opportunity	relief	suppress	versus
library	originally	religious	surely	vicious
license	parallel	reminisce	surprise	villain
lightning	peculiar	renown	suspicious	visible
loneliness	perceive	repetition	teammate	voyeur
magazine	permanent	resemblance	technical	vulnerable
maintenance	persistence	resistance	technique	wallet
manageable	personnel	rhythm	thorough	warrant
marriage	pleasant	ridiculous	tomorrow	Wednesday
miniature	politician	roommate	tragedy	whale
minor	prairie	sacrifice	truly	whisky
mirror	precede	scarcity	tyranny	wholly
mischievous	preferred	schedule	unanimous	woman
morale	prejudice	secretary	unconscious	women
mysterious	prevalent	sergeant	undoubtedly	wreak
necessary	privilege	several	unnecessary	wreath
neither	probably	similar	usually	writing
niece	prominent	sincerely	vacuum	
noticeable	pursue	sophomore	variety	

EXERCISE 1   Choosing the Appropriate Homonym

Underline or circle the appropriate homonym in each sentence. Example:

The letter was in (_plain_/plane) sight.

1. The new tax plan will (_affect_/_effect_) millions of Americans.

2. The hockey player was on the disabled list (_threw_/_through_) most of the season.

3. We make a good team because your curiosity (_complements_/_compliments_) my persistence.

4. The economic devastation caused by last year's floods has been greater (_than_/_then_) was predicted.

5. The escaped prisoner (_alluded_/_eluded_) capture for nearly a week.

6. By the time we got to the theater, the play had (_all ready_/_already_) begun.

7. People who are (_board_, _bored_) with their work may start making mistakes.

8. The team has decided to hold (_its_/_it's_) meeting behind closed doors.

9. He doesn't like to enter competitions if there is a chance he may (_loose_/_lose_).

10. (_Their_/_There_/_They're_) is a possibility that the Steins may sell (_their_/_there_/_they're_) house and move to Maine.

EXERCISE 2   Choosing the Appropriate Homonym

Underline or circle the appropriate homonym in each sentence. Example:

Snow fell so often that month that the sidewalks had to be shoveled (_every day_/everyday).

1. The (*presence*/*presents*) of a well-known theater critic made the actors nervous.

2. Mr. Zhang, (*who's*/*whose*) daughter is in the fourth grade, is active in the PTA.

3. I can (*advice*/*advise*) you as to what choices are available to you, but I cannot tell you which choice to make.

4. The candidate was disappointed, but he (*accepted*/*excepted*) defeat graciously.

5. It is (*to*/*too*) late for us (*to*/*too*) turn back now, even if we wanted (*to*/*too*).

6. After hiking for hours, we were finally within (*sight*/*site*) of the summit of the mountain.

7. The child's unceasing questions nearly exhausted my (*patience*/*patients*).

8. Commuters are not happy about the raise in bus (*fairs*/*fares*).

9. People who sit at desks all day should take an occasional (*brake*/*break*) and get up and walk around.

10. People unfamiliar with the Bible will not understand many of the preacher's (*allusions*/*illusions*).

EXERCISE 3 Writing with the Appropriate Homonym

Write a sentence for each word in the following sets of homonyms. Example:

conscience, conscious

His conscience will not allow him to lie at a job interview.
She was conscious of his presence but did not acknowledge him.

1. all ways, always

2. council, counsel

3. weather, whether

4. principal, principle

5. their, there, they're

6. waist, waste

7. eminent, imminent

8. all together, altogether

9. elicit, illicit

10. your, you're

Name _____ Section _____ Date _____

EXERCISE 4   Spelling by the Rules

Underline the correctly spelled word in each pair. Then use that word in a sentence. Example:

<u>logically</u>, *logicly*

I thought the result of the experiment was logically impossible.

1. neighbor, nieghbor

2. reviseing, revising

3. truely, truly

4. foreign, foriegn

5. magically, magicly

6. noticable, noticeable

7. beleif, belief

8. receed, recede

9. exploration, exploreation

10. proceed, procede

EXERCISE 5   Spelling with *y* or *i*

Keep *y* or change it to *i* when adding the suggested suffix to each of the following words. Examples:

lonely + ness: loneliness

study + ing: studying

1. messy + est

2. rely + ed

3. defy + ance

4. wry + ly

5. mercy + ful

EXERCISE 6   Deciding When to Double Consonants

Decide whether or not to double the consonant when adding suffixes to the following words. Example:

confer + ing: conferring

1. occur + ance

2. refer + ence

3. worship + ful

4. happen + ed

5. commit + al

EXERCISE 7   Spelling Plurals

Form the plurals of the following nouns. Example:

country: countries

1. nest

2. defense

3. brother-in-law

4. wrench

5. woman

6. scarf

7. solo

8. alley

9. executive

10. tooth

EXERCISE 8   Using Plurals in Writing

Use each of the following plural nouns in a sentence. Example:

knives

These steak knives need sharpening.

1. attorneys

2. churches

3. shelves

4. species

5. ideas

6. sketches

7. tests

8. pleas

9. memos

10. children

EXERCISE 9 Spelling Using the Schwa

For each of the following words, fill in the missing vowel. Then supply a related word that uses the same vowel in a stressed syllable. Finally, check your work by consulting a dictionary. Example:

friv lous: frivolous, frivolity

1. defin te

2. sed tive

3. cons lation

4. mir cle

5. preserv tive

6. rep titious

7. inst llation

8. hist ry

9. nec ssary

10. explan tory

EXERCISE 10 Spelling Words with Silent Consonants

Prove that the following spellings are incorrect, first by spelling each word correctly, and then by finding a related word. Example:

maline

malign; malignant

1. colum

2. bom

3. benine

4. condem

5. resine

6. paradime

7. contemp

8. mussle

9. abrup

10. (to) dam (someone or something)

EXERCISE 11   Spelling Compound Words

Decide whether or not to hyphenate the following compound words. Consult a dictionary to confirm your answers. Examples:

straight man: no hyphen

twenty one: twenty-one

1. straight out

2. string quartet

3. eighty seven

4. a well respected leader

5. chief executive

6. U turn

7. music box

8. un American

9. two thirds

10. community property

EXERCISE 12   Checking for Misspellings

In the following pairs of sentences, a word is spelled correctly in one sentence and incorrectly in the other. Cross out the incorrectly spelled word and write in the correct spelling. Example:

I am not familiar with his work.

                         familiar
Your face looks very ~~familar~~ to me.

1. Is this operation really neccesary, or are there other options?

   He sadly made all the necessary arrangements for his mother's funeral.

2. He felt no fear or loneliness despite working in the jungle by himself for six months.

   He was suddenly overcome by lonliness and panic.

3. The team has acquired an excellent young pitcher.

   After only a month in London, he aquired an English accent.

4. The new schedule is not very convienient for me.

Would it be convenient for you to meet with me this afternoon?

5. Mary's teammates elected her captain.

The center must learn to pass more to his teamates.

PART TEN

Punctuation and Mechanics

CHAPTER 35

End Punctuation

The period, question mark, and exclamation point are end, or terminal, punctuation marks. They indicate where one sentence stops and another starts.

35a Using the period

Use a period at the end of a sentence that makes a statement or gives a mild command.

STATEMENTS	Temperatures will be seasonal all this week. Last summer we went to the Grand Canyon.
MILD COMMANDS	Let your imagination roam. Please send me a copy of your article.

Use a period for an indirect question.

INDIRECT QUESTION	She wondered why some children learn to read by the age of four. [Direct question: Why do some children learn to read by the age of four?]
INDIRECT QUESTION	Commuters are asking why fares are being raised again. [Direct question: Why are fares being raised again?]

Most abbreviations take periods.

Mr.	B.A.	A.D. (*or* AD)	i.e.
Mrs.	M.A.	B.C. (*or* BC)	e.g.
Dr.	Ph.D.	a.m.	Jr.

R.N.   D.D.S.   p.m.   Sr.
U.S.A. (*or* USA)   M.D.   U.K.   Ms.

Note: Strictly speaking, *Ms.* is not an abbreviation, but a period should be used because *Ms.* is modeled on the abbreviations *Mr.* and *Mrs.* and because *Ms.* is the title of an influential magazine.

Do not use periods in the postal abbreviations for states.

FL   TN   CA   NY   MA   ME

However, you can write either *Washington, DC,* or *Washington, D.C.* Also, you can abbreviate the names of states with a period following the abbreviation: *Fla., Tenn., Mass., Conn.*

Do not use periods when abbreviating the names of organizations, companies, and agencies. Acronyms—abbreviations pronounced as words—also omit periods.

IBM (International Business Machines)
CNN (Cable News Network)
NASA (National Aeronautics and Space Administration)
MADD (Mothers against Drunk Driving)

35b Using the question mark

The question mark is used after direct questions. Direct questions usually begin with an interrogative word (*who, what, when, where, why, how*) and have inverted word order, with the verb or an auxiliary verb placed before the subject.

DIRECT QUESTIONS   When does the next train leave?

                    Where are you going?

                    It's late, isn't it?

                    How are you going to solve this problem?

                    You do remember me, don't you?

Question marks may be used within sentences to indicate questions in a series:

Working parents constantly ask themselves questions: are we neglecting our children? are our day-care arrangements satisfactory? do we have any alternatives?

You can punctuate a series of questions as independent sentences:

Working parents constantly ask themselves questions. Are we neglecting our children? Are our day-care arrangements satisfactory? Do we have any alternatives?

Both methods are correct, so choose the version that accomplishes your purpose. The single-sentence version moves more swiftly than the other version, thereby creating a sense of urgency. The version with separate sentences is slower paced and more deliberate.

The question mark can also be used to express uncertainty, especially about a date, number, or word. For example, a question mark is often used when the dates of birth or death are unknown or uncertain.

Giovanni da Verrazano (1485?–1528?) was an Italian explorer.

The fate of Judge Joseph Force Crater (1889–1937?) has never been discovered.

However, do not use a question mark in *statements* expressing uncertainty.

INCORRECT It will rain (?) all next week.

REVISED It may rain all next week.

Sometimes questions include quotations. When the question is part of the quotation, put the question mark before the closing quotation marks. Do not put a comma or a period after a question mark.

She asked me, "What was the happiest day of your life?"

The most frequently asked question is "When is the midterm exam?"

When the question is not part of the quotation, put the question mark after the closing quotation marks.

Who first said "A stitch in time saves nine"?

Do you agree that "Still waters run deep"?

35c | Using the exclamation point

The exclamation point is used to convey surprise or strong emotion or to give a command.

Help!

What a great game!

Stop that at once!

Do not use a period or a comma after an exclamation point in a direct quotation.

FAULTY He exclaimed, "What a great pass!".

REVISED He exclaimed, "What a great pass!"

Exclamations occur more frequently in speech than in writing, where they can be distracting and even annoying to readers. Using an exclamation point is a weak way to draw attention to an idea. Stress your important ideas by choosing your words carefully and by placing those ideas in emphatic positions in your sentences.

EXERCISE 1   Using Periods in Abbreviations

Add periods to abbreviations as needed in the following sentences. (Some abbreviations may be correct as given.) Example:

Warren has both an MBA and an MD.

Warren has both an M.B.A. and an M.D.

1. Nurses with only an RN do not have as many career opportunities as those with both an RN and a BS.

2. He received a DDS in 1985 from Columbia University.

3. Mr and Mrs Luna own a small sportswear store downtown.

4. Alexander the Great lived from 356 to 323 BC.

5. They make an annual donation to the NAACP.

EXERCISE 2   Using the Question Mark

Supply question marks as needed in the following sentences. (Some sentences may be correct as written.) Example:

Ms. Bailey asked, "Did you want to see me."

Ms. Bailey asked, "Did you want to see me?"

1. The lead editorial posed the question, "Has there been an upturn in the economy in the last year."

2. Where do you think you lost your history notebook.

3. She wondered where she had put her passport.

4. "Have any of you played tennis before," the instructor asked.

5. It is not a question of whether it will be hot but of how long the heat wave will last.

EXERCISE 3   Using the Exclamation Point

Add or delete exclamation points as needed in the following sentences. Examples:

What a jerk. He can never take a hint!
What a jerk! He can never take a hint.

Samuel Clemens's pen name was Mark Twain!
Samuel Clemens's pen name was Mark Twain.

1. Drop the gun. Raise your hands.

2. Help! Fire.

3. Hurry up. We'll miss the bus.

4. Anthony Trollope was a prolific author!

5. The weight of a newborn baby usually doubles in the first three months!

6. On your marks. Get set. Go!

7. The disk is full! You can't save any more files on it!

8. Oh no. It's raining! Not again!

9. It's impossible to watch television and do a good job on your homework at the same time!

10. He works as a bus driver during the day and as a security guard at night!

EXERCISE 4 Reworking Direct and Indirect Questions

Rewrite direct questions as indirect questions, and indirect questions as direct questions. Examples:

Bill asked, "Are you going to that meeting?"
Bill asked if we were going to that meeting.

Isadora asked if we had won the game.
Isadora asked, "Did you win the game?"

1. The candidate asked, "Are all the election results in?"

2. Mr. Smith wondered if he should retire soon.

3. Ms. Pena asked her son, "Where are you going tonight?"

4. People asked when the next aftershocks would come.

5. He wondered, "Was quitting my job a good or bad idea?"

6. The reporter questioned whether the witness was telling the truth.

7. Conservationists ask the question, "Will this project have a negative effect on the environment?"

8. They wondered what they would do if they could not find jobs.

9. "Will the investigation continue?" the reporter wanted to know.

10. She asked if she could take the day off.

Name _____ Section _____ Date _____

EXERCISE 5   Using Terminal Punctuation

Add the appropriate end punctuation to the following sentences. Example:

What are you going to do after class today

What are you going to do after class today?

  1. The police examination is not given every year

  2. How often does the car have to be inspected

  3. Biblical allusions are found throughout the works of Dante and Milton

  4. Who said "Winning is the *only* thing"

  5. Apple trees do not grow well at high elevations

  6. Help   The engine is on fire

  7. The supervisor asked me if I could train the new employee

  8. The reporter asked, "How often is the college president on campus"

9. Should the school year be extended

10. Do you agree that "All things come to him who waits"

CHAPTER 36

Commas

Unlike end punctuation, which indicates where a sentence stops, the comma indicates a pause within a sentence. Commas also help make writing clear by separating parts of sentences from each other, thereby making it easier for readers to see the relationships between those parts. Here is a list of comma uses.

USES OF THE COMMA

1. To separate main clauses linked by a coordinating conjunction
2. To separate introductory words and phrases from the main clause of a sentence
3. To set off nonrestrictive elements
4. To separate items in a series
5. To separate coordinate adjectives
6. To set off transitional and parenthetical elements
7. To set off absolute phrases
8. To set off contrasting elements, *yes* and *no,* direct address, and tag questions
9. To set off dates, addresses, place names, numbers, and titles
10. To set off quotations
11. To aid comprehension

36a Use a comma before a coordinating conjunction that links independent clauses

Use a comma to separate two independent clauses when the second clause is preceded by a coordinating conjunction (*and, or, but, for, nor, yet,* or *so*).

They got married in 1988, *and* their first child was born three years later.

The team reached the play-offs four times, *but* they never reached the finals.

The pianist broke her wrist, *so* her concert was postponed.

We have to pick the snow peas regularly, *or* the vines will stop producing.

Although a comma usually precedes a coordinating conjunction linking independent clauses, use a semicolon to link long clauses that contain internal commas.

Many supermarket tomatoes, although large, round, and red, are practically tasteless; *for* they have been genetically engineered for long shelf life, not for good taste.

When the two independent clauses are short and closely related in meaning, you can omit the comma.

We tried hard *but* we lost.

But even when the clauses are short, always use a comma if there is a chance that its omission could cause confusion.

CONFUSING   You have to be ready *for* the bus driver won't wait.

REVISED   You have to be ready, *for* the bus driver won't wait.

Be careful not to omit the coordinating conjunction between two independent clauses. Trying to punctuate two independent clauses with just a comma and no coordinating conjunction will result in a comma splice.

36b | Use a comma to set off introductory elements

Use a comma after an introductory word, expression, phrase, or clause. Introductory elements may be adverbs, conjunctive adverbs, transitional expressions, adverb clauses, participles, infinitives, or various kinds of phrases.

Unfortunately, it rained all weekend. [adverb]

You were irritating; *moreover,* you were rude. [conjunctive adverb]

On the other hand, fame can also mean a loss of privacy. [transitional expression]

After the tennis player started training with weights, he developed a stronger serve. [adverb clause]

Annoyed, he abruptly hung up the phone. [participle]

After a hard day of work, she relieves stress by exercising. [prepositional phrase]

The roads having been plowed, traffic was moving slowly but steadily. [absolute phrase]

Bowing and waving to the audience, the singer acknowledged the applause. [modifying participial phrase]

To save money, they do most of their car repairs themselves. [modifying infinitive phrase]

The comma can be omitted after short introductory elements if the omission does not cause confusion.

CLEAR   *After today* temperatures should rise.

CLEAR   *By the end of the year* the business should be earning a profit.

CONFUSING   *By seventy* judges in some courts have to retire.

CLEAR   *By seventy,* judges in some courts have to retire.

36c   Use commas to set off nonrestrictive elements

A nonrestrictive modifier does not limit or restrict the meaning of the words it modifies. All nonrestrictive elements are set off from the rest of the sentence with commas. Notice the difference between the following restrictive and nonrestrictive modifiers:

RESTRICTIVE	Sports commentators *who are very popular* sometimes earn multimillion-dollar salaries. [The modifying clause *who are very popular* is necessary to the meaning of the sentence because it specifies which sports commentators are highly paid. Therefore, the modifier is restrictive and is not set off by commas.]
NONRESTRICTIVE	John Madden, *who is a popular sports commentator,* earns a multimillion-dollar salary. [The clause *who is a popular sports commentator* adds information about the noun it modifies, *John Madden,* but it does not limit that noun. The clause is a nonrestrictive modifier and is set off by commas.]

Sometimes a modifying element can be interpreted as either restrictive or nonrestrictive. Look at these examples:

The children, *needing a bath,* were given one. [The nonrestrictive modifier suggests that all the children needed and got a bath.]

The children *needing a bath* were given one. [The restrictive modifier suggests that only some children needed and got a bath, while other children did not need or get a bath.]

Although the words in these two sentences are identical, the presence or absence of commas makes a significant difference in the meaning.

If you are not sure whether a modifier is restrictive or nonrestrictive, try reading the sentence without the words in question. If the words can be deleted without changing or confusing the meaning of the sentence, they constitute a nonrestrictive modifier and should be set off by commas. If the words are vital to the meaning of the sentence, do not use commas.

NONRESTRICTIVE	Ms. Lyman, *who is a marketing executive,* went to college in Boston.
	Ms. Lyman went to college in Boston. [The sentence makes sense without the nonrestrictive modifier.]
RESTRICTIVE	Meat *that has spoiled* should not be eaten.
	Meat should not be eaten. [The sentence needs the restrictive modifier to convey its meaning.]

1   Use commas to set off nonrestrictive adjective and adverb clauses

Use commas around only nonrestrictive adjective and adverb clauses. Do not use commas around restrictive adjective and adverb clauses.

NONRESTRICTIVE	They play softball at the town park, *which is well maintained.* [The adjective clause is marked off by a comma because it is not necessary to the meaning of the independent clause.]

NONRESTRICTIVE	The transit system, *even though it has its problems,* provides a vital service to the city. [The adverb clause is not necessary to the meaning of the independent clause; it is thus marked off by commas.]
RESTRICTIVE	The book *that I wanted* was not available in the local library. [The adjective clause is necessary to the meaning of the independent clause; therefore, no commas are used. Without the restrictive modifier, the sentence would not identify which book was not available.]

When you write sentences containing relative clauses, use the word *that* only for restrictive clauses. Although *which* may be used in both restrictive and nonrestrictive clauses, many writers prefer to use *which* only in nonrestrictive clauses (those requiring commas).

2   Use commas with nonrestrictive phrases

Participial and prepositional phrases can be either restrictive or nonrestrictive, although prepositional phrases are usually used restrictively.

NONRESTRICTIVE	Ms. Andrews, *delighted by Arizona's climate,* decided to move to Phoenix.
NONRESTRICTIVE	The rock star, *even with all his fame and wealth,* was a reclusive, unhappy man.
RESTRICTIVE	People *bored by their work* will start making careless mistakes.
RESTRICTIVE	The stand *for the Christmas tree* is in the hall closet.

3   Use commas with nonrestrictive appositives

An appositive is a noun or noun substitute that renames another noun. Use commas with nonrestrictive appositives. Do not use commas with restrictive appositives that are essential to the meaning of the sentence.

NONRESTRICTIVE	Sir Lawrence Alma-Tadema, *an English painter,* lived from 1836 to 1912.
NONRESTRICTIVE	*Mama Day, a novel by Gloria Naylor,* is a beautiful, evocative novel.
RESTRICTIVE	The American poet *Emily Dickinson* wrote nearly 1,800 poems, but only a few were published in her lifetime.
RESTRICTIVE	In 1994, the movie *The Piano* was unexpectedly successful.

36d   Use commas between items in a series, whether words, phrases, or clauses

Use commas to separate items in a series of three or more words, phrases, or clauses.

SERIES OF WORDS	The floral arrangement contained *asters, daisies, and ferns.*
SERIES OF PHRASES	The ball rolled *down the hill, off the sidewalk, into the street, and under a car.*
SERIES OF CLAUSES	I want to know *where you went, whom you met, and what you did.*

When one or more items in a series contain commas, separate the items with semicolons instead of commas.

> She watches only certain things on television, including sports, especially tennis and hockey; real-life court trials about divorce, prenuptial agreements, and domestic violence; and public television broadcasts of plays, operas, and ballet.

Some writers, particularly journalists, omit the comma before the coordinating conjunction, but doing so can sometimes result in confusion. Look at the following examples:

UNCLEAR	The dress is available in red, black, *blue* and green. [Is this dress available in four different colors, or is it available in red, in black, and in a mixture of blue and green?]
CLEAR	The dress is available in red, black, *blue,* and green. [Four different colors are available.]
CLEAR	The dress is available in a red, a black, and a blue and green version.

36e   Use commas to separate coordinate adjectives

Coordinate adjectives contain two adjectives that modify the same noun or pronoun. Separate coordinate adjectives with a comma or with a coordinating conjunction. Do not use both a comma and a coordinating conjunction to separate coordinate adjectives.

INCORRECT	The playground was filled with *noisy, and exuberant* children.
CORRECT	The playground was filled with *noisy and exuberant* children.
CORRECT	The playground was filled with *noisy, exuberant* children.

When adjectives are coordinate, their positions can often be reversed. However, the positions of cumulative adjectives cannot be reversed. Adjectives are cumulative when the adjective closer to the noun is more closely related to the noun in meaning. Do not use commas with cumulative adjectives. In the following examples, note the difference between coordinate and cumulative adjectives.

COORDINATE	She had a bowl of *delicious, hot* soup.
COORDINATE	She had a bowl of *hot, delicious* soup.
COORDINATE	She had a bowl of *hot and delicious* soup.

CUMULATIVE She had a bowl of *delicious lentil* soup. [The positions of these adjectives cannot be reversed, nor can *and* be put between the two adjectives.]

36f Use commas to set off transitional and parenthetical expressions

Transitional expressions include conjunctive adverbs, such as *however* and *therefore*, as well as other words and expressions used to join sentence elements. Parenthetical expressions add supplementary information or digressions; they are not essential to the grammatical structure of a sentence. Use commas to set off transitional and parenthetical expressions.

This car, *on the other hand*, gets excellent gas mileage.

The commissioner, *however*, would not answer reporters' questions.

The tests, *in fact*, indicate that the experimental medicine is safe.

Studies show that reading scores have, *surprisingly*, risen in the last twenty years.

36g Use commas to set off absolute phrases

An absolute phrase modifies an independent clause as a whole, rather than modifying any particular word or phrase in the clause. Absolute phrases may be placed anywhere in a sentence. Always use commas to set off absolute phrases.

Fingers gripping the handlebars, he rode his tricycle down the sidewalk.

We stopped hiking for a few moments, *a fallen tree serving for a seat.*

Mr. Travis, *his house damaged by the earthquake,* set up a tent in the yard.

36h Use commas to set off contrasting elements, *yes* and *no*, direct address, and tag questions

CONTRASTING ELEMENTS	The elderly, *not the young or middle-aged,* suffer most in extreme temperatures.
YES AND *NO*	*Yes*, the package was delivered yesterday.
	No, the store does not take personal checks.
DIRECT ADDRESS	*Mildred*, can you help me for a minute?
	Please answer the phone, *Jack.*
TAG QUESTIONS	It was the coldest day of the winter, *wasn't it?*
	This isn't a good time to talk, *is it?*

36i   Use commas with dates, addresses, place names, numbers, and titles

Use commas with dates, addresses, place names, and numbers. Also use commas to separate personal and professional titles from the name before them.

Dates

Use a comma to separate the day of the month from the year. Also put a comma after the year, unless the year ends the sentence.

He began his professional basketball career on *September 3, 1984,* and he retired on *September 3, 1994.*

When dates appear in inverted order, commas within the date are not needed.

The conference began on *15 June 1993* and lasted a week.

Commas are also not necessary when a date contains only a month and a year.

The new schedule goes into effect in *May 1995.*

Addresses and place names

Use a comma after each part of a place name, but do not use a comma directly before or immediately after a ZIP code.

Portland, Oregon, has a very different climate from Portland, Maine.

The address is Computer Concepts, 912 West 115th Street, New York, New York 10025.

Numbers

Use commas to separate numbers of more than four digits into groups of threes, moving from right to left. The comma in a four-digit number is optional.

More than *10,000* people attended the rally.

A mile is *5,280* [or *5280*] feet.

Do not use a comma in years, street numbers, telephone numbers, Social Security numbers, or ZIP codes.

What will you be doing in the year *2000?*

His last known address was *1569* Miller Place, Hinsdale, Massachusetts *01235.*

His Social Security number is *123-456-7890.*

Titles

Use a comma to separate a name and a title that follows the name. Also use a comma to separate a title from whatever follows it in a sentence. Note that the final period in an abbreviated title is included before the comma.

Ariane Reed, Ph.D., has joined the Department of Slavic Languages.

Andrew Eggers, Jr., is running for the city council.

36j   Use commas with quotations

Use commas to separate quotations from introductory words and from words that identify the source of the quotation. Place commas before the closing quotation marks unless the quotation is also the end of your sentence.

"English is the language of men ever famous and foremost in the achievements of liberty," wrote John Milton in *Areopagitica.*

In 1861, Ralph Waldo Emerson wrote, "A nation never falls but by suicide."

Do not use commas when explanatory words follow a quotation ending in a question mark or an exclamation point.

"This is unbelievable!" she exclaimed.

"When does the semester start?" he asked.

Commas are also unnecessary when the quotation is introduced by the word *that.*

Coleridge wrote *that* "One error almost compels another."

In *Walden,* Thoreau states *that* "Superfluous wealth can buy superfluities only."

Do not use commas in indirect quotations.

The conductor said that the train would be a few minutes late.

The governor announced that he would run for reelection.

36k   Use commas to aid comprehension

Use a comma in cases where lack of one would cause confusion or misunderstanding.

CONFUSING   As the professor walked in the class became quiet.

REVISED   As the professor walked in, the class became quiet.

CONFUSING   Although tired medical interns must work through the night.

REVISED   Although tired, medical interns must work through the night.

36l   Avoid overusing commas

1   Omit commas between subjects and verbs, verbs and objects or complements, and prepositions and their objects

UNNECESSARY   The defense lawyer, called his first witness. [incorrect separation of subject and verb]

REVISED	The defense lawyer called his first witness.
UNNECESSARY	The actor finally agreed, to be interviewed but insisted that no questions be asked about, his wife or his children. [incorrect separation of subject and verb, and of preposition and object]
REVISED	The actor finally agreed to be interviewed but insisted that no questions be asked about his wife or his children.

2   Omit commas around restrictive elements

UNNECESSARY	Buster Keaton's movie, *The General*, is both moving and comic. [The commas suggest, incorrectly, that Keaton made only one movie.]
REVISED	Buster Keaton's movie *The General* is both moving and comic.

(See 36c.)

3   Omit commas in compound constructions

Do not use a comma before or after a coordinating conjunction that joins two words, two phrases, or two dependent clauses of a compound construction.

UNNECESSARY	I quickly read my mail, and made some phone calls.
REVISED	I quickly read my mail and made some phone calls. [compound verb]
UNNECESSARY	We saw the truck skid across the road, and into the telephone pole.
REVISED	We saw the truck skid across the road and into the telephone pole. [compound prepositional phrases]
UNNECESSARY	Most people want lower taxes, and better municipal services.
REVISED	Most people want lower taxes and better municipal services. [compound direct objects]
UNNECESSARY	Citrus fruit, and leafy green vegetables contain vitamin C.
REVISED	Citrus fruit and leafy green vegetables contain vitamin C. [compound subject]

4   Omit commas before the first and last items in a series

UNNECESSARY	Her speech was, brief, informative, and amusing.
REVISED	Her speech was brief, informative, and amusing.
UNNECESSARY	Reading, gardening, and cooking, are their hobbies.
REVISED	Reading, gardening, and cooking are their hobbies.

EXERCISE 1   Punctuating Linked Independent Clauses with Commas

Add commas and/or coordinating conjunctions where necessary in the following sentences. Examples:

I could not call you for my phone was not working.
I could not call you, for my phone was not working.

We circled the block three times, we could not find a parking space.
We circled the block three times, but we could not find a parking space.

1. His winning the election was a surprise for no one had thought he had a chance.

2. The heat has not abated nor has the humidity gone down.

3. The library has a copying machine, it also has a fax.

4. Keep candles and flashlights handy or you may have problems during a power emergency.

5. I wanted to take a course in social psychology but all the sections were closed.

EXERCISE 2   Punctuating Introductory Elements with Commas

Insert commas after introductory elements in the following sentences. Example:

Whenever it rains heavily the gutters overflow.

Whenever it rains heavily, the gutters overflow.

1. By thirty one out of every three men may have some baldness.

2. Holding the trophy high the athlete posed for the cameras.

3. To stimulate sales the car companies offered large rebates.

4. Unfortunately more cold air and snow will arrive early next week.

5. As a result traffic was backed up for miles.

EXERCISE 3   Punctuating Nonrestrictive Elements with Commas

Use commas in the following sentences to set off nonrestrictive clauses, phrases, and appositives. Do not use commas with restrictive elements. Example:

The Mighty Ducks a new hockey team plays in Anaheim.

The Mighty Ducks, a new hockey team, plays in Anaheim.

1. Mr. Anderson whose dogs bark all day long has received many complaints from his neighbors.

2. People who let their dogs bark day and night are inconsiderate to their neighbors.

3. Beethoven's only opera *Fidelio* has been recorded by many singers.

4. Greta Garbo displeased by a negative review would not talk to reporters.

5. The heiress even with all her money and advantages did not seem happy.

6. Customers dissatisfied with the merchandise should write to the following address.

7. Harriet Beecher Stowe's novel *Uncle Tom's Cabin* contains some surprisingly radical views.

8. Ms. Richardson holding her diploma proudly smiled at her parents.

9. The boots that you are wearing look warm and waterproof.

10. This coat which I bought three years ago is reversible.

EXERCISE 4   Punctuating Items in a Series with Commas

In the following sentences, add commas where necessary to separate the items in a series. (Some sentences may be correct as written.) Example:

Her favorite sports are baseball tennis and hockey.

Her favorite sports are baseball, tennis, and hockey.

1. The athlete wanted to improve her speed endurance and strength.

2. Someone choosing a college has to consider the location of the school its course offerings the strength of its faculty and its cost.

3. Most of the runners were wearing dark-blue warmup suits.

4. I got a long informative letter from my brother.

5. The committee interviewed many candidates and chose the two best people.

6. Very young children have vivid imaginations they think that wishes can become reality and they often cannot distinguish between fantasy and reality.

7. The area is filled with many Italian Thai Vietnamese Chinese and Spanish restaurants.

8. The classroom was so crowded that students sat on the floor on their bookbags and on the radiator.

9. The coffee boiled over the toast burned there was no orange juice and the eggs were too well done.

10. He gave an accurate unbiased account of the conflict.

EXERCISE 5 Punctuating Transitional Expressions, Parenthetical Expressions, and Absolute Phrases with Commas

Use commas to set off the transitional expressions, parenthetical expressions, and absolute phrases in the following sentences. Example:

I agreed against my better judgment to lend her some money.

I agreed, against my better judgment, to lend her some money.

1. The streets having been plowed we could finally get to the store.

2. I am in fact astonished at how well you did.

3. The tests suggested that salt surprisingly is not always a cause of high blood pressure.

4. Stock prices however have not rebounded.

5. The new gym furthermore will not be finished until next spring.

6. On the other hand sharing a room can teach siblings to cooperate.

7. Six people stood at the bus stop the bus shelter protecting them from the cold rain.

8. The rock concert having been canceled customers got on line for ticket refunds.

9. The ambulance crew shockingly did not respond to the emergency call.

10. Nobody however will admit responsibility for the crime.

EXERCISE 6   Punctuating Contrasting Elements, *yes* and *no*, Direct Address, and Tag Questions with Commas

In the following sentences, use commas as needed with contrasting elements, *yes* and *no*, direct address, and tag questions. Example:

We never really talked about it did we?

We never really talked about it, did we?

1. He is interested in jazz not heavy metal.

2. Yes this office does have a fax number.

3. Your resume Mr. Romero looks very interesting.

4. It hasn't rained for the last two weeks has it?

5. No you cannot pay your library fine with a check.

EXERCISE 7   Punctuating Dates, Addresses, Place Names, Titles, and Numbers with Commas

Place commas where necessary in the following sentences. Example:

He lived in Juneau Alaska until he was fifteen.

He lived in Juneau, Alaska, until he was fifteen.

1. The book was published on July 11 1992 and quickly sold nearly 50000 copies.

2. They live at 425 Underhill Road Freeport Maine 04033.

3. Contestants came from both Manchester Vermont and Manchester England.

4. Maria Sanchez M.D. is the chief resident in pediatrics.

5. Flyers handed out throughout April 1994 announced that school board elections would be held May 10 1994.

EXERCISE 8   Using Commas with Quotations

Use commas with quotations as needed in the following sentences. (Some sentences may be correct as written.) Example:

The confused student asked "Where is the bookstore?"

The confused student asked, "Where is the bookstore?"

1. Thomas Carlyle stated "Society is founded on hero-worship."

2. "What a ridiculous notion!" she scoffed.

3. In *Poor Richard's Almanac* Benjamin Franklin states "A good man is seldom uneasy, an ill one never easy."

4. John Donne wrote that "No man is an island."

5. "This train does not stop in Omaha" the conductor said.

EXERCISE 9 Using Commas to Avoid Confusion

Place commas as needed to eliminate confusion in the following sentences. Example:

For Alice May was both a friend and mentor.

For Alice, May was both a friend and mentor.

1. When I walked in the room felt chilly.

2. Even when angry parents should try to remain calm.

3. Those who can help the others who can't.

4. For most snakes are frightening.

5. When she joined in the discussion was getting interesting.

EXERCISE 10   Using Commas to Alter Meaning

Rewrite the following sentences deleting *only* the underlined commas. Then explain how the omission of commas changes the meaning of each sentence. Example:

No, dictionaries are allowed.

No dictionaries are allowed.

Omitting the comma reverses the meaning. The original sentence states that the use of dictionaries is permitted; the rewritten sentence indicates that dictionaries are forbidden.

1. No, advance payment is required.

2. John Smith's book, *My Past,* was a best-seller.

3. I dislike the neighbors, who play their stereo very loud every night.

4. My son, James, is in fourth grade.

5. She has taught many students, who appreciate her no-nonsense style.

EXERCISE 11   Eliminating Needless Commas

Eliminate unnecessary commas from the following sentences. Example:

All children, should be immunized against polio, diphtheria, and measles.

All children should be immunized against polio, diphtheria, and measles.

1. The excited audience, cheered as the team entered the stadium.

2. Although your plan is a good one, the committee has decided, not to adopt it.

3. A buzzer sounds two minutes before time is up, and at the end of the period.

4. The runner took long, loping, strides around the track.

5. Nobody knew, the mayor was not planning to run for reelection.

6. Students can take, yoga, swimming, tennis, track, or basketball.

7. The nurse bathed the patient, and helped him to get dressed.

8. Spike Lee's movie, *Do the Right Thing,* was very well written.

9. The dean said, several classes had to be canceled because of low registration.

10. The book has, an exciting plot, an interesting setting, and intriguing characters.

EXERCISE 12 Using Commas Appropriately

Place commas where necessary in the following sentences. Example:

For some eggs and wheat cause allergic reactions.

For some, eggs and wheat cause allergic reactions.

1. The tracks were flooded so many trains were delayed or canceled.

2. To explain their new proposals the senators held a news conference.

3. They live in a rambling farmhouse which was built in 1790.

4. The ingredients of this dish include ginger garlic red bell peppers and chicken.

5. We will need a spacious well-lighted conference room.

6. The study showed that red wine surprisingly helped to lower cholesterol.

7. Eyes fixed on the ball the batter swung at the pitch.

8. Donald you did remember the concert tickets didn't you?

9. Mary Elders M.D. lives at 123 Main Street Roslyn New York 11576.

10. Euripides states in *Andromache* "Better to have an honest poor man for kin or friend than wealthy knave."

CHAPTER 37

Semicolons and Colons

SEMICOLONS

37a Use the semicolon to signal a close relationship between independent clauses

When two independent clauses are closely related in meaning, you can use a semi-colon to signal their relationship. In a sense, the semicolon [;] acts like a period, separating the end of one independent clause from the start of another independent clause. But unlike a period, the semicolon also links two clauses in one sentence. Use a lowercase letter after the semicolon, unless the word would be capitalized in any case.

Do not use semicolons between any two independent clauses; there should be a relationship between the first and the second clauses. Look at the following examples:

RESTATEMENT He wanted to continue his speech; he had more to say.

EXPANSION The youth center offers more than sports; children and teenagers can also get health services and academic tutoring there.

CONTRAST Our team plays a good running game; the other team's strength is passing.

BALANCE If you start exercising, you will probably lower your blood pressure; if your blood pressure decreases, you lessen your risk of having a heart attack.

37b Use a semicolon between independent clauses linked with a conjunctive adverb or a transitional phrase

Independent clauses joined by conjunctive adverbs (see 17c-4 in the *Workbook*) or transitional phrases need a semicolon between them. Look at the placement of semi-colons in the following examples.

He graduated from law school ten years ago; however, he has never practiced law.

She speaks five languages; moreover, she can read two others.

Most of the town budget was spent on snow removal; therefore, no funds are available to buy a new ambulance.

His grades are good, but not outstanding; on the other hand, he has won a distinguished science award.

She took eighteen credits last semester; as a result, she was overwhelmed with term papers and reading assignments.

Conjunctive adverbs and transitional expressions may not always be at the start of the second independent clause. When such expressions occur later in the sentence, use a semicolon between the two independent clauses and set off the expressions with commas.

The project will not exceed its budget; it will, moreover, be completed ahead of schedule.

Despite popular opinion, goldenrod does not cause allergic reactions; wind-pollinated plants such as ragweed are, in fact, the real culprits.

37c   Use the semicolon to separate long and complex independent clauses and those that contain commas

Sometimes compound sentences are long and involved, containing appositives, transitional expressions, parenthetical expressions, and the like. In such cases, use commas to separate the independent clauses.

More than thirty years ago, on January 11, 1964, a report on the effects of smoking was first issued by the surgeon general; and, in those thirty years, the percentage of smokers has decreased in most groups, but, sadly, has increased among women and teenagers.

37d   Use semicolons to separate items in a series

Usually, items in a series of three or more are separated by commas (see 36d in the *Workbook*). However, when a series has items containing commas or other punctuation, use semicolons to separate the main items. The semicolons help readers to see the demarcation between items.

Dance majors at that special high school can expect to take dance class three hours a day, including a ballet class and a modern dance class; to study anatomy, dance history, and first aid for dance injuries; and to choreograph a piece, lasting three to six minutes, for a group of dancers.

37e Avoid semicolon errors

1 Do not use a semicolon to separate an independent clause from a phrase or from a dependent clause

INCORRECT The team played its first game in the new gym; which is bigger and has more modern facilities than the old one had.

REVISED The team played its first game in the new gym, which is bigger and has more modern facilities than the old one had.

2 Do not use a semicolon to introduce a list or a series

INCORRECT We will read plays by four authors; Edward Albee, Eugene O'Neill, Tennessee Williams, and Anton Chekhov.

REVISED We will read plays by four authors: Edward Albee, Eugene O'Neill, Tennessee Williams, and Anton Chekhov.

(See 37g.)

3 Be careful not to overuse semicolons

OVERUSED Susan has had exhibitions of her paintings and other art in Rome, Italy; Munich, Germany; and Nice, France; a new exhibition is planned for Venice, Italy, next summer; her work is quite varied, including watercolors; embroidery using clothing labels; and mosaics.

REVISED Susan has had exhibitions of her paintings and other art in Rome, Munich, and Nice; a new exhibition is planned for Venice next summer. Her work is quite varied, including watercolors, embroidery using clothing labels, and mosaics.

COLONS

37f Use the colon to introduce a statement that summarizes, amplifies, or explains a statement in an independent clause

When an independent clause follows a colon, the first word is generally not capitalized unless it is a word that would be capitalized anyway. However, writers sometimes use a capital letter to emphasize the importance of the second statement.

She had had a very busy day: she had gone to college classes in the morning, worked at her part-time job in the afternoon, and then picked up her children at the day-care center and gone home.

This school has one major rule: Do nothing that will hurt others.

37g   Use the colon to introduce a list

Use a colon to introduce a list only when the words before the colon constitute an independent clause.

These are the qualities of a good parent: patience, good humor, and tolerance.

When they moved, they threw out many things: an irreparably broken lawn mower, years of old newspapers and magazines, and clothes that had been old fashioned twenty years ago.

37h   Use the colon to introduce long or formal quotations

To introduce a long or formal quotation or to introduce a quotation formally, use a colon before the quotation.

Here is the opening of his novel: "It was a dark and stormy night."

I will never forget the words of my friend: "Be what you want to seem."

When a colon follows quoted material, put the colon after the closing quotation marks.

This object was once called the "Cellini Cup": it had, erroneously, been attributed to Benvenuto Cellini.

37i   Use the colon to introduce delayed appositives

She was frightened of only one thing: rats.

The Bills hoped for only one thing that January: a Superbowl win.

37j   Use the colon in salutations, memo headings, hours/minutes, titles/subtitles

Also, use a colon between chapter and verse in references to the Bible.

FORMAL LETTER	Dear Professor Brown:
MEMO HEADINGS	To: Anita Ruiz
	From: Evelyn Richardson
	Re: Guidelines for Promotion

HOURS/MINUTES/SECONDS	5:37 a.m.
TITLE/SUBTITLE	*The First Amendment: A Brief History*
BIBLE REFERENCE	Genesis 2:5 [chapter 2, verse 5]

37k Avoid misuse of the colon

Do not use a colon after an incomplete sentence or a partial statement. Do not use a colon after such words as *including* and *such as*. Do not use a colon after a verb.

INCORRECT	We needed to buy: laundry detergent, shampoo, soap, and oven cleaner.
REVISED	We needed to buy laundry detergent, shampoo, soap, and oven cleaner.
INCORRECT	The movie dealt with themes such as: guilt, love, and responsibility.
REVISED	The movie dealt with themes such as guilt, love, and responsibility.
INCORRECT	I think the most important thing a hockey goalie needs to have is: quick reflexes.
REVISED	I think the most important thing a hockey goalie needs to have is quick reflexes.

EXERCISE 1   Punctuating Independent Clauses with the Semicolon

Place semicolons where necessary in the following sentences to indicate the relationship between independent clauses. Example:

Many people pass the driving test on the first try some fail it several times.

Many people pass the driving test on the first try; some fail it several times.

1. Strobe lights are used in this production people who have seizures should not attend the show.

2. Large hands can be advantageous for a pianist they can stretch with more ease and less tension than small hands can.

3. Mariela is a great basketball player she outscored all the other high school players, girls or boys, in the state.

4. Time dragged by very slowly I thought an hour had passed, but when I looked at my watch, it was only five minutes.

5. The tunnel underneath the English Channel has been nicknamed the "Chunnel" it opened to cars in 1994.

EXERCISE 2   Working with the Semicolon

Complete the following sentences by adding, after the semicolon, a second independent clause—one that restates, expands, or contrasts with the first independent clause. Example:

The car would not start;

The car would not start; the battery was probably dead.

1. The jury did not believe the witness;

2. The football player weighed only 165 pounds;

3. Many people regard old age as a disease;

4. Film can convey action very convincingly;

5. They had radical ideas when they were young;

Name _____ *Section* _____ *Date* _____

EXERCISE 3   Using the Semicolon with Conjunctive Adverbs

Place semicolons where necessary in the following sentences. In addition, use commas to set off conjunctive adverbs and transitional expressions. Example:

Until she was ten years old, she had never been in an elevator in fact she had never seen a building higher than three stories.

Until she was ten years old, she had never been in an elevator; in fact, she had never seen a building higher than three stories.

1. We did not receive your high school transcript therefore we cannot evaluate your application.

2. The elementary school has an afterschool athletic program in addition tutoring in reading and math is available.

3. He wanted to take a year off between high school and college his parents however were against the idea.

4. We had a very dry, hot summer as a result the water reservoirs are dangerously low.

5. That job pays well but sounds dull on the other hand this one looks exciting but is not well paid.

EXERCISE 4   Correcting Misuses of the Semicolon

Revise the following sentences to correct misuse of the semicolon. (Some sentences may be correct as written.) Example:

As far as the eye could see; there were endless wheat fields.

As far as the eye could see, there were endless wheat fields.

1. When the semester is over and this project comes to an end; we should try to keep in touch with each other.

2. Just ten feet away from the corner of the garage; grows a huge oak tree whose roots are beginning to buckle the pavement of the driveway.

3. Before approving this site for a drug-treatment center, we should consider three factors; access to public transportation, the cost to taxpayers, and the effect on the neighborhood.

4. In the past, students had to register in person; now they can do it by telephone.

5. He is allergic to a number of things; dust, pollen, cat hair, and mold.

EXERCISE 5   Writing with the Semicolon

For each topic that follows, write a sentence using the semicolon. Example:

Topic: Train fares

Excursion fares are lower than regular fares; excursion tickets, however, can be used only at nonpeak hours.

1. Airline food

2. A sport you do not enjoy watching

3. A favorite relative

4. Unusual laughs you have heard

5. A book you admire

EXERCISE 6   Using the Colon

Place colons where necessary in the following sentences. Example:

Remember this advice, talk little, listen much.

Remember this advice: talk little, listen much.

1. To make that special sauce, I needed the following items, peanut butter, tamarind paste, sugar, lemon juice, soy sauce, and garlic.

2. In a letter written in 1787, Thomas Jefferson wrote the following words about slavery "This abomination must have an end. And there is a superior bench reserved in Heaven for those who hasten it."

3. Only one thing impresses that coach hard work.

4. Dear Senator Feinstein

514

5. To   Professor Hawkins
   From Dean Roberson
   Re   Class size

EXERCISE 7   Writing with the Colon

For each topic or assignment that follows, write a sentence using the colon. Example:

Topic: The ingredients needed for a recipe

To make chapatis, you need only three ingredients: white flour, whole wheat flour, and water.

1. The following quotation from Benjamin Franklin: "In rivers and bad governments the lightest things swim at the top"

2. Money (use *money* as a delayed appositive)

3. The headings for a memo from yourself to a professor about the syllabus

4. The best time (hours, minutes, seconds) in a lengthy dogsled race

5. The title and subtitle of a book

CHAPTER 38

The Apostrophe

The main use of the apostrophe is to indicate possession. The apostrophe is also used to form the plurals of letters, numbers, and symbols, as well as in contractions to show the omission of a letter or number.

38a Use the apostrophe to form the possessive case of nouns and indefinite pronouns

The possessive case indicates ownership or possession or the relationship between two things. Use the apostrophe to form the possessive case of nouns and indefinite pronouns.

1 Add an apostrophe and -s to form the possessive case of singular nouns or indefinite pronouns

Please put the files on Ms. *Halperin's* desk.

Tonight I have a conference with my *daughter's* teacher.

It was *nobody's* fault.

Voting is *everyone's* right.

2 Add an apostrophe and -s (or just an apostrophe) to singular nouns ending in -s.

For singular nouns ending in -s, most writers add an apostrophe and -s to show possession.

I have read most of Henry *James's* novels.

Nobody believed the *witness's* testimony.

Here is Mr. *Rios's* office.

However, for singular nouns ending in *-s*, it is also acceptable to form the possessive by adding only the apostrophe. Whichever way you choose, be consistent; do not switch from one possessive form to the other in a piece of writing.

Nobody believed the *witness'* testimony.

Here is Mr. *Rios'* office.

If you choose to form such possessives with only the apostrophe, be careful not to put the apostrophe in the wrong place.

INCORRECT What is *Charle's* last name?

REVISED What is *Charles'* last name?

3 | Add an apostrophe and *-s* to plural nouns not ending in *-s*

For plural nouns ending in *-s*, add only the apostrophe.

The library is asking for donations of *children's* books.

The author Deborah Tanner states that *men's* modes of communicating are very different from *women's*.

The *boys'* clothing department is on this floor.

The company has an annual party for its *employees'* children.

4 | Add an apostrophe and *-s* to the last word in compound words and phrases

My *sister-in-law's* car was stolen last week.

This is *someone else's* responsibility.

The voters seem to like *John Reed, Jr.'s* style.

5 | Add an apostrophe and *-s* to the last noun only to show joint possession for two or more nouns

Bob and Ray's radio show was popular for years. [Bob and Ray worked as a team.]

Andrea and Tom's house is a converted barn. [Andrea and Tom own the house jointly.]

6 | Add an apostrophe and *-s* to each noun to show individual possession for two or more nouns

Mr. Truong's and *Ms. Best's* offices have computers, modems, and fax machines. [Mr. Truong and Ms. Best have separate offices with similar equipment.]

The *owners'* and the *players'* representatives met for several hours this afternoon. [The players are not represented by the same people who represent the owners.]

38b   **Do not use an apostrophe to form the possessives of personal pronouns and adjectives**

Possessive pronouns and possessive adjectives do not include an apostrophe. Do not confuse possessive pronouns and possessive adjectives with contractions.

PRONOUN	POSSESSIVE FORM
I	my, mine (*not* mines or mine's)
he	his (*not* his' or his's)
she	her, hers (*not* hers' or her's)
it	its (*not* it's or its')
we	our, ours
you	your, yours (*not* your's or yours')
they	their, theirs (*not* their's or theirs')
who	whose (*not* who's, whos', or whoes)

Be especially careful not to confuse the possessive form *its* with the contraction *it's,* which stands for *it is* or *it has.* Also distinguish between the possessive form *whose* and the contraction *who's* for *who is* or *who has.*

FAULTY   The college is changing *it's* registration procedures.

REVISED   The college is changing *its* registration procedures.

FAULTY   Luca, *who's* family is from Switzerland, speaks four languages.

REVISED   Luca, *whose* family is from Switzerland, speaks four languages.

For more on possessive pronouns and possessive adjectives see, respectively, 15d-3 and 16h in the *Workbook.*

 38c   **Use the apostrophe in contractions and to indicate missing letters, numbers, or words**

Contractions are words from which one or more letters have been omitted. They are two-word combinations that use apostrophes to mark the place where one or more letters have been left out. Contractions are common in speaking and in informal writing, but you should avoid them in most academic writing. Following is a list of the most commonly used contractions.

COMMON CONTRACTIONS

cannot—can't	let us—let's
could not—couldn't	she is, she has—she's
did not—didn't	should not—shouldn't
do not—don't	they are—they're
he is, he has—he's	was not—wasn't
has not—hasn't	we are—we're
have not—haven't	who is, who has—who's

I am—I'm   will not—won't
I would—I'd   would not—wouldn't
it is—it's   you are—you're

Apostrophes are also used to indicate omissions of letters and numbers in some common phrases.

ten of the clock—ten o'clock
the class of 1994—the class of '94

38d | Use the apostrophe to form the plural of letters, numbers, symbols, and words used as words

Many young children get their *b*'s and *d*'s mixed up.

The *1960's* were years of change, protest, violence, and excitement.

He likes to use a lot of *#*'s and *$*'s and *&*'s when he writes letters.

You have used too many *therefore's* in your essay.

It is also acceptable to form the plural of years and symbols without the apostrophe: *1990s, $s*. Whichever style you use, be consistent; do not switch between one usage and another in a piece of writing.

38e | Avoid using the apostrophe incorrectly

Do not use the apostrophe with present tense verbs in the third-person singular.

INCORRECT   Regular exercise *decrease's* the chance of heart trouble.

REVISED   Regular exercise *decreases* the chance of heart trouble.

Do not use the apostrophe to form a nonpossessive noun plural.

INCORRECT   We visited three *countries'* in South America last winter.

REVISED   We visited three *countries* in South America last winter.

INCORRECT   The apartment has three *bedroom's*.

REVISED   The apartment has three *bedrooms*.

Do not put an apostrophe before *-s* when indicating the plural possessive form of a noun. Use *-s* followed by an apostrophe for plural noun possessives.

INCORRECT   The legislators should listen to *citizen's* concerns.

REVISED   The legislators should listen to *citizens'* concerns.

INCORRECT   We have prepared a summary of these *scientist's* research.

REVISED   We have prepared a summary of these *scientists'* research.

Name _____ Section _____ Date _____

Insert apostrophes as needed to form the possessive case of the italicized words. Example:

I found *somebody* umbrella under the chair.

I found *somebody's* umbrella under the chair.

1. I could hear the *conductor* voice, but I could not understand what he was saying.

2. My private life is *nobody* business.

3. The group is planning to meet in *Dolores* office.

4. I have a bag of *children* clothes that my daughters have outgrown.

5. We will have to refund these *customers* money.

Write a sentence using each of the following words. Example:

yours

I have read you my paper; now read me yours.

1. his

2. its

3. mine

4. hers

5. yours

EXERCISE 3   Using Apostrophes in Contractions

Insert apostrophes as needed in contractions in the following sentences. Then rewrite each sentence spelling out the contractions. Example:

I shouldnt stay long because its getting late.

I shouldn't stay long because it's getting late.
I should not stay long because it is getting late.

1. Thats the most boring movie Ive ever seen.

2. Id like to take a vacation, but theres so much work to do.

3. You shouldve listened to my advice.

4. The police say that its unlikely theyll find your stolen car.

5. Does anybody know whos been sending these flowers every day?

EXERCISE 4   Using Apostrophes to Form Plurals

First form the plural for each of the following; then use that plural in a sentence. Example:

because

because's

You have used too many *because's* in your composition.

1. x

2. t

3. 1600 (the century)

4. and

5. thus

EXERCISE 5   Supplying Missing Apostrophes

Insert apostrophes where necessary in the following sentences. Example:

Its funny how many *nices* there are in Jims letters.

It's funny how many *nice's* there are in Jim's letters.

1. My father-in-laws office is located on the east side of town.

2. Andre got three As and two Bs last semester.

3. We werent expecting you, but were glad youre here.

4. My childrens rooms need to be vacuumed.

5. I wouldve called you, but there wasnt time.

EXERCISE 6   Using the Apostrophe to Indicate Possession

In each sentence, change the italicized phrase to a possessive noun. Example:

The excitement *of the children* was obvious.

The *children's* excitement was obvious.

1. The son *of Mr. and Mrs. Guzman* is in first grade.

2. The testimony *of the witness* lasted nearly six hours.

3. The goal *of the tennis player* was to win a Grand Slam tournament.

4. The accident was not really the fault *of anybody.*

5. Groups *of women* have protested the verdict.

CHAPTER 39

Quotation Marks

39a Use quotation marks for direct quotations

Put quotation marks around the exact words of a source, whether those words are spoken or written. Record the quotation exactly as it appears in the original source; do not change it in any way. Do not use quotation marks for indirect quotations, which summarize but do not record verbatim the words of a source.

> DIRECT "Can you work overtime next week?" the manager asked Ms. Reese.
>
> INDIRECT The manager asked Ms. Reese if she could work overtime next week.
>
> DIRECT Mr. Phillips said, "I can finish putting in the tiles this afternoon."
>
> INDIRECT Mr. Phillips said that he could finish putting in the tiles this afternoon.

39b Use single quotation marks for quotes within quotes

Use single quotation marks (' ') when you enclose a quotation within another quotation.

> Ralph said, "I think the new Pepsi slogan, 'Be Young. Have Fun. Drink Pepsi,' is too long."
>
> Ms. Pemberton said, "I have heard many versions of the Italian proverb, 'Little children, headache; big children, heartache.' "

Note: British usage is different from American usage. In Britain, single quotation marks are used for normally quoted material and double quotation marks for quotations within quotations.

39c Set off lengthy quoted passages

Quoted passages that exceed four typed lines are treated differently from shorter quotations. Begin a lengthy quotation on a new line and indent the entire quotation ten spaces from the left margin of your text. This format, which is called block quotation, does not require quotation marks. The block format visually differentiates the quotation from your text.

> In his speech on December 10, 1960, upon receiving the Nobel Prize, William Faulkner said:
>
> > He [the writer] must teach himself that the basest of all things is to be afraid; and, teaching himself that, forget it forever, leaving no room in his workshop for anything but the old verities and truths of the heart, the old universal truths lacking which any story is ephemeral and doomed—love and honor and pity and pride and compassion and sacrifice.

39d │ Use quotation marks with poetry as appropriate

Quote poetry as you would prose. Put verse quotations of fewer than four lines within the text, placing them within double quotation marks. Separate the lines of poetry with slashes, including a space before and after each slash.

> Tennyson's lines written in 1850, "Tis better to have loved and lost, / Than never to have loved at all," are very similar to those written by Congreve in 1700, "Say what you will, tis better to be left / Than never to have loved."

When the quoted poetry exceeds three lines, use the block format: begin the quotation on a new line and indent ten spaces from the left margin. Do not use quotation marks.

> In *A Midsummer Night's Dream*, Shakespeare writes of the power of the imagination:
>
> > Such tricks hath strong imagination,
> > That if it would but apprehend some joy,
> > It comprehends some bringer of that joy,
> > Or in the night, imagining some fear,
> > How easy is a bush supposed a bear! (V, I, 18-22)

39e │ Use quotation marks for dialogue

When you record conversations or dialogue, put the words of each speaker in double quotation marks. Indicate changes in speaker by starting a new paragraph; doing so makes it easier for readers to follow the dialogue.

> "When do you think you will have that report on sales projections finished?" Ms. Wilson asked.

> "I need to gather a bit more data and, as soon as that's in, I'll need two days to finish writing. So you should have the report at the end of next week," replied Mr. Rose.

39f   Use quotation marks to enclose titles and definitions

Use quotation marks when referring by title to short poems, short stories, articles, essays, songs, sections or chapters of books, and episodes of television and radio programs.

> William Blake's poem "The Human Image" was a first draft of his poem "The Human Abstract."

> In Hawthorne's short story "The Birthmark," a scientist kills his wife in trying to make her perfect.

> George Orwell's essay "Shooting an Elephant" is often anthologized.

> "Encounter at Farpoint" was the first episode of *Star Trek: The Next Generation*.

> Chapter 1 of Deborah Tannen's book *You Don't Understand* is called "Different Words, Different Worlds."

Use italics (underlining) for the titles of long works such as books, lengthy poems, plays, and films (see 42a in the *Workbook*). Italicize the titles of newspapers, magazines, and journals. Do not italicize the titles of your own essays, papers, or reports, except in cases where your title includes the title of a long work.

> The Use of Color in Hawthorne's Short Stories

> Hawthorne's Uses of Color in *The Scarlet Letter*

Definitions are commonly set off with quotation marks, though some writers italicize (or underline) them.

> The verb *exculpate* means "to clear oneself from alleged fault or guilt."

> The verb *exculpate* means *to clear oneself from alleged fault or guilt*.

39g   Use quotation marks for words used in special ways

Use quotation marks for words used in special ways; ironically, for example.

> The singer's "final" tour was the fifth of an eventual nine.

In addition, use quotation marks around any words that you (or others) have invented.

> I have no family; I am completely "relativeless."

Words used as words can be italicized (underlined) or placed within quotation marks. Whichever style you use, be consistent within a piece of writing.

> **INCORRECT**   The words "discreet" and *discrete* are sometimes confused.
>
> **REVISED**   The words "discreet" and "discrete" are sometimes confused.
>
> **REVISED**   The words *discreet* and *discrete* are sometimes confused.

39h | Avoid common misuses of quotation marks

Do not use quotation marks simply to emphasize particular words or phrases. In addition, do not use quotation marks with slang or colloquial language. Quotation marks are not used to give emphasis; if you wish to emphasize a word or phrase or idea, do so by careful word choice and word order.

MISUSED He was not a "perceptive" person, but he was "kind."

REVISED He was not a perceptive person, but he was kind.

MISUSED When he heard that he had failed the exam, he "freaked out."

REVISED When he heard that he had failed the exam, he became very agitated and angry.

39i | Follow established conventions for using quotation marks with other punctuation

1 | Place periods and commas before closing quotation marks

"We cannot afford to give our children a poor education," she said. "If we do not fund education adequately now, we will pay for it later."

2 | Place semicolons and colons after closing quotation marks

He punctuated his speech with too many "therefore's" and "whereas's"; as a result, he sounded ignorant and pompous.

"Cauliflower is nothing but cabbage with a college education": that is Mark Twain's definition of the vegetable.

Note: British practice places the colons and semicolons before the closing quotation marks rather than after.

3 | Place question marks, exclamation points, and dashes before the closing quotation marks if they are part of the quotation

Place them after the closing quotation marks if they are not part of the quotation.

PART OF QUOTATION

"Did you turn off the iron?" he asked.

"Don't do it!" she shouted.

"If you leave, I'll—" he threatened.

NOT PART OF QUOTATION

"Did you read "Benito Cereno"? she asked.

I can't remember any lines of the poem "Lycidas"!

"The whole nine yards"—that's an expression that makes no sense to me.

EXERCISE 1   Supplying Quotation Marks

Place quotation marks as needed in the following sentences. (Some sentences may be correct as given.) Example:

I am writing a paper on Henry James's short story The Beast in the Jungle.

I am writing a paper on Henry James's short story "The Beast in the Jungle."

1. In *Pride and Prejudice* Jane Austen states, Everything nourishes what is strong already.

2. The famous lines Age cannot wither her, nor custom stale / Her infinite variety are from Shakespeare's *Anthony and Cleopatra.*

3. The copy machine has stopped working, said Frank.
   I'll call the repair company, replied Jack.

4. Poe's short stories The Pit and the Pendulum and The Cask of Amontillado are studies in horror.

5. Dr. Martinez told Ms. Jones that she would have to give up smoking.

EXERCISE 2   Using Direct and Indirect Quotation

Rewrite the following sentences, changing direct quotation to indirect, and indirect quotation to direct. Examples:

The scientists said, "We are close to a breakthrough."
The scientists said that they were close to a breakthrough.

Ms. Ramos said she wanted to major in comparative literature.
"I want to major in comparative literature," Ms. Ramos said.

1. "The milk smells a bit sour," James said.

2. "Gertrude Stein's poetry is very difficult to understand," the professor stated.

3. President George Bush told voters to read his lips.

4. The instructor told students to use tenses consistently in their essays.

5. The student asked, "Is there a limit on how many credits I may take each semester?"

EXERCISE 3   Revising with Quotation Marks

Revise the following sentences by supplying missing quotation marks, eliminating unnecessary quotation marks, and moving quotation marks placed incorrectly. Example:

"In spite of many rejections", the poet said, I still kept sending my poetry to various magazines".

"In spite of many rejections," the poet said, "I still kept sending my poetry to various magazines."

1. Do you know the words to the Beatles song "Hey Jude?"

2. The losing candidate did not seem sincere when he said, I wish my opponent good luck during her first term in office.

3. He has confused the word imply with the word "infer" .

4. How often have you been told "Take a deep breath and don't panic?"

5. He insists that "computer" skills will be just as important in the future as "reading and writing" skills are now.

EXERCISE 4   Supplying Other Punctuation with Quotation Marks

Revise the following sentences by inserting commas, periods, question marks, exclamation points, dashes, colons, and semicolons where they belong. Example:

"That section of the course is closed" he said.

"That section of the course is closed," he said.

1. Was it Nathan Hale who said "I only regret that I have but one life to lose for my country"

2. "If you quit, I'll" she stammered.

3. "Hey" he shouted. "That's not fair"

4. Here is Mark Twain's definition of a classic "A classic is something that everybody wants to have read and nobody wants to read"

5. Most people do not know the source of the line "All hell broke loose" it is from *Paradise Lost* by John Milton.

6. "Stirring people up is easy" she said "but educating them is hard"

7. *To imply* means "to hint" *To infer* means "to guess"

8. A reporter asked the defendant "Do you intend to plead guilty"

9. "As long as I am head of this company" she said "there will be no lay-offs"

10. Here is the correct way to spell it "serendipitious"

CHAPTER 40

Other Punctuation Marks

This chapter covers dashes, parentheses, brackets, ellipses, and slashes.

40a | Using the dash

The dash interrupts a sentence to put in additional nonessential information. Pairs of dashes usually occur in the middle of a sentence, and a single dash occurs at the end of a sentence.

PAIRS OF DASHES   That sort of newspaper—with its gigantic headlines and lurid photographs—contains very little real news.

SINGLE DASH   He blamed all the woes of the modern world on one thing—permissive parents.

With most typewriters and computers, make a dash—by combining two hyphens (--). Do not put a space before, between, or after the hyphens. In handwritten papers, make a dash with a longer line than you use for a hyphen.

1 | Use the dash to insert an interrupting comment, whether for illustration, explanation, or emphasis

ILLUSTRATION   He looked at me with his usual expression—eyes narrowed and mouth pursed—and asked where I was going.

EXPLANATION   Colorizing old black-and-white movies is a desecration—like painting a mustache on the Mona Lisa—and should be stopped.

EMPHASIS   You must take this medicine before—not during or after—meals.

2 | Use the dash to indicate a shift in tone, a hesitation in speech, or a break in thought

SHIFT IN TONE   The children—how energetic they are!—run and play and quarrel and laugh.

HESITATION IN SPEECH   "I can't—I can't do it!" he stammered.

BREAK IN THOUGHT   His schemes were prospering, and he felt triumphant, but then—disaster.

3   Use the dash to introduce or comment on a list

INTRODUCING A LIST   At first he found everything intimidating at college—the other
                         students full of confidence, the dark dormitories covered in
                         ivy, the remote professors who seemed to be brilliant in a way
                         he felt he never could be.

COMMENTING ON A LIST   Stubbornness, willfulness, selfishness, and charm—these are
                         the attributes of the typical two-year-old child.

4   Use the dash to set off a parenthetical expression within another parenthetical expression already set off by commas

The park, set in an area of the city once considered so far uptown as to be practically out of the city—and now regarded as far downtown—and hopelessly unfashionable, is surrounded by a locked fence to which only residents have keys.

Like dashes, colons can be used to insert explanations or introduce lists. Dashes, however, are less formal than the colon. Since too many dashes can give writing a broken, choppy effect, use dashes sparingly in academic writing.

40b   Using parentheses

1   Use parentheses to enclose nonessential explanatory information

Nonessential parenthetical information may amplify, specify, exemplify, or expand what precedes it.

AMPLIFY   Her first poetry (written before her teens) was conventional, though
            promising.

SPECIFY   Queen Victoria's long reign (1837–1901) spanned a period of history that saw
            many important changes.

EXEMPLIFY   Although other opera singers had been very popular (e.g., Rosa Ponselle),
            Maria Callas became almost a cult idol.

2   Use parentheses to enclose numbers and letters with lists

The development plan will affect the neighborhood in three ways: (1) socially, (2) politically, and (3) economically.

Parentheses also can be used to restate a spelled-out number or to enclose a date, especially when identifying the year of a work's first publication or performance.

Payment must be made within twenty-one (21) days.

Willa Cather's novels *My Antonia* (1918) and *A Lost Lady* (1923) are set on the frontier.

3 | Use parentheses with other punctuation carefully

Periods

Place a period inside a closing parenthesis when the material inside the parentheses is a complete sentence. When the material inside the parentheses is not a complete sentence, put the period outside the closing parenthesis.

Applications must be filed by March 1. (Late applications will not be considered.)

See Dean Jordan for financial aid applications (and information about deadlines).

Commas

A comma may come after the closing parenthesis, but it may not come before the opening parenthesis.

Although not the most shocking short piece of literature (that distinction belongs to *A Modest Proposal*), the short story "A Rose for Emily" still horrifies the first-time reader.

Question marks and exclamation points

Put question marks and exclamation points before the closing parenthesis if the material inside parentheses is a question or an exclamation.

He tried to recall her face (how could he do so after all those years?) as he reread her letters.

Leontyne Price's debut at the Met (what a triumph!) was rewarded by a standing ovation and many curtain calls.

Quotation marks

Do not put quotation marks either before or after opening and closing parentheses. If words requiring quotation marks occur within parentheses, place the quotation marks inside the parentheses.

Melville's portrait of a passive clerk ("Bartleby the Scrivener") is an evocative description of depression anomie.

Use parentheses sparingly. Like dashes, overused parentheses can break up continuity, making writing choppy and hard to follow.

Choosing dashes, parentheses, or commas

Dashes, parentheses, and commas can all be used to set off nonessential material. The choice depends on the effect you wish to achieve. Dashes create a strong pause followed by heavy emphasis. Parentheses downplay the effect of the interrupting material and are less emphatic than dashes. Commas neither emphasize nor downplay the information, but simply include it. In the following examples, consider the different effects created by dashes, parentheses, and commas.

Her speech—though brief and calmly delivered—created a furor.

Her speech (though brief and calmly delivered) created a furor.

Her speech, though brief and calmly delivered, created a furor.

Note: Avoid using more than one set of dashes or parentheses in a single sentence.

40c   Using brackets

1   Use brackets to enclose material already in parentheses

The major problem (at least according to NASA [National Aeronautics and Space Agency] officials) is the lack of funding for the space program.

The geography of medieval Europe (see the map [and inserts] and illustrations on page 45) was quite different from that of the present.

2   Use brackets to enclose words inserted into quotations

In the following example, the bracketed words take the place of the words *she* and *it* in the original quotation:

Mr. Elvers stated, "[Ms. Danforth] has insisted that [the incident] was not important."

In this example, the bracketed words identify the team mentioned:

The manager said, "Many players from this team [the Albany-Colonie Yankees] have gone on to the major leagues."

The word *sic* (meaning "thus") in brackets usually indicates an error in punctuation, spelling, grammar, or usage in a passage being quoted. It tells your reader that the error is in the original source and is not your mistake. In the following example, the writer has misspelled the word *apologize*.

Sandy wrote, "I must apoligize [sic] for my hasty remarks."

40d   Using ellipses

Ellipses, three equally spaced dots (. . .), usually indicate that words have been omitted from a direct quotation. Ellipses may also indicate a pause or hesitation.

When you use directly quoted material in an essay, you may sometimes wish to use only part of a passage. If the part you want to quote includes words from different sections of the passage, you must indicate the omitted words with ellipses. Look at the following example.

ORIGINAL TEXT

"Socrates, a Greek philosopher generally regarded as one of the wisest men of all time, left no writings, and most of our knowledge of him and his teachings comes from the works of Plato and the memoirs of Xenophon. Socrates drew knowledge from his pupils by asking a series of questions, a method now known as Socratic dialogue."

OMISSION OF WORDS FROM THE MIDDLE OF A SENTENCE

"Socrates . . . left no writings, and most of our knowledge of him and his teachings comes from the works of Plato and the memoirs of Xenophon."

OMISSION OF WORDS FROM DIFFERENT PARTS OF A SENTENCE

"Socrates . . . left no writings, and most of our knowledge of him . . . comes from the works of Plato and the memoirs of Xenophon."

OMISSION OF WORDS AT THE END OF SENTENCES

"Socrates, a Greek philosopher generally regarded as one of the wisest men of all time, left no writings. . . . Socrates drew knowledge from his pupils by asking a series of questions. . . ."

In the preceding example, note that a period and three spaced dots are needed when an ellipsis coincides with the end of a sentence.

INDICATING PAUSE OR HESITATION

PAUSE   What I really need is . . . money.

HESITATION   And the winner of the sportsmanship award is . . . Sally Blair.

40e   Using the slash

INDICATING POEM LINE DIVISIONS

These lines of the verse shows Hemminger's humor: "Tobacco is a dirty weed. I like it. / It satisfies no normal need. I like it."

SEPARATING ALTERNATIVES

The supervisor does not want to be pushed into an either/or situation.

His attitude is "Heads, I win/Tails, you lose."

SEPARATING PARTS OF FRACTIONS

She started skating when she was only 3 1/2 years old.

SEPARATING MONTH, DAY, AND YEAR IN SHORTHAND DATES

3/3/33 [March 3, 1933]

EXERCISE 1   Using Dashes

Insert dashes as needed in the following sentences. Example:

The meeting will start we hope it will start at noon.

The meeting will start—we hope it will start—at noon.

1. Diet and exercise these are the keys to weight loss.

2. CD players have a big advantage over turntables portability.

3. The mayor seemed to raise taxes after never before an election.

4. The baseball players how young they looked ran onto the field.

5. "You should try to try to forget this horrible experience," he said.

EXERCISE 2   Writing with Dashes

For each topic that follows, write a sentence using a dash. Example:

Topic: An emotional plea

"Don't—please don't open that door," he begged.

1. Severe weather conditions

2. Different student groups at your school

3. A difficult decision

4. The qualities of a good tutor

5. A friend's one weakness

EXERCISE 3   Practice with Parentheses

Supply parentheses as needed in the following sentences. Example:

Several eastern European countries want to join NATO North Atlantic Treaty Organization.

Several eastern European countries want to join NATO (North Atlantic Treaty Organization).

1. The author a self-educated man who never went to high school set his first novel in Maine in the 1850s.

2. The award will be given to a person who shows 1 academic progress, 2 sportsmanship, and 3 athletic talent.

3. All bills must be paid within fourteen 14 days of receipt.

4. Eisenhower won both presidential elections 1952 and 1956 against the same opponent, Adlai Stevenson.

5. She said that the School of American Ballet often referred to as SAB gave excellent training in classical ballet.

EXERCISE 4   Selecting Parentheses or Brackets

Supply parentheses or brackets as appropriate in the following sentences. Example:

The Pleistocene epoch from 2 million to 11,000 years ago was an era of glaciation.

The Pleistocene epoch (from 2 million to 11,000 years ago) was an era of glaciation.

1. In her letter she wrote, "I have been intrested sic in fossils since childhood."

2. The medicine (according to FDA Federal Drug Administration officials) is safe for use on human beings.

3. The Chinese Han dynasty 202 B.C. to 220 A.D. saw the beginnings of the use of civil service examinations to recruit members of the bureaucracy.

4. Many groups hoped that the ERA Equal Rights Amendment would be accepted, but it was not.

5. Neanderthals 125 million to 35,000 years ago had a much larger brain than those of modern humans.

EXERCISE 5   Using Ellipses

Rewrite each of the following, leaving out some words and using ellipsis points to indicate your omission. Example:

Thomas Coram, an English philanthropist and colonizer, lived for a while in Massachusetts, where he worked as a shipbuilder.

Thomas Coram . . . lived for a while in Massachusetts, where he worked as a shipbuilder.

1. Marcus Garvey, an American proponent of black nationalism, founded the Universal Negro Improvement Association in 1914.

2. Aaron Copland, the American composer who lived from 1900 to 1990, used jazz and American folk tunes in his music. Among other things, he wrote music for ballets and for the movies.

3. Small children are very imaginative, but they cannot always distinguish between reality and fantasy.

4. Aztecs arrived in the Valley of Mexico near the end of the twelfth century and for some time lived a poor, nomadic life. By the early sixteeth century, they had become a powerful political and cultural group.

5. The defendant, a man in his early thirties who had worked for the company for about five years, was alleged to have forged his boss's signature on several checks.

CHAPTER 41

Capitals

41a | Capitalizing the first word of a sentence

Capitalize the first word of a sentence.

*H*as anyone seen Mr. Milenkovitch?

*T*he last two summers have been unusually hot.

In a number of cases, the writer has a choice about using capitals or lowercase letters.

Capitals with a series of questions

In writing a series of questions, you may use capitals for the first word of each question, or you may choose to use lowercase letters. Be consistent; do not switch styles in a piece of writing.

*W*hich do you think is the nation's most serious problem? *C*rime? *E*ducation? *U*nemployment?

*W*hich do you think is the nation's most serious problem? *c*rime? *e*ducation? *u*nemployment?

Capitals with parentheticals and dashes

When you use complete-sentence parentheticals, use a capital letter for any that function as separate sentences.

People who exercise regularly can significantly lower their chances of having a stroke. (*E*ven mild exercise for thirty minutes three times a week is beneficial.)

However, do not use capitals when putting an independent-clause parenthetical within a sentence, whether it is set off with parentheses or dashes.

No trains were leaving the station (*h*eavy snow had covered the third rails), so commuters had to check into hotels or stay with friends who lived in the city.

The committee decided—*t*he vote was unanimous—to keep the library open six days a week.

Capitals with sentences following colons

Practice varies for sentences following a colon. You may choose either a capital or a lowercase letter. Whichever style you choose, be consistent.

It is not true that a camel stores water in its hump: *T*he hump actually stores fat.

It is not true that a camel stores water in its hump: *t*he hump actually stores fat.

41b   Capitalizing the first word of a quotation

Always capitalize the first word of full-sentence quotations.

"Life is my college" could be said of many people in addition to the author who wrote the phrase, Louisa May Alcott.

In their report the scientists stated, *"T*he test results are interesting, but they are not conclusive."

Embedded quotations

Do not capitalize quotations incorporated into one of your own sentences, even if the original quotation begins with a capital. Use brackets to show how the quotation's first letter has been altered.

ORIGINAL	*"Hitch your wagon to a star."*
EMBEDDED	Most people have heard the saying *"[h]itch your wagon to a star,"* but they may not know it was written by Ralph Waldo Emerson.

Interrupted quotations

When you use words of your own to break up or interrupt a quotation, do not use a capital letter to begin the second part of the quotation. Capitalize the first part if it is capitalized in the original.

ORIGINAL	*"Time is a great legalizer, even in the field of morals."*
EMBEDDED	*"Time is a great legalizer,"* said H. L. Mencken, *"even in the field of morals."*

41c   Capitalizing the first letter in a line of poetry

Traditionally, poets capitalize the first letter of each line in a poem; some poets, however, do not observe this convention. If you write poetry, you can choose to capitalize or lowercase the first word of each line. When you quote poetry, capitalize or lowercase words exactly as the poet does.

ORIGINAL	these hips are big hips, they need space to move around in. —Lucille Clifton

QUOTED	Lucille Clifton's lines, "these hips are big hips, / they need space to / move around in" have an assertive, even proud, tone.
ORIGINAL	One day in the country Is worth a month in town. —Christina Rossetti
QUOTED	"One day in the country / Is worth a month in town," wrote Christina Rossetti.

41d Capitalizing nouns and adjectives

Use capitals for proper nouns.

Ariane *Belgrade*
Mr. Smith the *Eiffel Tower*

Do not capitalize proper nouns that are used in a common or everyday context.

some french fries
a danish pastry

Use capitals for proper adjectives (adjectives derived from proper nouns), but do not capitalize the articles (*a, an, the*) that accompany proper nouns and proper adjectives.

an *American* tradition
the *French* government
a *Chinese* custom

Some writers use capital letters in unconventional ways. Emily Dickinson did so routinely in her poetry.

We grow accustomed to the Dark—

When Light is put away—

Advertisers often use capitals unconventionally, to attract attention and to give emphasis.

Sensitive, Slouching, Bald. (How Much More Lifelike Can They Get?)

—from an automobile advertisement

How Do I Know Which Mutual Funds May Be Right For Me?

—from an advertisement for an investment service

Corporations and university administrations also use capitals unconventionally.

the Board of Trustees
the Faculty
the University

When you use a common noun alone, do not capitalize it. When you use a common noun as an integral part of a proper name, capitalize the common noun.

the *college*	*Reed* College
the *river*	the *Hudson* River
a *prize*	the *Nobel* Prize
a *street*	*Taylor* Street

Following is a list of words that are commonly capitalized:

COMMONLY CAPITALIZED WORDS

NAMES OF PEOPLE

Andrew Young	Alice Hoffman
Socratic method	Shakespearean actor
Whitney Houston	Mary Shelley

PLACES AND GEOGRAPHICAL REGIONS

Asia	Adriatic Sea
New Zealand	Mount Rushmore
Fort Smith	Pennsylvania Avenue

STRUCTURES AND MONUMENTS

Sears Tower	the George Washington Bridge
Hoover Dam	the Eiffel Tower
the National Cathedral	the Lincoln Monument

DAYS OF THE WEEK, MONTHS, AND HOLIDAYS

Monday night	a June wedding
the Veterans' Day parade	Sunday brunch
an August day	a Bastille Day speech

HISTORICAL EVENTS, PERIODS, AND MOVEMENTS

the Industrial Revolution	the War of 1812
the Inquisition	the Renaissance
the Stone Age	Modernist writers

OFFICIAL NAMES OF ORGANIZATIONS, INSTITUTIONS, AND BUSINESSES

the Democratic party	Simon & Schuster, Co.
the Girl Scouts of America	the New York State Senate
Swiss Bank Corporation	the American Museum of Natural History

ABBREVIATIONS AND ACRONYMS

NAACP	CBS	YMCA
NATO	MADD	IBM

RELIGIONS AND RELIGIOUS TERMS

Buddhists, Buddhism	Buddha, the Enlightened One
Christians, Christianity	Jesus Christ, the New Testament
Jews, Judaism	Moses, the Bible, the Hebrew Scriptures
Muslims, Islam	Allah, Mohammed, the Koran

ETHNIC GROUPS, NATIONALITIES, AND LANGUAGES

Latino, Latina	Vietnamese
Arabic	African American
Japanese trade agreement	Italian American
the Chinese mainland	Peruvian culture

TRADE NAMES

Froot Loops	Xerox
Ford	Reebok
WordPerfect	Levi's
Volvo	Nike

COMPOUND WORDS

Native-American groups	a French-Canadian writer
Asian-American communities	Indo-European languages

ACADEMIC INSTITUTIONS AND COURSES

Adelphi University	Skidmore College
History 104	Chemistry 200

1　Capitalizing titles of individuals

Capitalize titles that are used before a proper name. Do not capitalize titles following a proper name or titles that are used alone. Exceptions are titles of very important positions, such as *President of the United States* or *Prime Minister of Great Britain.*

Justice O'Connor	Sandra Day O'Connor, a Supreme Court justice
Governor Mario Cuomo	Mario Cuomo, governor of New York
Professor Ann Smith	Ann Smith, a professor of nursing
Dr. Ana Mendes	Ana Mendes, a local doctor

2　Capitalizing academic institutions and courses

Capitalize the names of specific schools, departments, and courses. Do not capitalize common nouns for institutions or areas of study.

University of Connecticut	a Connecticut university
the Psychology Department	a psychology professor
Economics 101	an introductory economics course
Truman High School	my high school

41e | Capitalizing the titles and subtitles of works

Capitalize most words in the titles and subtitles of books, articles, short stories, poems, plays, essays, films, musical and choreographic works, and paintings and other works of art. Capitalize the titles of your own essays.

Do not capitalize articles (*a, an, the*), prepositions (e.g., *in, of, on, to, for, with*), conjunctions (*and, or, for*), and *to* in an infinitive (*to* discover)—unless they are the first or last word of a title.

"My Wood"
"Shakespeare in the Bush"
"A Rose for Emily"
"The Raven"

The Kitchen God's Wife
The Daughter of the Regiment
One Flew over the Cuckoo's Nest
Hawthorne's Use of Color

41f | Capitalizing *I* and *O*

Always capitalize the personal pronoun *I* (except when quoting literary works that use the lowercase form). Capitalize the interjection *O* (an old form of the more modern *oh*). Capitalize *oh* only when it begins a sentence.

My sister is always irritable if *I* call her before eight in the morning.

Do not forsake us, *O* Lord.

"*Oh*, I wish I hadn't said that," he muttered.

There is *oh*, so much work to do.

41g | Avoiding the misuse of capitals

Do not use capitals inappropriately, particularly when they are not required.

1 | Avoid using capitals with words designating family relationships

Use capitals with words designating family relationships only when they are used as names or titles, or in combination with proper names.

INCORRECT   When she was in high school, *my Mother* took physics and calculus.

CORRECT   When she was in high school, *my mother* took physics and calculus.

When you substitute a word indicating a family relationship for a name, or when you use such a word as part of a name, capitalize it.

We plan to visit *Mother* next month.

We plan to visit *my mother* next month.

I have to send these photographs to *Uncle Van* and *Aunt Alice*.

I have to send these photographs to *my uncle* and *aunt*.

2 Avoid using capitals for words denoting seasons or parts of the year

summer vacation   spring term
winter weather   fall semester
autumn leaves   sophomore year

3 Avoid capitalizing words for compass directions, except when designating a specific geographic area

The hurricane traveled *north,* then *east.*

In early 1994, the *Northeast* was hit by one snowstorm after another.

EXERCISE 1   Supplying Capitals

Insert capital letters where needed in the following sentences. Example:

the best speech at the convention was given by governor richardson.

The best speech at the convention was given by Governor Richardson.

1. next monday in our lab for biology 101 we are going to dissect frogs.

2. of all the doctors mr. grant consulted, only dr. rogers had helped alleviate his back pain.

3. professor clinton's specialty is latin american politics.

4. have you ever heard philip glass's opera *einstein on the beach?*

5. "your tires," said aunt sarah, "are underinflated."

6. On our last visit to washington, d.c., we visited the lincoln memorial, the holocaust museum, and the smithsonian institute.

7. that indonesian restaurant serves a salad with a spicy peanut sauce.

8. the quality of mercy is not strain'd,
   it droppeth as the gentle rain from heaven
   upon the place beneath.   —Shakespeare

9. the civil war is sometimes called the war between the states.

10. the national council of churches is an organization of various christian denominations.

EXERCISE 2   Revising Incorrect Capitalization

The following sentences contain errors in capitalization, including misused capitals and missing capitals. In addition, some capitals are used correctly. Rewrite the sentences to correct the capitalization errors. Example:

Tom lehrer was a Professor of mathematics at Harvard university.

Tom Lehrer was a professor of mathematics at Harvard University.

1. My Uncle and Aunt are Physical Therapists who work at St. Luke's hospital.

2. the central character of *A man for All seasons* is Sir Thomas More.

3. there are two major jet streams, which run from West to East.

4. Do you know which Professor will be teaching Physics 303 next Fall?

5. Harriet beecher stowe's Novel *Uncle tom's cabin* was very influential in spreading abolitionist sentiments.

6. Some Universities allow students to spend their Junior year abroad.

7. "The reason i cannot accept your offer," he said, "Is that i just signed a contract with a Minor League baseball team."

8. Bertrand Russell, a mathematician and Philosopher, advocated Pacifism, except during world war II.

9. After church, Father Gordon went to see my Mother in the hospital.

10. Ms. Gratwick's favorite Opera is *the Marriage of Figaro.*

CHAPTER 42

Italics

Italic type is a style of printing in which letters are slanted to the right, *in this way.* Standard type, which is not slanted, is called roman type. Most computers and printers can reproduce italic type. If you do not have a printer that can produce italics, use <u>underlining</u> to indicate italics.

42a Using italics for titles

Use italics for the titles of long or complete works, such as books, plays, films, and periodicals. The titles of shorter works, such as poems, essays, and chapters, should be enclosed in quotation marks (see 39f in the *Workbook*). The following chart identifies the various types of titles that are italicized.

TITLES TO ITALICIZE (UNDERLINE)

BOOKS
Sense and Sensibility
The Plague Dogs

FILMS
High Noon
Do The Right Thing

NEWSPAPERS
the *Berkshire Eagle*
the *London Times*

MAGAZINES
Rolling Stone
Opera News

JOURNALS
American Political Science Review
Journal of Basic Writing

PLAYS
Waiting for Godot
Angels in America

LONG POEMS
Paradise Lost
The Dynasts

MUSICAL WORKS
Prokofiev's *Love for Three Oranges*
Mozart's *The Magic Flute*

TELEVISION AND RADIO PROGRAMS
N.Y.P.D. Blue
A Prairie Home Companion

RECORDINGS
Whitney Houston's *Bodyguard*
Harolyn Blackwell's *Strange Hurt*

PAMPHLETS

Common Allergies
Seven Steps to Better Health

PUBLISHED SPEECHES

Lincoln's *Gettysburg Address*
King's *I Have a Dream* speech

WORKS OF VISUAL ART

Da Vinci's *Mona Lisa*
Van Gogh's *Flowering Almond Branch*

Exceptions

The following exceptions do not take italics:

1. Sacred books, including the Bible and the Koran, do not take any special punctuation—neither italics nor quotation marks.
2. Public documents, such as the Declaration of Independence and the Bill of Rights, also take roman type.
3. The word *the* in the titles of magazines and newspapers is not italicized: the *New York Times*.

42b   **Using italics for words, letters, numbers, and phrases used as words**

Years ago, the main meaning of the word *broadcast* was "to scatter seed."

In Italian, when the letter *h* begins a word, the *h* is not pronounced.

Many athletes do not want to wear the number *13*.

According to H. W. Fowler, the term *in-law* derives from Canon Law.

Where did the expression *kicked the bucket* come from?

Note: You can use quotation marks instead of italics in any of these cases (see 39g in the *Workbook*).

Italics may also be used for words being defined.

A proliferation of *leucocytes,* the white or colorless nucleated cells occurring in blood, is symptomatic of the disease leukemia.

42c   **Using italics for foreign words and phrases**

English has acquired many words from foreign languages, including French, Greek, Italian, and Arabic words. Many such words—*spaghetti, chef, khaki, assassin, stasis*—have become part of the English language. These words should not be italicized. However, foreign words and phrases that have not become part of the English language should be italicized. If you are uncertain whether a word or phrase is considered foreign, check your dictionary.

The French verb *pretender* means "to claim," not "to pretend."

Many Americans mispronounce the phrase *coup de grace*; the final sound should be "ss," not "ah."

42d Using italics for names of trains, ships, air and spacecraft

Italicize the names of specific trains, ships, and air and spacecraft, but do not italicize general types and classes of these vehicles.

The space shuttle *Enterprise* is named after the spaceship from *Star Trek*.

They sailed to Europe on the *Queen Mary*.

Just for a change, they went to Europe on an ocean liner instead of an airplane.

42e Using italics for special emphasis

Italics can occasionally be used for emphasis. Overuse, however, creates a tone of insistent exaggeration that loses its force. It is better to create emphasis through conciseness, careful word choice, and proper sentence construction.

My eighty-year-old grandmother and her friends called themselves *girls*.

It may be *fast*, but I would not call this stuff *food*.

EXERCISE 1   Supplying Italics

Use underlining to indicate italics where necessary in the following sentences. Example:

A new recording of Handel's opera Semele has just been issued.

A new recording of Handel's opera <u>Semele</u> has just been issued.

1. He always reads both the New York Times and Newsday.

2. Westerns like Maverick and Bonanza were popular in the 1950s.

3. Lincoln's Gettysburg Address is one of the most quoted speeches ever given.

4. In Venice, one can buy pasta or other food by the etto.

5. That week, the skater's photograph appeared on the covers of Time and Newsweek.

6. The movie Soapdish did not stay in the theaters long, but it has been very popular on video.

7. Milton's Samson Agonistes is based on biblical subject matter but modeled on Greek tragedy.

8. The expression long in the tooth means that one is getting old.

9. She was confused when her son used the word bad when he really meant good.

10. I do not have the money to buy or the room to store the unabridged Oxford English Dictionary.

CHAPTER 43

Abbreviations

Abbreviations serve as a kind of shorthand, enabling writers to replace long names and titles with simple sets of letters. Thus, abbreviations allow you to read and write more efficiently.

43a Abbreviating personal and professional titles and academic degrees

Some personal and professional titles are abbreviated when placed before or after a name.

Ms. Carolyn Smith	Ms. Chang
Mr. Donald O'Neill	Mr. Gonzalez
Mrs. Laura Battista	Mrs. Murphy
Dr. Daniel Lofton	Dr. Lofton *or* Daniel Lofton, M.D.
St. Ursula	Mary Ellen McManus, Ph.D.
Matthew Jenkins, Jr.	Ronald Anson, Sr.
Frederick Otis, DFA	Elena Rios, LL.D.

Note that the abbreviations for academic degrees and for junior (jr.) and senior (sr.) are set off with commas.

Other titles, including religious, military, academic, and government titles, do not take abbreviations in academic writing. In informal, nonacademic writing, you may abbreviate them before a full name, but you should spell out titles appearing before a surname only.

Rev. Josephine Nicholas	Reverend Nicholas
Sen. Patrick Moynihan	Senator Moynihan
Prof. Margaret Mackey	Professor Mackey
Gen. George Patton	General Patton

Academic degrees can be abbreviated when used alone. Do not abbreviate personal or professional titles used alone.

ACCEPTABLE	After she got her M.B.A., she decided to get a Ph.D.
UNACCEPTABLE	He is known as a very demanding prof.
REVISED	He is known as a very demanding professor.

Do not abbreviate a single title twice with a person's name. You may use an abbreviated title before the name or after it, but not in both places.

UNACCEPTABLE   Dr. Erica Ashford, M.D.

ACCEPTABLE   Dr. Erica Ashford

ACCEPTABLE   Erica Ashford, M.D.

You may use two abbreviations for different titles:

Prof. Richard Roberson, Esq.

Using familiar acronyms and abbreviations

Acronyms are abbreviations that are pronounced as words, such as *MADD* (Mothers against Drunk Driving) and *NATO* (North Atlantic Treaty Organization). Initialisms, or initial abbreviations, are not pronounced as words; each letter is sounded. Examples are *ABC* (American Broadcasting Company) and *IBM* (International Business Machines).

If you use a term only once in a piece of writing, spell out the term rather than using the abbreviation. However, if you use the term repeatedly, spell out the term on first use, note the abbreviation in parentheses, and then give the abbreviation in all subsequent uses. Look at the following example:

The *North Atlantic Treaty Organization (NATO)* was formed in 1949. A military alliance, *NATO* had as its aim the safeguarding of the Atlantic community, particularly against the Soviet bloc.

43c   Using the abbreviations *a.m., p.m., B.C. (BC), A.D. (AD),* and symbols

Using *a.m.* and *p.m.*

The abbreviations *a.m.* and *p.m.* should be used only with exact times. Both are Latin abbreviations: *a.m.* stands for *ante meridiem,* meaning "before noon"; *p.m.* stands for *post meridiem,* meaning "after noon." Use *a.m* and *p.m.* only with numbers designating time of day, never with the word *morning, afternoon, evening,* or *night.*

INCORRECT   They met at *10:30 a.m. in the morning.*

REVISED   They met at *10:30 a.m.*

REVISED   They met at *10:30 in the morning.*

Using *B.C. (BC)* and *A.D. (AD)*

A.D. stands for *Anno Domini,* Latin for "in the Year of the Lord." *A.C.E.* stands for "After the Common Era." *B.C.* stands for "Before Christ," and *B.C.E.* stands for "Before the Common Era." In abbreviations for years, place *A.D.* or *A.C.E.* before the year. Place *B.C.* or *B.C.E.* after the year.

A.D. 1650   300 B.C.
A.C.E. 835   175 B.C.E.

Using symbols: *$, %, @, #, &, +, -, =*

Sometimes you will need to spell out symbols such as *$, %, @, #, &, +, -,* and *=.* As a general rule, do not use symbols in most academic writing, except in scientific and technical writing and in graphs and tables. It is acceptable to use the dollar sign before some figures: *$20 million.*

INAPPROPRIATE   Nearly *90%* of those eligible to vote came to the polls.

REVISED   Nearly *90* percent of those eligible to vote came to the polls.

APPROPRIATE   The hospital hopes to raise *$15 million.*

When you write scientific and business reports containing many numbers and symbols, using the symbols (instead of spelling them out) makes the writing easier to understand. Your decision to use symbols or to spell them out will be determined by the nature of your writing, your audience, and your purpose.

43d Using Latin abbreviations (such as *i.e.*, *e.g.*, and *etc.*) for documentation only

In general, do not use the following Latin abbreviations except when documenting the sources of concepts and quotations. Do not use these abbreviations in the body of your writing; instead, use English words or phrases.

i.e.   that is (*id est*)
e.g.   for example (*exempli gratia*)
etc.   and so forth (*et cetera*)
cf.   compare (*confer*)
et. al.   and others (*et alii*)
N. B.   note well (*nota bene*)

INCORRECT   There are many student clubs, *e.g.,* the Forensic Society, the Volunteers Club, the Chess Club, *etc.*

REVISED   There are many student clubs, *for example* , the Forensic Society, the Volunteers Club, the Chess Club, *and the like.*

Do not end sentences with abbreviations. Ending a sentence with *etc.* makes it look as if you ran out of examples or were too lazy to give specific examples.

43e   Using other types of abbreviations

Given names and academic courses

Do not abbreviate the names of people and of academic courses.

INCORRECT   *Robt.* is taking *Prof.* Stein's *bio* course.

REVISED   *Robert* is taking *Professor* Stein's *biology* course.

Months, days, and holidays

Do not abbreviate the names of months, days, and holidays.

INCORRECT   The winter break begins on *Mon., Jan.* 23.

REVISED   The winter break begins on *Monday, January* 23.

INCORRECT   Most businesses are closed on New *Yr's* Day.

REVISED   Most businesses are closed on New *Year's* Day.

Geographical designations

Do not abbreviate geographical designations. Exceptions include *Washington, D.C.,* and *U.S.,* which can be used as an adjective but not as a noun.

INCORRECT   It takes several hours to drive from *N.Y.C.* to Boston, *Mass.*

REVISED   It takes several hours to drive from *New York City* to *Boston, Massachusetts.*

CORRECT   The group gathered in *Washington, D.C.,* was protesting *U.S. involvement* in Somalia.

INCORRECT   He first visited the *U.S.* in 1979.

REVISED   He first visited the *United States* in 1979.

Units of measurement

Do not abbreviate units of measurement, except in scientific and technical writing. Exceptions include *mph* (miles per hour), *rpm* (revolutions per minute), and *cps* (cycles per second).

INCORRECT   The length of the room is twenty *ft.,* four *in.*

REVISED   The length of the room is *twenty* feet, *four* inches.

CORRECT   The car was traveling at *80 mph* when it crashed.

Company names

Do not abbreviate a company's name unless the abbreviation is part of the name. Similarly, do not use the ampersand (*&*) unless it is part of the company's name.

INCORRECT The Rexworth *Co.* makes copiers and fax machines.

REVISED The Rexworth *Company* makes copiers and fax machines.

CORRECT Sears, Roebuck *&* Co. is closing some of its stores.

43f Using abbreviations for reference information

In citing sources, it is conventional to abbreviate such words as *editor* or *edition* (*ed.*), *page* and *pages* (*p.* and *pp.*), *chapter* (*ch.*), and *volume* (*vol.*). However, it is not acceptable to use these abbreviations in the body of a paper.

INCORRECT The actual theft of the necklace occurs in the second *vol.* of Anthony Trollope's *The Eustace Diamonds.*

CORRECT The actual theft of the necklace occurs in the second *volume* of Anthony Trollope's *The Eustace Diamonds.*

EXERCISE 1   Correcting the Misuse of Abbreviations

Revise the following sentences to eliminate the inappropriate use of abbreviations. (Note that some abbreviations may be correct as given.) Example:

On Tues., I have an appointment with Dr. Mitchell, M.D.

On Tuesday, I have an appointment with Dr. Mitchell.

1. At. 8:30 p.m. this evening, Thom. Beecher will appear on national television.

2. My English prof owns a first ed. of *The Wings of the Dove* by Henry James.

3. Nearly 90% of the students in that h.s. are bilingual.

4. Ms. Chouth will graduate from medical school and receive her M.D. the yr. after next.

5. Eliz. Green was born in Ark., but she grew up in Calif.

6. The community center offers classes in many things, e.g., computers, automobile repair, aerobics, and cooking.

7. Ms. Rogers reminded us that all schools will be closed on Mem. Day.

8. My son Rbt. is only fifteen, and he is almost six ft. tall.

9. Gov. Reed has appointed Dr. Ellis and Rev. Pena to the long-range planning committee.

10. The prof asked us to read the first ch. of the chem book.

CHAPTER 44

Numbers

44a Spelling out numbers of one or two words and using figures for numbers of three or more words

If you can spell out a number in one or two words, do so. A hyphenated number is considered one word. Look at the following examples:

The class is limited to *twenty-four* people.

Eight hundred people watch the skater practice.

The soccer stadium holds *fifty-five thousand* people.

Use figures for numbers that cannot be spelled out in one or two words.

She won the election by a margin of *1,031* votes.

The small theater has *548* seats.

In addition, when a sentence contains some numbers that can be written in one or two words and others that cannot, write all the numbers as figures for consistency.

INCONSISTENT   One summer they hiked a *one-hundred*-mile stretch of the Appalachian Trail and later decided they would try to hike the entire *2,050* miles.

CONSISTENT   One summer they hiked a *100*-mile stretch of the Appalachian Trail and later decided they would try to hike the entire *2,050* miles.

44b Spelling out numbers at the beginning of sentences

Always spell out numbers that begin a sentence. However, sentences that begin with spelled-out numbers of two or more words can be awkward and hard to read. In such cases, revise the sentence so that the number is not the first word.

INAPPROPRIATE   *100,000* demonstrators or more gathered at the Lincoln Memorial.

REVISED   More than *100,000* demonstrators gathered at the Lincoln Memorial.

AWKWARD   *Two hundred twenty-eight million* dollars was the winning bid for the company.

REVISED   The winning bid for the company was *$228 million.*

When using more than one number to modify a noun, spell out the first number or the shorter of the two numbers to avoid confusion:

CONFUSING   I need *five eight-inch* slats.

REVISED   I need *five 8-inch* slats.

CONFUSING   They brought *twenty one-gallon* containers of paint.

REVISED   They brought *20 one-gallon* containers of paint.

44c   Using figures according to convention

Figures are usually used for the following: days and years; page, chapter, and volume numbers of books; acts, scenes, and lines of plays; decimals, percentages, and fractions; temperatures; addresses; scores and statistics; exact amounts of money; and the time of day when given with *a.m.* or *p.m.*

GUIDELINES FOR USING FIGURES ACCORDING TO CONVENTION

DAYS AND YEARS

April 12, 1945	A.D. 614
July 7th	55 B.C.
the 1930s	January 3, 1995

Exception: The day of a month may be expressed in words when the year does not follow: *March first.*

Note: Use ordinal numbers only for dates without the year: *October second.* In other cases, spell out ordinal numbers: *My first daughter was born on October 2, 1986.*

PAGES, CHAPTERS, AND VOLUMES

page 104	pages 53–57
chapter 12	volume 3

ACTS, SCENES, LINES

Hamlet, act 2, scene 1, lines 1–15   *or*   *Hamlet,* 2.1.1–15

DECIMALS, PERCENTAGES, AND FRACTIONS

64.2   89 percent   8 1/2

TEMPERATURES

38°F   15°C

ADDRESSES

853 Brandon Street, Apt. 2A, South Orange, NJ 07079

SCORES AND STATISTICS

101 to 87   a combined SAT score of 1150

AMOUNTS OF MONEY

$1.25 $1,743
$8.6 million

Exceptions: Round dollar or cent amounts of two or three words may be spelled out: *forty-five dollars, fifty cents.*

TIME OF DAY

6 a.m.   3:11 p.m.

Exceptions: When expressing time without *a.m.* or *p.m.,* spell out the numbers: *nine in the morning, four in the afternoon, eight in the evening.* Similarly, when using *o'clock* to indicate time, express the number in words: *four o'clock.*

EXERCISE 1   Using Numbers Appropriately

Revise the following sentences so that numbers are, according to convention, spelled out or written as figures. Example:

100 people applied for the job that starts on August second, 1997.

One hundred people applied for the job that starts on August 2, 1997.

1. My grandfather said that when he was a child, the bus fare was only 5 cents.

2. The total cost for the computer, the printer, and the software was one thousand six hundred and fifty-two dollars.

3. We had to memorize act two, scene five, lines five through thirty-five.

4. Children are often jealous when a 2nd child is born.

5. Water boils at two hundred twelve degrees Fahrenheit, at one hundred degrees Celsius, and three hundred seventy-three degrees Kelvin.

6. The last train leaves at eleven fifteen p.m.

7. Nearly eighty-seven percent of those responding to the questionnaire do not approve of more defense spending.

8. The final score was sixteen-fifteen, a very high score for a baseball game.

9. They live at eight hundred West One Hundred Fifteenth Street, Apt. five A.

10. To complete the jump correctly, the skater must turn three and one half times in the air.

CHAPTER 45

Hyphens

Hyphens are used to divide words at the end of lines, to form some compound words, to attach certain prefixes and suffixes, and to clarify word meanings in special cases. Do not confuse the hypen (-) with the dash (—).

45a Use a hyphen to divide words at the end of a line

Do not divide words in your writing unless it is absolutely necessary. When you must divide a word at the end of a line, divide it between syllables, putting the hyphen after the first part of the divided word only. If you are not sure where to divide a word, consult your dictionary, which indicates syllabication of all words. In addition, the following conventions should be observed when dividing words across lines.

CONVENTIONS FOR DIVIDING WORDS AT THE END OF A LINE

- Do not divide one-syllable words, even such long words as *strength* and *breadth*.
- Do not leave on one line or carry over to the next line only one letter. Leave at least two letters on each line when dividing a word.

INCORRECT   When it was a matter of skills assessment, he was a-
damant that standards should be kept high.

REVISED   When it was a matter of skills assessment, he was ada-
mant that standards should be kept high.

- Do not divide abbreviations, contractions, or numbers. It is incorrect to try to hyphenate such words as *U.S.A.*, *shouldn't*, and *100,000*.
- Do not hyphenate names of people and places. If the whole word does not fit at the end of a line, move it to the next line.

INCORRECT   We visited the homes of George Washington, Thomas Jefferson, and John Adams.

REVISED   We visited the homes of George Washington, Thomas
Jefferson, and John Adams.

- Divide words only between syllables.

  INCORRECT   rec-ess, not-hing, sch-olarship

  REVISED   re-cess, no-thing, scholar-ship

- Divide compound words only between the words that form the compound.

  INCORRECT   ho-mecoming, han-dbag, grou-ndnut

  REVISED   home-coming, hand-bag, ground-nut

- Divide words according to their prefixes and suffixes.

  sub-standard, pre-cognition, establish-ment, fair-ly

45b   Use a hyphen with compound words

Compound words are two or more words joined as a single word. Some are written as one word, others as separate words with hyphens, and others as separate words without hyphens.

ONE WORD   housework, skyline, spendthrift

HYPHENATED   sister-in-law, cross-eyed, nation-state

SEPARATED   identity crisis, senior high, ice cream

It is not always easy to determine whether a compound word should be hyphenated. Conventions change rapidly and are not predictable. Consult your dictionary for compound word hyphenations, and use the following guidelines.

1   Using a hyphen with compound adjectives

A compound adjective is two or more adjectives that function as a single unit to modify a noun or pronoun. Hyphenate a compound adjective when that adjective precedes the noun or pronoun. Do not hyphenate a compound adjective when it follows the noun or pronoun. Do not use a hyphen when part of the compound adjective ends in -*ly*.

He is a *well-known* author and lecturer.

The author is *well known.*

The *never-to-be* published manuscript was lost in a fire.

The manuscript was *never to be* published because it was lost in a fire.

He lived in a small, *poorly furnished* apartment.

2   Using a hyphen with coined compounds

A coined compound is made up of words that are not ordinarily joined. Use hyphens in coined compounds. Be aware that coined compounds are usually informal, so use them only sparingly in formal or academic writing.

We were all offended by his *it's-not-my-job* attitude.

She always had a *poor-pitiful-me* look on her face.

3   Using a hyphen with fractions and compound numbers

Use a hyphen when spelling out fractions to connect the numerator and the denominator. Use a hyphen to spell out whole numbers from twenty-one to ninety-nine, even when those numbers are part of larger numbers.

three-fourths

five-eighths

one thousand twenty-eight

twelve thousand four hundred seventy-three

4   Using hyphens in a series

Use a hyphen for a series of compound words built on the same base word.

The new curriculum is designed for *first-, second-,* and *third-grade* children.

Each individual must work by *him-* or *herself.*

45c   Use hyphens with prefixes and suffixes as appropriate

Prefixes are usually combined with word stems without hyphens:

*pre*fabricate

*dis*content

*over*indulge

When the prefix precedes a capital or when a capital letter is combined with a word, use a hyphen:

anti-American

T-shirt

X-ray

Certain prefixes take a hyphen when combined with words and roots: *all-*, *self-*, *quasi-*, and *ex-* (meaning "formerly"):

all-encompassing

self-explanatory

quasi-legal

ex-legislator

Very few suffixes take a hyphen. Two that do are *-elect* and *-some*.

the senator-elect

thirty-some people

Do not capitalize the prefix *-ex* or the suffix *-elect*, even in titles with proper names.

INCORRECT Ex-Mayor Dinkins

REVISED   ex-Mayor Dinkins

INCORRECT Senator-Elect Smith

REVISED   Senator-elect Smith

Use a hyphen to prevent confusion resulting from two identical letters being placed together:

CONFUSING antiintellectual

REVISED   anti-intellectual

Note: Some prefixes with double vowels do not use the hyphen: *reentry, cooperation*. Check your dictionary if you are not sure whether to use a hyphen.

45d | Use hyphens to keep your meaning clear

In special cases, the use of a hyphen can make your meaning clear to readers. For example, the word *reform* means to improve or to correct; with a hyphen, the word *re-form* means to form again. Similarly, without a hyphen the word *recreation* means refreshment or amusement, but with a hyphen *re-creation* means the creation of something again.

EXERCISE 1 Hyphenating Words at the End of a Line

Divide each of the following words into syllables. Then place a hyphen after each syllable that could be left at the end of a line. (Some words cannot be divided.) Example:

contract   con-tract

1. allusive

2. rebellious

3. dimensional

4. would've

5. national

6. Jesse Jackson

7. communicate

8. exult

9. dawdled

10. wealth

EXERCISE 2   Using Hyphens

Add hyphens as needed to the following sentences. (Some sentences may be correct as written.) Example:

He is celebrating his thirty ninth birthday.

He is celebrating his thirty-ninth birthday.

1. That book was first published eighty five years ago.

2. Two thirds of the class did very well on the final exam.

3. The baseball team had won four fifths of its games.

4. Several ex governors are now running for president.

5. His nose in the air manner irritated all of us.

6. Three fourths of the voters thought the election was properly conducted.

7. A badly drawn picture of a cow was scrawled on the wall.

8. The world famous singer has gone into seclusion.

9. It is better to be a has been than a never was.

10. The voting age was lowered from twenty one to eighteen.

```
┌─────────────────────────────────────────────────┐
│                                                   │
│              PART ELEVEN                          │
│                                                   │
│              Research                             │
│                                                   │
└─────────────────────────────────────────────────┘
```

```
┌─────────────────────────────────────────────────┐
│              CHAPTER 46                           │
└─────────────────────────────────────────────────┘
```

```
        ┌───────────────────────────────┐
        │                               │
        │         Avoiding              │
        │    Plagiarism: Using          │
        │    Sources Correctly          │
        │                               │
        └───────────────────────────────┘
```

Plagiarism is theft. It is stealing the words and/or the ideas of other writers and passing them off as your own. Plagiarism is not taken lightly; in many academic institutions, people who plagiarize risk failing a specific course or even being expelled. If you use the exact words of another writer, or if you take the ideas of another writer and put those ideas in your own words, avoid plagiarism by properly acknowledging the source of the words and ideas.

| **46a** | **Avoiding plagiarism and acknowledging sources** |

(Section 47j in the *Handbook.*)
When you quote the exact words of another writer in your essay, use the following guidelines:

- Copy the writer's exact words. (For information on how to use ellipsis points to indicate omissions from a quotation, see 40d in the *Workbook.*)
- Use quotation marks for short quotations that can be incorporated into the body of your text. (See Chapter 39 in the *Workbook.*)
- Use the block quotation format for long quotations that would take up too much room if incorporated into the body of your text. (See 39c in the *Workbook.*)
- Use proper documentation style. (Ask your instructor which documentation format is preferred, or consult Chapter 48 in the *Handbook.*)

1   Using short and long quotations

(Section XX in the *Handbook*.)

Short quotations (of up to four typed lines) can be incorporated into the text of your essay. Enclose such an excerpt within quotation marks. Document the source by using a parenthetical citation and a reference in your text:

```
Mark Twain disliked pomposity and pretentiousness in all its forms.
His comment from Pudd'nhead Wilson's Calendar, "Cauliflower is noth-
ing but cabbage with a college education," says as much about peo-
ple as it does about vegetables (XXX).
```

Long quotations (of five or more lines) should be typed in block form. Look at the following example:

```
The Greek philosopher Aristotle, in Politics, Book II, emphasizes the
value of the middle class.

          Those States are likely to be well administered in which
          the middle class is large, and larger if possible than both
          the other classes, or at any rate than either singly; for
          the addition of the middle class turns the scale and pre-
          vents either of the extremities from being dominant. (XXX)
```

2   Paraphrasing and summarizing

(Section XX in the *Handbook*.)

To paraphrase is to restate in different words what a writer has written. Paraphrasing is a useful way of knowing whether you really understand a text; if you cannot state the ideas of a source in your own words then you probably do not understand them. Paraphrasing is also useful in making difficult concepts clear.

To summarize is to take the most important points of a text and present them in a condensed version. A summary is much shorter than the original.

Both paraphrasing and summarizing involve using your own words. In addition, you must acknowledge the source of the ideas in your paraphrase or summary to avoid plagiarism. Look at the following examples:

ORIGINAL TEXT   Art is a jealous mistress, and, if a man has a genius for painting, poetry, music, architecture, or philosophy, he makes a bad husband, and an ill-provider.

                                                  —Ralph Waldo Emerson

PARAPHRASE   According to Emerson, art consumes all or most of a person's time and attention, so that a painter, poet, musician, architect, or philosopher does not do well as a spouse or a provider (XXX).

ORIGINAL TEXT   Money does not pay for anything, never has, never will. It is an economic axiom as old as the hills that goods and services can be paid for only with goods and services; but twenty years ago this axiom vanished from everyone's reckoning, and has never reappeared. No one has seemed in the least aware that everything which is paid for must be paid for out of production, for there is no other source of payment.

—Albert Jay Nock

SUMMARY   Albert Jay Nock argues that payment for goods and services can be made only with other goods and services; people have forgotten that money is simply a symbol of production, not a thing in itself (XXX).

EXERCISE 1   Using Quotations

Write a paragraph using each quotation that follows. Example:

1. It is perhaps the highest distinction of the Greeks that they recognized the indissoluble connection of beauty and goodness. —Charles Eliot Norton

2. I wish to preach, not the doctrine of ignoble ease, but the doctrine of the strenuous life. —Theodore Roosevelt

3. Physiological experiment on animals is justifiable for real investigation, but not for mere damnable and detestable curiosity. —Charles Darwin

4. I've never any pity for conceited people, because I think they carry their comfort about with them. —George Eliot

5. Until you have become really, in actual fact, a brother to every one, brotherhood will not come to pass. —Fyodor Dostoyevsky

EXERCISE 2   Paraphrasing and Summarizing

Write a paraphrase or summary of each quotation that follows.

1. Since I do not foresee that atomic energy is to be a great boon for a long time, I have to say that for the present it is a menace. Perhaps it is well that it should be. It may intimidate the human race into bringing order into its international affairs, which, without the pressure of fear, it would not do. —Albert Einstein

2. No man is an iland, intire of itselfe; every man is a peece of the Continent, a part of the maine; if a Clod be washed away by the Sea, Europe is the lesse, as well as if a Promontorie were, as well as if a Mannor of thy friends or of thine owne were, any man's death diminishes me, because I am involved in Mankinde; And therefore never send to know for whom the bell tolls; it tolls for thee. —John Donne

3. The moment an audacious head is lifted one inch above the general level, pop! goes the unerring rifle of some biographical sharpshooter, and it is all over with the unhappy owner. —Mary Abigail Dodge

4. Older men declare war. But it is youth that must fight and die. And it is youth who must inherit the tribulation, the sorrow, and the triumphs that are the aftermath of war. —Herbert Hoover

5. Literature is my Utopia. Here I am not disenfranchised. No barrier of the sense shuts me out from the sweet, gracious discourse of my book-friends. They talk to me without embarrassment or awkwardness. —Helen Keller